D1557337

Making Caribbean Dance

UNIVERSITY PRESS OF FLORIDA

Florida A&M University, Tallahassee
Florida Atlantic University, Boca Raton
Florida Gulf Coast University, Ft. Myers
Florida International University, Miami
Florida State University, Tallahassee
New College of Florida, Sarasota
University of Central Florida, Orlando
University of Florida, Gainesville
University of North Florida, Jacksonville
University of South Florida, Tampa
University of West Florida, Pensacola

# Making
# CARIBBEAN DANCE

Continuity and Creativity in Island Cultures

EDITED BY
SUSANNA SLOAT

University Press of Florida
Gainesville · Tallahassee · Tampa · Boca Raton
Pensacola · Orlando · Miami · Jacksonville · Ft. Myers · Sarasota

15    13    12    11    10    6    5    4    3    2    1

Library of Congress Cataloging-in-Publication Data
Making Caribbean dance: continuity and creativity in island cultures/
edited by Susanna Sloat.
p. cm.   Includes bibliographical references and index.
ISBN 978-0-8130-3467-6 (alk. paper)
1. Dance—Caribbean Area. 2. Dance—Anthropological aspects—
Caribbean Area. 3. Dance—Caribbean Area—African influences.
4. Dance—Caribbean Area—European influences. I. Sloat, Susanna.
GV1631.M35 2010
793.3'19729—dc22     2010001919

The University Press of Florida is the scholarly publishing agency for the
State University System of Florida, comprising Florida A&M Univer-
sity, Florida Atlantic University, Florida Gulf Coast University, Florida
International University, Florida State University, New College of Florida,
University of Central Florida, University of Florida, University of North
Florida, University of South Florida, and University of West Florida.

University Press of Florida
15 Northwest 15th Street
Gainesville, FL 32611-2079
http://www.upf.com

# Contents

# Illustrations

# Acknowledgments

First, a heartfelt salute to all the authors of the book. Out of impossible schedules, these scholars, dancers, teachers, choreographers, administrators, artists, writers, musicians, filmmakers, cultural leaders in so many ways, carved out the time to write fascinating and insightful chapters for this book. Thank you also to the translators. Many, many thanks to all.

Many thanks also to the authors of *Caribbean Dance from Abakuá to Zouk* who served as a brain trust for this second book, including Nathaniel Crowell, Suki John, Rex Nettleford, Alma Concepción, Halbert Barton, Dominique Cyrille, and Gabri Christa. It is with great sorrow that I report the passing of Thomas Osha Pinnock and VèVè Clark. Some of the authors of *Abakuá to Zouk* gave such extensive help that I can only offer special accolades, thanks beyond measure, and enduring gratitude to Melinda Mousouris, Lois Wilcken, Martha Ellen Davis, Cynthia Oliver, and Patricia Alleyne-Dettmers.

Much, much appreciation and many thanks to my husband, Don Burmeister, for assistance of many kinds, including working to make all the photographs ready for publication and help with many complicated (and exasperating) technical details. And thanks, too, to our sons, Abe and Tobias Burmeister, particularly for their computer expertise.

To editor Meredith Morris-Babb I offer gratitude for persistence in publishing *Abakuá to Zouk* and her interest, too, in wanting and helping along this second book. Thanks also to project editor Jacqueline Kinghorn Brown and copy editor Lucy Treadwell.

Thank you, Hostos Center for the Arts and Culture in the Bronx, New York, for all the special programs in Puerto Rican and Dominican folklore. Thank you, Centro León in Santiago de los Caballeros, Dominican Republic, for hosting the conference El Son y la Salsa en la Identidad del Caribe.

Thanks to all the friends and acquaintances who offered encouragement and information—in naming a few, I am sure to have forgotten many others to whom I am grateful, too—but thanks to Maria Lara, Ane Franco, Gail Yvette Davis, Sydney Hutchinson, Janny Llanos, Angelina Tallaj, Leonardo Ivan Dominguez, Winston Fleary, C. Daniel Dawson, Shannon Dudley,

Marisol Berríos-Miranda, Willard S. John, Julian Casanova, Merián Soto, Fayola Olufemi, Jean Paul D., Ruel Ellis, Beryl Easton, Claudia Whittingham, Diane Shepard, Wayne Alleyne, Jacqueline Yancey, Trajal Harrell, Stephanie Goldman, Susan Silvey, Rebecca Sager, Kenneth Bilby, Peter Manuel, Afua Hall, Catherine Evleshin, and Carl Paris. A special thank-you for help from Burton Sankeralli and Barbara Palfy. Thank you to Lisa Solon and Humphrey Taylor for hospitality in Jamaica and to Linda Leonora Greenidge for hospitality in Trinidad (and Keith's buljol, too).

I owe my dance teachers over the years much gratitude; through them I studied Dunham technique and many styles of Caribbean and African dance, and without them this book would never have been written. While I've been working on this book, Prisca Ouya has been my mainstay. Thank you, Prisca. And thanks to Mabiba Baegne, Crystal Harrison, Janice Tillery, Titos Sompa, the late Malonga Casquelourd, Pierre Desrameaux, Jackie Guy, Barry Moncrieffe, L'Antoinette Stines, and to Pearl Reynolds, Bernadine Jennings, Pat Hall, Jean Léon Destiné, Richard Gonzalez, Ricardo Colon, Xiomara Rodriguez, Norman Saunders, Pedro Soto and Maria Terrero, Esther Grant, Dele Husbands, Harold Pierson, Lygia Baretto, M'Bayero Louvouezo, and others, unnamed but appreciated.

"Tangled Roots: Kalenda and Other Neo-African Dances in the Circum-Caribbean" was adapted by Julian Gerstin from his article originally published in *New West Indian Guide* in 2004, vol. 78, nos. 1 & 2. It is used by permission of *New West Indian Guide*.

Portions of "Haitian Migration and Danced Identity in Eastern Cuba" by Grete Viddal originally appeared in her article "Sueño de Haiti: Danced Identity in Eastern Cuba" in *Journal of Haitian Studies*, vol. 12.1. Used by permission of the *Journal of Haitian Studies*.

Some of the material on Jamaican dance moves in Sonjah Stanley Niaah's "Dance, Divas, Queens, and Kings: Dance and Culture in Jamaican Dancehall" appeared in the chapter by Sonjah Stanley Niaah and Donna Hope, "Canvasses of Representation: Stuart Hall, the Body and Dancehall Performance," in *Caribbean Reasonings: Culture, Race, Politics and Diaspora*, edited by Brian Meeks, published in 2007 by Ian Randle Publishers, Kingston. Used by permission of Sonjah Stanley Niaah.

Lyrics to the calypso sung by Wayne "Poonka" Willock, quoted in Susan Harewood and John Hunte's chapter, "Dance in Barbados: Reclaiming, Preserving, and Creating National Identities," are by Anthony "Mighty Gabby" Carter and are used with his permission.

# Introduction

Music flows through the people of the Caribbean islands and it comes out in dance. It comes out on streets and stages, in homes and places of worship, at clubs and competitions. Whether the dance is old and full of surprising retentions, African or European (or a mixture of the two), or as new as tomorrow and constantly evolving, whether it is danced by a small subculture (sometimes just in one place) or spreads over a whole island or a chain of islands and into the world at large, dance in the Caribbean, as elsewhere, tends to reflect multiple elements of a culture and to encapsulate aspects of identity—national, local; religious, ritual, spiritual, ancestral; fun loving, sexual; creative, resistant, traditional, progressive; professional, amateur; communal, personal.

The Caribbean islands are crucibles of mixture. As boats and airplanes, electronic signals, people, and ideas move between them, they continue to influence each other. This mixing has been happening since the beginning of the modern Caribbean, after the Spanish claimed the islands they sighted. Existing populations were eliminated or left as small remnants through mistreatment, enslavement, and Old World diseases. Bringing enslaved people from Africa from the early 16th century on resulted in the African-European mix of cultures that characterizes the Caribbean.

Waves of takeovers and attempted settlements, chiefly by the French, Dutch, and British, left islands with mixed peoples, customs, languages—and dances. These European powers in the seventeenth and eighteenth centuries greatly expanded the labor-intensive sugar-growing industry and the numbers of enslaved Africans brought to the islands, with Spanish island colonies later following this expansive pattern. In the nineteenth century, as first British, then French, then Dutch, and finally Spanish colonies disavowed the slave trade and two or three decades later emancipated enslaved people, indentured laborers from many places—places like Portugal, China, Africa—as close as other Caribbean islands and as far off as India, were brought in to work the sugarcane fields. This arrangement continued into the twentieth century as U.S. interests turned to Caribbean sugar. Other im-

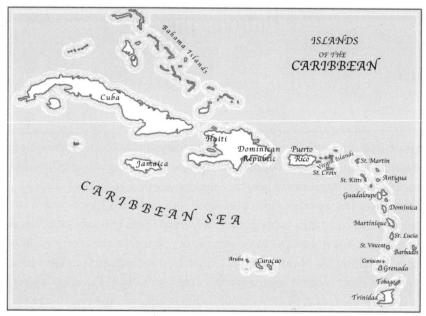

Map 1. The Caribbean Islands. Map by Don Burmeister

migrants were recruited or sought refuge or business opportunities in the islands.

Throughout their history, continuing today, people from within the islands visit and migrate to other islands, further complicating the hybrid nature of their cultures. Yet islands by their very water-surrounded definition do not melt into each other, so that each island retains its own history and specifics of culture, its own institutions and flavor, its own subtly or distinctively different collection of dances. We offer a chance here to trace shared connections and subtleties of difference.

*Making Caribbean Dance: Continuity and Creativity in Island Cultures* takes off from an earlier volume, *Caribbean Dance from Abakuá to Zouk: How Movement Shapes Identity*. It covers many topics, including entire islands, not discussed in the earlier book and greatly extends the discussion on many others, offering a faceted look at the way dance of all sorts reflects and is shaped by questions of identity, of individual and communal creativity, and the complications—of continuity and change—of hybridized and evolving cultures. Again, it sticks to the West Indian archipelago itself, even more so this time, with an unusual number of authors who are not only from the islands they write about but also still live there and contribute in multiple ways to the cultures they are a part of. Similar and related dance and music phenomena arising from the mixture of the African and the European and the Caribbean diaspora on the mainlands of the Americas are of enormous interest. We keep to the islands just to make the subject area more manageable.

Not every topic we would have liked to cover is here, nor is every island. We regret this. The culture of a smaller island can easily be eclipsed, but thanks to the Internet, news seeps out more readily than before. On St. Maarten, for instance, there has been a revival of the ponum dance. Ponum is a dance said to have been danced when slaves were emancipated in 1848, earlier than in other Dutch Caribbean colonies because then as now the island was shared with the French. Today it is danced to a song about emancipation and considered a national dance (called the only surviving folk dance), presented at regattas, book fairs, and for the visit of Queen Beatrix. But this is very recent. Ponum was almost extinct when dance teacher Carolyn Jenkins, then at the Motiance Dance School, began its revival in the late 1980s. Clara Reyes, founder of the Imbali Center for Creative Movement on St. Maarten, began interviewing older people about what they remembered about ponum in 1997 and wrote her master's thesis at SUNY Brockport about it. She has made a video about ponum.

In the NAGICO insurance company newsletter on its Web site, ponum is described by Clara Reyes: "It is a very powerful, riveting, high energy dance. It involves much jumping, prancing, pelvis gyration and sexual play between the male and female dancers. The couples, however, never actually touch each other. They use scarves as a connection between the partners. The man will fling a scarf around the woman's waist to pull her close." Ponum sounds exciting and very Caribbean, a dance revived for the twenty-first century.

The Caribbean as an arena for significant creation of modern dance was recognized by Culturesfrance, sponsor, in partnership with the Cuban Ministry of Culture, of the First Caribbean Dance Biennial in Havana, Cuba, from March 27 to April 1, 2008. This was a festival of dance from many places and a choreographic competition (like one the French initiated in Africa several years ago) open to all companies and choreographers from the Caribbean islands and Guyana and French Guiana. There were applicants from ten countries, with seven represented among the five company choreographies selected for the group piece competition and the seven solo choreographers (including our Barbadian coauthor, John Hunte) for the solo category. The president of the international jury was the dean of Cuban modern dance choreographers and our author, Ramiro Guerra. The winners were Awilda Polanco and Cecilia Camino of the Dominican Republic for *Exclamaciones*, which they choreographed for their company Blo a Blo, and Luvyen Mederos of Cuba for his solo, *Coca Cola Dreams*. Special mentions went to choreographer Sandra Ramy of DanzaAbierta of Cuba and solo choreographer Annabel Guérédrat of Martinique.

*Making Caribbean Dance: Continuity and Creativity* builds on *Caribbean Dance from Abakuá to Zouk*, though each book is independent of the other. For readers who do not know the first volume, it is useful to note what is covered there and to suggest a few of the many ways in which the earlier book interacts with this volume. It begins with two chapters on the African background of Caribbean dance. Brenda Dixon Gottschild elucidates the Africanist aesthetics that underpin so much dance on the islands with a set of concepts so useful that some writers in the current book, such as Janet Wason on Dominica, have built directly on them. Look to Cheryl Ryman's chapter on Jamaica in this book for an illuminating extension of Dixon Gottschild's predecessor, Robert Farris Thompson's definition of Africanist principles of movement. In the first volume, Nathaniel Crowell discusses some of what is Congolese in Caribbean dance, a subject touched on by others here, particularly by Julian Gerstin in his long, historical article connecting many islands through older dances.

Once again we move south through the archipelago, beginning with Cuba. In *Abakuá to Zouk*, Yvonne Daniel builds a strong base with a comprehensive overview of Cuban folkloric dance and institutions, Melinda Mousouris offers a portrait of Ramiro Guerra and his pioneering choreography for the first national modern dance company in Cuba, and Suki John describes the técnica cubana that Guerra and others built into a significant teaching and choreographic tool. In the present volume, a cornucopia on Cuba, Guerra himself writes about his continued experimentation; Graciela Chao Carbonero, also Cuban, takes a schematic look at African elements in various types of Cuban dance; Juliet McMains looks for links to ballroom rumba in Cuba; Jill Flanders Crosby finds a community of Arará worshippers that connects itself to Africa (and to her work among the Ewe there); and Grete Viddal looks into the tumba francesa and gagá of two different waves of emigrants from Haiti.

In the earlier book, Rex Nettleford offers an overview of Jamaican dance that connects to the dance of the entire Caribbean and leads to formation of the National Dance Theatre Company of Jamaica, and Thomas Osha Pinnock's memoir links his childhood as a dancing legsman in the slums of Kingston, the development of Rastafarianism and reggae, and his own choreographic experiments in New York. In the present volume, Cheryl Ryman shares a remarkably comprehensive view of the specifically folkloric in Jamaican dance, but first defines characteristics of the dance and the dance event that again connect to other African-derived dance in the Caribbean; Sonjah Stanley Niaah writes on creators of dancehall dances from those slums of Kingston; and Isaac Akrong takes a look at Kumina from a distinctly Ghanaian point of view.

In *Abakuá to Zouk*, Henry Frank gives a brief overview of Haitian folkloric forms, and Lois Wilcken discusses how folklore evolved in performance in Haiti and the diaspora. In *Continuity and Creativity*, Celia Weiss Bambara looks back at the concept of indigenism and how that is reflected or emended in the work of three current dancemakers, taking us into the present century in Haiti. Martha Ellen Davis, who contributes a thorough overview of the folkloric dance of the Dominican Republic to the first book, is back with an investigation into the dance and ceremonies of the rarely discussed Dominican *misterios*, extending her work from the earlier book. A piece by postmodernist Josefina Baez, who limns Dominican American identity with kuchipudi dance from India, is discussed by Ramón Rivera-Servera in *A to Z*; now we have a memoir by another witty and surprising Dominican American performance artist, Nicolás Dumit Estévez, who connects the dancing vedettes on Dominican television with a work of his own. Xiomarita Pérez offers a glimpse into the way a Dominican teaches the elegant Dominican son and the subculture of the sonero.

In the first book, Alma Concepción investigates Puerto Rican folkloric and social dance, and Halbert Barton discusses the challenges of Puerto Rican bomba, that island's most African form. Concepción also introduces the innovative dancemaker Gilda Navarra, who is only at the beginning of Susan Homar's searching look here into recent decades of Puerto Rican experimental choreographers. In the earlier volume Cynthia Oliver takes a thorough path into past and present dance in the Virgin Islands, particularly her native St. Croix; she is back, now, with our opening chapter on how calypso connects many islands, including St. Croix, and the Caribbean diaspora women, too, that she's invited to make a work about calypso with her. *Abakuá to Zouk* reaches zouk in Dominique Cyrille's extensive overview of the creole dances of Martinique and Guadeloupe. Look to Julian Gerstin's chapter here for more on Martinique and also for connections with chapters in this book on the bele and quadrille of Dominica by Janet Wason, the many personalities of St. Lucia as reflected in its dancing by St. Lucia-born and raised choreographer Tania Isaac, and the Big Drum complex of dances of the tiny island of Carriacou by Annette Macdonald.

The Big Drum of Carriacou has, through emigration, had a role in Trinidad and Tobago. This and other African and French influences that Gerstin discusses come more to the fore in Hazel Franco's overview of Afro-Trinidadian and Tobagonian dance here than they do in the earlier volume's investigation into the limbo as a wake dance by Trinidadian cultural and spiritual leader Molly Ahye, and Carnival expert Patricia Alleyne-Dettmers' discussion of African antecedents of Carnival masquerade and ways in which a children's Carnival band of Moko Jumbies encapsulates a symbolic history of the island. In *Continuity and Creativity*, we also have a reflection on the dance of Trinidad's very large population descended from India by Ravindra Nath Maharaj. In the first book, Gabri Christa describes the fascinating tambu and other folkloric dances of Curaçao; now we have a concentrated look at the many forms of dance on Barbados by Susan Harewood and John Hunte.

*Abakuá to Zouk* ends with three chapters connecting the Caribbean and the United States: by VèVè Clark on Katherine Dunham and her dance drama, *L'Ag'Ya*, by Susanna Sloat on dance on Caribbean themes seen in pan-Caribbean New York City, and by Robert Farris Thompson on the progression of mambo from Havana to New York's Palladium. The verve of Thompson on mambo innovators is hard to match, but we still offer surprises right to the end here; check out Harewood and Hunte on the Barbadian Landship and Barbadian carnival wukking up, or Franco on the dancing sailors of Trinidadian Carnival, with similarities to the Landship, though both are independent and unique, or Maharaj on the influence of Bollywood on Indo-Trinidadian dance.

Harewood and Hunte frame their chapter with a discussion of a perennial question on the islands that reflects issues of class, race, sexuality, religion, national origins, and different ways of looking at these questions and at the ways in which they interact with the many forms and possibilities of dance: decency and indecency. No one else puts it quite that way, but, from the first two chapters on (see Oliver and Gerstin on different approaches to the erotic in dance), the issue is one of the recurrent themes of *Making Caribbean Dance: Continuity and Creativity*, and it is one that cropped up from the beginning of the islands' mixture of the African and the European. With its exploitive colonial powers, angry indigenes, slaves and slave masters, escaped slaves, indentured laborers, criminals sent abroad, invaders and intruders of all sorts, sailors and soldiers, pirates, and adventurers, the early Caribbean was a place where "decency" could be hard to come by and was therefore treasured, even by those whose own actions might be questionable.

Julian Gerstin writes of the attitudes of early European observers— shocked, dismissive, admiring, or a combination of these—when they recorded what they saw of African-derived dance. Perhaps they felt a need to frame their descriptions in negative, Eurocentric, often racist terms; certainly they were fascinated. But the question of "decency" keeps coming up, over and over. It remains a tug between European and African ways of dancing and seeing dance and Caribbean notions of correctness and license, of religious propriety and danced religions, of the enjoyment of mastering every muscle of the body and the possibility of reining it all in. See, for instance, Tania Isaac's metaphoric descriptions of the personalities of St. Lucia as exemplified in dance.

The isolations of shoulder, torso, and, in particular, pelvis, that mark much African-descended dance sparked indignant cries about lasciviousness. European set dances are often very flirtatious. Combinations of the two modes invoke more avenues for indignation. When European-embraced dances (and of course the waltz was a scandal in its time) were transformed in the Caribbean, particularly when, as beginning in the late 19th century, people danced very close, with their whole bodies engaged, these new dances provoked censure. They still do—lovers do the grind in the Caribbean, and the newer perreo to reggaetón in Puerto Rico, Dominican Republic, and Cuba can involve explicitly sexual contact. But dancers are often more aroused by their own and their partner's skills than by ideas of eroticism. To master the many possibilities and subtleties of hip movements—revolutions and spirals that are quick or slow, small or larger, simple or intricate; shifts, thrusts, shakes, and shimmies—is to master a world of movement as complex and beautiful as that of the feet. And the pleasure of mastery—and of shocking the onlooker with one's daring—is why two strangers can wine together very closely on the streets of Port of Spain during Trinidad's Carnival parades without feeling any sense of invasion, just of dancing well.

Other subjects that one can trace through various chapters of the book (and the previous book, too) include the way folkloric and popular dance forms are changed by innovations in subject and choreography and merge with modern dance into new choreographies; the way dance can inform ritual and spirituality and how that is maintained or changes, including the influence of late (nineteenth century) arrivals from Africa; the way specific individuals are essential to the continuity of traditions as well as innovations within them; the way governments encourage the retention of folklore and a sense of local and national identity through national competitions or other policies; the way old dances like bele, much influenced by island migrations, appear on different islands; or the way new modes of dancing—from social ones like carnival wining or wukking up or fresh dancehall creations to professionals' experimental choreographies—reflect new senses of independence and the freedom to create. Another thread is about understanding and accepting the importance of the contribution of Africa to island cultures, taking different forms at varying times on different islands. At the same time, a cultural mixture itself born on the islands, or, as the French say, créolité, has also been celebrated. Look for other threads that glint and reflect and weave together throughout the book.

As in *Abakuá to Zouk*, the authors in *Continuity and Creativity* are a group of people with a truly impressive variety of talents, insights, and cultural contributions. Almost half live immersed in the places they write about here—Cuba, Jamaica, Dominican Republic, Puerto Rico, Barbados, Trinidad. Some have left the islands, living in the United States, but returning for sustenance. Other authors, born elsewhere, have gone to the Caribbean for long, immersive periods of island cultural study. Their viewpoints and approaches are also varied—literary or scholarly; out of ethnomusicology or cultural studies or performance practice; from personal interviews, personal experience, or extensive and diverse reading—or, most often, because these authors mix so many achievements and approaches in their lives, they take on their subjects in multiple ways from multiple perspectives, allowing readers a chance to see things from them, too.

Dance by its very nature is always moving, always transforming, and its history can be very difficult to pin down. This is certainly true in the Caribbean, where much remains unknown and perhaps unknowable—some authors here explicitly raise questions; other chapters will generate questions by readers, which we hope will lead to further explorations. The Caribbean islands, well off or poor, calm or strife-torn, exploited or, at least in small parts, pristine, are known for their beauty and the pleasures they engender. They have had troubled histories and face the future with the many problems that confront us all. "This is the visible poetry of the Antilles, then. Survival," said Derek Walcott in his 1992 Nobel prize for literature speech. Yet these islands can be places where communal and individual creativity is celebrated with an islandwide intensity, a long buildup of design and rehearsal that culminates in a carnival of costume, music, and dance. Other traditions are hidden. We invite you to investigate the Caribbean's dances, known, less known, barely knowable, with us here.

*Making Caribbean Dance: Continuity and Creativity in Island Cultures* opens with two very different chapters about dance and music genres that form a connective tissue between groups of islands. In "Rigidigidim De Bamba De: A Calypso Journey from Start to . . . ," Cynthia Oliver, choreographer, performer, and associate professor of dance at the University of Illinois, limns the twentieth- and now twenty-first-century arc of calypso and its offshoot, soca, connecting the Anglophone islands of the West Indies. She begins with her father's youthful glimpse of a Caribbean coming back to him over the air from Canada, though the song he remembers is, in the way that memory scrambles, actually from much later. In Oliver's childhood on St. Croix, every family member danced to calypso with his or her own distinctive flair. In twenty-first-century New York City, Oliver corrals a group of diaspora-diverse women to begin to delve into calypso hip circling wining and island memories, conflicted as well as joyful, for a collective investigation sure to have the island tang with which she tantalizes us here.

"Tangled Roots: Kalenda and Other Neo-African Dances in the Circum-Caribbean," which Julian Gerstin adapted from an article originally published in *New West Indian Guide* in 2004, starts with the many historical confusions about the names and variants of the dances kalenda, chica, bamboula, djouba, and bele. He collects a great many citations of these dances from the early eighteenth century on, focusing on the islands, but extending from New Orleans to South America. In the process, Gerstin, a percussionist and ethnomusicologist who studied bele drumming and dance in Martinique and who teaches at New England colleges, sees a pattern. With the exception of chica, he finds that these neo-African creole dances, born from mixtures on the islands, spread with French influence. Because of specific characteristics of the dance and music, and because the French increasingly moved their expanding slave-trading activities in the eighteenth century from the Bight of Benin into the Congo/Angola region, Gerstin sees evidence of Congolese origins in these dances. Of course, enslaved people from many regions mixed in the Caribbean; there was much cultural mixture in Africa, too, and many similarities of movement, and there is no one prototypical Caribbean dance, which Gerstin notes in his "Summary and Caveats." But the French influence, from France itself as well as brought from Africa, extends beyond the obvious from Cuba to Puerto Rico to Trinidad, and in this book you can follow the thread Gerstin establishes from the tumba francesa of Cuba to the dances of Dominica, St. Lucia, Carriacou, and Trinidad and Tobago.

Confusion about Caribbean dance and music terms is still with us. Rumba, for instance, has meant different things in movement and rhythm since it became a worldwide craze around 1930, and what the word suggests in Barcelona or Brazzaville is not the same as what it does in International-style ballroom dancing, or, very differently yet, in its homeland, Cuba. These two worlds, ballroom dancing and Cuban rumba, converge in the work of Juliet McMains, an assistant professor in dance at the University of Washington, author of *Glamour Addiction: Inside the American Ballroom Dance Industry*, and a former professional ballroom dance competitor. In "Rumba Encounters: Transculturation of Cuban Rumba in American and European Ballrooms," McMains searches for the lineage of ballroom rumba in Cuba, where Pierre and Lavelle, a professional dance couple whose version became the accepted international style in the 1950s, had studied before bringing it back to England. Cubans, to whom rumba today means three improvisational forms with an African thrust and complication (two with partners, the mild yambú and the fiercely competitive guaguancó, and the men's solo virtuosic form, columbia), had not heard of them or their Cuban teacher, nor were they were familiar with the expansive, upright stylizations of international ballroom rumba. McMains eventually discovers what Pierre and Doris may have encountered as she takes us on a journey of cultural confrontation that becomes a kind of detective story.

Ramiro Guerra is not only the fountainhead of Cuban modern dance, he is also one of Cuba's most important writers on dance. In "My Experience and Experiments in Caribbean Dance," Guerra looks back on his life and work, from a vivid remembrance of the cultural milieu of his childhood in the 1930s in Havana, to his early days of becoming a dancer and beginning to transcend the conventions of dance and theater, to his innovative work as founder of Cuba's national modern dance company at a time when modern dance was little known in Cuba. Since then, it has become a major art form there, with Guerra acknowledged as its founding father. When a daring site-specific piece he had spent much time developing was suspended by the government in 1971, Guerra withdrew from the company and turned to other work, exploring Cuban folklore, gesture, expressions, and humor; choreographing at times for other companies, including in 2000 for Danza Voluminosa, a Cuban company of very large dancers; and making other, highly experimental works, even in his own apartment house, very much for himself, with a questing creative nature that makes him well suited to the twenty-first century.

In "The Africanness of Dance in Cuba," Graciela Chao Carbonero, a veteran teacher and researcher of dance in Cuba and author of texts on teaching traditional dances, a recently published book on social dances up to today's casino, and one on the dances of the orishas, offers a schematic look at the ways in which African roots penetrate all levels of Cuban dance. She begins with some basics about the danced religions of African origin in Cuba and continues with the assimilation of movement from them into secular dances, including both African and European-based dances. With a distinctly Cuban point of view, Chao discusses lesser known dances like the sones miméticos as well as familiar ones, describes casino and casino rueda, and moves into the ways in which African-based movement has been incorporated into modern dance and nightclub and television dance styles.

Just how strongly Cubans can be attached to African roots is conveyed in Jill Flanders Crosby's "Secrets Under the Skin: They Brought the Essence of Africa." Flanders Crosby, a professor of dance at the University of Alaska Anchorage with a background in jazz dance, has spent years investigating the dance of the Ewe of Ghana and the related dance of the practitioners of the Arará religion in the small towns of Matanzas province in Cuba. In this chapter, she depicts two of these communities and individuals within them, detailing their Arará religious practices, including altars and fodunes, ceremonies and sacred places, and their abiding connections to their ancestors' African origins. These small-town ceremonies and dances are in many ways different from Arará in Matanzas city and the way the dancing has been codified in folkloric performance and teaching, echoing, as is so often the case all over the world, what happens when varied practice becomes reduced to one particular variant. In conclusion, Flanders Crosby goes back to Ghana and Togo and notes how relationships with Cuban practice are perceived there. Though adherents of the Arará rites may not be numerous or widespread in Cuba, their attachment to Arará has been enduring, from enslavement to the transcendent twenty-first-century ceremonial dancing with which the chapter closes.

The eastern end of Cuba, hundreds of miles from Havana, has a distinct culture influenced by two waves of emigrants from Haiti. Grete Viddal, a doctoral candidate at Harvard's Department of African and African American Studies, addresses the dance legacy that resulted in "Haitian Migration and Danced Identity in Eastern Cuba." She concentrates here on forms from the first migration, a consequence of the Haitian Revolution more than two centuries ago, particularly the tumba francesa, which combines African rhythms and French contredanse patterns, and from the second, by farm workers in the early twentieth century, on gagá, pre-Lenten carnivalesque processions. But she also discusses tajona, a rural processional form that may stem from the early migration, and the presence of choreography from Vodú, still going strong among descendants of later migrants. Viddal, who has been investigating the folkloric dance and ritual belief systems of eastern Cuba and Haiti for some time, finds that Cubans of Haitian descent have increasingly highlighted the value of their heritage through folkloric performance.

Cheryl Ryman's "When Jamaica Dances: Context and Content" offers an unprecedented view of the complexities and richness of Jamaican folkloric dance. Ryman first sets up a detailed context for her exceptionally complete description of the dances, giving insights into ways in which all distinct dance cultures as well as the Jamaican can be identified, the African aesthetics and spirituality that define Jamaican dance, and the way a dance event evolves, reflecting not only what happens in Jamaica, but also much of what takes place across the Caribbean. A former principal dancer with the National Dance Theatre Company of Jamaica who has produced a significant body of dance research dating back to the 1970s, she is a candidate for a PhD in cultural studies at UWI, Mona, and is also involved in film, television, and a cultural and historical tourist attraction, the Outameni Experience.

Ryman's extensive descriptions of such traditions as Jonkonnu, Bruckin Party, Buru, Maypole, Mento, Kumina, Tambu, the Nine Night dances, including dinki mini and guerre, Maroon Kromanti Play nation dances, Etu, Hosay, and Rastafari will not only greatly extend your knowledge of Jamaican culture, but also set you dancing.

As will Sonjah Stanley Niaah's "Dance, Divas, Queens, and Kings: Dance and Culture in Jamaican Dancehall," which takes us into the ever-creative world of the dancehall queens and kings and the dances they invent and pass on to others in a milieu in which dancing transforms people from their workaday lives. As both Ryman and Stanley Niaah show, the wellsprings of traditional Jamaican dance and culture provide a reservoir of movement for dancehall dances and such cultural manifestations as particulars of costume (a form of masquerade) and an intensity of involvement akin to possession. Stanley Niaah, a lecturer in cultural studies at the University of the West Indies, Mona, who has published and presented widely on dancehall and was the coordinator of the ACS Crossroads in Cultural Studies Conference at Mona in July 2008, gives a glimpse into the thoughts of dancehall stars like Bogle and Stacey about their roles, notes significant aspects of the subculture, including changing gender roles, and describes some of the dances themselves, as well as identifying an extensive chronology of the major dance moves, which have proliferated in recent years.

"All persons are 'others' sometimes," says Isaac Nii Akrong in "Ghanaian Gome and Jamaican Kumina: West African Influences." Here, Akrong, a candidate for a PhD in ethnomusicology at York University, Toronto, who has a masters in dance ethnology from York and directs the African Dance Ensemble (ADE) in Toronto, a multicultural city with a large Jamaican population, writes very much from inside the cultural perspective of his native Ghana. Both Ghanaian Gome and Jamaican Kumina have complex relationships with mixed African and Caribbean elements. Though Kumina has strong Congolese roots, it also incorporates influences from the Maroons, who have multiple origins, with Ghana predominant. Akrong also notes contact and trade between Central Africa and Ghana; moreover, many of the dance moves and musical practices of Kumina are very similar to those in Ghana. The cylindrical Kumina drum is modulated with the heel, as is the Ghanaian Gome drum, and the square Gome in turn has its roots in Jamaica, brought to Sierra Leone by Maroons (who still use a square drum on legs in Jamaica) and by Sierra Leoneans to Central Africa, where migrant workers from Ghana, in turn, developed square drums they brought back to Ghana to become part of the Gome tradition. Beyond these complex mixings back and forth of diverse peoples, it is the spiritual dimensions of the Kumina religious rites that Akrong recognizes and emphasizes as intensely African and deeply connected to ritual and "spi-ritual-ity" in Ghana.

In "Chimin Kwaze: Crossing Paths, or Haitian Dancemaking in Port-au-Prince," Celia Weiss Bambara takes us into the world of contemporary Haitian dancemaking by focusing on three important women of different generations whom Bambara interviewed, studied with, and/or worked with from the late 1990s until 2003. Each of these dancemakers, Viviane Gauthier, Florencia Pierre, and Nicole Lumarque, draws on the Haitian religious traditions of Vodou, but each has a different relationship with the concept of indigenism, of using Vodou as material for the stage as a way to project Haitian identity, which, Bambara explains, was first formulated by Haitian intellectuals in the first half of the twentieth century. A dancer and choreographer who received a PhD in dance history and theory at the University of California Riverside, and with her partner, Christian Bambara, has formed the CCBdance project, Bambara notes the different ways each of her dancemakers departs from the old indigenist idea. Gauthier uses the notable Haitian training technique kultur physik, while Pierre and Lumarque fuse other elements and extend ideas of folklore to make contemporary pieces, to which, for Pierre's program, *Chimin Kwaze*, Bambara herself contributed and danced in. The U.S. deposition of elected president Jean-Bertrand Aristide in 2004 produced a period of such chaos that many dance artists emigrated. But others, including the three featured here, stayed and are again producing work, Bambara notes, as she names artists who have been taking Haitian dance into the twenty-first century.

The *misterios* or spirits of the Dominican Republic are little known and infrequently discussed. In "Dance of the Dominican Misterios," Martha Ellen Davis explains how they and spirits of the dead manifest themselves in mediums trained to receive them. They are an aspect of what Davis terms Vodú-spiritism, with the misterios influenced by the Vodou of adjacent Haiti. She reveals its procedures, ceremonies, and distinctiveness, its relationship to folk Catholicism, and its less specific attachment to African origins than that of the complex religion of the neighboring country. Davis, an anthropologist and ethnomusicologist who does research for the National Archives of the Dominican Republic and has produced much about the culture and music of that country, including two documentaries, many articles, and three books, among them the prize-winning *La otra ciencia: el vodú dominicano como religión y medicina populares*, describes a continuum of practices ranging from the almost purely spiritual (as in the spiritism descended from Allan Kardec), to saints' festivals mixing the spiritual and the material, to a spirituality with a strong material component, here called Vodú-spiritism, which includes music, dance, and possession by los misterios.

The Dominican son descends from the Cuban son, but the dance and music have developed locally. To the son's irresistible rhythms and lilting guitar, the soneros, urban people who have developed a subculture that stresses elegance and who may belong to organizations devoted to the son, dance with grace and great style, hips moving to the lilt, men taking breaks for elaborate footwork or inventive body shifts, women and men partnering as one. Xiomarita Pérez, a widely published journalist on traditional Dominican culture with long experience as a dancer and director of folkloric organizations, is the founder of a dance school in Santo Domingo where, among other dance forms, she teaches Dominican son. In "How to Dance Son and the Style of a Dominican Sonero," based on a lecture demonstration Pérez gave at El Son y la Salsa en la Identidad del Caribe conference in Santiago de los Caballeros in April 2007, she discusses the dance, the teaching of it, and the characteristics of dance and personal style that mark a true Dominican sonero.

These days television is both a connector between islands (watching Puerto Rican reggaetón videos in Jamaica, for instance) and within an island (catching all the highlights of Carnival on Trinidadian TV), and Nicolás Dumit Estévez in "The Drums Are Calling My Name" shows us how powerful the impact of television culture is on the young, zeroing in on his Dominican boyhood watching larger than life singing and dancing vedettes. The over-the-top Iris Chacón from Puerto Rico (still probably viewable on YouTube), the Dominican Mayra el Ciclón del Caribe, and Tongolele, star of Mexican movies, were some of the notably endowed performers who made Estévez want to be one himself. Becoming a performance artist in New York City allowed him to invent a male vedette. The witty and inventive Estévez has gone on to many different projects, including the cape-wearing "Super Merengue," a dancing superhero whose flight by cape links the Dominican Republic and the United States, and "The Flag," which joins

U.S. and Dominican flags and also the historical contexts of their patriotic symbols. Both were seen at El Museo del Barrio in New York. Recently, Estévez has moved away from the irony richly imbuing such pieces including his vedette, the dancing Machete, to embrace something difficult for a performance artist, sincerity, in diverse pieces about art, service, Catholicism, and meeting all the people in a small town. He intends to go back to the Dominican Republic for a project tracing any possible Haitian heritage he might have. Estévez's methods and materials are mixed; here his medium is words.

Modern dance of the era of Graham never took hold in Puerto Rico, but postmodern or experimental dance has had notable exponents on the island. Susan Homar, a professor in the Comparative Literature Department at the University of Puerto Rico who teaches dance history and theory, has been paying keen attention to this phenomenon since its beginnings in the late 1970s with the group Pisotón. Her "Contemporary Dance in Puerto Rico, or How to Speak of These Times," reveals with illuminating depth how the most significant of these choreographers developed innovative ways to explore themes reflecting the ironies and dissonances of identity and gender in contemporary Puerto Rico. As experimentalists, each approached the challenges in a different way. Choreographer Viveca Vázquez, who with Merián Soto organized the postmodern festival Rompeforma, which galvanized local attention to new forms, uses arresting, fragmented ways of moving in dance that is, Homar says, "physically, conceptually, and choreographically risky." Her work, like that of such choreographers as Awilda Sterling-Duprey, Javier Cardona, and Teresa Hernández, attempts to subvert received ideas of sexual politics and nationality by complicating them with multiplicity and contradiction. In the twenty-first century, such experimentalists are not always as active, but Andanza, a new contemporary dance company that mixes styles, has created excitement with its charged dancing.

In 1986 Janet Wason, whose background is Guyanese and Canadian and who grew up on different West Indian islands, primarily Barbados, got the opportunity to go to Dominica, the island between Guadeloupe and Martinique, for six months to research, report on, and video its dances. She arrived from Canada with an MFA in dance history from York University— her specialties are sixteenth-century European court dance and nineteenth-century ballroom dance—an unusual, yet fruitful background for someone investigating Caribbean dance. "Bele and Quadrille: African and European

Dimensions in the Traditional Dances of Dominica, West Indies" focuses on two genres, the African-descended bele and the European-derived quadrille, though both, as Wason shows, have absorbed influences from the other continent. Now a library associate at the University of Waterloo, Ontario, Wason gives a brief history of nineteenth-century European social dance and pays meticulous attention to what is African and what is European about the dances she studied in Dominica. She revisits them in such detail that we can see that the bele of Dominica has similarities with the bomba of Puerto Rico (see Barton's and Concepción's descriptions in *Abakuá to Zouk*), though many bele steps seem more elevated, with more spring or bounce, and that quadrille on Dominica, though quite European in formation, is very much danced with an Afro-Caribbean inflection.

Tania Isaac lets you know the kind of choreographer she is right from the beginning of her chapter, "Helen, Heaven, and I: In Search of a Dialogue," suggesting an intense, complex experience that takes off from Caribbean dance in a transformative way. Helen, the beautiful, is the nickname of Isaac's native St. Lucia (she is now based in Philadelphia), and Isaac finds three more names with which to suggest metaphoric characterizations of the multiple selves of her island. She uses these selves to explore the movement of St. Lucian kwadril (quadrille), masquerade, calypso, and soca, of Carnival of the bands playing mas and the more individualistic Carnival of Ol' Mas, a synthesis of the personalities that particularly appeals to Isaac in its expression of possibilities. Isaac uses description and metaphor to suggest a density and variety of cultural information, a layering that can contain all contradictions. Circling back to her own creative impulse, she says, "What I find in quadrille, in calypso, in soca, in masquerade, is not a series of steps or moves, but a way of looking at the body." She shares that with us here, as a way to understand the complexities of St. Lucia and her own creative process.

As Susan Harewood and John Hunte tell us, little has been written about dance in Barbados. Their "Dance in Barbados: Reclaiming, Preserving, and Creating National Identities" reveals a wealth of information and insight about how a range of dance and policy on the island becomes part of this formation of identity, from the historical dances, to efforts after independence to use dance to promote nation building, to development of a government-subsidized modern dance company, to that uniquely Barbadian social organization, the parading Landship. Issues of class, of who gets government money and encouragement, of emphasis on the local or not, or on the primarily African-derived or European-derived, come to the fore within the framing question of decency and indecency. Harewood, a Barbadian who is now an assistant professor at the University of Washington, Bothell, and Hunte, a performer and choreographer who is a PhD candidate in cultural studies at University of the West Indies, Cave Hill, Barbados, go on to discuss the government's initiation of two cultural festivals, for independence day and the Crop Over summer carnival season, when Bajans get many chances to demonstrate their facility at wukking up to soca and calypso. Straitlaced disapproval of that is one factor that has led to a resurgence in ballroom dancing. Dance companies reflecting various communities, dance schools, the growth of liturgical dance are all part of this extensive overview of dance and complications of identity in Barbados.

The very small island of Carriacou, the southernmost of the Grenadines and politically a part of Grenada, has maintained an important and extensive set of old dances, the Big Drum ceremony, which includes sacred rituals and nation dances reflecting African origins, creole dances including different types of bele, and another category of secular dances called frivolous dances. Annette C. Macdonald, a documentary filmmaker and professor emerita of dance at San Jose State University, first visited Carriacou in 1966 for a master's thesis on the Big Drum, returning to the island in 1977 to do more filming of the ceremony, in 1996 for another Big Drum, and briefly in 2007 to interview Winston Fleary, a Big Drum leader, folklorist, and repository of island oral history. Her chapter, "Big Drum Dance of Carriacou" is based primarily on that interview and on the recent book *Folk Traditions of Carriacou and Petite Martinique* by Christine David, a folklorist and former school principal on Carriacou who describes the dances vividly. These two local experts, David and Fleary, bring us into the twenty-first century, with the Big Drum remaining a spiritual and cultural focus of the island.

In "Tradition Reaffirming Itself in New Forms: An Overview of Trinidad and Tobago Folk Dances," Hazel Franco braids the many strands making up the two islands' folk dance cultures with their histories. Franco, a choreographer, a dance educator at the University of the West Indies, St. Augustine, and a researcher into folk forms with a master of arts degree in dance ethnology from York University, Toronto, focuses on Afro-Trinidadian dances with their underlying African heritage and French, Spanish, and British infusions. She discusses Carnival traditions, from the balls of the French plantation owners and those of free coloreds, who had to have a "fandango license" for their segregated balls, to the development of traditional Carnival characters, to the heyday of the fancy stepping bands of sailors and ship's firemen following steel bands in the mid-twentieth century. Franco notes the different history of Tobago and its folk dances, how changes in government change the way folklore is viewed, including the importance of the Best Village competitions from independence until today, and the black power movement of the 1970s, which introduced an enduring emphasis on African heritage. Charting the development of new forms incorporating folk dance for the professional stage, she describes an arc of choreographers from the important pioneer Beryl McBurnie to Cyril St. Lewis, with whom Franco danced, to Astor Johnson, whose fusions moved into new territory.

The Indian population in Trinidad is very large. Hindu temples and prayer flags (and a smaller number of mosques) dot the towns and villages of the predominantly Indian parts of central and south Trinidad. The insufficiently known dance of this community, as Ravindra Nath Maharaj shows in "A Narrative on the Framework of the Presence, Change, and Continuity of Indian Dance in Trinidad," stems from folk traditions, dance dramas, and religious folk theater brought by indentured laborers from India from the middle of the nineteenth century into the beginning of the twentieth, but new sources from India, the West, and the Caribbean have added to the dance traditions of the Indians in Trinidad. Maharaj, known widely as Raviji, is active in community and Hindu religious life, is a newspaper columnist and has performed as a dancer, and leads a Ramdilla ceremonial folk theater group and Hindu festivals; his wife, Sujata Maharaj, was one of the first Trinidadians to study dance in India and came back to teach folk dances to children. He discusses the widespread influence of Indian films on Trinidadian music and dance, the changing roles of women, the beginnings of the teaching of classical Indian dance in Trinidad, the emergence of chatnee (or chutney), as well as the secular and Hindu folk traditions, including the Ramdilla, a large-scale community re-enactment of the Ramayana in a form that may be extinct in India today.

The bibliography is a compilation by all authors and will take readers into many interesting pathways, around the Caribbean and beyond. We hope you will add to them, using the book as a launching pad. Much remains to be explored and conveyed about Caribbean dance. Although only a few Web sites are listed in the bibliography, the Web is an obvious place to look for information at all levels of accuracy, including video examples of some of the dances discussed herein.

And now: music please. Rhythm, riddim, ritmo. Let us all dance.

*Susanna Sloat*

# ISLAND CONNECTIONS

# 1

# Rigidigidim De Bamba De

## A Calypso Journey from Start to …

CYNTHIA OLIVER

This thing happens in fragments. It is multilinear. I have looked for a beginning, journeying through first traumas (Hall 2001, 28) to African and French retentions, South Asian influences, shifting from songs sung extempore to processional jump up, for an end. Yet no matter how deep the dig, I return to the beginning. To de riddim. To hip shake, hip swill. So I will start where I might, and the beginning will inevitably circle round, circle back, and begin again.

Canada wafts over the radio. It is the 1930s or '40s, he says. Young Retty hears this tune, this lively music, and its storytelling of a man traveling back to the Caribbean on an airplane, resisting as his bowels threaten to deliver him to the toilet time and again, finally succumbing to his bodily function, and exiting the plane with a stink that makes all who hear this tune double over in laughter. This song, "Calamity," is more than a peculiarity. It is an emblem of the times. It is the sound of something new. Retty reconciles his familiar St. Croix cariso, that extempore song rife with commentary of local politics, gossip, or word play, with what he decides is "organized music," this new thing with horns and flutes, and drums all crescendo-ing into a sound that reverberates with the familiar, but catapults him into a new recognition of self. Him-self in relation to something else. To a broader Caribbean that spans oceans, that comes out of thin air in radio waves with flavors all melding in an archipelago of sound.

This is my father's introduction to calypso, his first awareness of a music that has shifted from the cariso of his memory to something so special it is worthy of transmitting airwaves right back to the region of its making.

Although he has collapsed time in his memory, between his first hearing of calypso and his recollection of "Calamity," which actually aired much later (Lord Nelson, 1966), he so clearly recalls calypso taking the world by storm. Gleefully summoning Lord Kitchener and Lord Caresser, whom he contends paved the way for a Sparrow, he lists them as part of a wave, making Caribbeans proud to reckon with their own music, even if some didn't yet know it was theirs. This music and its dance that circles and circulates are contemporary and come from right where he sits, not outside of him. This region has birthed modernity and no matter what their condition in what faraway place, calypso is the connective tissue, spreading through the collective body of Caribbeans like veins, delivering the bounce, the roll, de riddim, like the lifeline it is to the heartbeat of a national, geographical, spiritual, imagined consciousness.

## My Beginnings . . .

I grew up in St. Croix and heard calypso from the earliest days of my childhood. My father danced and swayed my mother around the house and their grins spread from ear to ear as the house swelled with the crooners Byron Lee and the Dragonaires, The Mighty Sparrow, Lord Kitchener, Lord Short Shirt, and Archie Thomas. I was in love with their grace. Their happiness was infectious. Calypso rhythms pulsed in the bodies of relatives moving fluidly. Uncle Mario was energetic and almost acrobatic in his gesticulations. With his furtive dose of "fire water," he would "leggo" with such fury that his hips and torso seemed to move independently of one another. My father and Uncle Gerald each swore he was the smoothest, most stylish dancer there was, and they were both right. Auntie Carol, my 300+ pound aunt, moved as lightly as a butterfly showing me the latest steps, chipping through the living room, dancing down the hallway singing. And my grandfather Elias, who refused to sweat, would shift his weight from side to side ever so lightly with each foot gently grazing the ground no matter what the music demanded. Witnessing this immense and impossible beauty has brought me back after years of love affairs with other music—to calypso, even as calypso has changed for my generation, moved from its early storytelling and commentary forms into the dance arena, from calypso to "soca." Some use this terminology interchangeably, though Lord Shorty coined the melded Indo-

Figure 1.1. Cynthia Oliver. By Michael Nemeth. Used by permission of Cynthia Oliver.

Caribbean elements with the calypso of before, "soca," and moved the party (Dudley 2004, 87). Still calypso carries on, literally and figuratively . . .

## Another Beginning . . .

It is 1999. I am in St. Thomas doing fieldwork on beauty pageants in the islands. Petra Maximay, a young woman once a contestant in the Miss Big and Beautiful contest, tells me of activities prohibited by the pageant for its contestants. The harbor "boatrides" are atop the list as they are deemed unrespectable for young ladies. Those jam-down events that young people swarm during carnival season take them from a pier in Charlotte Amalie out into the harbor, where they mingle and dance (or grind) the night away to sounds by the latest hottest soca bands in the islands. I am brought back to my own relationship with calypso. I want to claim it. I want to own it. Distance has made me desire and savor those things of home so much more than when I lived there. I want to own those portable recognizable things that will claim me, that will telegraph to those knowing eyes that I am you too.

I want to make this experience tangible, to express this connectivity, the politics of its history as we have moved away to work, to feed families, to experience freedom and its challenges, to find opportunity, to find modernity, even though we were making it, right here at home, right there as we traversed others' spaces, right now as we glimpse each other on videotapes, cable TV, the Internet, as we get off planes and flash our spirit. This calypso is spiritual, sexual, proper and improper. My father encountered it as he sat in his house on the island hearing his Caribbeanness come to him over the radio from Canada. My own re-encounter blooms as calypso summons me to familiarity and comfort as I myself move across oceans and geographies and encounter others embracing the selfsame thing.

## Another Beginning . . .

In 2005 I sent out a call to Caribbean artists. They had to be Caribbean, had to know something about calypso in their bones. In this project I didn't want to have to explain myself, translate my meanings, or dictate the dance. I wanted to be in a room and develop a work with folks who would need no translation. I had not yet figured how the performance work would ultimately translate to an audience. Remember, I was at the beginning. . . . I sent the call to friends far and wide and heard from many interested artists. But I had no funding yet for it and had to mark time. I had to dance in place, wine me wine by me'self until ah could afford to bring de people dem een an wuk it out. I had already named it. I called it Rigidigidim De Bamba De, remembering the name from a call to calypso, a recognition of its splendor and pleasure I had heard while at home in St. Croix on holiday. I decided then to store it until one day when I would have a chance to give it suitable space.

The piece would say something about the journeys of Caribbean people crossing water, crossing continents, coming together yearly at the very least, like church on Easter Sunday or Christmas mass, but this time under the complexity of de wine. Under what we could call the lexicon of our collective africentric movements, our collective root, spirit moves, rudegyal stylings, the contradictory "cova yo face becaz dem de goin ahn tuh bad" kinda moves. These very moves that I saw in the bodies moving from Trinidad to England, from Grenada to Brooklyn, from Montreal to the Bahamas, all in de winin' ah de wais, this identity marker, this infinity wine of de hips telegraphing national identity, that would inspire an artistic creation that might only begin to tell the story of this transnational dance and its resonances across lives.

Every time I delve into this dance I begin again. Talk about nation, begin. Talk about gender, begin. Sex. Class. Aesthetics. Begin and begin again . . . It is New York City, February 28, 2008. I arrive at JFK. I have invited a group of women to participate in a workshop with me so I can begin the process of casting this evening-length piece I will produce (there is finally money, though it is never enough) and present in the fall of 2009. I endeavored to make this coming together a space where we were sharing information, locating ourselves in the city, but carving out a private place for Caribbean gyuls to be themselves safely, unabashedly, without censor, and that is exactly what I got. And I was moved.

## I Asked Each Woman Questions . . .

Where were you born? Where did you grow up?

There was Nehassaiu, as beautiful as her name, from Toronto and Montreal and born in Trinidad of St. Vincentian, Grenadian, Guyanese, and Dominican heritage; swarthy and petite Debra from Guyana, the measure of respectability; chocolate brown Rosa, from Brooklyn, who as she says, is Trini-Gambian; spitfire Lisa from Toronto and Jamaica; sophisticated and sinewy Caryn from St. Croix; A'Keitha from the Bahamas; MarieLouise from Queens of Jamaican parentage; Ithalia from Liverpool, of St. Lucian and English-Irish folks and intent on discovering the Caribbean of her father through this music and this dance. This group of women move air and summon Oya, swirl winds and wind hips, level mountains, and alter topographies until the separation is no longer possible. We are together and it is good. There is music in the air even as the women speak and fill the silences. We can hear our selves in each other's lilt, in its disappearance, its eruptions.

Nehassaiu speaks of her family moving, to and fro from Guyana to Toronto, Trinidad to Dominica, Grenada to Montreal, to and fro until she—the blend of all their seasons—ends up here in New York, a shy mover who opens her mouth and poetry tumbles out with power and range. She jumps and she laughs between and around the crowd of sister voices. She drops to the floor on her belly, shouting, trying to make her diatribe heard. And though you can't hear her words distinctly, the world lights up. Rosa moves quietly with hips circling, describing the music in her childhood home, her parents' respectable hip wining restricted to a vertical pendulum-like move of the middle (body and class) that she had been so taken by until later as a young woman she realized the lyrics were not so respectable, that while her parents were doing the nice dance, the words were Sparrow's "Drunk and Disorderly." But Rosa's hands tell tales. They are delicate as doilies on a mahogany table. They pose dainty-like against a background of sweat. I imagine they shield against harsh traveling conditions, from homophobia to acceptance, discord to peace, staunch attitudes to freedom, despite which we long for home. We long to get on the curve of the wine both here and there.

I ask if there is a particular smell, taste, or sound that connects you with your Caribbean roots? Pepper pot, they say, plantain chips, the moaning sounds of sex in another room. I think of the thick humid air when the hatch of an arriving plane opens on an island tarmac and skin and hair swell to meet it like a lover.

How and or when did you first hear calypso or were conscious of it?

MarieLouise from Queens pulls out albums of a Caribbean Broadway show, *Ballad for Bimshire*, and recalls her fascination with its peculiar sounds, its distinct melodies, the Caribbean a distant reverie of her father's, a reference she would summon years later, now, as her body manages moving through the tensions of a life in N.Y.C. and returns to African and Afro-Caribbean dancing as outlet. A'Keitha, a tattooed and pierced Bahamian goddess who stands at six foot tall, towering above us all, activates the space above heads and circles down low. Calypso moves round her so easily. It slips and slides against her hips and falls off exhausted to the floor.

Were there taboos or other unsavory associations made with calypso in

Figure 1.2.
Caryn Hodge
and performers
of Rigidigidim
De Bamba De
rehearsing in New
York, 2008. By
Marcus Behrens.
Used by permission
of Cynthia Oliver.

your world? Do you connect with a Caribbean community? Where? Do you dance calypso? There are so many questions, so many pregnant and loaded answers. Of course there were taboos. It was winin' yo hips! It meant you were fass! Even if Lisa decries "freedom" to her folks, it was still calypso upside yo backside. Or upside a wall wid a bwoy. 'Tain' so innocent as she tinkin. 'Tain' so respectable. Yo must know it if you gon call yo'self Caribbean, but for goodness sake don' dance it. Not dat way. Not dere. History layin it European stink value 'pon it. We fightin dat. So here yo could dance it, in de street, in de parade wid yo people dem. Yo could be a flag gyul in a LGBT march, not just ahn Eastern Parkway. Yo could wine yo wine wid de woman and de man dem. You can acknowledge the heteronormative in the culture but the homoerotic in the moves.

Caryn hits a high-pitched whine, sounds like she's speaking in tongues, then breaks it down, murmuring slowly the words of an aunt's relentless reprimands in a childhood filled with the surreal, complicating sweet reveries of calypso with some harsher realities for young people in the islands, where they use it to express generational difference, a dense forest of sexual relations far from safe, where children make their way in minefields of adult complexity. Calypso is all this too. We watch this next generation, negotiate the landmines, find de wine and move it faster and hotter down the streets and in de parties pumping music.

Rhetta brings Trinidadian mass and mas to de studio. Rhetta, meh gyul, a broad beautiful woman wid wavy dense black hair, a Trini black belt who does hold she own and move spirit as she windin' word round her silky tongue. For a moment we feelin' like we chippin' down de street. We connecting owa moves wid de dirt, de grung, and de people dem in T & T. Dis explosive man! 'Tis mas. Wid de bodies packed an marching dung de road. We summonin in de studio and we gon summon ahn de stage. But den again, I rememba . . . dis jus de beginnin.'

And these are only the first moments. Again, though I have been thinking about this since 1999, I am once again at a beginning. All I know is calypso circling, circulating from the Caribbean to the metropolis and back, shifting each time for nationals, natives, tourists, expats, and enthusiasts alike as it moves, going and coming back in its traveling, in its refrain, in its relentlessness, in its contemporariness, in its badness . . .

Dis where we gon start . . .

Special Thanks to Caryn, Nehassaiu, Rosa, Lisa, Debra, MarieLouise, A'Keitha, Ithalia, Rhetta, Mario, Carol, Gerald, "Daddy" Elias, Mary, and Everett. You are an inspiration. Thank you Susanna for the invitation to be a part of this work a second time round. I am honored.

# 2

# Tangled Roots

## Kalenda and Other Neo-African Dances in the Circum-Caribbean

JULIAN GERSTIN

In this chapter I investigate the early history of what Roberts (1972, 26, 58) terms "neo-African" dance in the circum-Caribbean. There are several reasons for undertaking this task. First, historical material on early Caribbean dance and music is scattered, sketchy, and contradictory. Previous collections have usually sorted historical descriptions by the name of dances; that is, all accounts of the widespread dance kalenda are treated together, as are other dances such as bamboula, djouba, and chica. The problem with this approach is that descriptions of "the same" dance can vary greatly. As Samuel Floyd warns, "In studying this music, its constitution as a large, complex, and tangled array of musical genres . . . becomes apparent" (1999, 2–3).

I propose a more analytical sorting by the details of dance descriptions, such as can be gleaned. I focus on choreography, musical instruments, and certain instrumental practices. Based on this approach, I suggest new twists to the typical historical picture: namely, that Bantu-speaking enslaved people from the Congo-Angola area played a greater role in early Caribbean culture than is often understood—and that French slave trading played a major role in bringing them. The French were also particularly influential in spreading European dance and cultural forms such as contredanse and Carnival, adopted and adapted by people with African origins in the Caribbean.

Caribbean people today remain greatly interested in researching their roots. In large part, this article arises from my encounter, during ethnographic work in Martinique, with local interpretations of one of the most famous Caribbean dances: kalenda. (Kalenda is also spelled kalinda, calenda, and calinda. For the sake of simplicity I use the Martinican Creole spelling, except in quotes.) Martinicans today are familiar with at least three versions of kalenda. One is from the island's North Atlantic coast, a virtuosic dance for successive soloists (usually male), who match wits with drummers in a form of "agonistic display" (Barton 2002; Cyrille and Gerstin 2001). A second, from the south, is a dance for couples who circle one another slowly and gracefully. The third is a fast and hyper-eroticized dance performed by tourist troupes, which invented it in the 1950s and 1960s. In addition, a line dance known as mabelo is very like a 1724 description of kalenda by the priest Jean-Baptiste Labat, and a danced martial art, damié (danmyé, also known as ladja or l'agya), recalls the stick-fighting kalendas of other islands (though on Martinique it is done without sticks).

Sorting out these kalendas and kalenda-cognates is made more difficult by the ideologies that surround them. The name "kalenda" appears in descriptions of early neo-African dances from numerous islands. Despite differences between these descriptions, white observers soon stereotyped kalenda as a frenetically sexual and dangerous dance; as such kalenda became an emblem of slave identity. Martinique's tourist troupes obviously drew on the cachet and drama of this stereotype. (To differentiate tourist kalenda from the North Atlantic version, some Martinicans call the latter "calenda ticano," after the most popular song sung for that dance. In the first volume of *Caribbean Dance*, Dominique Cyrille [2002] uses this term in her article on Martinique.)

A contrasting perspective arose during the 1980s, when a younger generation of performers began researching and revalorizing more authentic folk dances. Many politicized members of this generation strongly reject touristic performance. They admire the nonstereotypical elements of Africanicity in the North Atlantic solo kalenda, and at the same time accept the African-European hybridity, or *créolité*, of the southern kalenda—another side of their identity. Yet a third perspective comes from a highly influential Martinican scholar, Jacqueline Rosemain, the first to publish serious studies of the island's dance history (1990, 1993). Unfortunately, Rosemain accepted the old stereotype of kalenda, offering a narrative of early Caribbean dance based on images of black eroticism and prerationalism. My effort to understand what may actually have happened in early Caribbean dance was sparked partly as a reaction to her work.

In this chapter, I will not dwell on Martinique's contemporary interpretations of dance history. I have discussed these elsewhere in the contexts of an ethnography of musical revival and political ideologies in Martinique (Gerstin 2000) and white representations of black Caribbean identity through dance (Gerstin 2007). Instead, I concentrate on sorting through the historical material. Some of this may be familiar to readers, as it has appeared in several well-known collections (e.g., Emery 1988, Epstein 1977). Other material is more obscure, although I hasten to add that I am an ethnographer, not a historian, and except where Martinique is concerned I have worked from secondary sources.

## Kalenda

One of the best-known descriptions of early black Caribbean dance was published by the priest Jean-Baptiste Labat in 1724:

> What pleases them most and is their most common dance is the calenda, which comes from the Guinea coast and, from all appearances, from the kingdom of Ardá [Ardra, in Dahomey]. The Spanish have taken it from the blacks, and dance it in all America in the same manner as the blacks. . . . The dancers are arranged in two lines, the one before the other, the men to one side, the women to the other. Those are the ones who dance, and the spectators make a circle around the dancers and drums. The most skilled sings a song that he composes on the spot, on such a subject as he judges appropriate, and the refrain, which is sung by all the spectators, is accompanied by a great beating of hands. As regards the dancers, they hold up their arms a little like those who dance while playing castanets. They jump, they spin, they approach to within three feet of each other, they leap back on the beat, until the sound of the drum tells them to join and they strike their thighs, [the thighs of] some beating against the others, that is, the men's against the women's. To see this, it seems that they beat their bellies together, while it is however only their thighs that support the blows. They back away immediately, pirouetting, to recommence the same movement with completely lascivious gestures, as often as the drum gives them the signal, which it does several times in succession. From time to time they interlace their arms and make two or three turns while always striking their thighs together, and they kiss

one another. We see enough by this abridged description how this dance is opposed to decency. Despite this, it has not ceased being really the rage of the Spanish Creoles of the Americas, and so strong in use among them, that it forms the best part of their divertissements, and even enters their devotions. They dance it in their churches and in their processions, and the nuns hardly stop dancing it even on Christmas eve upon a raised theater in the choir, behind a railing, which is open, so the populace have their part of these good souls giving witness to the Savior's birth. It is true that they do not admit men with them to dance such a devout dance. I would even believe that they dance it with a very pure intent, but how many spectators would one find who would judge them as charitably as I? (Labat 1972 [1724], 401–403; my translation)

Compare another description of kalenda, as well-known as Labat's and as often cited, written about Haiti and published in 1796 by the Martinque-born scholar and politician Médéric-Louis-Élie Moreau de Saint-Méry:

A dancer and his partner, or a number or pairs of dancers, advance to the center and begin to dance, always as couples. This precise dance is based on a single step in which the performer advances successively each foot, then several times tapping heel and toe, as in the Anglaise. One sees evolutions and turns around the partner, who also turns and moves with the lady. . . . The lady holds the ends of a handkerchief which she waves. Until one has seen this dance he can hardly realize how vivacious it is—animated, metrical and graceful (Moreau de St.-Méry 1976 [1796], 54–55).

Moreau de St.-Méry's choreography of a couple or couples within a ring of onlookers who also sing, clap, and take their turn in the ring is common for entertainment dances in West and Central Africa. It is quite different from Labat's formation, men and women in separate lines. This formation is not unknown in Central Africa (J. H. Weeks 1882, in Cyrille 2002, 229, 238); however, the duple line dancing observed by Labat may have been the slaves' adaptation of the latest Parisian craze, contredanse. Several contredanse styles continue to exist in Martinique today. Those on the island's North Atlantic coast, a distinctive musical region, are considered part of the lalinklè or "full moon" genre (so-named because they used to be done on nights of the full moon). One of these dances, mabelo, as noted above, fits Labat's description of kalenda (AM4 1992b, 51, 77; Bertrand 1966b). It is no coincidence that Labat observed this particular dance. While Labat does not state on which island he observed this dance, he managed a large plantation on Martinique's North Atlantic coast, just north of the town of Ste-Marie. In all likelihood he portrayed a scene from his own slave quarters.

In addition to Labat's and Moreau de St.-Méry's reports, kalenda is noted in Haiti in 1799–1803 (Descourtilz, in Emery 1988, 23). An 1881 newspaper article from Port-of-Spain, Trinidad, describes it in the pre-emancipation Carnival of the 1830s (Cowley n.d., 8). Anthropologist and choreographer Katherine Dunham watched a kalenda in Trinidad in the 1930s; she described it as similar to Moreau de St.-Méry's graceful couple dance, which she cited by way of comparison (1947, 6–7). Kalenda is also mentioned in a 1933 account from St. Croix, U.S. Virgin Islands (Cowley n.d., 17). Dances called Old Kalenda and Woman Kalenda are part of Carriacou's contemporary Big Drum ceremony (McDaniel 1992, 397; 1998a, 19). The sicá rhythms of Puerto Rican bomba include, among its variations, one called calindá (Barton 2002, 189; Vega Drouet 1998, 937). Martha Ellen Davis (2002, 136) describes the Dominican Republic's baile de palos as resembling Moreau de St.-Méry's calenda, including the use of a handkerchief as prop (137).

A double line dance from Peru, which included belly bumping à la Labat's kalenda, was reported in both 1747 and 1791 (Bastide 1971, 174–176; Crowell 2002, 16); Bastide also mentions the presence of kalenda, bamboula, and chica in Uruguay. In the United States, Le Page du Pratz noted kalenda in Louisiana in 1758 (Epstein 1977, 32). A better-known description is by George Washington Cable, in a celebrated article on dancing in New Orleans' Congo Square. Yet Cable's description is both brief and stereotyped. Here it is in its entirety: ". . . it was the favorite dance all the way from [Louisiana] to Trinidad. To dance it publicly is not allowed this side of the West Indies. All this Congo Square business was suppressed at one time; 1843, says tradition. The Calinda was a dance of multitude, a sort of vehement cotillion. The contortions of the encircling crowd were strange and terrible, the din was hideous" (1886; in Katz 1969, 42). Neither Cable nor his illustrator, Edward Windsor Kemble, were eyewitnesses to Congo Square's dancing, which was banned in the early 1840s (Southern and Wright 2000, 34).

## Chica

Another widespread early dance was chica, which Moreau de St.-Méry describes as follows: "This dance consists mainly in moving the lower part of the torso, while keeping the rest of the body almost motionless. To speed up the movement of the Chica, a dancer will approach his danseuse, throwing himself forward, almost touching her, withdrawing, then advancing again, while seeming to implore her to yield to the desires which invade them. There is nothing lascivious or voluptuous which this tableau does not depict" (Moreau de St.-Méry 1976 [1796], 61–62).

This description is distinct from both Moreau de St.-Méry's kalenda ("animated and graceful" rather than "lascivious") and Labat's kalenda (a double line dance rather than a single couple dance). Moreau de St.-Méry also distinguishes the two by placing chica in his section on creole dances and kalenda among the black dances, and by stating that it was chica, not kalenda as in Labat, that was danced by nuns at Christmas. In Curaçao, he adds, chica was danced by black women; it was widespread in Africa, particularly the Congo; it was a favorite of white society women; and, brought by the Moors from Africa to Spain, it was identical to fandango (Moreau de St.-Méry 1976, 60, 64–65, 67).

Labat and Moreau de St.-Méry introduced a confusion that has plagued many later writers. Cable wrote that New Orleans' Congo dance, "called Congo also in Cayenne [French Guiana], Chica in San Domingo, and in the Windward Islands confused under one name with the Calinda, was a kind of Fandango" (1969 [1886], 42). A book published about Haiti in 1889 equated bamboula with chica and quoted Moreau de St.-Méry's description of the latter (Spenser St. John, in Emery 1988, 26). By the twentieth century the chica/kalenda equation seems to have become taken for granted, and I have found it in Katherine Dunham (1947, 6–7), Janheinz Jahn (1961, 81), Jacqueline Rosemain (1990, 38, 40), and Sully Cally-Lézin (1990, 81).

That is my main point, but let me also note that chica is again mentioned in Cuba in the 1840s or 1850s (Bremer, in Emery 1988, 26). In contemporary Puerto Rico, "sicá" is a subset of rhythms in bomba. Kenneth Bilby suggests a Bantu origin for these terms, from Kikongo *sika* (to play an instrument), with the common New World creole shift from /s/ to /sh/ (Bilby, personal communication). Contemporary rumba guaguancó in Cuba uses the pursuit choreography described for chica by Moreau de St.-Méry, while adding kerchief and skirt play by the woman (as in Moreau de St.-Méry's kalenda) and the pelvic thrust of the man (as in Labat's kalenda).

## Bamboula, Djouba, and Bele

In 1881 in Trinidad, a newspaper article on the Carnival of the 1830s reported, "At carnival time our mothers and grandmothers have even danced the *belair* to the African drums whose sound did not offend their dainty ears, and our fathers and grandfathers danced the *bamboula*, the *ghouba* and the *calinda*" (Cowley n.d., 8). All these dances were widespread in the circum-Caribbean. We will begin with bamboula.

Bamboula forms the centerpiece for Cable's article on New Orleans' Congo Square. As noted above, Cable did not see the dancing, and his writing tends toward the fanciful. Here is a representative example from his passage on bamboula: "Yonder brisk and sinewy fellow has taken one short, nervy step into the ring. . . . He moves off to the farther edge of the circle, still singing, takes the prompt hand of an unsmiling Congo girl, leads her into the ring, and leaving the chant for the throng, stands her before him for the dance. . . . Now for the frantic leaps! Now for frenzy! Another pair are in the ring! . . . And still another couple enter the circle" (1969 [1886], 38).

Contrast Benjamin Latrobe's 1819 account, an eyewitness account this time: Congo Square filled with a large crowd and a number of dance rings; in most of the rings he observed "two women dancing. They each held a coarse handkerchief, extended by the corners, in their hands, and set to each other in a miserably dull and slow figure, hardly moving their feet or bodies" (Latrobe 1905, 180). Again the basic choreography is couples in a circle, but Latrobe depicts a same-sex version, the handkerchief recalls Moreau de St.-Méry's chica, and the dancers are reserved rather than frenetic.

Latrobe does not record a name for the dance he saw, but another report on Congo Square dancing, from 1808, names bamboula (Laussat, in Epstein 1977, 84). Bamboula was also reported in Trinidad in the 1700s (Cowley 1996, 7, 45) and in St. Lucia in 1844 (Breen, in Abrahams and Szwed 1983, 267; Emery 1988, 27). The bamboula in the U.S. Virgin Islands is either recently extinct or recently reconstructed (Bilby 1985, 188; Courlander 1954, Band 21, liner notes 4; Lieth-Philipp 1988, 8; Oliver 2002, 208–210; Sheehy 1998, 973). Earl Leaf states that the St. Thomas version was danced by pairs of women, like the dance Latrobe saw in New Orleans (Leaf 1948, 136–143).

The name is also found in Haiti for a dance performed "on the occasion of building a new house" (Courlander 1960, 136); in the Samaná region of the Dominican Republic (bambulá), where it is considered derived from Haiti (Davis 1998, 856; 2002, 142); and as one variation (bambulaé) of the sicá style of Puerto Rican bomba (Barton 2002, 189). An alternate name for one of Carriacou's Big Drum dances, quelbe, is boula, a shortened form of "bamboula" (McDaniel 1998a, 19).

In Guadeloupe bamboula is considered the predecessor of today's gwoka (Lafontaine 1986, 85–90; Rosemain 1986, 22, 53; Uri and Uri 1991, 38–39). Rosemain suggests the term was used in Martinique as well, but she is vague on the point (e.g., 1986, 50–51, 53). The only other reference I have found to bamboula in Martinique is by the journalist Lafcadio Hearn, who claims to have heard from an old drummer that a bamboula was a drumming competition (Hearn 1923, 82; AM4 1992a, 96). Hearn, a member of Cable's New Orleans circle, was something of a fabulist, and I would prefer more supporting evidence.

Djouba (*djuba, juba, yuba*) is another frequently reported dance. It is best known in Haiti, but the above-quoted newspaper article on Trinidad carnival also mentions *ghouba*. According to John Storm Roberts, djouba existed at one time in Guadeloupe (1972, 157, 223). Yubá is one form of bomba in Puerto Rico (Barton 2002, 186; Vega Drouet 1998, 937). One of the dances of tumba francesa, a contredanse style brought to eastern Cuba by the slaves of planters fleeing the Haitian Revolution, is yuba (Alén Rodriguez 1986, 169; Armas Rigal 1991, 29–32; Szwed and Marks 1988, 30). Juba is one of the Creole dances of the Big Drum ceremony in Carriacou (D. Hill 1980, 8; McDaniel 1998a, 19; Pearse 1956, 4).

Cable briefly mentions djouba in New Orleans: "The *guiouba* was probably the famed *juba* of Georgia and the Carolinas" (1969 [1886], 48). But this seems to me to be a case of one name being used for very different things. Djouba as performed in Congo Square would probably have been a drum dance, whereas the juba of the rural South was a body percussion style, "patting juba" (Epstein 1977, 141–144). Juba may also have been a character of folklore; he appears, for example, in a 1793 ballad (Hamm 1979, 110).

A recent publication cites Moreau de St.-Méry's description of kalenda— a couple dance—to illustrate Haitian djouba (Frank 2002, 111). In contrast, Dunham describes the Haitian version as "a 'set' dance of several men and women facing each other in two lines, with movement and attention directed to a partner" (1947, 45–46). The yuba of Cuban tumba francesa is a contredanse, and in French Guiana, djouba is a contredanse (Blérald-Ndagano 1996, 179).

The final dance complex I will discuss is bele. (The Creole orthography of this word varies greatly: bele, bèlè, bélé, bélè. We use "bele" as a neutral version.) This dance is found today on Martinique, St. Lucia (Guilbault 1993, 1, 3), Dominica, Trinidad, and Carriacou. (Among the sources for Dominica are Caudeiron 1988, 27; Guilbault 1998a, 841; Honychurch 1988, 36–37; Phillip n.d. For Trinidad, Tobago, and Carriacou, see Anon. 1994, 156; David 1994, 162, 164; Herskovits and Herskovits 1964, 158–159; McDaniel 1998a, 19; 1998b, 865; 1998c, 959; Pearse 1955, 30–31; 1956, 4; Roberts 1972, 117.) Puerto Rico's bomba complex includes a style known as belén. Bele formerly existed in Grenada (McDaniel 1998b, 865; Pearse 1955, 31); St. Thomas, where it was danced only by women (Leaf 1948, 184–190); and French Guiana (Beaudet 1998, 437). In the latter case, the contemporary kaseko dance complex is considered bele's direct descendant (Blérald-Ndagano 1996). In most of these places bele features couple flirtation in the center of a circle.

A number of authors describe bele as "creole." I take it they mean to portray bele as a fully Caribbean synthesis, as distinct from earlier neo-African dances. In fact, I do not find references to bele before the late 1700s and early 1800s. Women's costume for bele suggests creolization, as it is most often based on the French creole outfit of long skirts and petticoats, plaid waistcloth ("madras"), lace-trimmed blouse, and madras head scarf. (Men's costume varies more widely, but often includes the madras worn as a belt, plus a high-crowned straw hat.) In Trinidad, as in Martinique's North Atlantic, bele may use quadrille or contredanse choreography (Herskovits and Herskovits 1964, 158–159). On Carriacou, the dances of the Big Drum ceremony are grouped into three major categories: nation, creole, and frivolous. The beles belong to the creole category, along with Old Kalenda, juba, and quelbe (boula) (McDaniel 1998a, 19). Such details lend credence to the idea that bele was associated with the spread of French creole culture somewhat after the period of initial neo-African transculturations.

Overlaps between these dances indicate the importance of cultural ties between former French colonies. For instance, Haitian djouba is sometimes called *tanbou matinik* (Martinican drum) or simply *matinik*, and may be played in the style of Martinican North Atlantic bele with transverse drumming and sticks on the side. Gage Averill states that djouba/matinik also refers to a secular contredanse style (personal communication). In Vodou, djouba is the dance of the peasant lwa Zaka, who typically presents himself in farmer's clothing and carries a machete; in Martinique the dance mabelo (the duple line dance with pelvic bumping so similar to Labat's kalenda) is sometimes performed under the name *négryé* or *danse de la canne* (dance of the cane), the dancers appearing as cane-cutters, with stalks of sugar-cane and machetes. In Cuba, the Congolese-derived double line (with pelvic thrust) yuka dance is sometimes done with sugarcane stalks and machetes (Vélez 2000, 65).

Similarly, Trinidadian bele is also known as juba (Herskovits and Herskovits 1964, 159), and bélé juba is one of several bele dances in Dominica (Guilbault 1998a, 841; Honychurch 1988, 36–37).

## Eroticism Examined

The complexity indicated by descriptions of kalenda, chica, bamboula, djouba, and bele throws into relief the frequency with which chroniclers have reduced Caribbean dance to a single sensational image: frenzied black dancers revolving their loins and bumping together. This image appears to have formed fairly early. Diderot's encyclopedia (1751–1772) followed Labat in depicting "calinda" as an erotic line dance (cited in Rosemain 1993, 111). In numerous works since, compilers have lumped Labat's, Moreau de St.-Méry's, and other descriptions together as if they were the same, or as if the difference did not matter, ignoring their variety and focusing, in the main, on eroticism.

The reasons for such reductionism seem straightforward enough. White colonials created an image of black identity that embodied both their fears and their own forbidden desires. The stereotype was strong enough to influence even sympathetic and careful observers, let alone those more dismissive of black Caribbean culture.

But eroticism is a broad and variable realm. It is worth reexamining such concrete details as we can find, and let us start by returning to Labat and Moreau de St.-Méry. Their descriptions differ not only in choreography but also in sensibility: Labat's kalenda is "lascivious," Moreau de St.-Méry's "vivacious" and "graceful." The distinction may simply have lain in the eye of the beholders, Labat the righteous priest versus Moreau de St.-Méry the cosmopolitan traveler. Moreau de St.-Méry was not afraid to describe eroticism when he saw it; he called chica "lascivious" and "voluptuous." He simply did not see kalenda as outstandingly erotic.

Which brings up the element of subjectivity in all these dance descriptions. To my eye, for example, the movements of Martinique's southern bele genre (bele lisid, which includes the dance kalenda lisid) are graceful, minimalist, and reserved; dancers circle one another slowly, there is little pelvic isolation or overt flirtation, and no contact. Yet some Martinicans find the dance "*très lascive et sensuelle*" (AM4 1992b, 58–59). This recalls St.-Méry's "lascivious or voluptuous" chica, yet that dance, with its flirtatious advances and retreats, sounds more like Cuban rumba than like bele lisid—or, for that matter, more like Martinique's North Atlantic bele dances, which are full of flirtatious play.

Pelvic thrusting or bumping occurs in numerous dances throughout the circum-Caribbean: in Martinican North Atlantic bele this move is called *zabap* or *wabap*; in St. Lucian jwé dansé it is *blòtjé* (Guilbault 1998c, 943). The move may be seen in photographs of bamboula dancers on St. Thomas in the 1940s (Leaf 1948, 138–139). In some dances the contact is prescribed, as in Labat's kalenda, where bumping was a set part of the dance occurring regularly on the main beats, in contemporary Martinican mabelo, and in St. Lucian jwé dansé. In other dances contact is optional: the man pursues and the woman simultaneously entices and avoids him; whether they will make contact is left to their inspiration. Martinican North Atlantic bele is an example.

We can also distinguish between pelvic isolation (rotation or figure eights, pelvic shifts or thrusts) and pelvic contact. Many dances using isolation do not involve contact, even when they suggest it. Moreau de St.-Méry describes chica dancers as *almost* touching. The old Cuban dance yuka, considered the predecessor of today's rumba, includes a noncontact pelvic gesture called *ndoki* (Judith Justíz, personal communication), as does makuta, a dance related to yuka in that both are considered Congolese (Veléz 2000, 65). Perhaps the paradigmatic modern example of pelvic isolation is Trinidadian and Jamaican "winin," which usually does not include contact.

Conversely, there may be contact without pelvic isolation. In mabelo, partners grab one another's hips and pull themselves together, with full contact from belly through thighs. Labat is clear about this: "it seems that they beat their bellies together, while it is however only their thighs that support the blows." It is actually everything from bellies through thighs, and Martinican dance instructors are specific about this: the contact should be strong, not timid, so the force of the blow must be distributed. As one teacher, Pierre Dru, puts it, "If you go around thrusting your pelvis at people you'll hurt yourself." However, Labat comes very close for someone who in all likelihood never tried the dance himself.

Moreover, there are varying manners of signifying erotic contact; it is not always pelvis to pelvis. In Cuban rumba guaguancó, the man attempts to give the woman a *vacunao* (vaccination), gesturing toward her groin with his hand or foot as well as pelvis.

Finally, there are degrees of sexual intent. Often, dancers are simply or playfully absorbed in displaying their skills. In Martinique's North Atlantic bele, flirtation and even pelvic contact are usually treated as pleasant fun. One is rarely really pursuing one's partner, unless serious flirtation is going on outside the dance as well. All kinds of games may be played with eyes, hands, and body, with approach and evasion, and with props such as skirts and hats. Even in mabelo, where body contact is prescribed, partners signal their willingness to interact through meeting or avoiding one another's eyes, by withholding themselves tensely or meeting solidly. Some dancers treat the contact humorously. I once saw a large woman knock a smaller man over with the force of her *zabap*. Another woman turned aside from her partner to throw her long skirts over the drummer's head—bringing the music to a crashing halt, and bringing down the house as well.

Surely European observers understood sexual nuance in the context of their own dancing. Yet in the culturally unfamiliar, racially tense context of neo-African dance, they seem to have lost perspective.

## Challenge/Display Dancing

Challenge dancing (Crowell 2002, 12) involves "agonistic display" (Barton 2002) between a dance soloist and a lead drummer, in which the drummer tries to mark the dancer's movements in sound. I would expand the category of challenge dancing to include virtuoso solo display as well as challenge per se. This is a widespread African type and surely traveled to the New World, although I have found only a few colonial descriptions. An unnamed, men-only competitive display was performed in the Bahamas in the late nineteenth century (Edwards, in Emery 1988, 28), while an 1844 account from Cuba tells of a woman dancing competitively with a succession of men (Wurdemann, in Emery 1988, 27).

Modern examples include Cuban rumba columbia, Puerto Rican bomba, Jamaican "drop legs" (Pinnock 2002, 97) and more recent dancehall dances, and at least two Guadeloupean gwoka dances, toumblak and kaladja. Dunham described djouba as "primarily a competitive dance of skill" (Emery 1988, 27). In addition, some dances in the contemporary kalenda and bele complexes are competitive. Of Old Kalenda, one of the creole category of dances in the Big Drum of Carriacou, Pearse (1956, 6) writes, "The dance, which now often incorporates some of the eccentric and violent movements of stick-fighting, is by a man or a woman, and is a dramatic duel between the drummer and the dancer, in counterpoint. The drumming is extravagant and complex."

In the southern United States, the body percussion style "patting juba" often accompanied buck dancing, a solo male competitive/display style. The minstrel entertainer William Henry Lane billed himself as Master Juba, and, since minstrel dancing was based on buck dancing, Lane perhaps took his stage name from that source.

There may be elements of sexuality in challenge/display dances—the moving human body is almost always erotic—as well as dimensions of challenge in erotic dances, such as flirtation/avoidance between partners, or competition between men for a female dancer. But dances seem to emphasize either challenge/display or flirtation, not both. For example, Cuban rumba guaguancó may have challenge/display elements, but is clearly a couple/flirtation dance, while rumba columbia is a virtuoso solo display by a series of men (nowadays women as well), with some degree of dancer/ drummer challenge.

The style of kalenda danced in the North Atlantic region of Martinique (similar to Guadeloupean toumblak and kaladja) clearly fits the challenge/ display description. The dance is performed by successive soloists in the center of a circle, until recently always men. Some movements are fixed by tradition, but many dancers develop their own signature variations, which may be spectacular and acrobatic. Dancer and drummer match movements and drum rhythms together; there is an element of improvised reciprocity as well as competition. A well-known Martinican dancer from the North Atlantic region told Dominique Cyrille and me: "You make a turn around the circle before presenting yourself in front of the drum. . . . Now when you arrive before the drum and the drum goes tipitip and immediately marks for you whatever it is you have done. You come and the drum works with you; you come back and the drum is with you. Whatever you have done, the drum works with you" (Vava Grivalliers, interview). This is as neat a synopsis of the challenge/virtuoso aesthetic as any.

## Stick-Fighting Dances

Taking challenge dancing one step further, we find the name kalenda attached to yet another form of Caribbean performance: stick-fighting dances, done almost exclusively by men. The best-known example is the calinda of Trinidad. Stick-fighting calinda was part of Carnival in Trinidad and Grenada from the nineteenth to well into the twentieth centuries (Cowley 1996, 2, 14, 45, 78, 85; E. Hill 1972, 23–31). It spread to the Carnival of nearby Carriacou in the twentieth century (Anon. 1994, 156; Pearse 1955, 30; Pearse 1956, 6; D. Hill 1980, 9). It was also known on St. Thomas (Leaf 1948: 190). Courlander refers to a Haitian stick-fighting dance called mousondi, but identified by older Haitians as calinda (1960, 133). Courlander also mentions a stick-fighting "bomba calindán" in Puerto Rico (133). Gabali mentions a Guadeloupean stick-fighting art, though she switches between two different names, calinda and konvalen (1980, 91, 109). For Martinique I know of a single historical reference to a stick-fighting calinda, in the writings of the untrustworthy Lafcadio Hearn (1923 [1890], 146). Recently, Martinican cultural activists have reconstructed both stick fighting and mimed stick fighting traditions partly based on Hearn, but even among these researchers their reconstructions have been controversial (AM4 2003; Pierre Dru, Daniel Bardury, Maria Vincente-Fatna: personal communications).

It is not clear how the name kalenda shifted from dancing to stick fighting. The relatively late appearance of this usage may be another example of later creole synthesis, as discussed above for bele. (Ditto for the use of kalenda to designate satirical songs, discussed below.)

## Satire and Secularism

By the nineteenth century, kalenda and bele had become, in certain places, the vehicles of topical, satirical song. Cable (1886; in Katz 1969, 43) writes,

"In Louisiana, at least, [kalenda] song was always a grossly personal satirical ballad . . . it has long been a vehicle for the white Creole's satire; for generations the man of municipal politics was fortunate who escaped entirely a lampooning set to its air." Cable's discussion of kalenda songs and musical instruments is extensive (unlike his very brief account of kalenda as a dance) and he seems to have been familiar with these songs firsthand.

On Trinidad, Cowley and others describe both stick-fighting calinda and bele songs as satirical predecessors of calypso (Cowley 1996, 7, 45; E. Hill 1972, 11, 34, 63). In Martinique and Guadeloupe, we find references to nineteenth-century bele as "improvisations" or satirical songs of domestic slaves (Cally-Lézin 1990, 69–70) and of urban free blacks (Hearn 1977 [1924], 84; Rosemain 1993, 53–54). H. H. Breen, in 1844, described St. Lucian beles as songs sung without dancing by the La Rose and La Marguerite societies (in Abrahams and Szwed 1983, 263–265). In Martinique, bele songs provided the melodic basis for biguine (Rosemain 1993, 139–141), just as kalenda and bele songs did for calypso in Trinidad. In this context of emergent nineteenth- and early twentieth-century dance-band music, kalenda and bele were a vital part of urban, proletariat culture in the Creole-speaking islands.

All these dances—kalenda, chica, bamboula, djouba, and bele—appear to have been secular. Apart from Labat's and St.-Méry's nuns, I am aware of very few references to kalenda that specifically involve religion. Epstein (1977, 135) cites an 1885 report from New Orleans of a Vodou ceremony that included "the weird and strange 'Danse Calinda.'" Courlander (1960, 132) notes, "the word Calinda appears sometimes in songs of the Vodoun cult in Haiti" and also mentions the reputed existence of a Calinda secret society, though he is dubious about the latter's reality (166–167). Courlander mentions that the Haitian stick fight mousondi or calinda is associated with the Congo nation of Vodou (133). But these instances are few and far between. In this regard, it is worth noting Bastide's contention that Bantu influence in the New World—and as I shall argue below, all of these dances have strong Bantu roots—survives more strongly in secular folklore than in organized religion (1971, 11, 105–106).

The issue of religion is important because those who have attempted to counter the stereotype of hypersexuality in black dance have frequently insisted on the art's spiritual, ritualistic quality. The "sacred fertility dance" trope finds its origins in European Romanticism, animates *The Golden*

*Bough*, resurfaces in négritude, and continues today in New Age invocations of "spirituality" in regard to virtually everything. There may be truth in this, but too often it seems to be just another exoticizing, primitivist projection. Caribbean dance does not need this apology.

## Other Comparisons

Connecting the dots between descriptions of dances is only one way to trace dance/music history. Elsewhere (Gerstin 2004) I have tracked the names of musical instruments (drums, idiophones) associated with early Caribbean dances, as well as a drumming style—transverse drumming, with the drum laid on its side, the drummer seated on top and using his heel to modify its pitch, and very often sticks played as an accompaniment on the drum's side—closely associated with bamboula, djouba, and bele. Since this technique is considered to be of Congolese/Angolan origin by several authorities (Alén Rodriguez 1986, 170; 1998, 825; Bilby 1985, 187; Kubik 1998, 678; Lewin 1998, 898; Szwed and Marks 1988, 32), it is of particular interest to my thesis.

Other researchers have taken additional approaches. Samuel Floyd (1999) groups certain Caribbean styles by rhythmic motifs, specifically the "cinquillo-tresillo complex" (cf. Pérez Fernández 1986). One might also tackle melodies or lyrics. It is fascinating, for example, that the zydeco "Colinda" recorded by the Lawtell Playboys in Louisiana around 1976 (Spitzer 1976) has the same melody as a merengue recorded in Dominica around 1970 (Malm 1983) (thanks to Pete Simoneaux for this connection). The circles keep widening as one keeps looking.

## Accounting for Discrepancies

I have only scratched the surface of this tangle of names, places, and practices. It is obvious that certain dances were (and are) widespread, but that observers' reports of them differ, sometimes quite drastically. We have various dances with the same name, and similar dances with different names. We have eroticism of many shades. The historical records mix and match with bewildering complexity.

Several possible reasons exist for such a patchwork. Dances can change over time, or as they spread from island to island, even while keeping the same name. Written testimony by white colonials and travelers, which constitutes the bulk of the historical record, is not necessarily accurate. Having heard the name kalenda or chica in reference to one dance, they may have applied it indiscriminately to others. "It is evident," writes Courlander, "that writers tended to use a single name, such as Chica or Bamboula, to cover virtually any kind of dance festivity, much as many white Cubans refer today to all sorts of Afro-Cuban cult dances as Bembé" (1960, 127).

Many white writers were condescending toward or offended by black dances, attitudes that can lead to careless and superficial reporting. Even white observers who took on the task of describing slave dances seriously may have lacked the cultural knowledge needed to discriminate between dances, musical instruments, or the variety and meanings of African eroticism, flirtatiousness, and playfulness. "White commentators," Gordon Rohlehr points out, "tended to view Blacks as a single undifferentiated mass, and only a few would or could distinguish between nation and nation, let alone between dance and dance" (1990, 15).

Slaves often used a single term for multiple purposes, and this practice remains common among Caribbean people today. To take just one contemporary example, *graj* (*grajé*), which means "grate" or "scrape" in French Creole, is both a dance and a dance step in southern Martinique, one of the gwoka dances in Guadeloupe, a contredanse (Blérald-Ndagano 1996: 125–128) or perhaps another form of dance (Beaudet 1998: 437) in French Guiana, and in Haiti both a musical instrument (a metal scraper) and a method of strumming guitar (by analogy to scraping).

Etymology compounds the problem of polysemy. In the Caribbean, the derivation of words becomes a political issue, as people battle over the African and European sides of their heritage. For example, does the Guadeloupean dance term *gwoka* derive from Bantu *ngoka* or *ngoma* (drum, drum dance) (Gabali 1980, 91–96) or from French *gros ka*, "big quart," the rum barrels from which gwoka drums are made (Rosemain 1986, 102)? Does *bele* descend from Kongo *boela*, a dance (Cyrille 2002, 241), or from French *bel air*, "pretty tune" (Rosemain 1986)?

In the end, we may not be able to sort dances by name. The surviving names have too broad a sweep of referents, and doubtless a great many other names have vanished, but we can be assured that several basic choreographic styles existed, including successive couples in a ring, double line dances, challenge dances, and martial arts dances.

If the widespread recurrence of names and practices does nothing else, it provides evidence of the spread of creole culture—from island to island in the Caribbean and from Brazil to New Orleans. I believe that we can use this fact to advance two hypotheses. First, enslaved people from Bantu-speaking Central Africa played a large role in forming these early styles. Second, four of the five dances I have discussed—kalenda, djouba, bamboula, and bele— were particularly associated with the routes of French colonialism. Only the name *chica* seems to have been linked to Spanish rather than French slavery.

## Congolese/Angolan Influences

Much of the dancing I have described is of Central African (Congolese, An-golan, Bantu) origin. The Congolese contribution to New World black cul-ture is widespread. (For studies on this topic, see Bastide 1971; Crowell 2002; Kubik 1990; Thompson 1993.) Besides kalenda, chica, bamboula, djouba, and bele, we have numerous instances of religious cults or rites with Congo origins (Haitian Kongo rites, the Cuban Palo Monte religion, Dominican baile de palos) and quasi-religious nation dances with Congo components (Carriacou's Big Drum, for example).

Reports from New Orleans in the 1820s state that the Sunday afternoon dances of slaves were called "the Congo dance" (Epstein 1977, 132–133) and, of course, the place where dances were held was known as Congo Square. Two of the choreographies discussed here—couple dancing in the center of a circle with flirtation, pelvic isolation, and sometimes contact; and chal-lenge dancing between dance soloist and lead drummer—have also been associated with Central Africa. The former, according to Brandel, is "an in-tegral part of many Central African dances" (1973, 46; cf. Crowell 2002, 17; Fryer 2000, 95–102).

In Brazil, batuque and lundu appear to have been the early Congolese/Angolan syntheses. Peter Fryer (2000) traces the spread of batuque, an early Brazilian dance that featured couples in a circle, pelvic isolation, and pel-vic thrust or contact (called semba in Angola—one hypothetical source of the word samba—and umbigada in Brazil). Becoming popular by the late 1700s among white Brazilians and in the cities, batuque turned into lundu; incorporating Portuguese song in the 1800s, it turned into modinha; adding the salon dances polka and Cuban habanera, in the late 1800s it emerged as maxixe; and in the twentieth century, re-Africanized by the urban poor, it became modern samba. Fryer does not claim, reductionistically, that batuque is the sole ancestor of all Brazilian popular styles (as my synopsis may make it appear). Rather, a Congolese thread runs through numerous transculturations (see also Mukuna 1978, 74).

North of Brazil, Portuguese slave trading was not as intense. Congolese influences arrived largely on different ships: those of the French.

## The French Connection

The Spanish were the first to bring African slaves to the New World, but their chief interest lay in precious metals from the mainland of Central and South America, and they used mostly Amerindian slaves to work their mines. The Portuguese and Dutch dominated slaving through the 1600s, with the Portuguese controlling most shipments to Brazil and the Dutch those to the Caribbean (Fage 1999, 244–248; Thomas 1997, 256). The trade remained relatively small until the Dutch developed the sugar plantation system in the early 1600s. The Dutch system was soon copied by the British and French, who established their own plantations and slaving operations during the mid-1600s.

According to Hugh Thomas (1997), Angolans and Congolese formed the largest percentage of the slave population in the 1600s and early 1700s, mainly because of Portuguese involvement; however, most Portuguese slaves went to Brazil rather than to the Caribbean. The British concentrated mainly on the Gold Coast (present-day Ghana and Togo), Slave Coast (present-day Benin), and later the Bight of Biafra (southeastern Nigeria) and Angola (Eltis 2000, 252; Thomas 1997).

It seems, therefore, that the French were largely responsible for the Congolese impact in the Caribbean. The French began slaving in Senegal in the late 16th century and quickly moved their main trade southward, first to the Bight of Benin and then, increasingly, as the French slave trade reached its peak in the second half of the 18th century, to Congo/Angola. Half of the approximately 675,000 enslaved people brought to the Caribbean by French ships in the 1700s were from Central Africa.

Many islands now associated with the British, including St. Lucia, Dominica, St. Vincent, Grenada, and Carriacou, were originally French or passed back and forth between the two countries. Spain allowed the French to settle the eastern third of Santo Domingo, which became known as St. Domingue, France's largest Caribbean colony, and then became Haiti in 1804 after its successful revolution. The Haitian Revolution sent thousands of French slave owners, slaves, and free people of color to eastern Cuba, to Puerto Rico, and to Louisiana and New Orleans, among other places, with lasting influence on cultural practices and the dance and music of these areas.

Spain also invited French Caribbean planters with their slaves to settle in lightly populated Trinidad in the late 18th century, leaving an indelible effect on its culture, including its famous pre-Lenten Carnival. Kalenda, bamboula, djouba, and bele began appearing in Trinidadian records at this time. Even after the British took over during the Napoleonic Wars, French Creole speakers remained the largest population group, and the Franco-Creole cultural basis was refreshed by waves of French Antillean immigrants and those from the nearby French-influenced British islands.

Throughout the 1700s, France exerted a strong influence on white fashion. Then as now, Paris was a world center of style. The chief dance craze of the late 1600s, contredanse, originated there, and contredanse proliferated into various set dances (quadrilles, cotillions, lancers) through the 1700s and early 1800s. Later in the 1800s, couple dances (polka, mazurka, waltz) became popular in Paris. These fashions arrived in the Caribbean through the twin centers of French influence: St. Pierre on Martinique and Port-au-Prince in Saint-Domingue, France's two richest colonies. They were copied by the slaves, sometimes fairly strictly, sometimes in combination with neo-African traditions. Note that the spread of contredanse occurred during the same years as the spread of kalenda—again suggesting that French commerce was involved in both.

The wide scope of French commerce during the early years of Caribbean colonization is particularly important. Sidney W. Mintz and Richard Price (1992), reconstructing early Caribbean culture, write that adaptations and transculturations arose quickly, spread through commerce between islands, and laid down a basis for creole culture. Similarly, John Storm Roberts suggests that early musical transculturations spread rapidly and "provided the basis for the enduring elements in many mainstream Afro-American forms" (1972, 58). If the French were bringing numerous Congolese slaves during these years and transporting them from island to island once they had learned something of a new way of life, this could have had an enormous cultural impact.

A long-standing scholarly debate exists over the relative importance in black New World culture of creative adaptation (creolization, transculturation) versus the direct retention of African culture traits. Mintz and Price, cited above, argue for creative adaptation. Eltis (2000), in his studies of slave census data, makes a case for a greater homogeneity of African point of origin than previously thought, and thus a greater chance for direct retention. I do not intend to take sides in this debate, and in any case the presence of large numbers of Congolese slaves early in the slave trade supports both arguments. On the side of direct retentions, two of the earliest sources I have found here—Labat's description from Martinique in 1698, and a 1707 painting from Surinam (Price and Price 1980)—feature, respectively, belly contact and transverse drumming, which are purportedly Central African in origin. On the side of creative adaptation, kalenda provides evidence of the speed with which early transculturated styles spread. In Martinique, slavery began in the 1630s; an ordinance passed in 1654 prohibited slave dances; a second ordinance in 1678 mentioned kalenda by name; and the 1685 Code Noir extended the prohibition to all French possessions (Epstein 1977, 27–28).

So far, we have concentrated on the beginnings of Caribbean creole culture, but we should also consider the importance of late arrivals. In some cases, late arrivals were able to use the already established basis of creole culture as a foundation for their own practices, preserved fairly directly. For example, Cuban batá drumming is a reconstruction of Yoruban practices instigated in the 1830s by recently arrived African drummers and wood-carvers (Ortíz 1952–1955 vol. 4, 315–317). In Jamaica, Congolese indentured laborers arriving in the 1800s, after the end of slavery, are linked to the development of Kumina (Carty 1988, 20; Lewin 2000, 243–244). In other cases, however, it is difficult to be sure of the influence of latecomers. About 10,000 Congolese indentured laborers were brought to Martinique in the 1850s and 1860s, after the end of slavery (1848). These immigrants left the plantations behind as quickly as they could and founded their own communities, largely in the south of the island, which retained a distinct identity until very recently. Yet the southern bele style does not feature either the pelvic isolations and contact or the challenge dancing associated with Congolese dance. Martinique's North Atlantic dances seem to exhibit those features to a greater extent, yet most of the North Atlantic dances existed prior to the end of slavery.

## Summary and Caveats

To summarize, I suggest the following scenario: slaves from the Congo-Angola region brought dances of successive couples within circles to the New World, sometimes using pelvic isolation and contact, as well as challenge/ display solo dancing. Both these types were accompanied by transverse drumming with sticks on the side, or by upright drums played with the hands. The slaves adapted these practices into early transculturated forms known variously as kalenda, bamboula, djouba, and chica. Transported by the French, they carried the first three of these dances widely around the Caribbean. The places that recur in mentions of these dances were colonized by the French: Haiti, Martinique, Guadeloupe, St. Lucia, Dominica, Trinidad, Grenada, Carriacou, French Guiana, Louisiana. Kalenda, bamboula, and djouba may have been names for the same or similar dances; a wide range of variation is found in the historical material. Chica may have been similar to the others but was possibly associated with Spanish settlement, or with creoles (mulattos) rather than with black slaves. Some of these styles, for example kalenda and chica, were popular among white and creole as well as black dancers. The first dances laid a basis for later developments, some idiosyncratic and others widespread. The latter include kalenda stick-fighting dances, bele dances, and topical, satirical songs also known as kalenda and bele. Large numbers of Congolese/Angolan slaves arrived throughout the 1700s, and still later arrivals, even after the end of slavery, reinforced Central African influences.

We should treat this scenario cautiously. The Bight of Benin was also important to the French slave trade. This was especially true during early years, from the beginnings of the trade around 1650 up until about 1725, when French activity in Congo-Angola increased.

Certain dance styles and musical practices appear Congolese/Angolan in nature, yet few if any unambiguous cases of direct ancestry exist. The history of each Caribbean island is complex and includes various waves of migration and influence. A few examples, in no particular order, should suffice to show the degree of caution necessary.

Pelvic isolation, even including contact, cannot be considered diagnostic of Congolese/Angolan influence. Kubik warns that dances in Central Africa focus on different parts of the body, not always the pelvis (1994, 38–39). Conversely, pelvic isolation and sexy couple dancing occur in many places in Africa, including the stretch from Liberia through Nigeria that sent large numbers of enslaved people to the Caribbean. I have spoken of challenge dances as Congolese, yet dance and music competitions exist in other places as well (cf. Chernoff on musical "cutting" in Ghana: 1979, 81). Very specific dancer-drummer interaction, as is found in challenge/display dancing, is certainly not absent outside the Congo.

Elements from different parts of Africa blended in the New World. In Cuba, the Yoruban sacred dances are usually played on the Yoruban-derived batá, but may be performed instead by an ensemble combining shekere gourds (West African) with a conga drum (Congolese). Transverse drumming with sticks on the side occurs in Cuban Abakuá ceremonies (Vélez 2000, 18–19), but Abakuá is from northwestern Cameroon and southeastern Nigeria, not Congo/Angola. Histories of musical practices and of dance in Africa and the Caribbean are very incomplete. Somewhere along the line, adaptations were made. We must also take into account changes over time. It is difficult to know just what has been retained and what has evolved.

Nor should we neglect possible European influences. Southern U.S. buck dancing appears to fit the African solo male challenge/display type, but what about flat foot, its white counterpart? In Martinique's North Atlantic bele, each couple in turn performs a monté tanbou (approach to the drum) as a dramatic climax to the dance and an opportunity for dancers to show off their best moves. This is a seemingly African moment, yet European and American contredanses may also include a salute to the musicians, performed by each couple in turn.

Conversely, what appears to be European influence may not be. I have suggested that the double line formation of Labat's kalenda stemmed from French contredanse, yet a very similar dance—lines of dancers bumping bellies—was reported from the Bakongo area in the late 1800s (J. H. Weeks 1882, in Cyrille 2002, 229, 238). On the other hand, by that date European contredanses may have reached Central Africa as well.

I especially want to correct the assumption that a single proto-Caribbean dance gave rise to the rest. This notion informs a great deal of popular literature, tourist performance, and even scholarship throughout the circum-Caribbean. In the French Antilles, kalenda, with its many historical references and its eroticized, romanticized re-creations by tourist troupes, is put into this role (e.g., Rosemain 1990, 1993). Even serious Caribbean writers, tracing roots, are apt to seek very specific African provenances for one or another custom. This is understandable: the search for origins can easily become a search for a singular, undeniable beginning.

But we should not jump to the conclusion that every time we see the name kalenda we are reading about the same dance. A fresh approach would treat the labels attached by early chroniclers with caution, and look instead at the details of the descriptions. If all mentions of circles and lines, or of sexuality, are not assumed to be the same, then we may begin to track a range of expression, a welter of creativity, that passed from island to island and was adapted into distinctive forms. The result might be less conclusive but more accurate, and liberating in a different fashion.

This chapter is a revision of an earlier article (Gerstin 2004). I wish to thank Susanna Sloat and Gage Averill for pointing out several unclear points and additional citations. I owe many thanks to John Cowley and Dominique Cyrille for allowing me to share their knowledge and insights and, in John's case, for the unpublished manuscript from which I have drawn several references. Ken Bilby read an early draft of this chapter and provided many pertinent comments. Richard Price and the anonymous reader of *New West Indian Guide* provided corrections and suggestions on the submitted manuscript. In Martinique, as ever, many people have aided my research, particularly Paulo and Mayotte Rastocle, Siméline Rangon, Daniel Bardury, Etienne Jean-Baptiste, Maria Vincente-Fatna, Charly Labinsky, Georges and Pierre Dru, and the members of AM4.

CUBA

# 3

# Rumba Encounters

## Transculturation of Cuban Rumba in American and European Ballrooms

JULIET MCMAINS

While teaching an undergraduate ballroom dance class, I asked my students to read Yvonne Daniel's description of Cuban rumba published in the first volume of *Caribbean Dance* (Daniel 2002, 47–51). Her depiction of the rumba guaguancŏ as an improvisational polyrhythmic dance in which an assertive man attempts to sexually possess a flirtatious woman who easily foils his pelvic thrusts (*vacunaos*) departed so sharply from the ballroom dance of the same name they were learning, they felt duped. Watching videos of the Cuban rumbas only heightened their confusion. The Cuban styles feature dancers with bent knees, torsos pitched forward, and buttocks thrust behind, in contrast to the straight-legged vertical posture of ballroom dancers. The basic foot patterns and rhythmical structures appear completely unrelated, as does the music, which consists only of percussive instruments and human voice in the Cuban videos and European melodic instruments in the ballroom dance styles.

The Cuban dancers do not even touch each other (and as a result the female dancer can lead the timing and direction of movements as the man chases after her), whereas the female ballroom dancer moves only where she is guided by a physical lead from her male partner, whose hands are almost always in contact with her body. The subtle, sudden movements of Cuban dancers in which limbs, shoulders, and ribs constantly contract inward after sharp outward thrusts contrast directly with the long, languid movements of ballroom rumba dancers whose extensions of limbs and torsos carve out expansive shapes that stretch and melt into space. Differences among Afro-

Figure 3.1. Belkis Quintana and Annier Sanchez of Rumba Morena performing guaguancó at the Callejon de Hamel in Havana, August 2007. Photograph by Grete Viddal; used by permission.

Cuban rumbas (including yambú, guaguancó, and columbia) and among ballroom rumbas (including American and international social and competitive styles) not withstanding, the differences between the Afro-Cuban and ballroom styles are so startling as to leave any viewer astonished that they could share the same name. Aside from an emphasis on hip movement and a narrative of courtship, other similarities are difficult to find.

Most histories of ballroom dance account for the stark divergence between ballroom and Afro-Cuban rumba by clarifying that rumba as practiced by ballroom dancers is actually based on the Cuban son (American Rumba Committee 1943; Buckman 1978; Leymarie 2001; Murray 1938, 1942; Stephenson and Iccarino 1980; Veloz and Yolanda 1938). Admittedly, much of this discrepancy can be explained by the once common usage of the word *rumba* as a general term for any Cuban dance or music, resulting in the exportation of sones, boleros, and guarachas under the name rumba. According to ethnomusicologist Robin Moore, the troubled history of appropriation and reinterpretation of the Afro-Cuban rumba began on the island of Cuba itself in the late nineteenth century when white Cuban performers imitated and mocked black rumba musicians and dancers in *teatro vernáculo*, a theatrical genre similar to American blackface minstrelsy (Moore 1995, 1997).

The subsequent exportation of this "commercial rumba" to Paris in the 1920s and the United States in the 1930s led to an international "rumba craze," in which a wide range of Cuban (or more generally Latin American) music and dance styles were performed under the name rumba. Even these early exports departed drastically from the rumba music and dance styles developed by poor, primarily black Cubans in the late nineteenth century. Capitalizing on an international fashion for consumption of black culture (reflected in white fascination with the concept of *négritude* in France and with the Harlem Renaissance in the United States), many white Cuban musicians with little direct experience of Afro-Cuban rumba became international rumba ambassadors, creating a new genre of music and dance born from a mix of popular Cuban music and dance styles and international exotic fantasy.

Although Cuban hotel and cabaret owners had previously considered rumba too low class to be included in their floor shows, pressure from international tourists compelled Havana's nightlife establishments to stage rumba shows by the 1930s. For the first time, mulatto and black performers entered the commercial rumba sector, although their shows included little Afro-Cuban street rumba but were instead based on the hybridized, some might say bastardized, commercial rumba their audiences had seen in European cabarets. Some of these mulatto cabaret dance artists, including notables René Rivero and Estela (Ramona Ajón), who performed at the 1933 Chicago World's Fair, incorporated some movements from Afro-Cuban rumba, such as spectacular tricks of the male columbia soloist who dances while balancing a glass of water on his head or with sharp swords grazing his skin. These rumba steps were interspersed, however, with movements from many Cuban dances (son, danzón, guaracha, conga, and Santería rituals) as well as European dances (paso doble, ballet, ballroom). Thus, even when mulatto and black Cuban dance performers began traveling internationally to perform, the rumba they exported had little in common with the traditional rumba practice of black Cubans.

This fascinating and troubling history of exhibition rumba music and dance, which reveals much about the racial and national politics invoked through international circulation of expressive culture as commerce, has already been documented by other scholars (Moore 1995, 1997; Leymarie 2001). These historical records, however, do not address the social practice of rumba dancing in Europe and the United States. Descriptions of rumba in American dance manuals written in the 1930s and '40s, which consistently identify rumba as the Cuban son, are remarkably similar to each other in their instructions for the dance (American Rumba Committee 1943; Murray 1938, 1942; Veloz and Yolanda 1938), its technique and steps remaining relatively unchanged over the next sixty years (Buckman 1978; Don 2002; Engel 1962; Murray 1954; Stephenson and Iccarino 1980). To assume that the ballroom rumba is merely another name for the Cuban son, however, does not take into account the history of rumba/son export, in which Cubans themselves created a pastiche of many dances to appeal to the exotic obsessions of their foreign consumers.

Furthermore, it does not explain the rather dramatic split between American-style rumba (called the box or square rumba in Europe), and the revised English version sanctioned by the Imperial Society of Teachers of Dancing in 1955 and now used worldwide in competitions under the name "International style rumba." This International style ballroom rumba differs from the box rumba in its basic foot pattern, its vocabulary, and, most significantly, its rhythm. Whereas the box rumba uses a square foot pattern and four-count rhythm that matches squarely with the music, the English version uses a diamond foot pattern and begins on the second beat of the measure instead of the first. If ballroom rumba was based on the Cuban son as other historians have claimed, what accounted for the two different interpretations in ballroom practice?

Not satisfied with my own ability to adequately explain the relationships between and among the Cuban, American, and European rumbas to my students or to myself, I set out for Cuba in December 2005. The forty-three-year-old American embargo (or blockade as I was continuously reminded by those on the island) on trade with Cuba had resulted in a cultural isolation that I had not anticipated given the speed at which cultural expressions are shared, co-opted, and fused in the twenty-first century. Afro-Cuban street rumbas (yambú, guaguancó, and columbia) were celebrated and enjoyed throughout Havana with virtually no knowledge of or concern with rumbas practiced by ballroom dancers. Without access to the Internet (the use of which was illegal for most Cubans in 2005), international media, or travel, few Cubans had ever seen ballroom-style rumba. This lack of expo-sure resulted in myriad difficulties of translation.

When I tried to describe ballroom rumba as rumba *de salon*, Cubans as-sumed I was referring to rumba performed in Cuban cabarets for tourists, which, although more theatrical than traditional Afro-Cuban rumba, bears little in common with International or American style rumba practiced in ballroom studios or competitions. I tried to explain that people in Europe, Asia, and North America dance a rumba that differs radically from their own, but the contemporary Cuban cultural understanding of rumba is so unified, and their memory of the export of hybrid commercial rumbas in the 1930s and '40s so faint, that I was routinely met with the quip "rumba is rumba." They could not imagine any rumba beyond their own. I resorted to putting my iPod to people's ears when explaining my research, blasting them with a romantic love ballad that departed so sharply from the poly-rhythmic drumming of Cuban rumba that people would either look at me suspiciously as if I were playing a crude joke or break into outright laughter at the mere thought of dancing rumba to such music. The music used by ballroom dancers for rumba is not rumba music by any Cuban definition, but is most frequently identified by Cuban musicians as bolero, guajira, son, or balada.

I had traveled to Havana to research the relationship between ballroom rumba and Afro-Cuban rumba to discover that none of my informants had ever heard of ballroom rumba. Many of them told me that no relationship existed between the two, and I began to question it myself. Was the relation-ship coming into existence only through my own academic exercises? Did it have any relevance to those practicing either form? I had only to reflect on the relative demand for Afro-Cuban rumba and ballroom rumba in the United States (there is maybe one student of Afro-Cuban rumba for every hundred studying ballroom) and the relative incomes of Afro-Cuban versus ballroom rumba teachers (Cuban artists are not appearing on *Dancing with the Stars*) to know that it did. Even in Cuba, the lives of *rumberas* were af-fected by tourists whose ideas about rumba had been shaped by a century of its misrepresentation in the West. I forged ahead.

I had embarked on my journey armed with a few fragments of history. The English rumba was introduced by M. Pierre (whose surname Zurcher is known by very few, since Pierre used only his given name throughout his professional life) and Doris Lavelle in the late 1940s. Pierre immigrated to England from France, which was the portal through which Latin dances entered European high society throughout the first half of the twentieth century, and was considered England's foremost authority on Latin dances in the 1940s and '50s. His partner, Doris Lavelle, was a young English dancer, born Doris Davis, who trained for seven years under Pierre before becoming his professional partner and adopting the stage name Lavelle (presumably to further the illusion that she too was French and thus a more "authentic" Latin dancer). In December 1947, Pierre traveled to Cuba to study the Cuban rumba, returning four more times with Doris before the revolution in 1959. After his first excursion, Pierre began teaching an entirely new rumba to the English public that was eventually accepted by the Imperial Society in 1955. Realizing that few Cubans would have heard of Pierre and Lavelle, I began my search for information about their Cuban teacher—"the famous professional Pepe Rivera" (Lavelle 1965, 1).

Havana has an impressive array of specialized research libraries with knowledgeable research staff, and I spent many hours looking for information on Pepe Rivera and his partner Suzy in El Museo de la Danza, La Casa de las Americas, La Unión de Escritores y Artistas de Cuba (UNEAC), Fundación Fernando Ortiz, La Casa de la Música, La Biblioteca Nacional de la Cultura, and several days in La Biblioteca Nacional, where I met Cuban ballet historian Francisco Rey Alfonso, who said he'd been in the library nearly every day for more than ten years reading archives for references to dance and had never come across Pepe's name. After three weeks of combing libraries, I met only the second person in Havana who recognized the name Pepe Rivera. Helio Orovio, Cuba's foremost scholar on Cuban music, told me with all the authority of an academic superstar that I would not ever find a written reference to Pepe and Suzy, at least not in Cuba. He vaguely recalled that they were dancers of little significance in Cuba teaching rumba to a white clientele.

When pressed to describe the style of this rumba, Orovio confirmed what had already been relayed to me by Alfredo O'Farrill, a well-known Cuban dancer and professor of Afro-Cuban folkloric dance. Pepe Rivera likely taught a cross between rumba yambú and son danced by whites in Cuba in the 1940s that has almost entirely vanished from current historical or popular memory. What seems certain, however, is that white Cubans

Figure 3.2. Pierre and Lavelle, 1938. Photograph taken at the Blue Cafe, Leamington, England, of Doris Lavelle dancing a solo rumba accompanied by Monsieur Pierre on the bongo. Photograph by Walden Hammond. Used by permission of Bruce Davis, nephew of Doris Lavelle.

of a class high enough to interact socially with European tourists were not dancing guaguancó, the Afro-Cuban style now associated with the name rumba in Cuba. Although rumba may have achieved international success in the 1930s partly because of its association with blackness, Afro-Cuban rumba was still not accepted by the white elite in Cuba in the 1950s. It was only after Castro's government embraced traditional Afro-Cuban rumba as a symbol of national culture in the 1970s that Afro-Cuban rumba was widely celebrated by all sectors of Cuban society.

Between trips to archives, I was studying dance with two different Cuban teachers: Pilar, a teacher who catered to tourists and rarely taught anything beyond beginning level salsa, and a dance teacher at La Escuela Nacional de Arte, whom I will call Maritza (a pseudonym). One day when I returned from a son lesson with Pilar, I showed the video of my dancing to my Cuban friends. That's not son, they decried with outrage. When I had a lesson later the same day with Maritza, I learned that the dancing I had been doing earlier, while sharing some of the footwork patterns of son, had the accents in all the wrong places. I had transposed the movement, which in son is accented in the rib cage, to the hips, and I had entirely missed its relationship to the music. My tourist teachers had been teaching me modern-day Cuban salsa to son music.

It was at this moment that my Cuban friend Claudina gave me a precious insight. "I'll bet this Pepe and Suzy you're looking for were like these teachers you went to see today," she told me; "just regular people who knew a little bit about dancing trying to make a few pesos off the European fascination with Cuban dance." No wonder the Americans and the Europeans got the rumba so mixed up, my Cuban friends concluded. Pierre and Lavelle would not have been able to study with someone like Maritza, someone formally trained in dance, dance pedagogy, and dance history. Social and folkloric dances were not taught in Cuba until after the revolution, when the Cuban government reorganized education and began teaching Cuban folkloric dance alongside ballet and modern in specialized art schools. In the 1940s, Cubans did not learn social, popular, or folkloric dance in formal classes. They learned by growing up in the culture, imitating their elders in daily life. There would not have been any rumba teachers for Pierre and Lavelle to consult, except those who catered to tourists—shrewd business people who adapted the Cuban dances to suit the abilities, tastes, and expectations of their foreign clients.

After I returned from Cuba, I was lucky enough to locate and visit Doris Lavelle's nephew, who graciously offered me copies of the diaries she had kept while traveling through Cuba and a precious film fragment of her dancing with locals in Havana. This film confirms that Pierre and Lavelle were indeed studying son. The silent film also shows Pierre playing the clave to accompany Doris's dancing, offering evidence that Pierre and Lavelle understood the centrality of clave to Cuban dancing. Whatever shortcomings their Cuban teacher may have had, he taught them son in the rhythm as it was commonly danced in Havana at the time—*contratiempo*. Literally translating to "against time," contratiempo dancing in the case of son means starting each step at the end of the measure (count 4 of a 4-count measure), refraining from stepping on the downbeat (count 1), and then continuing to step on beats 2 and 3. It was this Cuban contratiempo rhythm that Pierre and Lavelle brought back to England, which then became the basis of international rumba.

Having concluded that the new "Cuban system rumba" Pierre introduced to English ballroom dancers in 1947 was indeed based on the son, I still was not certain about the Cuban antecedents of American rumba. At least since the 1940s, Americans have been teaching rumba using a square footstep pattern that begins on the downbeat. Although it appears to depart dramatically from the Cuban son danced contratiempo, it is possible that the American rumba was also an adaptation of the Cuban son, which, although commonly danced contratiempo, can also be danced *a tiempo*—on the downbeat. It is also possible, however, that the American rumba dancers drew more heavily from the Cuban danzón, which was more often danced a tiempo than the son and frequently made use of a step referred to as the *cuadro*, or box. Regardless of whether early American rumba dancers invented their steps after watching Cubans dancing danzón or son (or more likely both), their most significant misinterpretation of Cuban dancing may have been in assuming that the steps, rather than the music, define the dance. Although the steps and even the rhythm for Cuban social dances are variable, the dances do not exist independently from the music for which they are named. Pierre's interest in learning to play claves and the many records with which he and Lavelle returned from their travels demonstrates their awareness of the interdependence of Cuban music and dance, knowledge that faded with subsequent development of rumba in England and the United States.

When I presented some of this research to an audience consisting predominantly of Cuban exiles in Miami, I performed, with a partner, an International-style rumba for them to a popular bolero used in ballroom competition. Our audience asked us, "Why does it look like you are dancing off-time?" I fear that Pierre and Lavelle would have been heartbroken at this reception of their legacy by the Cubans. In the English attempt to mathematize the dance, they may have missed the point. Dancing contratiempo does not just mean breaking on beat two; it also means anticipating the downbeat and then landing on the next upbeat after a slight delay. But above all, it has to do with a specific relationship to the clave, the two wooden sticks that establish an underlying rhythm in both rumba and son music. Without the clave, which is rarely used in pop ballads to which ballroom dancers commonly practice rumba, the rumba-on-2 rhythm is not merely contratiempo but entirely outside the rhythm.

After the Cuban revolution of 1959 and the U.S. embargo imposed in 1962 curtailed cultural exchange between Cuba and the West, the subsequent development of rumba by European and American ballroom dancers on the one hand and by Cuban dancers on the other occurred in virtually nonintersecting "parallel traditions," a phrase introduced by dance scholar Anthony Shay to describe divergent practices of a single genre when performed in different contexts and communities (Shay 2002, 17–18). Competition ballroom dancers began incorporating arabesques, pirouettes, and splits into their rumbas, further distancing their practice from its social roots. In contrast, the Cubans re-embraced the traditional Afro-Cuban street rumba, relinquishing the cabaret rumba-as-variety-show spectacle in favor of outdoor rumba events without costumes or stage. Increasingly in the 1980s, Cuba's national folklore company began performing Afro-Cuban rumbas on international tours, and by the mid-1990s Cuba began encouraging "cultural tourism" in which Europeans came to watch or study traditional Afro-Cuban culture, including rumba. As a result of these cultural exchanges, and the defection of many Afro-Cuban dance artists to Europe and North America, the parallel traditions have once again begun to cross, and many people, like my ballroom dance students, are bewildered by the encounter.

It may be tempting to identify the Afro-Cuban rumbas now seen weekly at *el sábado de la rumba* or Callejón de Hamel in Havana as the "authentic" rumbas and the ballroom versions as foreign impostors. Such a reading, however, discounts the multiplicity of rumbas that proliferated on the island of Cuba before and during international exportation and transculturation throughout the first half of the twentieth century. It also fails to recognize the efforts of people like Pierre and Lavelle who, however limited they may have been by their own history, were deeply invested in understanding and appreciating Cuban culture as the Cubans lived it, not as a reflection of English or American exotic fantasy. Doris Lavelle's diaries of her trips to Havana reveal that she and Pierre conscientiously avoided tourist locales and instead sought out *academias* (public taxi dance halls) where at least Cuban men danced for their own enjoyment rather than employment (the Cuban women in these dance halls were in fact employed as taxi dancers).

So if the actual steps and techniques of the American rumba and the English rumba more closely resemble the Cuban danzón and son, respectively, where is the Cuban rumba in the Euro-American versions? Is the relationship only one of economics, wherein the ballroom rumba dancers have at times displaced Afro-Cuban rumba dancers from representing and profiting from rumba in international markets? I suggest that the Afro-Cuban rumba, which was legally banned in Cuba in the early twentieth century (Moore 1997, 170) because of its association with the black underclass from which it developed, lives on in European and American rumbas in two important ways. First, the illicitness and the blackness of rumba was important for its initial success in Paris in the 1920s and in the United States in the 1930s. The idea of rumba as a forbidden black dance made it particularly appealing. The fact that the rumba performed and sold in Europe and America was not actually the forbidden black dance did not hamper its success as long as it carried the association of scandal through its name. Even today, ballroom rumba continues to tantalize Western audiences through its illicit, implicitly black, sexuality.

Second, I believe that the visual narrative performed by competitive ballroom dancers today is the same as that told by Afro-Cuban rumba dancers. The story embodied in guaguancó—the unending chase of a coquettish woman by a boasting man whose advances are continuously thwarted by her cunning and elegance—can also be seen in ballroom rumba. The female ballroom dancer alternately accepts and rejects the advances of her male pursuer in a continual interplay of acquiescent dips and coy retreats. Is it possible that the ballroom dancer's rapid closing of her legs in fan position, the sudden covering of her feminine jewels after inviting contemplation of her inner right thigh, is a remnant of her deft reply to his vacunao in guaguancó? Perhaps the rumbas of the ballroom and the Afro-Cuban street tradition are not as utterly unrelated as they first appear to be. It is naive to conclude that these rumbas have only a name in common. They share a complex history that reveals both a deeply troubling racist legacy and the resilience of rumba to reassert vital characteristics throughout a century of appropriation, recontextualization, and transculturation.

Versions of this paper were presented at the World Dance Alliance Global Assembly, Toronto, Canada, July 21, 2006, and the Congress on Research in Dance, Tempe, Arizona, November 3, 2006. I would like to thank all my friends in Havana, who so graciously helped me in what must have appeared to them a fool's errand. In the United States, I would like to thank Neri Torres for her patience as I tried to make my ballroom-trained body learn Afro-Cuban postures and rhythms. I would also like to thank Bruce and Barbara Davis for so generously sharing their treasured family archives with me.

# 4

# My Experience and Experiments in Caribbean Dance

RAMIRO GUERRA

TRANSLATED BY MELINDA MOUSOURIS

The boy was twelve years old, still in elementary school, already an avid movie fan. He had saved for a ticket to a movie premiere in one of Havana's fashionable neighborhoods. The film was *A Midsummer Night's Dream*, by the famous German director Max Reinhardt with an all-star Hollywood cast of the 1930s. Reinhardt's cinematic production of Shakespeare's classic had astonished the film world, and the boy walked all the way from his home far away to the Teatro Campoamor, solemnly, full of expectation.

The entrance of the King of the Night, flying through the air to earth with his courtiers to dance with the wood nymphs in the forest, was a beautiful ballet to the music of Mendelssohn that left him astonished. Going home in a state of ecstasy, midway he was nearly crushed by a car. So intense was his transport that he didn't hear the horn's warning. Only a great leap that he seemed to remember unconsciously having just seen in the film saved him from catastrophe.

So began the adventure of a boy already in the fourth year of a Catholic school paid for by his godfather and uncle, as he lived with the family of his mother, whom he had lost at age five.

We lived in the neighborhood of Cayo Huseo. If not exactly poor and marginal, the neighborhood was rich in households of black families who drummed and danced the religious rites of Santería and also the popular dances such as rumba in the courtyards. Extended families lived together in narrow rooms that faced on the common courtyard. Through the courtyard, they shared the collective life of an African community.

It was a "hotbed" neighborhood in which the boys played dangerous games: throwing stones, flying kites from the roofs with razor blades attached to the long tails, gangs competing in war games for dominance. The sound of drums filled the nights, coming from religious ceremonies or simply from parties.

I, protagonist of this story, wasn't permitted to share in the neighborhood games. I lived submerged in a large family of thirteen, ten women and three men. Among us were widows, married women, and some single women. They were bank employees, businessmen, and, one, a mechanic. A strong matriarchy ruled, as was natural. I lived with the three men in the bedroom that faced a roof and my grandmother's garden. Dinner was a noisy affair, animated by political discussion, a subject of much controversy in those years in Cuba. My life combined school with reading comic books and an eclectic assortment of old books pulled from the family bookcase; Chaplin, Keaton, and Laurel and Hardy comedies; and movie romances with beautiful women on the arms of Valentino-like men. Music from the radio also filled the house and so did radio serials, popular with everyone. All this made me a huge fan of big musicals, full of songs, chorus lines, and tap dancers moving in the geometric choreographies of Busby Berkeley.

All this delighted me, even though I was not too strong as a boy and a little neurotic in the midst of this agitated family life. I played marbles, making geometric formations, humming the popular songs of the day. As an adolescent, I fashioned myself into a dance star invited to entertain the teenagers at block parties held to celebrate birthdays and anniversaries. At this time I was living with my godfather and going to high school in Old Havana. There, to the radio, we danced danzóns, fox-trots, pasodobles, and even tangos, which we came to know through Argentinean movies. One day, for a masquerade party, it occurred to me to dress as Pinocchio. The costume caused a sensation and transformed a timid boy into a fifteen-year-old masked seducer. The girls left their boyfriends and even their fiancés to dance with me because they could shine as my dance partners. But I finished these dance parties alone, rejected by the girls I liked or pursued by the ones I didn't.

I graduated and went on to university. By this time I had a steady girlfriend who was a ballet student and impressed upon me that to dance seriously, you had to study seriously. But, in the 1940s in Cuba, for a man to perform ballet or modern dance on the stage would be a mortal sin. Yet I decided to do this and started classes at the Pro-Arte school. Pro-Arte was the center of international culture in Havana, at whose concerts I had been able to see Ted Shawn and Miriam Winslow.

From there I went on to study with Nina Verchinina, a key figure in a touring Ballet Russe company that had based itself in Cuba. In addition to ballet technique, Nina taught me the technique of the German school of movement that was so influential in the birth of international modern dance.

During this period, many Cuban dancers like Alicia, Fernando, and Alberto Alonso and Luis Trapága were already leaving Cuba to join companies based in the United States. I began to dance in Pro-Arte premieres, and I adopted a pseudonym to shield me from the scorn of my family and others in my daily life. Mostly because the people I knew didn't attend Pro-Arte concerts, I was never discovered. Later, I joined a company started by Verchinina, who took me with her when she rejoined Colonel de Basil's Ballets Russes de Monte Carlo. The company toured Brazil and New York, where I left it, looking to study at the Martha Graham School.

When I returned to Cuba, I began to teach in the new environment of national Cuban dance that was emerging. My university law degree was in my pocket, never used after convincing my family that to be a dancer was neither dishonorable nor a social deprivation, a concept that was acknowledged in my family, if not completely in the general social consciousness, which caused me some trouble from time to time.

I traveled to Colombia as a teacher and later to Paris and Madrid, where modern dance was hardly known. Back in Cuba, I was performing wherever I could, being practically a one-man show, from raising the curtain, playing the music from old records, changing costumes, and improvising the lighting to answering to the applause or hisses of the audience, who began to recognize me as a personality performing outside the mainstream. At least in the world of art and theater, I began to be respected as belonging to the avant-garde.

Political and social changes of the 1960s opened horizons hardly explored before in Cuban national art. The study of popular, folkloric, and modern dance underwent a series of expansions as state-subsidized companies were created. The support given to the already prestigious classical ballet was now extended to Cuban folkloric, vernacular, and modern dance, to build new dancers and repertory, performing for audiences receptive to a dance ever more open to innovation with respect to tradition.

Thus as a director I had at my disposal a company, some thirty dancers, whom I carefully selected in equal parts representing our racial mix—ten whites, ten blacks, and ten mulattos. They were trained by me in modern dance, and after barely one year of exhaustive work on a repertory—very Cuban in theme and dance movement, with music and set design by Cuban artists, and in which modern dance and Cuban folklore were well fused— we performed in Paris.

The Theater of Nations, a prestigious international festival created specifically to present the cultural diversity of international arts, invited us to perform. I was the first to be surprised at the critical acclaim with which we were received. After two weeks in Paris, we were invited to tour Russia and various socialist countries.

Upon returning to Cuba, we began an annual season of performing throughout the island in April and May, not only in theaters where they existed, but also in parks, at student and worker meeting places, at the sugar refineries, and in the open gathering places, on portable stages, where farmers came on horseback to see perhaps the first dance performance of their lives.

In Cuba, we created a national network of amateur performing groups, and in Havana developed a group of teachers that set out to establish dance classes throughout Cuba, teaching Cuban, Latin American, and European folkloric dance. The amateur groups performed in regional festivals that culminated with the companies from all the provinces coming to Havana for a finale performance. Taking part in this national arts program gave me the opportunity to teach and supervise festivals and to give workshops, as well as to train dance teachers to disseminate dance throughout Cuba, work that laid the groundwork for the creation of the National School of Dance as a branch within Cuba's National School of the Arts, known as ENA (Escuela Nacíonal des Artes), established in Havana. ENA's graduates, who were selected from dancers nationwide, joined the regional companies that were formed later.

At the same time I continued to work at developing, in the bodies of my dancers, a style of movement informed both by the concepts of modern dance and by the unselfconscious manner of moving that Cubans have, coming from their African roots, expressed in Cuban popular dances, and in the African religious rites that are very much alive in Cuba. A mix of African dance and the Spanish in Cuban daily life is present from the simplest gestures to the virtuosity of movement of religious observers and street dancers.

Thus was created a strong dance movement language differentiated from the Spanish style by adding the Cuban-ness of the street and its expressions, alive with sensuality and full of human warmth, in which I also discovered an elegance, not at all elite, but vital and spontaneous. The torso and pelvis communicate, along with arms, head, and feet, to project a clear and precise meaning, uniquely transmitted, across space.

An extract of my technique class with the title *Ceremony of the Dance* was adapted to the stage, prompted by Maurice Béjart, who on a visit to Cuba encouraged me to show it to the public. For *Ceremony of the Dance*, Jorge Berroa composed aleatory music for each performance as in each improvisatory dance class. The music was very creatively synthesized to create a sonorous unity with the dance. It utilized piano chords and live singing, and made use of orchestral recordings and also of a well-known promo from Radio Reloj with its trademark tic-toc and the voice of the newscaster giving the news schedule, emphasizing the measure and passage of time. All these auditory elements combined well with the spatial dimension of dance.

The search for national identity was a strong stimulus not only in dance, but also in the other arts, as Cuban artists worked to crystallize expressions that, if not universal, would make strongly personal impressions.

Beginning with the 1960s, the international spread of culture allowed us, without losing our identity, to open it to further exploration at the creative edge. Not only dance, but culture in general called out for exchange between the arts, very separate until then. In this way, dialogues between the arts began that enlarged the possibilities of art and moved forward quickly, changing the relationship between the arts and the public.

I then began to train my dancers in the other performing arts, in singing, voice production, and theater, involving them in special experiments not common in dance performance. A national identity needn't be altered by these explorations. Rather, they preserved us from falling into a sterile and closed folklorism and let us keep the doors open to inspiration. We were able to benefit from the new aesthetics of international culture without violating our own.

Figure 4.1. Ramiro
Guerra on his
apartment terrace in
Havana. By Melinda
Mousouris; used by
permission.

Thus my dancers assimilated the values of contemporary theater and were able to achieve a personal and unconventional relationship with the spectators as they invaded the theater aisles, climbed up walls, hung by ropes from the second balcony, and flew above the heads of the audience. We created new scenic impressions, adding film images, and we moved outside to the street. Traveling vignettes are not unusual now, but they were when my dancers made use of the open spaces around the National Theater of Cuba in my work *Decalogo del Apocalypsis* (Decalogue of the Apocalypse). After a year of enormous work at state expense and of rehearsals open to the public, because of the ruling of bureaucratic administrators, this choreography was suspended.

Dating from the suspension of *Decalogo* in 1971, I realized that my presence in the company was reduced to that of merely an administrator and not an artist and creator, and I withdrew. I threw myself deeply into other projects. I wrote on theoretical problems of dance and on conclusions drawn from my choreographies and artistic experimentations, pursuing the implications raised. I worked with the Conjunto Folklórico Nacional, Cuba's national folkloric company. Here, I faced other challenges inherent in dance, such as adapting folkloric material to the stage without losing its traditional values. I concentrated on creating work from other regions with very distinct traditions that had not been incorporated into the Conjunto. I choreographed *Triptico Oriental* with material from eastern Cuba and *Trinitarias* from an all-night festival of Villa Clara in central Cuba. *Trinitarias* introduced, for the first time on the stage, dances on stilts.

In my work on bringing Cuban folklore to the stage, I also turned to the street songs of the colonial era, the *trovador* tradition, the *congos reales*, and the masked carnival dances of the city of Trinidad, distinct from those of Havana.

I also threw myself into a work exploring Cuban gesture and common Cuban expressions. *Refranes, dicharachos y trabalenguas* (Sayings, jokes, and tongue twisters) made abundant use of the rich, soulful gestures of my dancers, and we achieved an extremely amusing work with which the audience felt a strong rapport.

At the invitation of Fernando Alonso, I choreographed *Two Nightingales*, based on a story by Hans Christian Andersen, for the Ballet of Camagüey. I created it as a personal vision, passing from medieval China to Japanese kabuki, utilizing this style of theatrical dance. In addition, I used the expanded vocal technique of the dancers and the total space of the theater, requiring the dancers to go up and down from the orchestra pit to the stage in a dangerous passage across a platform built on top of the orchestra. The music was a collage of Stravinsky's opera *Song of the Nightingale* and an orchestral version of the same by Ernest Ansermet, using a metronome on stage synchronized with a recording of "The Nightmare of the Emperor's Shadow."

The set by Julio Castaño was constructed with various rolling cylinders the dancers carried and with which they formed the image of the lake, the nest of the nightingale, the imperial palace, and the bedroom with the emperor's bed. I created the solo of the emperor's desperation completely in silence. From the beginning, scenic puppeteers, as in Kabuki theater, delivered a comedic ongoing commentary to the audience in a pseudo-Japanese language made of brand names of well-known Japanese products like Toshiba, Sanyo, etc.

I can say that from the time I had a company of dancers made to my own creative measure, I never stopped advancing my choreographic investigations. Once I had accomplished the fusion of modern dance with folklore in my country, my dancers were capable of giving themselves over to dance improvisation and the study of other systems complementary to choreography. They trained in drama, studying for their roles in *Orfeo Antillano* (Orpheus of the Antilles) by penetrating their characters. Using the Stanislavsky method, they were able to create biographies for each one, prior to encountering them in the work. I have held onto their biographies for their psychological insight.

Since *Suite Yoruba* was filmed as a short documentary by ICAIC (Instituto Cubano de Arte e Industria Cinematográficos) filmmaker José Massip and was a prizewinner in the Leipzig Film Festival of 1961, I decided to include scenes filmed in nature in the live stage actions. Thus the battle between the gods Ogun and Shango was seen on screen during the actual confrontation, mythically enlarging the event on stage. And when it finished, the choreography continued live. I imported the film image into the work not as a decorative form, but to give the performance a new dimension. This was the first break in my work with theatrical conventions. Today it is not uncommon, but it was in the early 1960s. There was not yet a public for new work. Even as we toured in Europe, audiences were not yet comfortable.

In *Orfeo Antillano* I used dynamic changes of recorded music to emphasize events during the carnival sequences. The slowing of the speed of the conga *toques* from 78 to 45 or 33 rpm created a distorted atmosphere in which the dancers slowed, or wildly and madly accelerated their movements, while the soloists remained frozen in the middle of the tumult, emphasizing the fundamental drama of the events in contrast with the exultation of the carnival. This situation was reversed at times, with the suspension of the carnival dancers, so that only main characters developed the conflict. The murder of Orfeo occurred actively in dance, while the rest of the carnival remained paralyzed like a frozen image outside the drama. This surreal dynamic had a big impact on audiences.

This work also used a combination of live music of the carnival drummers over a recording of *The Veil of Orpheus*, electronic music by Pierre Henry, conveying multiple levels of reality and myth in Orfeo's mind.

Humor, from burlesque to sarcasm, was the means I used to break with the intensely dramatic cycle of my preceding work, and also to create a new reality that reflected an aggressively politicized world and that aimed to break the rules under which art could not trespass below a certain tone. I sought to use Cuban humor—shameless, insolent, useless—with critical significance in the world in which I was living. In that way my Cuban identity didn't suffer. I made a turn onto the political and economic terrain of which I had been part for a long time, even when universal dance theater had no name, with a burlesque sense of humor, aggressive and irreverent.

The use of space was one of my main methods for developing new themes in flexible spaces, using the conventional properties of theater space, incorporating skylights, passages, balconies, and lobbies; exteriors and their surrounding parks, gardens, exterior walls, windows, even roofs, garage entrances, and nooks of large buildings like Cuba's Teatro Nacional, and including unusual spaces like the tower of my apartment with its interior duplex, iron stairways, and two small terraces. These were locations for developing repertory that included *Impromptu Galante, De la Memoria Fragmentada* (From Fragmented Memory), *Time of Phantoms* and *¿Fedra?*

In *De la Memoria Fragmentada* in 1990, I created a montage to celebrate the thirtieth anniversary of my first company, using dancers from the founding and current generations. The work referred with some irony to works that were nearly forgotten because they had not been preserved as repertory and had disappeared from the official choreographic memory. Working through a minimalist expressionism, I chose fragments from my works danced by the original company, dispersed through the theater's spaces.

As the audience entered the lobby, they encountered ghostly images. The dancers moved like souls in purgatory through all the areas of the theater, creating flashbacks recognizable to the audience, until they reached the stage, full of smoke fumes, where they disappeared in the density of forgetfulness. The same images were projected, in distorted variations, on a large screen as if exploded from a cannon. They were surrounded by puppets moved in wheelchairs like invalids, recognized by Cuban audiences, who screamed at the images, as bureaucrats. Dancers striding on stilts, with large suitcases in hand, like travelers, were recognized by Cuban audiences as opportunists, benefiting from my company to leave the country. There were conflicts between the old and current company members, at times violent, at others merely ironic or sarcastic, seasoning the work. These events appeared as metaphors for the bitter situation that arose when the government appointed young dancers trained at the National School of the Arts to replace the founding dancers, the force of whose work created the base of the company. I depicted in dance the scorn of the new dancers for the founding members.

In the final sequence, incongruous choreographic fragments flow into one another like fleeting images in a dream; in a kind of celebration their characters emerge as a solid group from all the factions of the company. I used the words of an old bolero: "Absent is forgotten / to say 'fog' is to say 'never.' / Birds can return to the nest / lost souls never return," as the curtain fell slowly. When the curtain rose for the dancers' second bow, only the empty wheelchairs were on stage to receive the applause, my final irony.

In 1992 I produced *Ordalias*, another spatial dance experiment for my dancers, in the tower of my own apartment, located on the top floor of a high-ceilinged building in the art deco style. I had seating room for only seven people in this unique space. A wrought iron spiral staircase leads to a trap door you must climb through to gain access to two small terraces and another floor which is the building's tower. There, with three dancers and me handling the lights, music, set, and costume changes, we performed this work portraying an adolescent initiation rite in our contemporary world.

The youth entered nude down the wrought iron staircase. In the choreography he came very near to the audience, separated by only one or two meters. A strange character suddenly appeared who was the guru or maestro, launching tests of intellectual and sexual knowledge and submission to power, while the spectators dressed the boy, and little by little he began to acquire knowledge. These events and others demanded that the dancers and audience walk on ledges and explore unusual spaces that were part of the architecture and functioned as the scenery. Sometimes the dancers even had to run personal risks, as when they had to dance on terrace walls fifteen stories above the ground. This created an intense and significantly compromised relationship between the dancers and spectators. After the performance, as we all sat in my apartment, drinking tea, we discussed their reactions. The male and female nudes practically brushing the bodies of the

Figure 4.2. From *De la Memoria Fragmentada*. Photograph by Lissette Hernández. Used by permission of Ramiro Guerra.

audience created strong sensations, positive and frightening, worthy of being heard. Someone who came casually without her husband and was seated on the floor found herself wondering what would have happened if her husband had been there when the nude male passed very close. For another, the naked man appearing at the top of the mysterious cubicle proved very disturbing until the light increased and the nude was joined by the guru.

*Tiempo de Quimeras* (Time of Phantoms) was created in 1992 with the Danza Libre Company of Guantánamo in eastern Cuba. Danza Libre was a very professional group, with a strong background in improvisation based on Cuban social gestures. This was an area I had already explored with the National Folkloric Company, but in this case we were working with the specific theme of current events, such as the food shortage of the 1990s and the lines to obtain food products; the mix of popular religions, fused with universals; myths of power; comedic impressions of some popular celebrities, and other events associated with the years called "the special period." When the Eastern European socialist bloc disappeared, it came to me to create this with ironic humor. I made use of Cuban sayings and popular refrains. Even in the most elaborate stylizations of Cuban folklore, I was mindful of not losing the roots. Working with a young company whose improvisations were fresh and uninhibited enabled me to create an easy flowing piece that audiences in Havana and throughout Cuba thoroughly enjoyed without feeling weighed down by a complex choreography with sophisticated meanings.

*¿Fedra?* (Phaedra), made in 2000, was my last work and based on ancient characters in classical theater that had a direct relation to our national way of life and contradictions.

A very unusual group of heavy dancers called Danza Voluminosa was the interpretive vehicle through which I could liberate the perception of dancers' bodies from prejudices, which, like other phobias concerning minorities, have dominated society. I made strong use of travesty. The queen, desperately in love with her husband's son, was portrayed extravagantly by the group's director, Juan Miguel Mas.

The recitative of the Greek chorus, half song and half speech, was transformed using the rhythms and cadences of Cubanized rap. I used the historical dance technique of Isadora Duncan, shorn of balletic dogmatism to choreograph the sequences of the heavy dancers. Hipolito and also Fedra expressed themselves in live and recorded operatic arias, while King Teseo's vocal language was a stream of discourse of consonants unsupported by vowels, an excited tirade of absurd chatter. Aphrodite appeared as the goddess Oshun of Cuba's Santería rites, singing and dancing her grievances against Hipolito to the melody of the famous "Guantánamera." Hipolito and his gay friends did a sort of striptease to rock music based on the popular theme of Cuban transportation, after entering on a bici-taxi (that product of Cuban inventiveness combining the bicycle with an upholstered back seat for passengers). In this way, the piece tells the story of the tribulations of the queen. The element of visual surprise plays a big part in the work. The toques and dances of Oshun become background for a celebratory can-can by the heavy dancers, and a pas de deux of ballet technique with difficult lifts is danced by Fedra and Hipolito, gallantly executed by these dancers without falling into caricature.

The ancient work provokes reflection on today's world with reference to an intertextuality, far off in time, but passing from the classic to the postmodern with an intense critique of the contemporary world.

This, my last work brought to the stage, I believe incorporates all that I have gathered of my experience and experiments with the synthesizing of dance styles: working with themes that translate from myth to daily life; incorporating historical dance styles into theater dance; making critical studies of the convulsed contemporary world of the twenty-first century in which we are living; creating an entertainment that breaks with sexual identities and confronts the right of minorities to have a place for expression in contemporary culture, without negating their own identity on this globalized and globalizing planet on which it is our lot to live.

# 5

# The Africanness of Dance in Cuba

GRACIELA CHAO CARBONERO

TRANSLATED BY MELBA NÚÑEZ ISALBE

This work is humbly dedicated to Don Fernando Ortiz,
who inspired us with his *Africanía de la música folklórica cubana.*

The African-rooted legacy we inherited from the enslaved men and women of this continent in past centuries is present in many aspects of Cuban culture and in the traditional culture of the Cuban people.

In different traditional cults and religions of African origin, dances play a leading role in rituals whose main aim is to pay tribute to divinities, entities, forces, and spirits. In these ceremonies, possessions help create a direct communication with the various deities. Among these religions are Regla de Ocha, or Santería, the cult of the orishas; Regla de Palo Monte, of Bantu origin; Regla Arará, the vodunes or fodunes cult from the Ewe-Fon culture; and the Abakuá secret society introduced by slaves who belonged to the Efik and associated peoples who came from old Calabar in what is today southeastern Nigeria and the adjacent region in Cameroon.

Regla de Ocha or Santería encompasses various types of Yoruba-based ritual ceremonies in which people sing and dance for the orishas. The Güemilere or Tambor de santo is the most important of these rituals and is where the sacred batá drums play an important part. Among the initiation rites, the presentation to the drums constitutes a key element. Those new initiates known as *iyabos* must dance for the first time in front of the batá drums to finalize the initiation ceremonies.

In the different sects of Congo origin, Palo Monte, Briyumba, Kimbisa, and Mayombe, whose practitioners are commonly known as *paleros*, palo dance integrates their ceremonies and rites. The Ararás also dance for their deities, fodunes or vodunes.

Drum rhythms, dances, and chants in all three cases have different forms and qualities. Years ago I investigated Santería dances and steps in the Güemilere ritual and could differentiate twenty-two steps; however, steps are not the most important aspect of these dances. The principal element to be considered is chest movement coordinated with arms, hands, and the entire body. All of these contribute to the meaning of arms and hands moving in gestures in which the sea, thunder, and wind are among the aspects of nature and human life that may be represented.

Congo dances, on the contrary, are characterized by simple steps with strong movements. (In Cuba, the steps of Congo-derived palo, yuka, and makuta are considered simple when compared with the twenty-two steps of Santería dances.) Dancers kick hard on the ground and jump, and shoulders and arms join in the dance as a consequence.

Arará dances are distinguished by a rapid and sustained shoulder movement. The Haitians who migrated to Cuba in the first decades of the twentieth century were also vodunes or fodunes worshippers. As a consequence, their dances also incorporate shoulder movements. What is known in Cuba as Arará came from the Ewe and Fon cultures in Africa, in and near the kingdom of Dahomey (present-day Benin and adjacent Togo and eastern Ghana), the same area from which were brought many enslaved people to Haiti, where their religion is known as Vodou (and in Cuba, Vodú).

In the Abakuá secret society exclusively of men, only íremes or diablitos dance, wearing their hooded garments. As íremes are mute, they communicate their thoughts through gestures, but in this case no trance is achieved.

We have mentioned four of the ritual manifestations of African origin in Cuba where dance plays a key role. These examples alone would suffice to highlight the importance of the African antecedents, but ritual dances, like music, have transcended their initial frontiers and reached other manifestations of the traditional culture not related to religious factors. The different styles of rumba (yambú, guaguancó, and columbia) are good examples of this. So, too, are the carnival congas or parrandas practiced nowadays in cities and towns of the entire island.

If we analyze the steps and movements of these dance forms we will see that many of them derive from ritual steps that have been assimilated. For example, the woman's basic step in guaguancó is similar to the step danced for the orisha Ochún in the distinctive Iyesá tradition of Yoruba religion. No doubt some men's movements in columbia come directly from Abakuá íreme dances.

Other examples could include the similarities between the basic step of Havana and western Cuban carnival comparsas and one much used in Santería, the step dedicated to Ochún in the chant *Eladde Ochún*. Another is the hip and body movement characteristic of gagá and Vodú, both of Haitian origin, with the particular style of the conga of Santiago de Cuba, which is marked with accentuated hip movements.

In peasants' traditions, especially in the annual celebration of the Fiesta de los Bandos in Majagua Ciego de Ávila, we can see how they execute several *sones miméticos* (mimetic sones). In sones miméticos the song text tells the dancers the mimetic movements they must execute. Among them are El papalote (the kite), El gavilán (the hawk), and El chivo capón (the gelded goat). There are many others. La Chindonga or El Perico Ripiao constitute good examples of strong Congo influence in the torso and hip movements. (In Cuba El Perico Ripiao is a son mimético. In the Dominican Republic it is a merengue típico.) Its basic step can be compared with the basic step of Colombian cumbia, also of Congo origin.

We have reached the border raised by some scholars between folkloric dances and those known as ballroom dances of European influence introduced in the seventeenth, eighteenth, and nineteenth centuries. People slowly transformed these European dances, such as contradanza, vals (waltz), polka, and others, by incorporating new ways of doing them. They also created new styles. The habanera, danzón, danzonete, mambo, and cha-cha-chá were born out of contradanza or Cuban danza.

As early as 1836, Esteban Pichardo, in his dictionary of Cuban voices, commented on the African influence on the Cuban danza in its musical sense and on dancers' flirtatiousness. This influence translated to all the ballroom dances previously mentioned. It is amazing how we can compare a cha-cha-chá step with one of Ogún's basic steps in Santería ritual ceremonies, or see traces of rumba in the man's style in all these dances. We cannot forget that those men and women who dance for their orishas in a ritual dance are the same people who entertain themselves with a rumba or a popular dance in the Havana club La Tropical. At each venue they dance differently, but somehow movements, steps, and styles translate from one dance to another in a natural and spontaneous manner.

At present this process can be particularly well analyzed with casino, the most popular couples dance in Cuba. Casino is not a musical term; it is the name with which Cuban popular dancers baptized a new dance style in the parties celebrated in the club Casino Deportivo in Havana around the 1960s. At the Casino, a fashion emerged for dancing in a circle formation. When those same dancers attended other clubs and parties they said, "Let's make the circle exactly the same as in Casino." The name remained and even now casino is the most popular dance in Cuba. It can be danced to salsa, to a modern son, or to a timba criolla, timba being a newer dance music style that takes son as a base, with musicians playing various percussion instruments at a faster pace in timba's rich interplay of rhythms. But casino is a dance style born before salsa music. It is danced mainly with the steps of the Havana or urban son or the danzón. Casino can be danced in couples or coordinated into a ring or wheel (*rueda*) of interacting couples, directed by a caller. This form is called rueda de casino and has attracted enthusiasts, developing their own steps, in many places around the world.

Casino also bears traces of African roots integrated into many steps, like the half turns women make under the instructions of the leader or caller, which, though characteristic of many turns or figures, are in a way similar to the half turns typical of dances for the orisha Ochún to the batá drums of the Yakotá toque. When the caller instructs a new turn, all men lead their women into the new figure. African roots are also present in the hip and shoulder movements and in the step improvisations men make in the figure *ni pa ti, ni pa mi* (neither for you nor for me), which is related to rumba.

This African influence can also be perceived in other Cuban nontraditional popular dances like mambo, mozambique, and pilón, which are styles in which professional dancers or even musical authors themselves created the steps (or some of the steps) later imitated by the population. In many cases steps were created following some movements in ritual dances. For example, one of the steps of mozambique is very similar to the basic step of the orisha Elegua in which he practically supports his body on one foot.

We will now briefly discuss what happens in the diverse styles of theatrical dance in Cuba. We'll begin with one of the major contemporary achievements of Cuban culture: the Cuban ballet school. In *Alicia Alonso, diálogos con la danza*, the investigator and journalist Pedro Simón (1986, 19) makes reference to the influence in all theatrical dances of the folkloric exuberance of Spanish and African musical and dance roots. This is the first factor that must be considered when explaining the very successful development of theatrical dance manifestations in Cuba, including the Cuban ballet school.

African-based dance movements, dynamics, and gestures have been directly incorporated into the Cuban technique of modern dance, highly acclaimed abroad (see John 2002). Using Martha Graham's technique as a base, Ramiro Guerra, company director and choreographer, trained dancers in the Conjunto Nacional de Danza Moderna (now called Danza Contemporánea de Cuba) in the early 1960s. He counted on the American teachers Lorna Burdsall, Elfrida Mahler, and Waldeen de Valencia, and on Elena Noriega from Mexico. Years later the company's dancers studied other techniques such as José Limón's, but early on Guerra himself and other Cuban choreographers realized the necessity of creating a technique that would fully incorporate the Afro-Cuban movements necessary for the essential Cubanness of their choreographic pieces. Master teachers such as Eduardo Rivero, Arnaldo Patterson, and Victor Cuéllar, in close collaboration with Guerra, helped create a new technique, the técnica cubana, which continued to develop in succeeding years. At present the students of all dance schools are trained in this technique, rich in Afro-Cuban ritual dance elements.

The variety dance style is a different sort, one used by choreographers in nightclub and cabaret shows and on television. The leading exponents at present are the dancers and soloists of the Cuban television ballet and of the world-renowned club Tropicana. Luis Trápaga, Cuban teacher and choreographer, was the creator of a technique in the 1950s to train dancers in this style. He based it on a barre with closed or parallel positions incorporating hip, torso, and shoulder movements, characteristic of rumba. Years later numerous teachers and choreographers developed this style; among the most recognized are Cristi Dominguez of the television ballet and Santiago Alfonso of Tropicana. Santiago Alfonso, trained in Danza Contemporánea and in the Conjunto Folklórico Nacional, has nourished the variety dance technique with elements of Afro-Cuban ritual dances.

The Africanness of dance in Cuba can be visualized as a ladder at whose base are ritual dances. The first step corresponds to those dances of strong African influence, but detached from any religious base. The second step amalgamates abundant African elements of body movement and style into European frameworks such as sones miméticos and ballroom dances. The third step belongs to theatrical dances of a variety of styles.

# 6

# Secrets Under the Skin

## They Brought the Essence of Africa

JILL FLANDERS CROSBY

WITH MELBA NUÑEZ ISALBE, SUSAN MATTHEWS,
AND ROBERTO PEDROSO GARCÍA

## Introduction

"Aaaaafrica" is a cry that rings out over and over above the insistent sound and sight of the drumming, singing, and dancing during Arará religious ceremonies in Perico, Cuba, as the energy level ratchets up another notch as more deities arrive by manifesting themselves in the bodies of community worshippers. "We are from Dahomey" is the response from residents of a nearby town called Agramonte when we query them on details of Arará history in their community. Elders in both communities who are great-grandchildren of former enslaved Africans speak with determination of the stories of their relatives who were tricked into climbing onto a slave ship, or proudly of relatives who brought their drums, deities, and necklaces for those deities from Africa. Elders insist that Arará in their individual communities is the "original" or "first" Arará in Cuba, based on the fact that the deities, drums, and necklaces did "arrive here directly" from Africa. Their roots in Dahomey (present-day Benin, West Africa) are fundamental to their identities as Cubans in communities where the Arará danced religion is practiced. Africa is proudly their source.

Of course, few material things could be brought by enslaved Africans as they endured the passage across the Atlantic, but once in Cuba, African peoples found ways to remake representations of their deities from memory with objects found in Cuba. Religious rituals also continued from memory in whatever way they could be practiced. Drums were eventually remade. Rhythms, songs, and dances were remembered, revitalized, and reinvented as individual Africans from different ethnicities and diverse villages came together in singular locations under the weight of slavery. In Matanzas province, located on Cuba's northern shore, the revitalizations and reinventions of their danced religious expressions became known as Arará.

This narrative is based on a long-term study, 1991–2008, exploring the connections of the Ewe and Fon peoples of West Africa to those of the Arará peoples living in Cuba as a result of the slave trade. The study informing this narrative spans the countries of Ghana, Togo, and Benin, West Africa, across to Cuba. Flanders Crosby began this project after observing during a 1992 Ghanaian research trip that the Ewe peoples' religious dances bore striking similarities to Arará dances she had learned in Cuban dance classes in New York City. Cuban coworkers Melba Nuñez Isalbe and Roberto Pedroso García of Havana joined the project in 2005, assisting with additional Cuban research and with Cuban interviews, translations, and transcriptions. Susan Matthews joined in 2006, providing musical and visual art analysis for the project. Flanders Crosby has traced the retentions of Ewe and Fon religions and religious music and dance expressions from Africa to the Arará religion and religious music and dance expressions of Cuba. Flanders Crosby has also looked at the differences and similarities between Arará as a performance form developed by folkloric companies such as Conjunto Folklórico Nacional de Cuba and Arará as it exists in ritual (see Flanders Crosby 2008). Together, Flanders Crosby, Nuñez, Matthews, and Pedroso have researched the uniqueness of Arará as it developed in Cuba by documenting the individual histories of Arará in Matanzas province, in particular, the towns of Perico and Agramonte.

This chapter provides a historical overview of Arará in Perico and Agramonte. The narrative details the oral histories of several elders, reveals the beliefs that continue to strongly attach them to Africa, and concludes with a broad overview of connections between Ewe and Fon religious practices and Arará religious practices in Perico and Agramonte. At first, this project's focus was to research the artistic form of Arará dance and music; however, it is the historical contexts, evocative oral histories of elders, and stories of African connections that resonate so strongly and stand out so boldly inscribed over the research data landscape. It is these contextual histories,

stories, and connections that underpin, inform, and are embodied in Arará dance, music, and ritual. Therefore, the focus of this narrative will be the evocative stories and contexts of Arará rather than specific steps, songs, or rhythms. For all of us involved in this project, the stories and contexts of Arará have added weight and substance to our own individual performance practices and identities as dancers, musicians, visual artists, religious practitioners, and/or Cuban nationals.

## Arará in Cuba

Arará is the name given to the Ewe and Fon people who arrived in Cuba, as late as the 1860s, often through Allada in the former Dahomey, as enslaved Africans to work at sugar refineries and mills in Matanzas province (Basso 1995; Daniel 2002, 2005; Fernández 2005). (Slavery was not abolished in Cuba until 1886.) The Ewe and the Fon share not only a physical proximity to each other in West Africa, but also a cultural heritage and common attributes of artistic and religious expression (Daniel Avorgbedor, interview, March 2, 2008). In the center of Matanzas province, former enslaved Africans and their descendants who eventually settled in the Perico area worked primarily at a sugar refinery called España. According to those we interviewed in Agramonte, people who settled in the Agramonte area worked at a sugar operation called Unión de Fernández. (Others also may have come from the nearby Santa Rita Baró refinery.)

For Ewe and Fon people brought to Cuba as enslaved Africans, their religious musical and dance expressions, according to many we interviewed about their ancestors, were their identities as a people torn from their homeland. In Cuba, they continued their religious practices to the best of their ability. The Arará religion, as it was eventually named, both is and is not a continuation of Ewe and Fon religious expressions as they exist in West Africa. The West African roots permeate, underpin, and inform Arará; however, Arará is its own revitalization and reinvention of the Ewe and Fon religious expressions by the people who practiced them as they endured slavery and later worked together to rebuild a new life in Cuba.

Arará as a religious expression in Cuba did not adopt a homogenous form across Matanzas province any more than homogenous religious forms exist across the Ewe and Fon areas of West Africa. The Ewe and Fon peoples had (and still have) multiple variations of music and dancemaking (Avorgbedor 2005) along with diverse deities from their respective West African communities; however, common attributes can be identified—shared and discernible larger deep structures across these diverse music and dance expressions (Flanders Crosby 2007), along with shared deities, often with slightly different names depending on location and people (Daniel 2005; Fernández 2005). These commonalities and diversities met each other in multiple locations across Matanzas province. As people were isolated in individual forced labor communities, Arará evolved differently at each site; thus, individual Arará variations are prevalent.

However, just as deep unifying structures are discernible across Ewe and Fon religious, music, and dance expressions, it follows that shared and discernible underlying deep structures exist across the various sites where Arará is practiced. Core aesthetic similarities can be seen in dances, rhythms, and ritual procedures, and in religious deities and their physical representations (known as *fodunes* or *fundamentos*) that evolved from the shared attributes among the Ewe and Fon. Likewise, the interviews we conducted with elders revealed very rich individual oral histories in Perico and Agramonte, but through each interview runs a shared theme of transformation and retention, pride in the roots in Africa, remembered stories about relatives who were slaves, and insistence on objects arriving "directly from" Africa. Also striking were the fundamental beliefs of these elders that, somehow, tradition, rituals, and the memories of key elders who endured slavery and who created Arará must be retained, practiced, and remembered.

## Perico

The most revered person in Perico in relation to the birth of Arará is Ma Florentina Zulueta. Ma Florentina, a former Dahomeyan princess called both Tolo-Ño and Na-Tegué, was captured and brought to the refinery España to work under owner Don Julián de Zulueta y Amondo around the 1860s (Alonso 1997). According to a document located in Perico's cultural museum, she was only fifteen years old when she arrived. Because enslaved Africans in this area were given the same last name as their owners, she was called Florentina Zulueta in Cuba (Basso 1995; Ortiz 1975). After she was free, Ma Florentina, as she is known in Perico, eventually settled in Perico and was instrumental in starting La Casa de la Sociedad Africana (The African Society House) in 1887 (Alonso 1997). According to elders, Sociedad

Africana was the heart and soul of Arará in Perico, functioning as a collective aid society and as a center of religious activities. Such societies were called *cabildos*. According to oral history, early members initially housed their individual fodunes together under the roof of Sociedad Africana. Over time, the various fodunes were dispersed and went to live in houses of individual family members.

Apparently many of these fodunes were made by enslaved Africans who lived and worked at España, while several others were made by their first descendants. The fodunes are still cared for and revered by the current descendants of their original owners. They not only are a direct link with the first practitioners of Arará, but also appear to provide a direct link to Africa since so many are believed to have "arrived here" from Africa. The fodunes of Ma Florentina, along with the fodún of Victoria Zulueta, who was raised by Ma Florentina, are to this day housed in Sociedad Africana, which is currently under the direction of Victor Angarica, known as Prieto, the grandson of Victoria Zulueta. Prieto is an important member of the community and critical to the survival of Perico's Arará tradition. Not only has he agreed to take on the responsibility of running Sociedad Africana, but he is also a drummer conversant in all the rhythms and bell patterns used to call the deities. Drummers enjoy special status in the religious community, as it is primarily through ritual drumming and dancing that the deities can be brought back into the realm of the living. Vocalized prayers in the creole language of the slaves, specific rhythms played on drums and bells, dance steps, and ritualized gestures laden with meaning have been carefully preserved and passed down in cabildos such as Sociedad Africana.

Ma Florentina and Victoria's fodunes, along with the drums that were brought to Perico by Ma Florentina, still receive annual ritual blessings by Prieto's extended family and other important drummers and religious leaders in Perico. According to local legend, the drums were brought by Ma Florentina from Africa, although Prieto says they were bought from a nearby community. True or not, the legend of the drums' African origin is strongly believed in Perico.

On December 27, 2007, the fodunes and drums were carefully placed inside a small religious *casita* (shrine) to receive their "feeding" of the blood of animals that would feed everyone involved in the ritual. Ma Florentina's original fodún takes the form of stones imbued with an Arará deity called Hebioso. These sacred stones that once belonged to Ma Florentina, along

Figure 6.1. Hebioso's stones inside the bowl in Perico. By Susan Matthews; used by permission.

Figure 6.2. Altar to Hebioso in Perico. By Susan Matthews; used by permission.

with Victoria's Arará fodún for San Lázaro, reigned over the site and were prominently placed in front of the drums that so many believe came directly from Africa. Inside the metal bowl filled with Ma Florentina's stones stand two worn, wooden statues representing Hebioso, one a full-body representation, the other shaped like a head and face. As legend has it, the statue in the shape of the head and face also came directly from Africa. As Prieto tells us, Ma Florentina carved both from her memory of Africa. The family also fed two of Ma Florentina's other fodunes, located at the front gate of the outside compound. Known collectively as the "guardians," one of these is also believed to have come directly from Africa. Again, true or not, the legend of the African origin of these specific fodunes is strongly believed. For this family, their roots are in Africa, and Africa is clearly their source.

Armando Zulueta, born in 1923, was another influential figure in the history of Perico. As a small boy, he was at his grandmother's house when San Lázaro manifested himself in Armando. When a deity manifests itself in (or "possesses") someone, the person enters a trance state during which he or she is able to perform ritual movements and gestures recognized by the community as attributes of that particular deity. As Armando's niece María Eugenia Zulueta describes it:

After the possession he remained at my grandmother's and didn't know how to get back to his mother's. Ondesia [his grandmother] told him, "Let's go. I'll walk you over to Teresa's [his mother]." And when she arrived with him she said, "Teresa, Teresa." "What?" "Here's Armandito, do not beat him because San Lázaro danced over his head." He was never possessed by any other than San Lázaro, not even by his guardian angel. When he celebrated for his deity, he spent all the money he had and that means we cannot let it die. (María Eugenia Zulueta, interview, December 18, 2005, transcription and translation by Melba Nuñez Isalbe.)

Armando would become well known throughout the area for his generosity and healing powers, either by helping others receive San Lázaro, or by helping them overcome illness through what is known as the Aguán ceremony, held every year on December 18th. The Aguán involves cleansing for all people in attendance with fowls, plants, and food offerings of dried corn and other grains and legumes. Attendees cleanse themselves by passing handfuls of the various food items over their bodies before receiving additional cleansing with the fowls by sanctioned elders and religious practitioners. All items used for cleansing are then placed in a large *canasta* (basket) carried away by a runner to an undisclosed location so that all the impurities go outside city limits. Upon the return of the runner with the canasta, an evening of ritual music and dance follows, and the runner cleanses himself with plants and herbs that he brought back in the canasta. In former times, the runner would go to a small hill near España called Ducaqué, a place of much resonance with the people of Perico despite its associated slave history.

Hilda Zulueta, an important elder in Perico, took us to Ducaqué late one afternoon, shortly after the Aguán still held at Armando Zulueta's house by María Eugenia Zulueta in honor of her uncle and the tradition she says must not die. In the late afternoon sunlight, a sea of tall, electric green sugarcane stalks rustled in the wind against the stark red of the soil set against a deepening orange sky as we stood at Ducaqué and felt the presence of so many before us. Moments earlier, Hilda had taken us to an enormous ceiba tree located right beside the now crumbling España. The ceiba tree, so reminiscent of baobab trees in Africa, had been an important ceremonial site for former enslaved Africans, as ceiba trees are considered sacred sites (Cabrera 1996). Here at this tree, she tells us, enslaved Africans and their descendants would make offerings to the deities. She shuddered when she got near that tree, for too much power still existed there for her to go too close.

Justo Zulueta, Hilda's grandfather, was a foreman at España and had a fodún called Oddu Aremu. Reinaldo Robinson, Justo's son, still lives in Justo's house and takes care of Oddu Aremu (although Reinaldo insists that Oddu Aremu takes care of him). Oddu Aremu lives behind a white cloth underneath an elaborate old altar.

Before describing Justo's altar, it is important to understand that eventually Arará adopted characteristics of what is called the Lucumí religion (or Santería), the most widespread African-derived religion in Cuba, similar in many ways to Arará, with origins in an area adjacent to Dahomey. Under the weight of slavery, Lucumí emerged from the meeting of the Yoruba peoples' traditional religious practices with those of the Catholic religion. Since many of the predominantly Yoruban deities (orishas) shared similar attributes with Catholic saints (as well as with Arará deities), the Yoruba deities have both an African name and a Catholic name. As Africans were not allowed to practice their religion openly, the Catholic representations lived

Figure 6.3. Hilda Zulueta in today's Ducaqué. By Susan Matthews; used by permission.

out in the open, while the African representations were frequently hidden under altars. Thus, the Arará fodunes may also have Catholic and Lucumí representations and live underneath altars as well.

Additionally, according to many we interviewed, the various Afro-Cuban religions, or "all things religious," are related. Thus, it is normal during an Arará ceremony with Arará rhythms on Arará drums for a practitioner's Lucumí saint to come down. As well, many elders passed away before passing on information on how to "give" their Arará deities to new practitioners. The exception is the Arará San Lazaro, since Armando Zulueta made sure that that knowledge was passed along. But Lucumí has grown in importance in both Perico and Agramonte as well as in Cuba on the whole.

Justo's altar for Oddu Aremu is filled not only with multiple statues of the Catholic representation of Oddu Aremu—Our Lady of Mercy—but also with statues of several other Catholic representations such as Santa Barbara for Hebioso. The statues, some more than a hundred years old, are prominently displayed as well as tucked up into the recesses of the altar. Photo-

Figure 6.4. Justo Zulueta's altar in Perico. By Susan Matthews; used by permission.

graphs of living and deceased relatives, vases of plastic and fresh flowers, and glasses filled with feathers have also been placed on the altar. At the top of the altar is an enormous and beautiful statue of Our Lady of Mercy that Reinaldo says was brought for the altar around 1948.

Behind Justo's house, as is true at so many houses where the fodunes live, is a well where another Arará deity lives. Although Reinaldo is not sure of the deity's name, he believes it is most likely Malé, a deity that represents the snake. Wells are important for Arará deities, as, according to elders, several Arará deities like to live in water (Valentín Santos Carreras, interview, December 18, 2007). Behind Sociedad Africana is another well where Malé also lives, and according to Hilda, there is another old well at España where Malé lives.

## Agramonte

In December 2007, we all spent an afternoon in Agramonte, sitting on the porch of 93-year-old Melao (Hilario) Fernández Fernández as he narrated stories of Manuela Gose. According to oral history, she and another elder called Ta Andres "Coso-Coso" were both tricked into getting on board a slave ship and were brought to Cuba to work at Unión de Fernández. After her freedom, Manuela continued to live in the small community of Unión de Fernández before moving to Agramonte.

Next, we went to the house in Agramonte where Manuela Gose had lived and talked with Israel Baró, husband of Manuela's great-granddaughter Onelia Fernández Campo. When Manuela came to Agramonte, say Israel and Onelia, she brought her fodunes and established an African Society at her house sometime in the late 1800s. Unlike those of Perico, all the fodunes of Agramonte were not housed in Manuela Gose's house; rather, the fodunes stayed with the individuals who carried them to Agramonte. According to Israel, the African Society's function in Agramonte was to serve as the vehicle for receiving permits from local authorities in order to conduct religious ceremonies.

One of Manuela Gose's many deities, they tell us, is Nanú, a serpent with the colors of a rainbow that is syncretized with San Manuel. Israel and Onelia are adamant that the fodunes came with Manuela Gose when she was transported as a slave.

Figure 6.5. Melao Fernández in Agramonte. By Susan Matthews; used by permission.

Following are excerpts from an interview by the four of us with Israel Baró, Onelia Fernández Campo, and Mario José Fernández, an important religious practitioner in Agramonte, on December 31, 2007. Transcriptions and translations are by Melba Nuñez Isalbe.

*Melba: Do you know how she brought them from Africa?*
*Israel: No, but she brought them. That's been talked about a lot because it was difficult to bring any object from Africa; however, she brought them. That's why this is so important here since it was so difficult to bring things from there.*

*Mario José: Maybe you see some attributes they didn't bring from Africa, but they brought the essence . . .*

*Melba: Yes, their memories.*

*Mario José: Just like my great-grandmother Ma Jacinta. She was born with a secret in her hands . . . and she brought it from Africa inside her hand. And that's how they brought their things, sometimes they swallowed them . . . then they vomited those things here, they expelled them, they got them out; I don't know how, and then they created a "fundamento" using the experience they had with them. It is not that they brought that whole cauldron with everything it contains; they brought the essence and they brought the spirits and summoned them here. . . . Attributes are one thing, but many of them brought their deities, their secrets, and that's how they brought them. Some brought stones; others brought the power inside the shackles traders made them wear when they were enslaved. That is in their feet or maybe they had it under the skin . . . In Dahomey they had those secrets under the skin . . . and once they got here they got them out. They made a fundamento out of the things that were similar. They found similarities in some elements here and established a syncretism just like the ceiba tree. There was no need to have the original cauldron here, but you may ask one of the elders, "Is that from Africa?" and he/she will answer, "Yes."*

It is said that Manuela Gose could make rain fall whenever and wherever she wanted. Comments Mario José: "She made rain fall on her property. She spoke her Dahomeyan language and threw her bucket of water and rain fell. It didn't matter if it wasn't raining in any other place . . . it rained. I didn't see it; those were the stories my godfather Chicho used to tell me." (Mario José Fernández, interview, December 31, 2007)

## Connections

The connections between the Ewe and Fon and the Arará practices and people are the living links between two worlds. Some connections are already well known in the field, others are more obscure, while still others reside in the spirit and beliefs of those who have been interviewed for this project. The connections described below are but a sampling of a richer tapestry.

Hebioso, in Arará, is a deity that, broadly stated, represents the power of thunder and lightning. Xebioso (with the X pronounced like a guttural H) among the Ewe and Fon also represents the power of thunder and lightning. Similarities in visual representation between Hebioso and Xebioso include the color red, and the fact that the Xebioso/Hebioso representations are frequently in the form of stones believed to have been cast from the sky during thunderstorms. Among the Ewe and Fon, Da, who is the snake, "walks" beside Xebioso and has a revered spot in the religious pantheon. Malé, as the snake is known in Perico, is also an important divinity (Basso 1995). Xebioso and Malé live in water.

San Lázaro, another important divinity in Perico and Agramonte, is known as Sakpata in Togo and Benin (Basso 1995; G. E. K. Amenumey, interview, June 9, 2006; G. K. Nukunya, interview, May 25, 2006). Representations of both deities are strikingly similar. Inside a small family shrine compound for Sakpata in Adjodogou, Togo, dwells a revered tree for Da. Da, according to my Togo and Ghanaian sources, can also "walk" with Sakpata. According to sources in Perico and Agramonte, San Manuel, also known as Malé (the snake) is another personality or possible representation of San Lázaro.

In Ghana, there is a dance called Togbui and the steps are almost a mirror image of an important Arará step. When I showed Cuban elders the way one dances for Togbui, they would smile with glee when they recognized Togbui's deeper dance structures that are the same for most Arará dances: the rise and drop of the shoulders in a successive double-time feel, two rise drops right next to each other, pause, and again. All is in harmony with the tap in and then placement out of the foot, with the rhythm of the shoulders, as the hands follow the rhythmic feel with the feet; together open, together open.

This same step can be seen in a dance known as Atsia in Ghana and Togo. When I showed videos from Cuba to my colleagues in the Dance Department of the School of Performing Arts at the University of Ghana, they remarked not only on the similarity of the steps, but on the sound of the rhythms as well. "It sounds like Atsia," exclaimed Patience Kwakwa, dance professor. When I showed Atsia, as I videoed it in Togo, to community members at Sociedad Africana, they cried, "You see, there it is," falling into the double rise and drop of the shoulders and placement of the feet on the correct place in the Togo rhythm, even though at that particular point in the video, a different movement for Atsia was on the screen. Other cries included comments on the similarity of faces to their relatives: "That could be my brother, uncle, grandmother." When I would play Arará music and songs for my Ghanaian coworker, Johnson Kemeh, master drummer from the Anlo-Ewe area of Dzodze and music instructor at the University of Ghana, he would often exclaim, "I know this song," or "I know this rhythm," or "I know what melody or rhythm will come next." When I tell Israel Baró and Onelia Fernández Campo that many scholars believe San Manuel is the equivalent of Da and that Da is an important serpent divinity among the Ewe and Fon in Africa, their faces reflect a calm sense of newfound connections.

Israel remarked, "Yes, and it is incredible how things fit together. That was the saint who danced on the head of my deceased aunt Esperanza, and when she was possessed, she crawled all the time" (Israel Baró, Onelia Fernández Campo, interview, December 31, 2007).

Israel and Onelia told us that people from Agramonte often go to Jovellanos, about thirty minutes away, for Arará ceremonies. On January 1, 2008, Flanders Crosby, Matthews, and Pedroso went to Jovellanos, accompanied by Mario José, to attend an important ceremony for San Manuel, known as Da in Jovellanos. Earlier in the day, we all went with Mario José to the ruins of Unión de Fernández. But, before the ruins, he took us to a nearby lagoon where enslaved Africans once ran away to hide in caves tucked into a rock face. The lagoon was also a site for important religious ceremonies. For all of us, the power at the lagoon that day was deeply felt and became a moment we would talk about for days to come.

In Jovellanos that night, the ceremony began, and almost immediately, Miguelina, the matriarch of the Baró family in Jovellanos, became possessed. The energy was high. A bell hung in the middle of the ceiling with a rope attached to the wall. The rope was frequently pulled so the bell joined in with the rhythms of the drums, heightening the intensity of the ceremony. As the intensity grew, Mario José's dancing became deeply evocative as he enfolded and unfolded into and out of the creases of his body, seemingly reaching into the deeper well of meanings and pulling forth the histories, stories, and contexts of Arará in Agramonte. Watching Mario José dance, one could smell the lagoon and see the ceremonies, hear the sounds at Unión de Fernández, and glimpse Manuela Gose speaking her Dahomeyan language, throwing her bucket of water with rain falling around her. It is the histories, stories, and contexts that infuse his dance with such passion. It is the histories, stories, and contexts embodied in Arará music and dance that continue to give it power and life.

# 7

# Haitian Migration and Danced Identity in Eastern Cuba

GRETE VIDDAL

I arrive at Santiago de Cuba's Teatro Oriente to see a small crowd of locals and tourists waiting outside. We are here to see Ballet Folklórico Cutumba, one of eastern Cuba's premier folkloric dance troupes. Although the theater is run down and no longer has electricity or running water, its former elegance is apparent. As we enter, we see that lush but tattered velvet drapes flank the stage and ornate architectural details adorn the walls underneath faded and peeling paint. Light filters in through high windows. As the performance starts, women in elaborate ball gowns enter this dusty stage. They must hold up their voluminous skirts to keep yards of fabric from dragging on the floor. Men sport white topcoats with tails and matching white cravats. The costumes, modeled on eighteenth-century French court attire, may lead the audience to expect a re-enactment of an *ancien régime* ball.

Instead, the performance space fills with the driving rhythms of African-style drums. This is the tumba francesa (French drum), a striking dance genre with roots in what is now Haiti that developed in eastern Cuba.

I had seen many different Havana styles portrayed in documentaries about Cuban dance. I'd read extensively on Cuban music and culture; however, I was completely unprepared for the exciting folkloric manifestations of Afro-Franco-Haitian-Cuban origin found in Cuba's eastern provinces. In 1998, I traveled for the first time to Santiago de Cuba to participate in a study program hosted by Ballet Folklórico Cutumba, a group specializing in performing the dances of eastern Cuba. Cutumba's mission is to research, collect, conserve, and present these dances.

Figure 7.1. Cutumba performing Tumba Francesa. By Grete Viddal; used by permission.

Santiago de Cuba, the "capital of Oriente"—the island's eastern provinces—has been home to thousands of Haitian immigrants and retains a special culture that strongly differentiates it from Havana. Haitian Creole, referred to by speakers as *patuá*, is considered Cuba's "second language." It is estimated that more than 400,000 Cubans have at least "some familiarity" with Creole (Martínez Gordo 1989).

The eastern provinces of Cuba were host to two major waves of migration from Haiti, one during the time of the Haitian Revolution in the early nineteenth century, and another in the early twentieth century, when almost half a million Haitians were recruited as manual labor for eastern Cuba's expanding sugar industry. Both waves of migrants brought well-defined, and quite different, traditions of music and dance still practiced in Cuba today.

## The Tumba Francesa (and Tajona)

In eastern Cuba, the remaining tumba francesa societies and professional troupes such as Cutumba specialize in performing this intriguing dance genre. In Ballet Folklórico Cutumba's version, dancers in ornate costumes enter the stage promenading in stately rows. Tumba francesa is danced to the beat of a battery of African-style drums: the *premier* or *maman* (which improvises and solos), the *segonde*, the *bulá*, and the *catá* (an ideophonic drum, in this case a hollow log struck with two sticks). When Cutumba's musicians play, they fill the performance space with robust sound.

According to Ernesto Armiñán Linares, Cutumba's choreographer and an authority on regional performance, domestic slaves living in the households of the francophone plantocracy created the tumba francesa. They danced it wearing the cast-off finery of the masters. Later, free blacks of means and mulatto elites adopted these dances as well. Even before emancipation in Cuba (1886), tumba francesa clubs or societies were formed. Members held offices, such as that of *presidente* and *presidenta*. Public dances started with salutations to the organization's titleholders, then other visitors and local elders. Armiñán Linares explained to me that in later decades, heroes of Cuba's wars for independence were also ritually saluted by the societies. Today, two urban societies with their own buildings still exist, known as La Caridad in Santiago and La Pompadour in Guantánamo. A third group, the Tumba Francesa Bejuco, survives in an isolated mountain village in Holguin province.

The Santiago tumba francesa society and various professional troupes such as Cutumba also perform a dance called tajona (sometimes spelled tahona). According to Armiñán Linares, the tajona was a rural *comparsa*, or a festive procession of coffee plantation laborers taking advantage of a break in the work schedule to celebrate, parading along mountain roads after harvest time, singing and dancing. Before emancipation, the festivities of Holy Week gave slaves on mountain plantations an opportunity to visit relatives or friends on other estates. Armiñán Linares characterizes early tajona as a "dance of the field slaves," in contrast to tumba francesa's origins as a "dance of domestic slaves."

Musicologist Zobeyda Ramos Venereo (1997) hypothesizes that tajona has been influenced by and absorbed forms from other festive processional dances and music, particularly those associated with urban Santiago's carnival clubs and saint's day festivals after post-emancipation population movements introduced rural dances to towns and cities. Antonio Pérez Martinez, currently the artistic director of Santiago's annual Festival del Caribe and a founder of Conjunto Folklórico Oriente, believes that tajona adopted steps and postures from the rumba of Havana and Matanzas in the early twentieth century, a period when cane cutters in search of work migrated from western to eastern Cuba. Concurrently, in 1912, the Cuban state banned a political party promoting civil rights for black Cubans, and the army was dispatched to the eastern provinces to prevent unrest. Some of these soldiers settled in the east and were also carriers of the rumba traditions (interview, December 15, 2008).

When Cutumba performs tajona, dancers enter in procession behind the *mayor drapo*, who carries a flag, and the *bastonero*, or baton carrier, who directs activities. Men and women execute steps reminiscent of the flirtatious pursuit and conquest patterns classic to Cuban rumba. The grand finale of Cutumba's tajona is a maypole dance. Dancers congregate around a tall pole festooned with ribbons and perform a complex series of interweaving steps around the pole to plait them. To unbraid the maypole, Cutumba dancers reverse their actions at double speed, jumping, twirling, and diving. According to troupe members, tajona processions are no longer active in the Cuban countryside; however, the tradition is maintained by tumba francesa societies and during Santiago's carnival, as well as by folkloric groups like Cutumba.

The city of Guantánamo, near but completely separate from the infamous U.S. military base, lies two hours drive east of Santiago de Cuba. Here, the tumba francesa society Santa Catalina de Riccis, locally known as Pompadour, gives weekly concerts. Demeanor is dignified and formal during masón, the dance that initiates Pompadour's performances of tumba francesa. Couples parade with curtseys and bows. Decorous and reserved dance steps are counterbalanced by dynamic percussive music. Next, the group presents the livelier yubá (also spelled jubá) and choreographies become more animated. As the music speeds up, couples begin to twirl and execute complex patterns.

To finish, Pompadour dances frenté, a competitive dance performed only by men. To begin, the men gather into a circle and fasten colored scarves to the arms, legs, and chest of a soloist. The player of the largest drum pulls his instrument into the circle, flips it sideways, sits on it, and begins to play quick riffs and sequences. Frenté is a friendly competition between dancer and musician, with displays of fancy footwork responding to challenging rhythms played by the lead drummer. Musicologist Olavo Alén explains in a Winter 1995 article in *Ethnomusicology* (56), "the premier player will always try to make his rhythmic improvisations so complex that the dancer will lose the rhythm or simply be unable to follow it; otherwise the dancer wins the challenge. When the duel between drummer and dancer is very close, the winner is determined by the applause of the spectators."

Watching tumba francesa performances made me curious. How did this dance genre arrive in Cuba? Had it really been performed in the eastern provinces for more than two centuries? Was this part of what made Oriente different from Havana? I began to learn about the colonial history of eastern Cuba, and the ways in which it was changed by events on a neighboring island.

## Saint-Domingue and Cuba

Migrations resulting from the Haitian Revolution altered the cultural landscape of the Caribbean. In 1804, the colony of Saint-Domingue became Haiti, the western hemisphere's first independent black republic. Saint-Domingue was France's most prosperous colony until a slave insurrection in 1791 spread across the country, eventually defeating even Napoleon's armies. As war engulfed Saint-Domingue in the years leading up to 1804, much of the French plantocracy fled, some with households that included domestic slaves. Free blacks and mulattos also joined the flood of refugees.

A large portion resettled in eastern Cuba, particularly in Santiago de Cuba and Guantánamo. By 1799, Calle Gallo, one of Santiago's main streets, had been renamed Grande Rue. By the end of the first decade of the nineteenth century, one of every four people in Santiago had come from what was now Haiti (Guanche 1983; Millet and Brea 1989; Bettelheim 2001; Duharte 2001).

Over the course of the next decades, former members of Saint-Domingue's colonial elite established coffee plantations (*cafetales*) in the hills and mountains surrounding Santiago. The planters of Saint-Domingue had experience growing coffee, a crop new to Cuba. The French taste for coffee, its spreading popularity in Europe, and the business acumen of the Saint-Domingue plantocracy combined to inaugurate a new economy in eastern Cuba. The *franceses*, as these immigrants were called, brought to the eastern provinces a repertoire of ballroom dances known as contredanse in French (eventually contradanza in Cuba) including quadrilles, the minuet, and cotillion. However, "The musicians who played for the Cuban contradanzas were black" (133) explains musicologist Ned Sublette in his 2004 book *Cuba and Its Music*. In Oriente, *franceses negros* took the European ballroom dances and remade them for their own pursuits, setting them to drum rhythms and creating their own tumba francesa. While the original ballroom dances of the white plantocracy faded from custom over the years, black franceses preserved their own versions of these dances.

Both enslaved and free blacks gathered for mutual aid and cultural expression in *cabildos*, social organizations active in Cuba since the early colonial period. Cabildos functioned as support networks. They also held dances and sponsored processions on holidays. The black franceses from Saint-Domingue began to form their own cabildos, which became known as tumba francesa societies, after the dances held there (Alén 1991).

In the decades following the arrival of the Saint-Domingue refugees, Franco-Haitian society in Cuba underwent a number of changes. With war in Europe between France and Spain in 1809 came an expulsion order, and French citizens living in Spanish colonies who had not pledged allegiance to the Spanish crown were ordered to leave. Many coffee plantation owners left for New Orleans, almost doubling that city's population (Sublette 2004). In the 1840s, hurricanes devastated eastern Cuba. Many cafetales were converted to sugar plantations or abandoned (Thomas 1998 [1971]). Cuba's first war of independence from Spain, the unsuccessful Ten Years War, lasted from 1868 to 1878 and further debilitated eastern Cuba's economy. As for the white franceses, Sublette describes their fate this way: "The coffee planters of Oriente, who had fallen on hard times already by 1840, saw their industry destroyed; what remained of the French coffee bourgeoisie was ground down to a rural middle class" (2004, 245). While the ballroom dances of the eighteenth century faded from the salons of affluent whites, they have remained a tradition among black franceses for more than two centuries.

After the 1959 Cuban Revolution, the Cuban state took over the funding and supervision of all public cultural organizations, including tumba francesa societies. Today in Cuba, dance troupes are classified in three categories. Members of *profesional* groups are full-time state-salaried performers. Troupes officially categorized as *aficionado* or *portador* are provided with costumes and transportation by the government, but members maintain other jobs. Portadores are groups with family, neighborhood, or ethnic ties to a particular tradition, such as tumba francesa societies, carnival congas active since the early twentieth century, groups comprising descendants of Haitian, Jamaican, or Chinese laborers, or rural bands performing regional specialties such as chancleta or other country dances brought by Spanish immigrants.

In 2003 UNESCO, partnering with the Cuban government, provided funds for the renovation of Santiago's tumba francesa building under the auspices of the Convention for the Safeguarding of Intangible Cultural Heritage. Tumba francesa societies are potential tourist attractions and may help the eastern region capitalize on its distinctive cultural patrimony.

Santiago de Cuba is Cuba's second largest city, with a population of almost half a million. Although Havana dominates as the administrative hub and the governmental seat of power, where more than two million Habaneros enjoy the capital's hustle and bustle, cosmopolitan reputation, and erstwhile ties to Miami, a lively rivalry exists between these two cities. Santiagueros are proud to live in Cuba's most "Caribbean" city, pointing to their municipality's flavorful local culture, slow pace of life, animated carnival, neighborhood musical rivalries, and friendly population.

## Gagá (and Vodú)

Gagá arrived in Cuba more than a century after tumba francesa. It was danced during the weeks leading up to Lent, when revelers paraded down roads and streets for miles, playing music, singing, displaying choreography and costumes, and vying to outdo other bands. This tradition came to Cuba with the Haitian labor migrants of the early 1900s. Specific sociopolitical conditions brought gagá to Cuba.

The United States entered the Cuban War for Independence in February 1898, fighting against Spain in what is known in U.S. history books as the Spanish American War. The war ended in Cuba's liberation from Spain in August of the same year, but the new country was independent in name only. President McKinley installed a military government and created the Platt Amendment, effectively making Cuba a U.S. dependency. By 1905, only 25 percent of land in Cuba was still owned by Cubans (Helg 1995); most of the rest now belonged to U.S. corporations and speculators. Expanding Cuba's sugar industry became a top priority, and this required intensive, inexpensive manual labor.

In the years following the war, former Cuban liberation fighters rallied for their rights with strikes and insurrections. The United Fruit Company, with extensive holdings in eastern Cuba, needed a servile workforce to toil on its growing plantations. According to Thomas, "in late 1912, after the Negro revolt, the United Fruit Company asked if they could bring in 1,400 Haitians to work on their plantations in Oriente. . . . In succeeding years, a torrent of black labourers came, Haitians and Jamaicans" (1998 [1971], 524).

Meanwhile, in Haiti, the United States responded to a period of internal political turmoil by invading the country in 1915, ostensibly to promote peace in the region, but in reality eager to protect U.S. investments and business interests. The United States Marines occupied Haiti for almost two decades, carrying out policies that caused trauma and displacement of the peasant population. Wages on Cuban sugar and fruit plantations, although meager, were higher than in Haiti. Between 1913 and 1931, some scholars believe that as many as 500,000 Haitians (and 75,000 Jamaicans) entered Cuba (James, Millet, and Alarcón 1992). Many of these migrants, called *braceros* (referring to "strong arms"), went to work on plantations in the eastern provinces.

The arrival of more than half a million Antillean immigrants during the first decades of the twentieth century profoundly changed eastern Cuba's cultural mix. Many Haitians never returned to Haiti and settled in Oriente, both rurally and in Santiago, Guantánamo, and Camagüey (Guanche and Moreno 1988; McLeod 2000). They brought with them, and in many cases maintained, their own traditions, religious beliefs, and music, a fact that has received relatively little notice in official narratives about Cuban cultural history.

Investigation into eastern Cuba's distinctive St. Dominguan-Haitian heritage raises many questions. Conversations with the Cuban ethnomusicologist Olavo Alén highlighted the possibility that tumba francesa music and dance may have changed as former slaves from the plantations moved to towns and cities. The role of the descendants of free St. Dominguans of color in the establishment of the urban tumba francesa societies needs further study. Furthermore, when the second wave migrants of the early 1900s found more than century-old populations from Saint-Domingue in eastern Cuba, did the new arrivals identify with the earlier group's culture?

Figure 7.2. Gagá performance by Grupo Folklórico Thomson. By Grete Viddal; used by permission.

Could they "dance the same dances," or were there clashes? At present, the tumba francesa societies identify their dances as "francés," but other folk-loric troupes describe the same repertoire as "franco-haitiano."

Today Ballet Folklórico Cutumba's performance of gagá never fails to elicit gasps and cheers from the audience. After the musicians have settled onstage, scouts enter and theatrically scrutinize the audience and theater. When the area is declared safe, the flag carriers, baton twirlers, and a dancer with a giant, colorful, beribboned headpiece called the *roi diable* follow the scouts. The references to defense and protection within festivity and celebra-tion are unmistakable. Traditionally, gagá bands are competitive. Choreog-raphy typically includes theatrical feats of bravery and skill, such as twirling machetes, throwing and catching torches, leaping, tumbling, walking across broken bottles, and deftly lifting tables laden with glasses of water and vases of flowers. Alexis Alarcón (1988) theorizes that gagá spectacles implicitly carry historically important cultural messages. They impress upon specta-tors that Haitians and their descendants, the poorest and most vulnerable migrant workers of the early twentieth century, are capable of dramatic feats of daring and skill, and in this way craft a protective stereotype for Haitians in Cuban society.

Known as *rara* in Haiti, this art form can be subversive. In her 2002 book *Rara!*, Elizabeth McAlister collected rara songs that comment on local and national issues or poke fun at elites. Many rara bands in contemporary Haiti are associated with Vodou congregations and traditional religious leadership. Whether gagá in Cuba once played a role similar to that of rara in Haiti is an intriguing question my research seeks to answer.

The repertoire of Haitiano-Cubano folkloric performance includes choreographies inspired by the religious dances of Vodou, typically spelled Vodú in Cuba. Haitian spiritual practices have been maintained by descendants of Haitian migrants in Cuba. Although Vodú is most typically practiced in the countryside, Vodú believers are in contact through networks across the whole island. Well-known Vodú priests and priestesses cross Cuba to take part in ceremonies on saint's days or attend state-sponsored festivals. Several also direct folkloric troupes and leave their towns on trucks and buses to perform in Santiago's Festival del Caribe, Guantánamo's carnival, or Ciego de Avila's spring dance festival. During an excursion to the village of Thomson in Santiago province, I found a hamlet with a six-student school, one tiny bodega, and a twenty-five-member Haitian folkloric dance troupe, complete with musicians, instruments, costumes, flags, banners, and rehearsal schedules.

Such local groups as well as professional ones like Cutumba perform dances from Vodú religious rites, adapted for the stage, including ibó, nagó, and yanvalú. (Some of these names reflect African ethnic groups brought to Haiti as slaves: the Ibo from what is now southeastern Nigeria, the Nago also from Nigeria and today known as Yoruba). Secular dances include merengue haitiano, a couple dance for festive occasions, and congo layé, with its mimed flirtatious pursuits between male and female dancers (not to be confused with carnival congas, in which dancers wind their way through the streets of Santiago de Cuba, shuffling conga style with a step that emphasizes the hip, and sometimes breaking into kicks, wiggles, and more complex improvisations as they follow carnival musicians).

The Cuban state is highly centralized, with many academies, institutes, and organizations headquartered in Havana. The music, arts, folklore, and religious traditions of the region surrounding Havana have been privileged in the distribution of resources, and in many cases have become synonymous with Cuban culture in general. But Havana's story is not Cuba's story. Scholarship on Cuban religious and performance culture has focused on Havana and its surrounds, equating the island's capital with its core, but lively customs set Oriente apart, contributing to the creation of a distinctive regional identity.

While some Cubans of Haitian descent hide their heritage or have assimilated, the pride-building efforts of specialized performance troupes and the emergence of regional folklore festivals sponsored by local cultural institutes are beginning to bear fruit. During an annual folk-dance festival in Violeta in Ciego de Avila province in April 2009, I found that five of the seven groups specialized in Haitiano-Cubano dances. The festival even featured an open-to-the-public Vodú ritual hosted by a local family of Haitian descent. Cubans of varied ethnic heritage across the skin color spectrum attended, enthusiastically imitated dance steps, and joined in the call and response songs. On the final evening of the festival, youthful spectators ignored a DJ spinning reggaetón hits to cluster around a performance group of rural villagers of Haitian descent performing gagá and Vodú dances. In eastern Cuba, members of a historically marginalized and denigrated population are using folkloric performance to challenge marginalization, build cultural capital, and cultivate regional pride.

Tumba francesa fused elite French court dances with African music. Gagá tells the story of Cuba's understudied and unheralded Haitian heritage. Dance can function as a kind of "embodied history," enriching and extending our understanding of migration and identity.

# JAMAICA

# 8

# When Jamaica Dances

## Context and Content

CHERYL RYMAN

## Introduction

Jamaican dance and music are inseparable, if not as tangible reality, then certainly by way of perceived reality. The adage, with reference to African, neo-African, and African-based creole dance and music, is that one "hears the dance and sees the music." When one element is employed, the missing component may be conjured into reality by "hearing the dance" or "seeing the music." Notably, the dance is never performed without music, even if it is the body that is used as an instrument to produce percussive, rhythmic sounds.

In the traditional, theatrical, and popular dance-music spaces, a musician/singer often accompanies the performance with movement. On the flip side, the dancer employs the body not only to move in response to external musical instrumentation, but often as part or all of the musical instrumentation. The use of claps, slaps, stomps, and nasal or vocal simulation of a variety of musical instruments, in addition to use of the voice to sing, constitutes the music-making sounds of the body. This use of the body illustrates the instinctive response to create a holistic dance-music reality and highlights the corporal component of musical performances in the Jamaican/Caribbean context.

Professor Rex Nettleford, artistic director and choreographer of the National Dance Theatre Company of Jamaica, often employs an additional musical instrument through the dance and the dancer's body; that is to say, he will introduce an "unsounded" rhythm to which the dancers respond as part of the "seen" music that accompanies the dance. In this case, the audience is forced to see rather than hear at least some of the music employed in the dance performance.

This dance-music synergy warrants ongoing investigation as we explore the rich heritage of dance in Jamaica through the dance spaces of the "yard" (street or community traditional), dancehall (popular), and stage (modern, contemporary). For this kind of evidence to be gathered, the content and context of Jamaican dance has to be viewed through two distinct but related lenses. One could think of them as bifocal cultural lenses. The first lens, the "New Eye," is one that allows the viewer to be highly attuned, more perceptive, and alert to the content and context of Jamaican dance. The second, the "New I," is the more internal lens, the third eye or Rastafari's "I and I," which reflects the vision of a culturally conscious and spiritually grounded beholder. This Eye/I is important because such is the nature and substance of Jamaican and Caribbean dance: culturally conscious (including the intuitive or collective consciousness) and spiritually grounded.

Woven into this approach to seeing (and hearing) the world of Jamaican dance is the need to know the relevant cultures that have contributed to the formation of what we have inherited as Jamaican culture. Much of this inheritance has been achieved through the process of creolization in which accommodation of different cultures takes place in a new environment, on soil foreign to all the contributing culture bearers. What is retained and transformed is more likely those cultural features that find resonance with the operative culture—in Jamaica, the majority cultural purveyors and innovators from Africa. This majority group, Africans, was forced to find accommodation first among themselves, from the variety of African ethnic groups that were brought without consent to this foreign land. They were simultaneously forced to find an uneasy and unequal relationship between themselves and the respective European colonizers who wielded power over them. By contrast, Africans were able to find a more equitable accommodation with the indigenous people of the island who were the first escapees from colonial enslavement, the first Maroons—the Taino.

In the main, the Africans recreated the culture of the homeland and that of their specific ethnic ancestry with retentions that today may be described as the ancestral forms of their African antecedents. More importantly, African people created a new culture in the time and space made available to them, then as now. Out of necessity and instinct, the ancestral dance-music forms morphed into homegrown creolized forms, as was the case with the language, food, dress, customs, beliefs, et al. of the people of Jamaica and of the rest of the Caribbean.

The peculiar cultural features that are dissonant with the other cultures encountered in this context tend to lead to two general consequences. The first is that the peculiar features fade away over time with the reduction in number of the specific group in subsequent generations, particularly where limited opportunities existed for expression and transmission. The second speaks to the survival of the unique features that remain more or less intact but operate in a restricted culture-specific environment as do Kumina and Etu, two ethnic-specific dance-music ritual forms.

In dance, as in other aspects of the culture, one must be mindful that the primary sources and retentions of Jamaican traditional dance context and content may be readily traced to Africa and Britain and to a much lesser extent to India. Nevertheless, the common and unifying force, the creolizing crucible in which elements of different cultures found resonance and morphed into new forms on Jamaican soil, was African.

## The Historical and Cultural Context of Jamaican Dance

The cultural pool from which the Jamaican/Caribbean and the wider diaspora drew its elements and from which the Jamaican culture evolved took shape over several centuries. During that time, many different cultures had an impact on an ever-changing society in its march toward independence and coexistence on a global stage. The people who came and the cultures they brought were re-created and became subject to adaptation on foreign soil. This mix of peoples and cultures tells the story of Jamaican dance and Jamaica dancing.

Tainos, the earliest inhabitants, contributed far more to the overall cultural pool of Jamaica, and to the world for that matter, than they have been given credit. Their collaboration and close association with the Spanish and British slaves who ran away to the mountains to join the early Taino Maroons have been grossly understated. Their possible contribution to Jamaican dance and music as we know it today is still largely unexplored.

Spanish rule for more than 150 years and a close relationship between Jamaica and both Spanish and French colonies—Cuba, Venezuela, Dominican Republic, and Haiti—predisposed Jamaicans to music and dance from these regions. The African soul and aesthetic in these dance-music forms found ready resonance in Jamaica, so that, for example, mento dance and music is enriched by the rumba box (*marimbula*), a larger variant of the African *mbira* (thumb piano), borrowed from our Latin American counterparts. The Spanish creole forms have found acute resonance on both sides of the popular dance-music culture found in former English- and Spanish-speaking colonies.

The African contribution dates back to the early sixteenth century, when the first slaves were brought to Jamaica as servants, herders, hunters, and laborers on large farms. Even given the predominantly West African source of slaves brought to the Americas, the people of Africa, although sharing many commonalities, were and are not homogenous in their cultural sources and expressions. Their entry into the island, forced and stripped of many of the conditions and paraphernalia to ensure continuity, heralded a major paradigm shift in the ways in which this variety of African ethnic groups achieved accommodation with each other and contributed to the rise of neo-African and Caribbean creole cultural institutions like Maroonage and Jonkonnu.

The vast majority of Africans who were brought to Jamaica came from the west coast (Senegal to Angola) and included ethnic groups like the Mandingo, Ewe/Fon, Yoruba-Nago, Ibo, and Ndongo, with the strongest ethnic influence and retentions drawn from the Akan- or Twi-speaking people from what is now Ghana. The most dominant among this latter group was the Asante. Among post-emancipation indentured laborers from Africa, those from Central Africa, as far south as Angola, came in larger numbers than previously, notably including Bakongo people, whose distinct influence is still felt in traditional forms like Kumina, Pukkumina, Kongo, and Tambu. Yoruba people from what is now Nigeria also arrived post emancipation, and their presence is found in the Etu and Nago traditional forms.

In 1655 the British wrested control of the island from the Spanish and by 1660 had succeeded in routing the last of the Spanish creole settlers and their African slaves. It was not until several years later that the island was officially handed over to the British by the Spanish. The long tradition of

British quadrille, in its original "ballroom" but heavily creolized style and its more "rootsy" "camp" style, remains one of two dance-music forms found in every parish in the island until approximately twenty years ago. The other is revival, particularly the Zion 1860 order, which is more overtly Christian in its orientation. Pukkumina, also known as pocomania, quickly emerged by the following year as the 1861 order, displaying distinctly African orientation.

East Indians arrived in Jamaica initially between 1845 and 1917 as contract indentured laborers to fill the labor gap after emancipation of the enslaved Africans. In the areas where the predominantly Hindu Indians were dispatched (Westmoreland, St. Thomas, St. Mary, Portland, and Clarendon), their influence on the cultural expressions of the African population was then and even now significant. So it is that in St. Thomas and Westmoreland, the Babu character in Jonkonnu is highly visible, and Clarendon is the primary parish in which the Hosay Indian Festival is still celebrated every August. Their love of jewelry and the making of it introduced affordable jewelry to the African population, but perhaps their most lasting impact on the African population in Jamaica was the introduction of plants and of curry seasoning. It was not only foods like mango, tamarind, plums, and curry goat and chicken, but also the cultivation and use of Indian hemp—marijuana, ganja, or the "holy weed/herb"—that became Jamaican staples. The latter carried an appeal for Jamaicans to effect physical and spiritual healing. Rastafari brethren have elevated its use to a sacrificial/religious dimension.

Several European countries, including those of the dispersed homes of the Jews, contributed settlers to Jamaica, with post-emancipation European and Asian immigrants following the indentured Africans and Indians. Such immigrants, including people from China, Germany, and Lebanon and Syria, all contributed their unique characteristics to the creolization process in Jamaica, some to a greater extent than others.

Later cross-cultural exchanges with the United States (its closest state, Florida, being approximately 580 miles from Jamaica) served to feed modern Jamaican theater and dance theater as well as popular dance-music culture. Similarly, the cross-cultural exchanges between the English-speaking islands (Trinidad, Barbados, Cayman Islands) and Spanish-speaking circum-Caribbean countries (Cuba, Costa Rica, Panama, Venezuela) point to the emergence of even greater shared experiences and cultural expressions. At the turn of the twentieth century, Canada aligned itself with Jamaica, primarily on economic grounds.

Radio stations from the 1940s and even into the 1960s featured American country and western, Trinidadian calypso, and Latin American rumba dance music, all sharing popularity with the indigenous Jamaican mento and creole quadrille, which moved seamlessly from the traditional to the popular dance-music arena. The continuing immigration patterns of Jamaicans introduced American rhythm and blues, rock and roll, and jazz music and dance, forcing onto the stage a further synergy with local popular and traditional forms to produce the first indigenous contemporary popular dance music, called ska. It was only a matter of time before ska gave way to rock steady and in turn to reggae and the misnamed "dancehall" dance music. In each phase of this evolution, dance and music remained virtually inseparable.

## The Aesthetic Context: African and African-derived Dance and Music versus Other World Cultures

For Jamaica's rich dance heritage, one needs to outline the aesthetic context in which African and African-Caribbean dance and music can be distinguished from other world dance cultures. In so doing, one must face the irreducible truth: people of all cultures are confined by the limited possibilities of movement allowed by the human body. How, then, does one attempt to prescribe individuality or uniqueness to one dance-music culture over another?

First, one needs to have an appreciation of the possibilities of movement by the body. These possibilities include such basic features as isolation of its components—head, shoulders, upper and lower torso, the limbs (legs, feet, arms, hands)—and the associated range of movement facilitated by the joints. These components may be employed individually, one at a time, or at the same time. They include the positions of the limbs—lifted at various heights, curved, straightened, articulated inward, outward, or in circular patterns or at various angles; positions and movement of the body—stand, bend, lunge, tilt, crouch, leap, step, turn; locomotory direction and patterns versus nonlocomotory movement executed in a stationary position—ripple, twist, stretch, contract/release, hyperextend, etc.; and dynamics or quality of the movement—strong/weak, pushed/pulled, fast/slow, suspended/sustained, tensed/relaxed.

The extent to which some or all of these human movement capabilities are employed, the ways in which they are employed, and the frequency with which they are employed signal the distinctive cultural features associated with one cultural group versus another. In terms of similarities versus differences, virtually no differences per se can be found in the way the body can be moved. The comparisons are in the combination and treatment of a particular set of movement features that occur with greatest regularity. It is that frequency of application of one or any combination of principles that establishes the distinctiveness of the dance expression of any cultural group.

That would explain why, for example, the iconic Cossack step of Ukrainian or Russian dance can also be found in African dance and in Jamaica's Jonkonnu, but would not be considered a unique feature of African and African-derived dances per se. The historic and aesthetic context of each dance-music culture shapes the peculiarities that present as signifiers of each distinct culture. In the case of the Caribbean, it is the proverbial "melody of Europe playing on the rhythm of Africa" (Nettleford 1985)—the "rhythm" being the operative musical force in this metaphor as it relates to Jamaican and Caribbean dance.

The types of instruments known to human cultures and the way they are played and to which the body will respond are also limited and include wind (flutes, horns), string (single and multiple strings), percussion (drums, bells, gongs, cymbals, tambourines, shakas/maracas, xylophone, rumba box), which are struck, plucked, shook, or scraped, and the human instrument of the body (slaps, claps, etc.) and, in particular, the voice. All of these types of musical instruments—manmade and made of man—have been employed in Jamaican music, albeit with important modifications, as in the case of the bamboo flute used in Jonkonnu, the bamboo saxophone in mento (made famous by saxophonist Sugar Belly), or the kerosene tin drum in etu (a Yoruba-based traditional dance-music form found in the hills of Hanover). Beyond this type of adaptation is the creation of a new type of drum, the square single-headed drum, gumbay (also spelled gumbe, gumbeh, etc.), which is seen worn around the neck of a musician in a print of Jonkonnu masqueraders by the nineteenth-century artist Isaac Mendes Belisario.

Even string instruments like the banjo are played rhythmically by plucking the strings or by infusing heavy spurts of speed, syncopation, and breaks (suspension of the beat). I have already made reference to the technique of introducing an "unsounded" rhythm that can only be "heard" by seeing the music "played" by the dancer.

Africa and Europe: fossilized, preserved, and evolved in a crucible of the phenomenon of the island continent (splintered, yet unified) which is at the heart of the "what" and "how" that has taken place in the Caribbean region over the past 500 years. Africa and Europe were both intruders on an already inhabited continent. The Tainos, Arawaks, and Caribs had already discovered and transformed their environment, imbuing it with the distinctive traits of preference and identity.

The clash of cultures, power, and control, then as now, served to define the different paths of evolution and creolization for the two protagonists. Suffice it to say that the cultural force in the African arena prevailed, shaping and defining the peculiarities of Jamaican/Caribbean culture and its dance/music components. The spiritual/religious synergy that prevails within the dance and music environment is described in Robert Farris Thompson's *African Art in Motion* (1974), Yvonne Daniel's *Dancing Wisdom* (2005), and, closer to home, the dancing powerful spirits and ancestors of Jonkonnu, Kumina, and the Maroons in Jamaica.

## African and Neo-African Context and Content in Jamaican Traditional and Popular Dance

Dance is central to the preservation and unveiling of Jamaican culture, cutting across class, race, gender, space, and generations. To move is to live or to affirm life. Not to move is to herald the end of life. That is why in Jamaica the body moves in response to internal and external impulses. That is why when someone dies, a Nine Night or Set Up is held with dance as the central theme amid other activities. The movement is usually vigorous and celebratory and carries sexual overtones—all aimed to cheer the bereaved as much as to affirm human power over death by the ability to generate life. This prowess is pitted against people's relative powerlessness over death and, where applicable, it is also pitted against a life that offers limited possibilities for self-fulfillment.

An important note in outlining the unique characteristics of how Jamaica dances is that the overriding African aesthetic prevails and transforms the content of even the most closely adapted non-African dance-music forms. It is significant that the following discussion about the content and context of the Jamaican dance experience holds true for both the traditional and popular expressions and to a lesser extent for Jamaican dance theater.

Within the context of African and neo-African principles of movement, the synergy of Jamaican music and dance almost always carries spiritual elements, if not overtly perceived and expressed, then hovering just below the surface, even in the popular dance-music arena. Dance is viewed as an integral part of being—as a condition of life and of sustaining the life of the living and the "living dead"—the ancestors and powerful spirits. The latter revisit the corporal world through possession of the living, enjoy their temporary reincarnation by sharing in the dance-music experience with the rest of the community, and, in return, give important advice and instructions to the community of the living.

The vital forces and keys to access supernatural powers are to be found in herbs, flowers, blood (the life force invoked through animal sacrifice), water, rum, sweet drinks, fruits, breads, meat, starchy food, colors (manifest in cloth and candles), fire, and iron. The devices of music, dance, and the mask are used as symbol and manifestation of the supernatural through which the spirits communicate to the living.

Feasting or the sharing of a meal with ancestors, primary performers, and nonperforming participants is integral to the dance event. In fact, among the Etu/Nago people, a common reason for holding a dance event is feasting. The significance is great in Etu since the food itself (fufu and chicken stew with annato) and the associated rituals allow the Nago people to recreate an important part of their Yoruba heritage.

The content of Jamaican traditional dance must be viewed in terms of the recurring features associated with movement: the steps, use of body, music, costume, ritual sequences, and paraphernalia. Strength, verve, energy, forcefulness immediately come to mind as qualities of movement most admired; hence, a sense of attack and dynamism—without sharp edges—is achieved by the element of surprise that frequently follows a mesmerizing routine-ness of movement in the warm-up phase of the dance experience. This can be broadly described as a "break," which in performances enjoins the collaboration of dancer and drummer. No apologetic or unsure move-ment is applauded. In short, it is better to be "wrong and strong" than to be "right and weak." The former quality is what will receive the accolades of onlookers cum participants.

All of this must be accompanied by a controlled but relaxed face, de-scribed by Robert Farris Thompson as a sense of cool. In Jamaica in the 1960s, during the rude boy era of popular dance-music, this was termed "cool and deadly." This characteristic is different from the sense of effort-lessness that forms part of the Western/European folk and theatrical dance aesthetic and that of unchallenged balance associated with Asian dance.

This sense of cool and deadly on top of strong, forceful, and sometimes athletic or acrobatic movement is a feature that is paramount in Jamaican and African-derived dance, since this is what expresses the regeneration of life and youthfulness. Even older and aging participants are able to display this sense of youthfulness by virtue of their ability to subscribe to these principles and qualities of movement: suppleness, agility, athleticism, and correctness of response to the music. The skill of the dancer in displaying this aesthetic confirms his or her status in the community.

The ability of the dancer to hear, direct, and respond correctly to the music cues amid highly complex and multirhythmic structures, articulating different parts of the body, is far more important than achieving the correct dance form. Without a doubt, this ability to dance to the music is the stron-gest aesthetic in Jamaican and African-derived dance and supersedes any perceived correctness of form.

The ranking and perception of correct dance form clearly does occur in the pantheon of Jamaican aesthetics, but falls much lower on the scale in comparison with other cultures. Rather than precision of predetermined form or clearly defined lines produced by the individual body or grouping of bodies, the Jamaican dancer tends to move constantly and collectively in mass formations. These formations do not generally demand the kind of precision of form for which European dance cultures ask in a freeze-frame or paint a picture-in-space aesthetic. The Jamaican formations are most commonly in a circle, rough processional lines, double line formations, or grouped loosely in the open cutout phase of the dance experience. The lat-ter may be described as a free-for-all, although an inherent organization still exists whereby improvised solo or duet performances are readily and frequently accommodated.

Performers are constantly moving as long as music is playing, even if it is an easy on-the-spot movement or during the warm-up phase of the dance event. Both body and dress as well as accessories like a rag, towel, or shawl are employed to capture space and increase the illusion of constantly moving and blurred mass, rather than defined lines and formations. Who more eloquently personifies the use of costume—in this case a full-body mask—in extending the sense of blurred, ever-moving mass than Pitchy Patchy in Jonkonnu?

A basic sequence of performance modes or format in a Jamaican dance event is in evidence even in the popular arena. Phase 1 is the "Greeting," in which a formal acknowledgment of all participants is made. This may start with a libation to the spirits, both friendly and unwelcome. The musicians greet each other by playing short riffs on their instruments, equivalent to a testing mode. Dancers greet each other, then extend the greeting to the musicians and finally to the onlookers. Singing in call-and-response mode and basic percussion is usually part of this phase, with dancing only beginning when other instruments, especially the drums, are introduced.

Phase 2 is the "Warm up," which, as the name suggests, heralds the beginning of the regular dance-music event. The performers use this phase to "catch the beat" and "build the vibe" through dance and music, with singing playing an important part. The warm-up phase may include procession, "profiling" in front of the larger group of nonperforming participants or onlookers, dancing in a continuous easy mode, or with spurts of individual dancing.

Phase 3, "Open Cut Out" or "Open Break Out," moves the more structured formation of the dance event into free form. This is perhaps the most energetic phase, when individual or coupled performances compete for a nondefined space. This phase allows not only for individual/couple performances, but also for viewing them. One should bear in mind that no exclusive space is created that is commonly used by the individual performers.

There are ways of participating in a Jamaican dance event without falling within the range of the "video light." This may take the form of singing and clapping along with the musicians and dancers, encouraging the active participants, and helping to "build the vibe" in the dance arena. Of course, there is dancing "in place" or "on the spot" without entering the defined dance space. This aspect is critical because it underscores how active the participation is in a Jamaican dance event, whether one is actively performing or observing in a traditional ceremony like Kumina. Even an apparently passive onlooker may become possessed within a highly charged dance-music environment, since it is the spirit of the ancestor that chooses the body through which to dance and enjoy him/herself.

Methods of showing appreciation for the active participants vary, but are consistent with West African modes. Appreciation may be shown by a finger pointed above the head; in the dancehall setting, two fingers are used to simulate a gun salute (a practice of actually shooting off a gun in the air, which has been largely discouraged), accompanied by "bouyaka!" or in more recent times, by "Pram! Pram!" with the open hand waved in the air from side to side and in time to the music; "shawling" or "crowning"—placing a shawl around the neck of a dancer or placing a hat on his or her head; or by entering the dance space and dancing with the dancer, described in popular lingua as "tekking a dance."

The characteristic posture is that of knees bent or relaxed, trunk inclined forward, sometimes tipped back or upright, always with a bearing of controlled relaxation and alertness without being taut, elbows bent and close to the body, one or both feet flat and often bare—close to Mother Earth.

The hands are often used as an isolated body part, responding to and emphasizing specific rhythms; at times one finger is used to punctuate a particular movement. They may be used in a symbolic gesture of praise and appreciation, twirled, flicked, held relaxed at the side of the body or in a more affected limp-wrist style. The hands may be held open, but more often they are left partially closed or fully closed to form a fist, or placed strategically for emphasis on the body, for example, at the side of the head, across the stomach, or akimbo, on the hips.

The feet, often bare, may slide, shuffle, drag, kick, brush, leave contact with the ground in hops and leaps, but always they return to and make contact with the earth—on the beat. Therein lies the crux of one of the features of Jamaican and by extension, Caribbean and other African-derived dances: deliberate contact of the feet with the ground on the beat, with the most important being the first beat of the bar.

The relationship of the dancer to the lead musician/drummer is an intimate one and is linked to the primarily religious motivation of humans (in the Jamaican/African-derived traditional dance context) to assert life and create communion with the Supreme Creator and the ancestors. In the most overtly spiritual context, the drum is the voice or the "carrier of the spirit" (as the fundeh drum of Rastafari is sometimes referred to) and the primary communicative device between the natural and supernatural worlds. At the level of mere aesthetics, the significance of the close relationship between the music/musician and the dancer has already been raised, with the added ability of the dancer to indirectly affect the performance of the music/musician on occasion.

The response of the dancer to different drum rhythms, simultaneously or consecutively, and the response engendered in the musician by the dancer is a feature that persists beyond the traditional into the popular dancehall arena. Here the selector (previously called the disk jockey or DJ, but referred to here by the Jamaican term "selector" to distinguish from recording artist DJs) will enthusiastically encourage and stimulate the performers and their performance in particular directions. The selector controls the dance experience but is also guided by the dancer or dancers who have entered the "video light." Solo or duet performance of dancers is encouraged and highlighted by one of the videographers shining the video light on the performers while recording the dance sequence. The video light has become integral to the Jamaican dancehall experience and is frequently referred to in the lyrics of popular artists.

The climax of this intimate and symbiotic relationship between dancer and musician is expressed in the "get down" feature that forces the performances of both participants to build to a peak of intensity, ending in a "break," which is often personified by a closer-to-the ground prelude, with the final climactic movement sometimes actually ending on the ground. The break itself comes in four parts: a "pulse" or "break away" movement initiated by the musician (and less often by the dancer) on the "and" beat, followed by a series of movements building up to the final emphatic sounding of the beat and corresponding movement, immediately followed by a perceptible suspension of movement and music—on the "and" beat—before returning to the regular music and dance patterns.

All four components of the break carry an element of surprise to the onlooker, but are discernible to the initiated ear and eye. For example, the intensification of movement involved in a break is regularly expressed in Kumina and dinki mini, consisting of a sharp "relaxed but controlled" pulse before continuous and increasingly "get down" characteristic turns—with the back almost parallel to the ground—or rapid footwork followed by a climactic tilt to the side, a sharp dip in the knees, a leg raised over the drum or toward another dancer with the hips meeting (or almost meeting) and held momentarily, followed by another pulse on the "and" beat before a return to the regular movement and music patterns. This exemplifies the need to experience the dance event, in particular, this break/get down feature, in order to deepen one's appreciation for the features described above by "hearing the music in the dance" and "seeing the dance in the music." The level of appreciation will depend on whether one is an active performer or an onlooker.

Mimicry, mime, and buffoonery are critical features to be read and understood in the Jamaican dance event whether traditional, popular, or theater. An appreciation of these often combined features will allow the viewer to sense an aesthetic that permeates even the most apparently sexually charged or violent movement sequences, such as the mimicry, mime, and buffoonery of the sexual play in Jonkonnu. Here, two characters (obviously male) engage in simulated copulation, either with the male standing behind the bent-over female character, sometimes ending with the "act" being performed on the ground, or the simulation being acted out entirely on the ground. The fact that this is not seen as vulgar and is laughed at, and the fact that two males in Jonkonnu performing this kind of act is tolerated by a partially homophobic audience speaks volumes about this particular aesthetic. This aesthetic spills over into the perceived bastion of Jamaican homophobic sentiments—the dancehall, where men cross-dress as women in the context of specific "masks" or characters. These characters are not only tolerated but also celebrated and captured by the video light in the live dance event and in music videos.

Significant features of Jamaican dance include the bounce, which in walk and movement is the single greatest signifier of Jamaican dance, traditional or popular. Its persistence is suggested in the experience of Sheila Barnett (pioneer dance educator and founding member/choreographer of the National Dance Theatre Company), who was chastised repeatedly for her inability to do the quadrille the English way as taught at college in the United Kingdom. In frustration, her tutor shouted, "take the bounce out of your steps!"

The Jamaican wine and the Latin roll are both hip-centered, but direction and quality is different. In the soft Latin roll, hips move side to side with a sustained undulation of the upper torso, while the Jamaican wine consists of rotation and largely sustained movement of the hip, but with intermittent change of pace and "breaks" or suspension, that is, a pulse, followed by rapid movement ending with a definitive stop—a dip, leg lift, hip contraction, or, in a popular context, with a split on the ground. The Trinidadian "chip" or sway in soca employs a continuous rolling action of the hip versus the Jamaican soca, which employs a sharper whipping action of the hip.

## Naming and Claiming Jamaican Traditional Dances: Typology and Classification

Naming and claiming the cultural lexicons of our environment is critical to owning and celebrating one's identity. With identity comes confidence to coexist and share with others comfortably. Dance is at the heart of Jamaican and Caribbean identity, the single most significant force and reservoir of who we are as a people—connected to all mankind, yet distinct in our approach and purpose.

Jamaican traditional dances have tended to travel from dance-music forms expressed initially as a celebration of ethnic specificity and origin to become accommodated and creolized within larger core dance forms that in turn break away into distinct forms suited to changed circumstances. A combination of the core types, related dances, and offshoots of the original dances speaks to the rich dance heritage that is continuously drawn on and plumbed for inspiration and content, instinctively in the popular and contemporary arenas, and consciously by the individual artist in the visual and performing arts.

The core traditional forms that emerge in more or less descending chronological order are Jonkonnu, Maroon Kromanti Play, Myal, Kumina, Revival, Hosay, and Rastafari—all contributing to and feeding on each other. The forty traditional dance-music forms identified as active within the last fifty years (Ryman 1980) demonstrate a tight network of interconnectedness even among the core types.

The predecessor of all known dance-music-religious forms identified in Jamaica is Jonkonnu, which was first recorded in the early 1700s by Sir Hans Sloane. It became the traditional dance-music-masquerade-religious form embodying ancestry and representing a historical and cultural repository of all peoples and cultures that have shared the Jamaican space. Traditionally, all the masquerade characters are played by men or young boys, although women have played some of the female characters in more recent times, especially in staged presentations.

What is preserved even now in the hills of St. Elizabeth, close to the Maroon town of Accompong, is an overt religious significance in the primary Jonkonnu figure (horned, or wearing a house or houseboat) who once danced alone as a "Kunu," with musicians and followers who cried out, "Jonkonnu, Jonkonnu!" Subsequent descriptions reinforce this, drawing strong parallels with the African male and female secret societies and masquerade traditions of the Egungun, Poro, and Sande. These and similar traditions span wide culture groups along the west coast of Africa from Senegal to Angola.

More than seventy characters have been recorded, encompassing a wide range of masquerade types: human, animal, and vegetal, as well as ethnic and social representations. The popular Pitchy Patchy, covered in many-colored strips of cloth and wearing a wide variety of headdresses, including horns, is reminiscent of the Egungun masqueraders of the Yoruba of Nigeria. Pitchy Patchy is to be found in almost every type of Jonkonnu or masquerade band, with the other primary figures, Horsehead, Cowhead, and House Jonkonnu, found only in certain parishes and locations. During the late eighteenth and early nineteenth century, the House Jonkonnu and Koo Koo or Actor Boy were very prominent figures in the Jonkonnu parade, as were the Set Girls, primarily Red and Blue Sets, along with sets of every gradation of skin color and dress style, reminiscent of the "crews" in today's dancehall environment. The Queen or Ma'am of the Sets and the Jack-in-the-Green are companion characters to the Set Girls.

Social commentary is often expressed with a distinct brand of humor, seen in the performance of characters like Belly Woman, Babu, Sailor, Whore Gal, and Policeman. Stilt dancers, last seen coming down from the hills of the Portland Maroon area, sport a quasi-military, vegetal camouflage with a grotesque mask, reminiscent of the Moko Jumbie, the dancing spirit/ancestor character of West African masquerade and closer to home, of Trinidad, St. Kitts, and St. Croix. The Devil became a twentieth-century favorite in most Jonkonnu bands islandwide and carries a frightening lead role in the bands. The lead character in Jonkonnu almost always embodies frightening and forceful characteristics. Less frightening characters include the Royal Sets (Queen, King, Queen Granddaughter, Prince, and a variety

Figure 8.1. Jonkunnu group on parade (2001). Courtesy of African Caribbean Institute of Jamaica/ Jamaica Memory Bank; a division of the Institute of Jamaica.

of Courtiers), Warrior or Warrick, Champion, Executioner, Jockey, Flower Girl, Wild and Tame Indians, Hobby Horse (related to both British mumming and the horse figures of the Efik of eastern Nigeria as well as the Kathgora of the East Indians), Reindeer, Monkey, Donkey, and male and female Sweeper.

The fife man is considered the key character by both the musicians and dancers. It is he who calls the tune by directing the pace and the start and end of each dance-music sequence, including the promenade or parade from one point to the next, the individual and couple dancing, and eventually the open cut-out phase of the Jonkonnu event. A wide range of instruments can be used in Jonkonnu. The bass drum keeps a basic 4/4 rhythm, with the rattling drum playing a slightly more complex rhythm, together with a grater maintaining a regular four beats to the bar with a doubling on every other beat. A departure from this norm is found among the Buru masqueraders in Clarendon, where the fundeh and repeater drums are included in the ensemble, and in Lacovia, St. Elizabeth (Maroon country), where the gumbay drum is still used. The gumbay drum carried around the neck was once a feature of nineteenth-century Jonkonnu bands, along with half a jawbone, teeth intact, scraped with a stick. Wooden knockers, shakas, a garden fork, stamping bamboo, bottles, calabashes, and even the wheelbase of a car have been used as improvised instruments.

Dance steps and mimetic movements are at once true to the traditional antecedents of earlier forms as well as being highly inventive and, more often than not, aim to introduce elements of humor. The play within the play (mimed skits) is a feature of the masquerade form of Jonkonnu in the western parish of Westmoreland, which presents courtly British characters, all of whom are transformed and infused with African models. The death and resurrection doctor plays are reminiscent of their Irish counterparts, but death and renewal is a recurring theme in all African based dance-music forms. Here the science/medicine/doctor man performs his magic of resurrection and renewal, calling upon the spirits from the four corners of the world with the dramatic spraying of white rum from the mouth, or signing at the four corners of the space occupied by the performers. Stick and sword fighting are common features in this context, with the vanquished being the object of the resurrection ritual.

With changing circumstances, offshoot Jonkonnu forms like Bruckin Party developed. Bruckins or Bruckin Party emerged after Emancipation in 1838 as a specific group of costumed characters who arose from the rivalry between the Jonkonnu Set girls and, in particular, between the Red and Blue Sets, led by their respective Kings and Queens. This celebratory dance music highlights the dramatic break from a military-controlled plantation environment to freedom from slavery. Nevertheless, both the music and dance reflect military influence. The early form of the bruckins dance is reminiscent of the slow-march step of the military, heavily embellished by a bruckin movement—a subtle to sharp contraction/release in the upper torso. The younger, post-1980s generation's reinterpretation of this dance emphasizes the bruckins quality (sharp contraction-release of the upper torso followed by a step to the side or forward) and de-emphasizes the slow march and graceful dipping, gliding movement of their elders.

Eventually, Bruckin Party gave rise to further offshoots, Queen Party and Brag, all of which were once part of the Set Girl tradition within plantation Jonkonnu. Both the Queen Party and Brag are performed independent of the Bruckin Party. The Queen Party consists of the elaborately dressed, veiled, and mysterious Queen accompanied by her entourage of daughters and granddaughters. There she is "auctioned"—first for her to enter, then for a peek under her veil, and finally for her to leave the gathering. Queen Party and Brag appear at Tea Meetings or any other type of traditional community-organized entertainment, especially fundraising events.

Brag is the actual processional dance of the Queen Party, which is done by the Queen and her party as they move toward a predetermined location. The Queen is also accompanied by two attendants who hit sticks over her head as she walks.

Another closely related masquerade form is Buru. Buru differs from Jonkonnu in its masquerade characters, musical instruments, and distinct dance and music traditions. The unique set of masquerade figures (horizontal cow, horse, reindeer, and alligator), related to similar British, East Indian, and African traditions, boasts a primary female "fertility" effigy, Mada Lundy, surrounded by her entourage of young female dancers. They unashamedly display provocative pelvic movements. The rolling, seductive Buru rhythm, resonating from the fundeh and repeater drums, demands no less of the dancers. The front foot flat on the ground with the back foot on the ball of the foot and rotating pelvises punctuated by small hops in sync with the slap of the fundeh drum are broken up by purposeful and continuous pelvic rotations as the young dancers slowly descend to the ground, only to ascend to their original position in one emphatic movement, a hop. Buru's influence on mento and the later popular ska and reggae forms was inevitable. The Rastafari adoption of this set of drums speaks to the link between Buru and Nyabingi music, if not the dance.

Buru as a musical tradition is processional in nature, with nomadic troupes of musicians who would set up the night before. In the morning, they would go to the homes of important community members while playing and singing en route, ending with a final performance in a central part of the town for the larger community. This tradition was observed as recently as some five years ago in Old Harbour, St. Catherine. Buru, like Jonkonnu, carries spiritual connotations that provoked much ridicule in the emerging modern Jamaica, particularly in the self-government, pre-independence era of the 1940s–1960s. Kenneth Bilby, a musicologist and anthropologist, has been unearthing religious and secular Jonkonnu retentions throughout the Caribbean over the last ten years. His interest in the closely related Buru, especially the musical tradition, has yielded much.

The quadrille and maypole are significant retentions of secular traditional forms that carry a more overt British/European influence. The quadrille remained in vogue as a social event up to the 1970s, although waning in popularity even among older practitioners. The group-set square dance in the ballroom style most authentically represents the British dance tradition in Jamaica. The transformed, highly Jamaicanized/Africanized camp style is presented in two lines of male and female dancers facing each other. The movement in the camp style is far more lively, being accompanied by equally lively mento music. In fact, the fifth figure of the quadrille—the "brawta" figure—is called the mento figure and is to be found in certain parishes like Clarendon, Manchester, and Trelawny. The four main figures include a number of European dances or movements like the polka, schottische, vaspian, mazurka, jig, chassé, balancé, and promenade, which is used to enter and exit the dance space.

In the maypole, spring and its fertility overtones come alive and are enhanced by the Jamaican belief in the fertility and special powers of the koratoe plant. The koratoe bears a tall flowering pole used by some of the earlier practitioners not only in maypole, but as the center pole in Kumina. Here again, mento or some other lively music is employed. The dancers move around the pole, weaving and unweaving intricate patterns with the many-colored ribbons anchored to the top of the pole. Dancers usually move in opposite directions, in and out in a figure-eight fashion to form a variety of weaves, including the grand chain and the single or double basket. More complex patterns like the spider or cobweb are formed by one set of dancers moving around their stationary counterparts holding outstretched ribbons. The maypole, like quadrille, forms an important part of the annual Jamaica Festival Competitions among school groups.

In fact, educational entities—from basic school to high school level—have been primary vehicles for the preservation of many traditional forms. The surviving adult traditional groups assist in workshops for students and are included in the annual Jonkonnu Festival in December. This festival, a Jonkonnu display and competition in different categories among schools, constitutes an important event in the annual Jamaica Festival schedule of activities. The adult traditional Jonkonnu groups perform in a noncompetitive context, offering a firsthand exposition of traditional Jonkonnu performance to young competitors and spectators alike. The recognition of traditional performers serves as both an accolade and a motivation to preserve the traditions for future generations in Jamaica and the world.

Less popular secular forms in the past 50 years are the bram, shay-shay, and yanga. Bram is an old-time dance step done spontaneously to mento-type village or country band music and is characterized by softly rolling but suggestive hip movements. Shay-shay has come to be used as a generic term for any lively or vigorous dancing ascribed to an African source. The shay-shay has two more specific references, as a figure in quadrille or as a dance style in Tambu, described later. The yanga, like shay-shay, has both specific and generic meanings. In fact, the yanga, in its generic usage, could be considered the saleone of tambu in that the body or a part of the body is shaken or made to tremble in a shimmy. This movement persists in popular Jamaican dances, previously in "the cockroach" and, more recently, as a regular part of the female dancehall repertoire, where the main body part shaken is the buttocks.

Specific steps attributed to yanga are the Jamaican "show-me-your-motion," very similar to the Haitian bamboche, in which the dancer, with hands on hip, pushes the pelvis and knees alternately forward and backward as she jumps in different directions. Yet another step described as the yanga involves a twisting of the hips, knees, and feet in the same direction while moving sideways. Even the kongo step (front foot flat and the back foot on the ball, moving forward with a push on the back foot) has been called the yanga.

Mento, on the other hand, is both traditional and popular, overlapping in function with the buru bands that played at private and public functions like "Coney Island" and village fairs. Mento bands often accompanied maypole and quadrille dance groups as well as performing at nine-night death observances. At one point in the 1950s, mento was absorbed into the tourism market, misnamed as calypso. It became an integral part of the popular Jamaican music of ska to reggae that has been exported all over the world.

Mento was the first home-grown, distinct type of music to be played in urban as well as rural settings. Mento boasts a wide range of instruments, including saxophones, flutes, bamboo fifes, guitars, banjos, rumba boxes, double basses, rhythm sticks, shakas, and sometimes drums played with both hand and stick. This was the live music in urban Jamaican settings like clubs and staged dance sessions up to the early 1960s, before it gave way to ska, rock steady, and reggae. The dance is a slow, winding, sensuous movement that may be performed separately or in intimate contact with a partner. The latter feature came to be called the "dry grind," "rent a tile," and "dub" or "rub a dub." Nice girls were not supposed to be seen in public dancing the mento, especially with a male partner not considered their "significant other."

The question of source and origin continues to be blurred as other forms like Myal may be both specific and generic by definition. Myal is specifically a dance-music, healing, spirit-invoked traditional form that seems to have had its African-creole genesis among the Maroons, but at the same time became specifically manifest in gumbay, found just outside Maroon communities and sharing the unique and indigenous square drum of the same name. Myal is closely associated with the generic description of the religious Revival movement of the post-1838 emancipation period, which at first resembled a renewed Apostolic Christian fervor. It was not long before it became overpowered by the more African Myal, soon to be named the Great Revival Movement of the 1860 and 1861 orders. The 1860 order, or Revival Zion, was and is the more overtly Christian expression of the movement, while the 1861 order or Pukkumina (little Kumina), also known as Pocomania, is more African in its orientation. The connection to Kumina is evident here, given the centrality of Myal and "catching Myal" in Kumina and Pukkumina ceremonies. As I wrote in "Kumina—Stability and Change" (Ryman 1984, 81), this "poses and resolves the contradictions of ethnic focus and creole content in Kumina."

Kumina is a Jamaican traditional dance-music spiritual form distinguished by adherents who refer to themselves as part of a distinct Bongo nation or family. At the same time, they subscribe to an Afro-creole aesthetic and content. That Kumina is limited culturally and geographically to a specific Kongo antecedent and a primarily eastern Jamaica locale in the parish of St. Thomas belies the fact that it incorporates the Afro-creole form Myal. There are two forms of Kumina: "bailo," the more recreational, secular, and public form that employs creole songs and in which possession is actively discouraged, and "country," the more ancestral, spirit-oriented form.

Kumina displays both creole and specific ethnic Bakongo features expressed in language, dance, and music. In the music, a close relationship exists between the drummers of the playin' cyas (or kyas) lead drum, the kbandu rhythm bass drum, and the dancers, with the drumming distinguished by the Kongolese style of heeling the drum. Once the singer raises

Figure 8.2. Queenie's Kumina Group, Waterloo, St. Catherine (1989). Courtesy of African Caribbean Institute of Jamaica/ Jamaica Memory Bank; a division of the Institute of Jamaica.

the appropriate song at any point in the day(s)-long ceremony, the call and response action of the musicians and dancers effect the desired outcome of the Kumina play. The ancestral spirits—sometimes referred to as the *nkuyu*—are invited and enticed to possess the dancer. It is through this medium that the nkuyu's presence and satisfaction may be expressed and achieved, allowing specific requests for assistance by the living members of the Kumina family.

In the Kumina dance, the flat-footed inching and shuffling of the feet, facilitated by bent knees and either a slightly forward-bent or an upright but relaxed back, is accompanied by a side-to-side, forward thrusting or upward heaving of the hip. Whether the feet are placed one slightly in front of the other or side by side, the weight is not evenly distributed. This facilitates the

punctuation of a drop step on each strong beat as the hips move continuously. Several stylistic and specific variants of this basic form may be found
in the Kumina dance repertoire. Regardless of the variants, Kumina dance
constitutes the thread that weaves together all the elements of the carefully
manipulated sequence of events that compose the Kumina ceremony.

Dances directly related to the Kumina dance complex, excluding Pukkumina and Buru already discussed, include Kongo, Tambu, Makumbe,
Warrick, and Kittihali.

Kongo is a secular song-music-dance closely related to Kumina in rhythm
and movement, albeit much faster and more vigorous. The main departure
in movement is the kongo step, found in Ghana in the Kpanlogo dance,
in other parts of the Caribbean, and even in the Etu and Guerre dances in
Jamaica. The lead foot is flat, and the back foot is on the ball of the foot. To
move forward, one pushes off the back foot and steps on the front foot in
continuous and successive movements. The energetic hip movement closely
resembles the Kumina movement. The demographic profile of Kongo participants is distinctly younger, usually pre-adolescent and adolescent, in
comparison to the generally more mature Kumina functionaries and participants.

Tambu is performed primarily in a celebratory nine-night context for
deceased members of the Kongo family and their relatives by marriage. The
dance-music form takes its name from the name of the drum. Tambu is
linked to Kumina by a common ethnic Kongo bond and by similarities,
particularly in the drums, drumming style, and rhythms, as well as in the
basic movement before the climax of the recurring dance sequences. The
Tambu people of Trelawny make reference to an ongoing interaction between themselves and the Kumina people of St. Thomas. (The bailo or lighter
recreational style of drumming within the Kumina and Maroon plays is
also referred to as tambu.) The drum, although similar in appearance to the
Kumina drum set, is slightly larger, and only one is played at a time. If two
are present, they are played in unison.

The dance has three main recurring components, shay-shay, saleone,
and mabumba. Shay-shay refers to the bulk of the dance, which features
a rotating action of the hips (reminiscent of mento), shuffling along with
one foot on the ball (reminiscent of the Kumina-kongo step), and jumps
landing with a dip through the knees (reminiscent of the hop in Buru).
The saleone marks the prelude to the climax of the dance sequence. As the

drum increases in intensity, so does the dancer, with an increasingly vigorous trembling or shimmying of the whole body, ending in a leg lift by the male toward his female partner. The break that immediately follows the saleone is called the mabumba and includes the male pressing his hip against that of his female partner or a definite dip or drop in the knees signaled by an emphatic drum beat. Couples face and advance toward each other using the three-part sequence outlined above, although a more free form style may be employed.

Makumbe seems to be part of the Kongo dance-music family, having been located in the primary Kongo area of St. Thomas and to a lesser extent in Portland. Ancestral spirit possession, the ritual language, and some beliefs and practices that originated from a Bantu-Bakongo source are common to both Makumbe and Kumina. Unfortunately, direct descriptions or examples of the dance or music are not known.

Warrick is a stick-fighting dance tradition that parallels a wide variety of stick-fighting practices in Africa and the diaspora. It has been preserved within the Kongo-Kumina complex, performed in its natural environment and for staged events. Warwick (creole Warrick), a British character, appears in the Jonkonnu masquerade tradition primarily in the parishes of St. Thomas and Trelawny, which exhibit traditional dances with strong Kongo influences. Kittihali is a related stick-fighting tradition found among the East Indians in Jamaica.

### Nine-Night Dances

The Nine-Night complex of dance-music traditional forms is perhaps the most common reason for almost all the traditional dances to be held. Traditional forms like those of Kumina, Tambu, Revival-Zion and Pukkumina, Convince, Flenkey, Etu, Nago, Kromanti Play, and Nyabingi are performed for, though not exclusively for, death or post-death celebrations, to ensure that the dead are properly sent off to their spiritual homes. In so doing, it is felt that the spirit will not become an "unwelcome spirit" that will roam at will as a troublesome or haunting "duppy," tormenting the living, or liable to being caught and manipulated by a "science" specialist to wreak havoc on the living.

Unlike the aforementioned wider traditions, a number of dance-music forms fall into a more specialized category of Nine-Night dances, so ascribed by the belief that a spirit cannot properly rest or be put to rest until nine nights have passed. The first night may or may not be merely a set up, with singing and general comforting of the bereaved, but the ninth night is the most important night of all for sending off the spirit of the deceased. It is usually treated in a more solemn tone, when religious music, albeit lively, is played, Sankeys (Christian hymns) are sung, and, traditionally, fish, hardo (hard dough) bread, hot beverages, soup, and drinks—soft and hard—are served, though the fish and hardo are now often replaced by a more substantial meal, typically curry goat and rice. More recent Nine-Night celebrations in both rural and urban areas will see a sound system or live band replacing the traditional singing and music. Popular religious reggae music is included in the repertoire, with the participants singing along and dancing to the music.

The other seven nights are devoted to cheering of the bereaved and singing, dancing, and feasting until the appointed ninth night. These celebratory, cheering dance-music forms include bele, calimbe, combolo, dinki mini, ring games, gucrre, and wake.

Calimbe is an old African dance performed by men. It requires strength, agility, and dexterity to execute the balancing and almost acrobatic movements demanded by the dance. It used to be performed primarily at wakes, the term associated with the first and last (ninth) night of death observances. The dance is said to signify death and resurrection. With its transmission to a more secular, tourism entertainment realm, it became known as the bamboo dance. The dancer is required to jump in and out of two bamboo sticks, held low and parallel to the ground, that are snapped together and released rhythmically, accompanied by singing and clapping. The dancer is expected not to tire or to lose the rhythm lest his feet get caught between the snapping sticks. A greater test of the dancer's prowess comes with his mounting of the sticks, now held much higher off the ground, forcing the dancer to balance on the sticks while riding them as they are moved apart sideways or as each stick is moved simultaneously forward and backward—all in rhythm. Calimbe is performed within *Gerrehbenta*, a dance choreographed by Professor Rex Nettleford for the National Dance Theatre of Jamaica. The other dances showcased in this work are all dances performed at Nine-Night celebrations and include Etu and dinki mini.

Combolo, found in the Kumina parish of St. Thomas, is far less popular today, but falls more into the ring games category of Nine-Night integrated song and dance, meaning that the dancers sing and dance at the same time rather than being accompanied. The movement carries erotic overtones with the theme that runs through all of the Nine-Night dances—a demonstration of man's capacity to generate life in the face of death.

Dinki mini remains one of the more popular Nine-Night celebrations, originating in the northeast parish of St. Mary. A closely related form, zella, is also found in this parish. It is performed on the second to eighth nights after the death. For the first three or four nights, dancing in couples and singing is accompanied by lively mento-type music, with a low twanging sound emanating from the benta, an instrument made from a length of thick bamboo with two or three joints and a string, lifted from the outer bark of the bamboo, stretched and tied at either end. The benta is placed on top of a stump of wood with two musicians sitting at either end. One musician presses a dried calabash along the string, producing a low twanging, while the other uses two bamboo sticks to strike the string. Other instruments that accompany this dance may include shakas, bamboo clappers and scrapers, and a large bamboo tube, open at both ends, that produces a deep thumping sound when hit on the ground rhythmically. By the sixth or seventh night, ring games, Anansi storytelling, and riddles dominate the proceedings. By the ninth night the climax takes the form of a wake with specific rituals designed to send off the "mature" spirit properly. The singing of hymns from the Sankey and Moody hymnal accompanies the proceedings. The mix of dancing and ring games is closely related to guerre on the western end of the island.

The dinki mini dance is characteristically sexually provocative and has two main formations and two movement styles that tend to be male dominated. The first formation is a circular ring-game pattern, and the second is the "Open Cut Out," in which the couples dance together in a free use of space. The corkscrew movement, with upper torso moving up and down and around simultaneously, is accompanied by a rotation of the hip with one foot flat in front and the other behind on the ball of the foot. The placement of feet and action of the hip is similar to the kongo step and more so the buru step, except for the marked corkscrew action of the upper torso. The second movement that tends to be most visible in male performers is a knock-kneed brushing action of the feet that occurs while the upper torso continues its corkscrew action. With the knees pressed together and bent deeply, the foot of the working leg brushes the ground to the side and alternately dabs and brushes to the front and back in either a stationary or a locomotory mode. The arms and shoulders pump on each brush, emphasizing the impulse and suspension-of-the-beat quality that defines the dinki mini movement. Also characteristic is an impulse/suspension and break turn, with an inclination of the upper torso to one side, or with sharp pelvic contact with the female partner.

Guerre (gere, gerreh) is best known on the western side of the island (where bele has also been reported, but not described) and employs the kongo step in what can only be described as very vigorous, sexually provocative movement. The performers form two lines, with males and females facing each other. Couples are called by the leader or cantor, who "dances" them as they meet in the center between the two lines, using the kongo step. There, they dance energetically with each other, the man often crouching and holding the woman loosely around the waist, with breaks against each other, leg lifted and hips meeting sometimes sharply on the beat. The non-dancing couples sing and clap. Guerre may be described as vigorous ring games, executed in a circle or two lines, reputed to reduce the best laid lawn to a dirt patch at the end of a night's activity. Typical ring games recalled are Appleton Train, Gal and Boy, and Planti Grass a Hetti oh. These sessions may take place over the first two nights after the death of an individual or up to the night before the burial, depending on the resources of those left behind to offer refreshments to the attending community.

Wake or Set Up conjures up an Irish contribution similar in purpose to that exercised by the slave population and their descendants, even today. Wakes can be on the first and ninth night after death or any night between not marked by one of the celebratory Nine-Night dances described above. Wakes may be more staid and marked by the singing of Sankeys and prayers, with accompanying refreshments, but reference to a Wake that includes dancing invariably refers to one of the many Nine-Night dance-music forms, usually dinki mini or guerre.

Before dealing with the last two core dance-music types, Maroon Kromanti Play and Rastafari, it is good to point to the closeness of the Maroon-Kumina relationship, particularly between the St. Thomas Bongo (Kumina) Nation and the Moore Town–Portland Maroon Nation, or what Kenneth Bilby records as sometimes called the "Kyatawud" Nation (Bilby 2003). There is a mutual admiration and respect by each, particularly on the part of the Bongo Nation for the acknowledged spiritual science expertise of the

Maroons. This closeness is based on a long history of interaction between these two groups, although the Bongo Nation emerged some 100 years after Maroon independence was established within Jamaica, following the signing of the 1738–39 treaty with the British.

Shared elements in both these distinct nations include songs in the bailo mode; spirit possession termed Myal with reference made to mounting by the spirit; the preeminent role of the ancestors; a special ritual or spirit language (Kikongo for Kumina and Twi and Fanti from Ghana for the Maroons); together with the importance of healing and use of the weed or bush (sometimes marijuana) in healing. Maroons have become familiar with and capable of playing the Kumina drums and performing the Kumina dance. Becoming possessed by a Maroon *granfa* (ancestor) is possible within the context of a Kumina play; however, there is a difference in the way possession by the Kumina and Maroon ancestors is treated: the striking of a match above the head of the possessed works to attract and appease the spirit of a Maroon ancestor, but with the Kumina ancestors, fire repels the spirit.

Between the traditions of the Bongo and Maroon is the Flenkey-Bongo-Convince tradition, closely related to the Great Revival. Flenkey and Convince are used interchangeably or together to describe a ritual with possession as the objective. The ritual is characterized by hymn singing, playing (with the hand) a tall drum that is mounted, and dancing with contortions and jumps, accompanied by heavy smoking and drinking of white rum with a distinct inclination to climb trees when possession by a Bongo spirit occurs. Bongo spirits seem to be among the most powerful possessing spirits in both the Kumina and Convince/Flenkey groups, although the Maroon influence is generally acknowledged.

Maroon Kromanti Play is a composite of different nation dances that form part of the celebratory activities of the Maroons. This is a product of the creolization process that took place over time between the various African ethnic groups in the context of the Maroons' isolation. Here a greater sense of identity and autonomy than that of their plantation counterparts pertained. The ethnic groups exerted greater or lesser influence by virtue of their numbers or natural leadership and fighting acumen. The Akan-Asante, coming from a royal court culture, had an aggressive and successful tactical war background.

Other specific attributes were offered by non-Akan-Asante ethnic groups, including "science" expertise, the ability to deal with ancestral and other spirits who provide medicinal/herbal and practical prescriptions to the benefit of the living. The Ewe people were particularly known for this. The commonly termed "Juju" operation in "science" matters in the Ewe Volta region in Ghana bears a close resemblance to that of Jamaica's Kumina and Obeah concentrated in St. Thomas and Maroon communities. The Maroons acknowledged for their Myal or "medicine" expertise are also known as science men. Nanny, the eastern Maroon female leader, a national hero, exhibited such legendary science prowess that she was said to catch bullets in her buttocks to repel and redirect them at her enemies. Maroon culture drew on the constant renewal of its numbers and its cultural pool, while in turn offering either source or inspiration for many of the practices in the larger Jamaican society.

The Kromanti Play, in its entirety or in part, depending on the occasion, includes ambush, masumba, saleone, and paw-paw (pa-pa or popo). Other nation styles that form part of the "business" dance music of the Maroons include the Mandiga (Mandingo), Ibo, and Tambu. The Tambu is related directly and indirectly to the Bongo nation and in particular to Kumina dance music and to the Tambu found in Trelawny.

Ambush is a reenactment in mime of the guerrilla fighting tactics of disguise. Camouflaged with bush and plant fiber, the western Maroons ambushed their British enemies repeatedly, eventually winning their freedom with the peace treaty of 1738–39. Camouflaged dancers form a guard of honor to pay homage to a distinguished visitor, a returning Maroon, and on January 6 in Accompong in the parish of St. Elizabeth, at the annual celebration of the signing of the peace treaty and birthday of Kojo (Cudjoe), the freedom fighting leader of the western Maroons.

The "pleasure" dance commonly displayed to outsiders is a creole Akan-influenced dance music in which two main drums are played upright, the prenting and the gumbay square drum. Other instruments include the spirit-infused abeng (a cow's horn), along with percussion instruments like calabash shakas, the quart (kwat)—a length of bamboo struck with two sticks, and the adowa—a cutlass struck with a piece of metal. Adowa is the nation dance music of the Asante in Ghana.

Masumba is a dance for men that demonstrates the agility and strength of the fighting Maroons. Like the now touristy limbo, it employs the same movement of pressing through the hip with the trunk tipped back and knees bent as the dancer inches under a pole held parallel to the ground. The pole is moved increasingly lower to test the prowess of those who dare to try. In the dance, the stick or pole starts at navel height; the Maroons believe that the strength of the body resides in the navel, and this is the area that must pass under the pole in order to successfully transition from one side to the other.

Saleone moves into the realm of nation dances and music that make up the full Kromanti Play, performed as part of the "business/medicine dances" among the Maroons and specifically as a song-music style among the eastern Moore Town Maroons. Saleone also appears as part of the Tambu dance, found in Trelawny on the western side of the island. The word seems to have its origins in the name of the West African country of Sierra Leone. Paw-Paw, like saleone, is performed as one of the nation dances within the context of the "business/medicine" dance music of the Kromanti Play. Here reference is made to an ethnic antecedent, the Paw-Paw or Ewe people found between Ghana and Nigeria.

After Emancipation in 1838, British, German, Indian, Chinese, and free Africans were brought into the country under a variety of contracts to work or settle the land. Among the Africans brought to Jamaica at that time were Yoruba people. Dances associated with these people are Nago and Etu, one of the two ethnic-specific dance-music forms in Jamaica. Although a distinct, surviving ethnic dance-music form, the people and their dance have weakened to virtual extinction in the last fifteen years. Nevertheless, a recent heroic effort as part of the Ph.D. work of Dr. Sandra Hamilton demonstrates the tenacity of cultural identity. The Etu families found in Kendal, Hanover, in the western end of the island, claim Yoruba ancestry, evidenced in their language, food, dance, and music. Another group who refer to themselves as Nago reside in a hill town (Waterworks District) in the parish of Westmoreland bearing the same name as a similar hilly town found in Nigeria called Abeakuta. The Nago people hold traditional dance, music, and feasting events referred to as a "play" primarily for nine-night and forty-night death celebrations as well as for weddings and "dinner plays." A dinner play is a community gathering involving dance, music, and feasting, with feasting being the primary objective.

Etu is distinguished by two drums: the achaka or kerosene tin drum and the irre, a two-headed oval drum. The achaka is played by hand and produces a largely unique 6/8 compound duple rhythm that has been identified among only one other group, the Maroons. The irre drum plays more intricate and spontaneous rhythms, but is largely drowned out by the singing and riveting sound of the achaka. The dance tends to exhibit great variation in movement as it relates to each family's dance style; however, some common movements may be identified. The hips move rapidly and continuously from side to side to the 8-beats-to-the-bar rhythm of the achaka, while the feet pivot on the ground, moving the hips, and end with a brush left and right alternately on every third count. The movements of the female dancers tend to portray a hippy, teasing quality, while the men exhibit more strength and agility. The dance moves from the individual performances to the open cut out group dancing.

Shawling, a ritual appreciation for the dancing of an individual, will see the Queen or a principal female member of the community rise to dance with and throw a scarf around the neck of the performer. More than one scarf may end up around the neck of a dancer, or sometimes tied around the waist, depending on the level of appreciation. Male dancers who demonstrate particular virtuosity tend to be "crowned," that is, to have a hat placed on their heads. In both cases, the person showing appreciation will ceremoniously dip the dancer back from the waist "to give him strength" and raise the dancer's arm above the head in a gesture of congratulations for a good performance.

Hosay refers to the specifically Muslim (but shared with Hindus) celebration of the massacre of the grandsons of the prophet Mohammed. Some Afro-Jamaicans participate in these celebrations, primarily as musicians. The Tazia, an elaborately decorated replica of the tomb of the martyred brothers, is built over a nine-day period and forms the centerpiece of this festival, which ends on the tenth day in a processional dance and extravagant feasting. The Tazia is carried through the streets amid drummers, dancers, stick fighters, and a large contingent of followers. It is released into a river or the sea, where it is allowed to sink into the sunset.

Hosay as a core form subsumes the wider contribution and sharing of East Indian and African cultures, evidenced by an Indian spirit as one of the strongest spirits in Revival, the comical and sexually charged Babu in Jonkonnu, and curry goat as the primary meal in Kumina. Curry goat has become one of Jamaica's national dishes, ranking in popularity next only to ackee and salt fish. In some cases Indians and Africans actually traveled together on the same ship as contract indentured laborers, signaling a close and continuing relationship between the two groups when they arrived on the island.

Rastafari—the most recent creole development—has been included here since it straddles African ancestral, traditional, and urban contemporary elements. It evolved from an acute African, primarily Ethiopian, consciousness with a strong back-to-Africa theme and a belief in the divinity of Emperor Haile Selassie—Ras Tafari. It took its early form and dance-music expression primarily from Revival (street meetings, large borrowings of songs, and use of the bass or thunder drum), mento, buru (fundeh and repeater or akete drums), and to a lesser extent from Kumina. Like its earlier Maroon antecedent, Rastafari evolved from an isolationist environment in the 1930s with its most significant center, called Pinnacle, found in the hills of St. Catherine. Although Rastafari eschews what may be described as the creole "corruption" or "Babylon" found in many of the traditional forms, it nevertheless drew heavily on the form and substance of these earlier traditions. Over time, it has developed its own distinct music and dance, best exemplified in Nyabingi (also Nyabinghi) celebrations. Rastafari is noted for its nondogmatic belief system, diet, philosophy, and most of all, a holistic lifestyle referred to as "Livity." In fact, Rastafari brethren will assert that Rastafari is not a religion but Livity.

The music style of Nyabingi resembles the role and function of the two main drums in Kumina and Buru. The Rastafari fundeh maintains a strong steady rhythm while the repeater, the smallest and most high-pitched of the set of drums, carries a sometimes steady rhythm with regular breaks, but more often the lead repeater drummer breaks out into dramatic slaps and syncopated utterances that are highly improvisational. Literally or symbolically the fundeh is perceived to be the "carrier of the spirit." It is difficult for the dancer not to respond to these impulses with the typical posture of bent knees and backs slightly forward, shifting the weight from one leg to the other, punctuated by suspended breaks that feature a low-impact hop on one leg in response to the last two beats of the bar. Spins and turns while hopping on one leg on the break are not uncommon. For the men, vigorous shaking of the locks is often a part of the dancer's response. Bob Marley in performance often subscribed to the movement sequences and styles described here.

## Continuities with Popular Dance—and Meaning and Function in Traditional Dances

The pervasive continuities in Jamaican popular and contemporary dance have been repeatedly demonstrated throughout the description of Jamaican traditional dances. The common threads that run through the dances are shown not only in the steps, movement patterns, and quality of movement, but also in the many principles of movement that have been designated African and African based.

The mask-dance-music triad of Jonkonnu persists even in dancehall, as much in terms of content as in context. Continuing features are found in a number of dancehall steps from the Bruckin Party's upper torso break, to the butterfly of Jonkonnu, to the log on, made popular by Elephant Man, together with a plethora of new rhythms specifically called Jonkonnu and Diwali (after the Hindu holiday)—all with the corresponding movements. Masking is evident in the exaggerated style, fads, and fashions of dancehall—shiny, elaborate, bizarre, topical, and comical. These serve to transform and transcend the everyday reality of the participants. The devices employed in the popular arena mirror those of the traditional in codes of behavior, sequencing, and protocol of dance-music events, the relationship of dancer to musician, the use of a "secret language," and the use of space and patterns of performance.

Jamaican traditional forms convey meaning through signs and symbols as well as through specific vocabulary and language in the dance and music. They may be described as cultural codes retrieved at conscious and subconscious levels and similarly deciphered by the participants. The level of initiation into a specific cultural group or subset will determine the level of understanding and meaning derived from what is heard, seen, and experienced. Traditional dance-music forms provide a tangible connection with the past through the re-creation of rituals and other elements of our heritage contained in the dress, food, language, songs, and musical instruments, transformed and refashioned. Possession and "spiritual schools" form part of the process of transfer and continuity. Meaning is found in the symbols and "keys" referred to as "nkisi" by the Kumina people. These keys unlock and enhance the spiritual forces that may be at man's disposal, if desired, and if one has knowledge about their use. They are found in the masks of traditional Jonkonnu—reinterpreted and refashioned in the popular dance-hall context.

Perhaps the most common function of traditional dance forms is to achieve specific objectives in the rites of passage from birth to death, in physical and mental health, and in happiness and general well-being. This includes the power to "tie" (hold or attract) a loved one or the object of one's affection and the diagnosis and resolution of problems like influencing the outcome of a pending judicial judgment or exercising judgment in the settling of scores. Another function at both the conscious and subconscious levels is the affirmation of life and man's power of procreation, especially when confronted with personal loss at an individual and community level. This explains the sexually charged and celebratory nature of dances performed at death observances in the Nine-Night complex of dances. They are a conduit between the family of the living and the "living dead"—the ancestors.

Traditional dance-music forms provide a vehicle for subversive responses and aggressive resistance to oppression, evidenced in the dance of Jonkonnu and today's dancehall. At the same time, the lyrics of mento and buru songs incorporate humorous and coded language to convey the full meaning and intent of subversive and antioppression messages. Traditional forms make a link with the past—bridging ancestry and contemporary pedigree. They create a sense of place and space and establish rootedness or a sense of identity within a specific culture amid the criss-crossing movement of global cultures and people, by generating symbols with specific meanings and codes of Being. In the contemporary world, consider the powerful branding brought to Jamaica and Jamaicans by Rastafari and reggae and their inspiration to the world. They provide, too, the inspiration and basis for consciously developing a national dance theater form.

Among the many functions that served our ancestors and continue to serve present generations and those to come, that of transformation and transcendence is paramount. It is achieved most effectively through the convergence of the triad of mask-dance-music. These traditional forms facilitate transformation and transcendence of the world of the mundane and even hopelessness to that of the extraordinary and magical—that is, to *luminosity*.

# 9

# Dance, Divas, Queens, and Kings

## Dance and Culture in Jamaican Dancehall

SONJAH STANLEY NIAAH

What do the names Kid Harold, Baskin, Pam Pam, Carlene, Labba Labba, Bogle, Stacey, Craigy Dread, Spongebob, Ding Dong, Mad Michelle, Keiva, Colo Colo, Sample Six, Sadiki, Ravers Clavers, Shelly Belly, Blazay, Timeless, Shortman, Cadillac, and John Hype have in common? All have made indelible marks on the repertoire and performance style of popular dance in Jamaica since the 1930s, from dance events at Marcus Garvey's Edelweiss Park (see Hamilton 1988) to more contemporary dancehall events such as Passa Passa and Dutty Fridaze in West Kingston (see Stanley Niaah 2004a).

There is a consensus that the definition of dancehall goes beyond that of a musical genre. It is the way of life for a group of people, largely disenfranchised youth—who are sustained by it in real, symbolic, imaginary, and material terms. In dancehall the act of dancing takes on connotations of slavery. Dancers and other patrons take on the toil of ridding their mind of daily troubles, becoming slaves, not (solely) in a capitalist (post)modernity that disenfranchises, but also in a somatic and kinesthetic sense. As if they were "slaves to the rhythm" that beats around them and inside them against the social ills of everyday Jamaica, in the way Grace Jones (1985) suggests in her song of the same name; the exerting body on the contemporary dance floors of Jamaica symbolically replaces the exerting body on the plantations that preceded them. The use of this analogy becomes even more critical when one considers Hartman's analysis of dance throughout the period of slavery and on the popular stage, acknowledging the terror and violence "perpetrated under the rubric of pleasure" (Hartman 1997, 4), and that slavery and freedom are inextricably linked with mechanisms of law, identity, and liberties. This is the body that through contestation, exploitation, discrimination, and oppression preserves itself through performance to tell the tales of history, while dance venues become de-localized for just a moment when they transcend time and produce the inevitable "congregational kinesis" (Brathwaite 1995, 46).

Much public debate about dancehall moves has revolved around evaluative judgments. This chapter examines some of the central and arguably underexposed creators of dance moves and by extension their personhood within the dancehall and everyday life. Their voices are mostly mediated through those of the DJ, selectors of music, and singers, but dancers have not been totally silent. Their expressions are mostly through movement as a tool of celebration; with the body as their instrument, they make their mark on Jamaican history, politics, and nationhood, as well as on the world. The discussion of dance moves that follows has been generated primarily from the dancers as key informants and the movement as key texts. What is the general character of these dance moves? At what periods have they been most prolific? Are there identifiable gender demarcations? Can kinesthetic genres be mapped? Do the dances reveal insights about recruitment patterns or the politics of location? Ultimately, this chapter establishes the central place of the dancer within dancehall through the presentation, translation, and interpretation of his or her own language, with emphasis placed on the dancer's practice.

## Ol' time somet'ing come back again

I wish to first take a historical look at Jamaican dance moves by telling a story. On October 30, 2006, an article in the *Daily Gleaner* (Turner 2006) reported that Tanisha Henry suffered fatal injuries due allegedly to her performance of the "dutty wine" dance at a school uniform party (a type of dancehall event) in the parish of St. Catherine. Coverage in the mass media included commentary from medical doctors, academics, dancers, and others with opinions on the cause of the incident as well as calls for banning the "dutty wine." The dance was created and popularized by Dyema Attitude, who explained on CVM Television's "Direct" (November 1, 2006) that the dance, designed to exhibit the rotation of hair extensions with its characteristic simultaneous rotation of the head and buttocks, was not being performed with enough caution. DJ/Selector Tony "Mentally Ill" Matter-horn, a.k.a. Anthony Taylor, selector and recording artist, further popular-ized the dance with his 2006 hit song of the same name. He explained on CVM Television's "On Stage" (June 24, 2006) that "the girls weren't getting involved . . . [and] the dances are created by men for a good period of time now," so it is time for girls to return to center stage.

Debate about the dance centered on the danger it posed to the neck, and on the association of its pelvic moves with lewd, licentious, devilish behav-ior, a reputation that has clouded black dance for some time. Interviews and archival research confirmed similar conversation about dance moves such as the yank, jerk, and twist. This debate is not new. For example, dancers have been threatened with expulsion from church. In particular, the yank was an infamously "dangerous" dance that emphasized the jerky movement of the hips. The yank was reputed to have "yanked out" people's hips, as well as caused performers to collapse after doing it. So infamous was the dance that a sign at the old St. James Hospital in western Jamaica reportedly read "no bed for yankers" (Milton Blackhall, interview, December 2, 2006).

Dance moves such as yanga (mento dance), yank, jerk, and those in ska that emphasize domestic activity (washing clothes, bathing), recreation (horse racing, cricket), or anything that appealed to the ska dancer (Reckord 1997, 6–7), are antecedents of popular dancehall moves such as the butterfly, log on, dutty wine, and gully creeper. So are moves such as "legs," performed by such famous dancers as Pam Pam and Baskin of the early years (White 1984, 72), the chucky, and horseman scabby.

### African Continuities

As descendants of African movement and aesthetics, dancehall moves con-vey continuities such as emphasis on the beat and on natural bends—elbow, head, pelvis, torso, and knees (see Dagan 1997, 102–119)—in the movement pattern, as documented in various African dances. Welsh Asante (1985, 71) recognized that commonalities in all African dances have an inherent con-nection to ancestral Africa "through epic memory and oral tradition, even though these dances represent different languages, people, geographies, and cultures." On the basis of these commonalities, she identified seven founda-tions or senses in African dance: polyrhythm, polycentrism, curvilinearity, multidimensionality, epic memory, repetition, and holism, which are all evident in contemporary dancehall moves.

Closer to home, specific aesthetic qualities have been isolated. Cheryl Ryman (2003, 170–171) discusses the connection to ancestral rhythms and moves through an explanation of the characteristic wining of the hips, the bounce (facilitated by natural knee bends), and an S-shaped stance in both male and female dance. The S-90 skank (1970s), mimicking the actions of the Rude Boy on his motorcycle, is an example, as well as traditional movement forms such as in Revival, gereh (or guerre), bruckins, and mento. Ryman discusses the seeming preoccupation with sexual (hip-centered) movements within the context of African principles:

> If we understand that procreation was/is considered vital to the African's survival in life and death, in Africa as well as the diaspora, then we can perhaps understand their apparent preoccupation with 'sexual' movements. Further, it is not unusual, as in Jonkonnu, for the traditional treatment within the context of the dance to be such as to allow for what the folk themselves define as "sexual play." It is simply a representation in dance-movement. (Ryman 1980, 4)

The characteristics pervade traditional and contemporary movement and have utility outside the dance. The agile pelvic movements help with uphill walks, especially with heavy contents on the head. In this sense it acts as a "shock absorber" (Eskamp and de Geus 1993, 56). Other characteristics such as bent knees, grounding of the body rather than lifts, rhythmic complexity, and parallel feet have also been documented.

## The Role of the Dancer

Former dancehall queen Denise "Stacey" Cumberland (crowned 1999) is clear about the role of the dancer in dancehall: "The dance can't happen without dancers. They are the crowd pleasers; if the music has nothing to vibrate on, the dance can't be nice." In discussing the recent proliferation of new dance moves, Stacey highlighted a special synergy between dancer, DJ, the young, the old, the friend, and the enemy: "I have seen dancehall taking out old people; dancehall never so nice in the history of dancehall . . . because it is not modeling, not hype again, just enjoyment and everybody together uniting, everybody [dancing]"—so much so that you forget your enemy on the dance floor. In fact, Stacey acknowledges that the proliferation of dance moves creates a synergy between dancers and DJs because there is always a new dance for DJs to sing about (Cumberland, interview).

## Gerald "Bogle" Levy—The Unnamed King (1966–2005)

Bogle was born in 1966 in Trench Town, West Kingston, and after being unable to take full advantage of the school system decided to go with what God seemed to be telling him: "you are a star." He dedicated his life to dance even after receiving a copious amount of the strap from his mother, who had no faith in that vocation. He started early and by the 1970s had appeared on the Louise Bennett Saturday morning show, "Ring Ding," televised on the Jamaica Broadcasting Corporation, and in the 1980s, the Saturday evening program "Where It's At" on the same station. Contemporary Jamaican dance has been significantly influenced by Bogle's popular dance creations (Gerald Levy, personal interview, June 7, 2002).

Bogle was Jamaica's unnamed dancehall king. He contended that the popular media-proclaimed dancehall queen Carlene Smith had been given recognition, but no one had said Bogle is the king. In an interview with Chicagoreggae.com, Bogle asked, "You ever heard of Carlene creating a dance in Jamaica? . . . Who create all of the dance in Jamaica? . . . You ever hear them crown me King?" To these questions the interviewee answered, "No." Bogle was not just a dancer, but a creator and ethno-choreographer as well. No other dancehall dancer has been credited with creating and popularizing as many dance moves as Bogle. These include (1) zip it up, (2) log on, (3) l.o.y., (4) pelpa, (5) pop the collar, (6) pick it off, (7) genie, (8) gwanie gwanie, (9) mission impossible, (10) hot 97, (11) urkel, (12) flip, (13) butterfly, (14) world dance, (15) imitation bogle, (16) bogle, (17) wave, (18) row like a boat, and (19) jiggy, among others. Bogle often released the moves to the media before exposing them on the dancehall stage. He was also present at many events promoting the moves, and sometimes not only dancing, but also taking the microphone from a selector to speak to the audience. Previously, he had thought of becoming a DJ, but didn't pursue this until just before his untimely death (he was killed in a drive-by murder in January 2005), when the popular hit "All dem deh" was released with the aim of silencing emerging dancers blinded by the spotlight into thinking they were more skilled than Bogle.

Bogle said, "I am dancehall. Because of me . . . everybody wanna dance! Everybody wanna dance right now." In Bogle's opinion, the "dance don't change until Bogle come . . . You never see any difference in the dance until Bogle come." And, he was confident about his ability to allow any DJ to reap success from a song if only Bogle were to create a dance for it. Bogle took credit for the success of such DJs as Beenie Man, Bounty Killer, Buju Banton, and Junior Reid, who sing songs describing Bogle's dance styles or built on Bogle's lyrical suggestions. He said there are phrases such as "Mr. Mention," used by Buju Banton, who has an album and single of the same name, that spring naturally from the Bogle fountain of creativity, but often go unacknowledged. Apart from DJs who use his phrases in their song lyrics, there are others who forget to mention or honor his creativity and place as dance creator. One such example is the single "Log On," about the dance of the same name created by Bogle. The song names "Keiva," who purportedly has a "dancing school" to which she should take those in need of dance tutelage, but does not acknowledge Bogle. As the adage says, "The king is not crowned in his own country."

Because of Bogle's presence in the dance, the number of popular male dancers has increased along with financial opportunities for their advancement, albeit with Bogle himself not benefiting in ways that he would have liked. These include John Hype, who received a contract with the Shocking Vibes recording company, which also managed DJ Beenie Man. Other examples include Sadiki, Craigy Dread, Shortman, Spongebob, Ding Dong, Sample Six, Blazay, and male crews such as Colour Colour, Ravers Clavers, and Cadillac.

## Reaping Rewards from Dancehall

The dancehall constitutes a space in which various rewards are reaped. For the dancer, these vary from personal and private to public and communal. Rewards include personal satisfaction from attending dance events, a U.S. visa, or cash from an admirer who later becomes a partner. Similarly, one male dancer acknowledged meeting all his baby mothers and girlfriends at dance events. For Carlene it was the ability to step into another part of herself that she eagerly wanted to develop—the sexy persona the entire world wanted to see and through which she felt fully ignited. On the other hand, there are those who gain purpose, a space in which they are anonymous but well known and appreciated for their style. Most importantly, dancehall offers a means of escape from real hardships. For example, Bogle conceded that dancehall kept him out of a life of "badness" and disrepute.

The benefits exist at the conscious and unconscious levels. Dancers report the ability to perfect dance moves in the realm of dreams; on the other hand, dancers have also reported feeling as if in a different world when dancing. The intense blurring of dream with reality, the ease with which a dancer steps outside his or her physical reality to enter an ethereal one, is consistent with many traditional performance practices in which varying states of possession are experienced (see Ryman 1980, 2–13). What is clear is that dance allows the dancer a particular kind of flight, the possibility of a permanent and instant lift in daily life beyond sadness, pain, and disenfranchisement. The sheer pleasure of the dance is also not to be overlooked. Many dancers acknowledged the importance of crowd approval as part of that pleasure.

In addition to high levels of satisfaction, dancehall constitutes a means of survival in financial terms. Perhaps the most important reward not yet fully investigated is a social one. From my research, preliminary observations suggest that the high points of increased dance creations, events, and spread of dancehall have been periods in which no general elections with attendant political tensions and violence were held.

## Masking in the Dance

The dance event invokes other sides of the self, other roles enacted, and the wearing of masks is important for the transition to other selves and roles. Masking in the dancehall is defined by the dress, hairstyles (wigs, braids), and behaviors adopted (language, profile) in the milieu of social celebration. The masks are aggrandizing tools for the self, a tradition with roots in Fancy Dress and related forms of masking in Jamaica, for instance, in Jonkonnu. Indeed,

> Jamaican masquerade (Jonkonnu) flourishes today not only in dance hall but also in the masquerade the ladies and gentlemen of quality in upper St. Andrew and Mandeville have adopted via Byron Lee's enterprises. . . . Among the "people from below" the device of "masking" (in fancy-dress) persists with a vengeance. . . . The ambush of a less than just society under the cover of festive masquerades has been one

way of experiencing control, if only a temporary one. . . . The actual dress is important. For the costume is a mask helping to transform the persona to do wild and uninhibited things. (Nettleford 1993, 1D)

In addition to impression-management schemes embodied within such practices as dress (new outfit, new hairdo, no borrowed clothes), the wearing of a different mask at each dancehall event ensures readiness for the video light that signifies the eventual broadcast of not just a self, but a visual product as well.

Figure 9.1. Dancer Shelly Belly poses with a female friend. By Sonjah Stanley Niaah; used by permission.

## Attributes of a Good Dancer

All the interviewees described how they learned to dance as well as to assess a good dancer. Most admitted to being self-taught, learning the dance primarily through observation. Stacey and Bogle are the most notable in terms of distinct creations and trends in movement, and they saw themselves as having natural talent. In respect of judging a good dancer, Sandy said, "If the hip nah move, yuh nah move," and further, "If nobaddy paying yuh any mind [is] like yuh nah do nutten." For her, excellence is reflected in the acrobatic movement of the waistline, and knowledge of all the dance moves, current and past. For Pinkie, "You have to know all the up-to-date dances; people hope to learn from you. That's what a dancehall queen is." Essentially, she acknowledges, as part of the role of the dancehall queen, pedagogical responsibilities in relation to those who hope to learn the moves, adding to the others named below.

Spandex highlighted specific attributes such as the ability to convey mood and emotions while dancing and the ability to elicit crowd response with exciting, frisky, and neat movements. In a similar vein, Stacey offered that the dancer must make an impression with appearance, creativity, attitude, confidence, and movement. The dancer's unique appearance should be accented with an attitude of self confidence that conveys the movement effectively to his or her crowd. Interviewees made the distinction between dancing and "mogelling" (modeling), the latter being attitude without real ability or talent; however, it was acknowledged that the act of dressing up has its own appeal that, in turn, propels the appeal of the dance arena. Modeling and profiling are seen as essential.

## Gender Demarcations and Negotiations in Dance

Male/female partner dancing was very popular in pre-1990s dancehall. Whereas women would attend dance events with male partners in the 1970s, for example, the 1990s ushered in an era when women attended events on their own or with a female "crew." A contributing factor is, arguably, the degree of independence some women achieved as a result of economic activities such as "higglering" (lower-class vending). One dancer observed that in the late '80s and early '90s, "Girl just give yuh a dance and any amount a dance," due among other things to "personal" security. One male dancer admitted, "If dance a keep, wi go to get a girl." In an acknowledgment of the mid-1990s shift, dancers admitted that they did not attend dance events with male partners, but rather with girlfriends, as attending the event with one's partner reduced the degree of freedom the dancer could exercise in dance moves and choice of dance partners. The 1990s could be said to have ushered in an element of free play among women as new levels of economic and social independence were reached.

The facts support a resurgence of other kinds of masculinities within dancehall, paralleling the legsmen of the 1960s whose dance skills found no contradiction with the macho, aggressive, and tough masculinity prescribed by the Jamaican social context. Bogle and those inspired by him occupy a space in which they can express new brands of masculinity. These include nonaggressive modes of being, centering around the improvisational nature of the individual and, increasingly, group creative dance process. Males dance with males, females with females, as well as males with females within both group (or crew) and couple modalities. There is less emphasis on sexuality and more on expanding the space and performance of dance styles outside of the every day. This does not mean that macho masculinities are not also performed by dancers, but this is less visible in male dancers' performances than it is of the male DJ.

Dances can be classified according to the sex for which they are intended. Bogle, major dancehall dance master or ethno-choreographer, is an important figure in dancehall. As the unnamed king, Bogle's contribution to dancehall choreography is unmatched, much like a twenty-first-century legsman whose dance repertoire reflects twenty-first-century politics, lifestyle, and tensions. Most importantly, Bogle has created a platform for other male dancers, some of whom testify to dancehall's life-saving role in their lives.

In discussing his creations, Bogle acknowledged that the bogle dance move is really for men, while the butterfly is for women (Reyes 1993, 48). While many dances are performed by women, those such as the one foot skank, legs, cool an' deadly, get flat, and, more recently, the chaplin, are performed mostly by men. On the other hand, the head top, body basics, sketel, bike back, position, and the various wines—wine an' go down, go go wine, and bruk wine—have been performed mostly by women. A larger number of dance moves, especially the more recent ones, are performed by both sexes: the world dance, bogle, tatti, screetchie, angel, tall up tall up, higher level, curfew, log on, row like a boat, wave, parachute, blazay, and signal di plane.

Female dances are generally those where the essential point of articulation is the rotation or thrust of the pelvic girdle, while male dances emphasize complex leg and hand-coordinated movements, and moves performed by both sexes are multidimensional in nature. The latter are not centered on the pelvic girdle or hand/leg coordination; they emphasize individual memory rather than dance skills, and the entire community can execute these moves. In other words, the criteria for recruitment are significantly less for unisex dance moves, ensuring continuity of the characteristic sociability in the dancehall space. Everyone can participate.

I want now to look specifically at the movement pattern of the most popular female dance steps. The butterfly reigned supreme in 1992. With the hands and spread legs, the life force of a butterfly is depicted. The butterfly is danced with the knees bent, a characteristic feature of African and diasporic movement patterns, with the feet flat, supporting the dynamic displacement of the hips, shoulder girdle, and legs while the fluid rotation of the knees laterally on a horizontal axis is achieved like the flapping of the butterfly's wings in flight. While the butterfly has clear connections with its North Atlantic cousin, the charleston (with its roots in an Ashanti ancestor dance), with its quick spreading and crossing of hands on the knees (Jones 1963, 17; Eskamp and de Geus 1993, 60), there are differences. For example, the forward and backward thrust of the hip which supports the opening and closing of the legs allows for increased degrees of variation on the movement style.

An important component for female dance moves is the skill of wining: winding the waist in a smooth, generic bubble or rotation of the hips, wining like a go-go dancer, or wining on the head top (in a head stand). There are various songs that encourage wining and a developed wining skill. Elephant Man's "Wining Queen" (2002) asks the question of who is going to be the next wining queen, the next wining machine. His "Fan Dem Off" (2003) encourages the dancer to wine up her body like a snake in the vine. Captain Barkey's (1996) song "Go Go Wine" sings of the dancers wining their waistline, their chest, and their rumps because they have no problem: they have fed their children, and they are hotter than the competition. Patra's "Bruk Wine," Admiral Bailey's "Stuck," and Shabba Ranks' "Girls Wine" are all wining incantations to the dancer.

Figure 9.2. Dancer in the groove at Dutty Fridaze, September 2007. By Sonjah Stanley Niaah; used by permission.

A crucial component of the wining capacity dancers must have is control of the buttocks. In various body positions, the dancer's buttocks can shimmy, thrust, rotate, release and contract, push, press, and pump, in a light, heavy, frantic, sharp, fluid, or jerky manner. Moves such as the bike back, position, and sidung pon it are examples; not only do they require fluid movement of the hips, they also feature a particular aesthetic of the buttock. Johnny P's (1991) recording about the bike back move is captured in a song of the same name in which he describes the movement of the experienced female bike rider/dancer. He explains, essentially, that as the dancer hoists her derriere, with bent knees facilitating rotating and flashing movements, perfect balance and control are mastered and maintained on the highly fashionable Kawasaki motorbike, so much so that she upstages the competition and passersby. Obviously, the large derriere, which is celebrated in dancehall and more widely in Jamaican culture, matters in such a move. It is the dancer with buttocks that are visible and can be manipulated who will command attention. As Johnny P explains, such a movement is best executed with a large but flexible derriere because girls with flat bums cannot effectively ride the bike back.

## A Preliminary Chronology

Some of the major dance moves throughout the period 1986–2007 are highlighted in the list below. This chronology was developed based on the production year of songs about the dance, memory of informants, mass media coverage (the *Gleaner*, *Star*, and *Observer*), and other secondary sources. They are considered major because of their popularity. The dance moves presented are by no means the extent of creations within the dancehall space. It is important to note that some dance moves have no name, such as variations of the generic bubbling, a characteristic rotation of the hips done mostly by women. In addition, not all dance moves become popular beyond a community or corner. It is popular personalities such as Bogle who have consistently and strategically added new dance moves to the repertoire.

Among other things, the chart illustrates the dynamic nature of dance creation and naming in the contemporary years, especially throughout 1990 to 1994 and 1999 to 2004. Like the musical rhythms—punawny, taxi, sleng ting, rampage, old dawg, dewali, fiesta, wicked, nine night, and tai chi—that have maintained a dynamic naming system, dance moves have names that tell stories. These include stories of cross-fertilization, identification with or of characters, vibes, phenomena, or body parts. For example, the "jerry springer" and "urkel" present interesting names for an analysis of dancehall within the text of two television characters originating in the social milieu or melee displayed in America's visualscape. Jerry Springer hosts a talk show known for high levels of controversy and public display of interpersonal feuding. The urkel, on the other hand, is named after a nerd from the series "Family Matters."

## Chronology of Major Dance Moves

The Early Years (1940s–1970s)—yanga, shay-shay, yank, twist, jerk, charleston, boogaloo, legs, funky, fox, shuffle, ska, s-90 skank, cripple skank, rema, cockroach, rub-a-dub, chucky, rocksteady

1980–1989—cool an' deadly, water pumpee, horseman scabby, heel an' toe, bubble, pedal an' wheel, body move, shoulder move, bounce, duck, jump 'n spread out, stuck, wine an' go down, get flat, one foot skank, della move

1990/91—crab, head top, poco man jam

1991/92—bike back, big it up, roun' di worl, santa barbara, bogle

1992/93—imitation bogle, butterfly, armstrong, bruk wine

1993/94—worl' dance, tatti, soca bogle, position, limbo, kung fu

1994/95—mock di dread, body basics, a capella

1995/96—urkel, go go wine, ol' dog

1996/97—sketel

1997/98—mr bean, pelpa, the flip

1998/99—jerry springer

2000/01—angel, screechy

2001/02—l.o.y. (lords of yard), zip it up, log on

2002/03—on line, drive by, curfew (taliban), tall up tall up, higher level, party dance, wave, karate or martial art, blaze, row like a boat, pon di river pon di bank, signal di plane, chaplin, parachute, fan dem off, propeller, hand cart, shake dem off, elbow dem, rock away, nah nuh head

2003/04—shelly belly, internet, gallop, krazy hype, jiggy, thunder clap, fall the rain, hop the ferry, scooby doo, thunder clap, shankle dip

2004/05—chaka chaka, sesame street, wacky dip, out an' bad, willy bounce, spongebob, back to basics

2005/06—bad man forward, gangsta rock, tick tock, dutty wine, stookie

2006/07—mad a road, live red, craigy bounce, bounty/killa walk, killa swing, prezi bounce, spread out, hoola hoop, beyonce wine, hot f/wuk, raging bull, tek weh yuself, drunkin' dance, drop dead, earthquake, statue of liberty, energy, rum ram

2007/08—no linga, gully creeper

The stylization of the everyday is particularly pronounced in this proliferation of movement patterns. Whereas dance moves like urkel, a capella, and bogle in the early 1990s depicted characters and aspects of life, dance moves during the current high point have served to magnify Jamaican style of life. In other words, everyday acts are more visible and have taken on new expressive proportions through dance. Such practices as "burn a spliff" or "give dem a drape" (grab by the collar or waist), as the police are well known to do to dance patrons, are enacted through dance. Similarly, row like a boat, fan dem off, thunder clap, and fall the rain are other examples. As has been said of the blues, dancehall movement went back "to the individual, to his completely personal life and death" for its "impetus and emotional meaning" (Jones 1963, 67).

What stories do these moves tell? Some of the messages to be read from the dance moves include tangible sociocultural and anatomical scriptings. For example, dances that comment on social ills include the curfew and drive by. The movement in curfew represents policemen carrying guns while searching for criminal elements in inner-city communities under attack by gang warfare and/or warring political factions. With the characteristic bent knees, sometimes to very low grand plié levels, the dancer walks in a forward motion with hands mimicking the shape of a rifle while looking forward and back. The get flat dance, popularized by the Bloodfire Posse band through a song of the same name, is an early replica of the curfew.

The drive by represents two things. First it comes into common Jamaican usage because of the "importation" of drive-by shootings from North America, as a sign of more complex criminal activity in Jamaica. Added to this is the representation of the actions of driving a car. The dance moves through a sequence of actions, including steering, gearing down, turning left, indicating, braking, and parking. With increased access to cars by a wider cross-section of the middle and lower classes since the influx of reconditioned cars in the late 1990s, one could argue that the drive by also represents the coming of age of car culture in Jamaica.

Alongside such imports as cars and technological advancements, as it were, others such as the Internet and the concept of logging on are reflected in dance names of internet and log on. In the case of the log on dance, however, its movement and description in song are not strictly related to information technology. The lyrics by Elephant Man instruct the dancer to log on and step on a "chi chi" man, with a lift of the leg followed by a twist to the side before stepping down. Apart from the reference to the chi chi bus (popular 1970s Jamaican public transportation), popularized by Jamaican poet Louise Bennett, there is the reference to homosexuality which the dancehall moral code denounces as a social ill. In the late 1990s, the meaning of chi chi transformed to refer primarily to a homosexual male rather than to a transportation mode.

Explicit spiritual themes can also be seen in dancehall dance. The poco man jam and angel are examples. The poco man jam highlights the move-

Figure 9.3. Swizzle Body Girls take center stage at Dutty Fridaze, September 2007. By Sonjah Stanley Niaah; used by permission.

ment of a Pocomania (also known as Pukkumina and closely related to the Revival religious group) dancer who is possessed or on the verge of possession. The head, hands, and feet are the central points of articulation. The dancer's head moves (sometimes erratically) from side to side with sharp jerky movements, while the body is propelled forward with thrusts on the right foot and rhythmic thrusts of the right hand. This movement pattern is characteristic of the Revival religious groups and described as the trumping step (see Simpson 1956, 354; Carty 1988, 68–74; Baxter 1970, 142). The angel is characterized by a side shuffle that moves the body to the left and right. In Harry Toddler's song "Dance the Angel," the dancer is instructed to dance the angel in what Toddler describes as a salute to the angels, adding that if you are not doing this you are with the "devil angels" (Toddler, The Party, CVM Television, May 25, 2002).

## Conclusion

Dance moves are created overnight and, in a similar vein, those created can disappear. In spite of power plays within the dancehall space and from external forces, the moves exist on every street corner and are accessible to each citizen, including the blind, the deaf, and the crippled, according to Beenie Man (1994) in his song about the "world dance." Beenie Man explained that he had found a new dance, the "world dance," being performed on the streets, lanes, and corners, that is, everywhere, by or for everyone.

The documentation of these moves has been undertaken (consciously or unconsciously) primarily by videographers since the early 1990s. What I have contributed is a record of the dynamic creation of dance moves within a cultural system of embodied elocution that holds dance as a sixth sense. It is by this sixth sense that many key participants articulate their likes, dislikes, loves, burdens, prejudices, and, ultimately, their identities. As Elephant Man eloquently puts it, dancing is Jamaica's middle name.

Some of the material on Jamaican dance moves is contained in the chapter by Sonjah Stanley Niaah and Donna Hope (2007), "Canvasses of Representation: Stuart Hall, the Body and Dancehall Performance" in *Caribbean Reasonings: Culture, Race, Politics and Diaspora*, edited by Brian Meeks. Information on dancers came from interviews conducted and sourced during the period 2000–2006. My special thanks to Patrice Eriata, Willie Blackhall, Cheryl Ryman, Tipper, CPTC, and Hype TV for assistance with compilation of the chronology.

# 10

# Ghanaian Gome and Jamaican Kumina

## West African Influences

ISAAC NII AKRONG

### Introduction: Bring the Drums

"Bring out the drums!" This is a signal of an unpredictable event to come in an African performance scene like Kumina. So, too, the drums come from trees that grow with green leaves, fruits, and feed the world—life itself. African practices on the mainland and in the diaspora have, over the years, presented unique puzzles to scholars. I wish to present a perspective on African performance practice that brings to the foreground an understanding of the making of the old, the margins of the new, and the connections between both. When I first started thinking about the links between Ghana and the Caribbean, Gome and Kumina immediately came to mind. I saw a clear Ghanaian-Jamaican connection through the arts of Kumina, Pocomania, Goombeh (Jamaican), Kple, Oshi, Oge, Gome, Tigari, Akom (Ghanaian), and others. In this chapter I will share a Ghanaian insider's perspective on the relationship between ethnic groups in the Caribbean and West Africa, as well as in Central Africa.

This scholarship seeks to foster an ongoing discussion among all who are interested in the similarities that bring nations together, as well as in elucidating fluid interpretations of rituals, spirituality, and holistic performative arts. This is an additional view in the spectrum of myths and stories that my predecessors have shared on Kumina. Kumina in today's context becomes a symbol of the past, yet it is alive. My story is told from a traditional African cyclic method of storytelling, based on the notion that the earth is round, spinning, rotating, orbiting, a spontaneous and symbolic affirmation of life's discourse connecting paradigms and drawing on analogies with an emphasis on oral tradition. This approach is opposite to linear presentations, and I encourage the reader to read with open-mindedness in this forum. Returning to Kumina, I have chosen two "green leaves," one from Ghana and one from Jamaica, representing a window into the culture, with ideas carefully threaded together. Where these leaves are located is a good place to begin.

We start our African story in Ghana. Named for the medieval Ghana Empire, it is a country of nearly 239,000 square kilometers positioned in the West African subregion. It is washed on the southern coast by the Gulf of Guinea; on the north it is bordered by Burkina Faso, and on the east and west by Togo and Ivory Coast, respectively. The Ghanaian populace, more than 23 million strong, speaks nearly seventy-nine different ethnic languages, and each ethnic group has numerous sets of rituals. A former British colony, Ghana attained independence under Dr. Kwame Nkrumah in 1957 (Cooper 2002, 81). Under colonialism, Ghana was called the Gold Coast because of its rich mineral resources (Webster 1980, 284). Cape Coast Castle, Elmina Castle, and the Christiansburg Castle in Osu were hubs of slave transactions involving various European nations. Turning now to the Caribbean, Jamaica is an island country of almost 11,000 square kilometers representing about 5 percent of the land mass in the Caribbean Sea. Like Ghana, Jamaica is a former British colony, gaining its independence in 1962. With about 2.7 million people, Jamaica has three counties comprising fourteen parishes; its people are largely of African descent, but in its multiethnic mix, small numbers are of East Indian, European, Chinese, or Lebanese origin, and about 7 percent are multiracial. The creole element of Jamaican language, called patois in Jamaica, is an indication of the existence of West and Central African influences that survived through traditional oral practice.

The African people and their ethnic languages predate the imperial geopolitical boundaries of contemporary Africa. The Maroons of Jamaica, among others, are important in the discourse on Kumina (see also Cheryl Ryman's chapter on "the closeness of the Maroon-Kumina relationship"), in a consideration of culture as a negotiation of African ancestry. Prior scholarship has fostered perspectives on Kumina's African history. Lewin (2000, 164) offers that "Links had been made when the Kumina people arrived from Central Africa as post-slavery indentured labourers during troubled times in St. Thomas [Jamaica]." The Congo basin shared trade and fishing links with the people of Cameroon, Nigeria, Benin, Togo, and Ghana. As an aside, it is worth noting that the "indentured labourers" and the free existed on the same island in "different" capacities. Technically, the commodification of "indentured" people is a camouflage of slavery in the form of "replacements."

## Kumina: Roots and Influences

According to the Tabanka Crew performers' Web site, Kumina is "a cultural form indigenous to Jamaica." Many scholars suggest that it originated in the Congo from roots and influences including the "dancing of the Bantu-speaking peoples of the Congo" (Tabanka Crew). In this forum we shall see that music, dance, ritual, and the embodiment of history through Kumina are strong phenomena that span many generations, roots, and influences across the African continent and the diaspora, including West African influences and traces among the Yoruba, Akan, Ewe, and Ga-Adangme (my personal roots). Rituals can be for goodness and blessings, cleansing or purifying, agriculture, war, nature, celebrations of events, or other things, depending on the local ethnicity. There are Kumina influences that span a variety of rituals connecting the soul, mind, and body.

## Historical Connections between Ghana and Jamaica: Slavery and Colonization

In an attempt to explore Kumina, the need arises to focus on the geographic mappings and political underpinnings of yesterday. Africa, the source of humanity, has for years been filled with people who mingle and trade in many forms, with Timbuktu and Djenne only two of the many learning centers (Jegede 2000, 261; Nwauwa 2000, 304). The advent of slavery and colonization changed the location of millions of Africans over a period of about four hundred years. This process included transplanting of human "commodities or properties" to the Caribbean. This commodification speaks to all nations involved in slavery, but in the Jamaican context specifically to the British transatlantic slave trade. In these events, we need to understand the history of Ghana and Jamaica that shaped their performing arts. As John Collins (1992, 190) says, "The musical similarities or analogues between Africa and the black Americas stem largely from the fact that millions of African slaves were taken to the New World during the black diaspora, taking their culture and music with them. And this has remained, either in transmuted form or—particularly in South America and the Caribbean—more or less intact."

Through their shared roots, Ghanaians and Jamaicans, or West Africans and Caribbean people for that matter, show many commonalities. I have met many Jamaicans on different continents who resemble an acquaintance or relative in Ghana to a degree that is striking. This phenomenon resonates with other Ghanaians when they mistakenly greet visiting Jamaicans in the native Twi or Ga languages, and then have to switch to English. Beyond a shared history of colonization by Britain, the histories of the two countries go further, through Liberia and Sierra Leone as well as most of the coastal lands of West and Central Africa. The people taken from Africa to Jamaica played the major role among the mixed workers used on the island for British gain, and many were from what is now Ghana. In Jamaica enslaved people and Maroons from Ghana, including the Ga-Adangme, Ewe, and Akans, were known as Coromantees (Lewin 2000, 155). While I am not here to talk about "reparations," I share the belief that civilized nations or people that enslave(d) human beings should be held accountable for their deeds in the twenty-first century, to appease the souls of the past, refresh the present, and smile from the heart of humanity (see Osabu-Kle 2000, 334 for more on this subject).

As a Jamaican will put it, to "over-stand" the network of performance derived from the African traditions brings us to the lecture hall of the unholy business of slavery and its geographical and political underpinnings. "The majority of Maroons [in Jamaica] originally came from West Africa" (Harris 1994, 36). The Bight of Biafra, Congo, and Angola saw about 40 percent of humans transplanted to Jamaica between 1792 and 1807 (Whylie and Warner-Lewis 1994, 139). The transplanted groups resisted their new situation, and "the unequivocal repudiation by the Maroons [of enslavement] created an atmosphere charged with life-giving oxygen for the lungs of sanity" (Harris 1994, 36).

Whylie and Warner-Lewis (1994, 139) cite Higman in noting that "half of the Jamaican . . . slaves were drawn from . . . among the Akan and Ga-Adangme peoples of the coastal strip of present-day Ghana." They interacted with many of the Jamaican peoples inhabiting the island, as is evidenced by shared common values and Jamaican names of Ghanaian origin such as Kofi, Ama, Afua, and Ananse (Agorsah 1994, 31). They also shared similar versions of songs, dances, drumming, and games. The Ghanaian word Gome sounds like Jamaican Goomeh/Gumbeh in pronunciation. Jama performance refers to people jubilating or resisting with songs and sometimes drumming in Ga communities (as Jamaicans do, too), reminiscent of Ghana's fight for independence, as narrated to me by Otu Lincoln, the originator of Kpanlogo dance (Akrong, 2003, 22).

## Kumina and Gome Connections

Just as we cannot talk about the sea without discussing its salt, to understand Kumina is to understand human survival and resistance during times of oppression. Hall-Alleyne (1982, 3–40) notes the importance of understanding the Maroons' history and culture as a path to appreciation of the music (see also Lewin 2000, 152). Other pieces of the puzzle are the complex links between Gome, Ghana, Congo, and Jamaica that reflect, among other things, Maroon performance traces. In "Strictly African Dancing—Biographies" from the BBC Press Office Web site for June, 20, 2005, the bio of Tessa Sanderson notes, "An exciting celebration dance, the Gome is a social dance performed at funerals, wedding ceremonies and festivals. It has been danced in Ghana from the 18th century, brought in by the Congolese fisher folk—the dance first being performed for the fisherman on their return." Some Ghanaians also went to other places in Africa to work, including the Congo region, encountering other cultures and other migrants. Connecting further, the African Rithyms performing group writes that

> Gome is social dance music associated with the Ga people of Ghana. In the 1940s, Ga men worked in Cameroons and Fernando Po as migrant laborers. They learned carpentry skills which are evident in the box-like shape of the Gome drum. When they returned to Ghana, they brought Gome with them. Recent research has traced the roots of this music to earlier migrant laborers from Sierra Leone who brought this music to Cameroons and to other parts of Africa. According to this research, Gome can be traced back even further to the Maroons of Jamaica who immigrated to Sierra Leone in 1800. Gome is truly a trans-Atlantic music that is 200 or more years old. ("Gome," African Rithyms Web site).

Figure 10.1. Gome drum, two views: in front of a mirror, enabling an inside view; the four-legged Gome with open frame. By Isaac Akrong; used by permission.

John Collins (1992, 188) elaborates on such links: "The black music of the New World has and is playing a part in the African pursuit of autonomy and identity, and this influence can be traced as far back as the introduction of Jamaican gumbey or gombe music to West Africa in the 1830s."

That given, tradition is fluid, and I believe, from a lifetime of cultural practice, that African traditional music, dance, songs, chants, sweats, and gatherings are only the "icing on the cake" of that tradition. The various layers in the "cake" are where history is embedded. Exposure to spiritual music and dance is the first layer. Decoding the drum language, special chants, social functions, and spiritual energies invoked is a special skill of the initiated interlocutor. Growing up in Ghana, I heard many stories about hunters and herbalists who were able to pick fresh leaves from dry, barren trees. This story, among others, confirms the "visioned" community practitioners who heal in many ways. In the same way, in Jamaica, they are able to transmit these energies through the Kumina dance, music, rituals, and ceremonies.

## Traditional and Choreographic Commonalities

To understand the choreography beyond the aesthetic, one must transcend the surface and go to the core of the beliefs embodied by the performers. These spiritual strengths take them through the journey of the music and dance of Kumina and its roots, and we tend to see commonalities in many traditional dances in Africa. Let us look at Gahu dance as an example. This

Ewe dance has a circle that moves a single file of dancers in anticlockwise motion (the same as in specific Gome dances), which is an element shared by Kumina. As Lewin (2000, 27) points out, "Kumina prayer, sung in call and response style and accompanied by drums and percussion, signals the official start of the ceremony. The leader 'salos' to the drums with a bow or curtsy and slow waving of the hand, then leads the bands round the table in an anticlockwise direction." Vocal imitation and communication are highlighted through call and response, and are embedded in African performing arts. The oral transmission of practices hinges on the core beliefs of their existence and stays with the practitioners forever.

Welle shaa, the rhythmic pulsating of the waist that coordinates the subtle muscles of the pelvis and buttocks, can be seen in Gome dance. Torso movements in Agbadza, pelvic rotation in Bamaya, whirling possession in Akom, Tigari, Kple, and Kanja, and the steps of the Wulomo (the chief priest of the Ga) at the Kpatsonshi ceremony during the Homowo festival—all these Ghanaian performance practices have similarities with Kumina. The Ga have a saying: "He fee heni akpe wie ye, ejoo," implying that the potency of the spice *wie* is the same wherever and whenever you chew it. In the same way we can trace the features of Kumina, which are characteristic of many people from one source, Africa, sharing Kumina over space and time.

Gome has embodied dance and drama elements that share story lines about community experiences, politics, religion, comedy, economics, healing, and education. Ga fisher folk, on their coastal expeditions to neighboring countries, shared integrated nuances of Gome, Oge, Kpanlogo, Twensi, and other performances in their structural forms and presentation, all of which are linked deeply with Kumina. In spirit, Blekete of the Ewe, Orisha of the Yoruba, Kple of the Ga, Tigari of the Dagbon, Akom of the Akan, and the Bantu lineage of the Congo and surrounding families all share deep ties with Kumina. I have chosen Gome in this context, for it imitates or includes some of these practices, sacred or not.

I grew up in Ghana on the beach of La and enjoyed folk music and dance forms, both recreational and ritual. As a cultural insider, one enjoys a tradition to some extent, one lives with the tradition, and there are days when one has to step back and look. Where are we going from here? Who influenced what, and when? For instance, the Gome dance and music I am describing are also highly connected to Ga dance forms such as Kolomashie, Oge, and Kple. The broad Gome sound-range pattern resonates quite fre-

Figure 10.2 Isaac Akrong playing the Gome drum, front and diagonal views. By Leonard Williams. Used by permission of Isaac Akrong.

quently within the Jamaican Kumina practice. Though the Kumina drum is cylindrical, the posture of the drummer and that of the Gome drummer, the tuning of the drum, and the angle of the heel of the foot against the drum of the master drummer in Kumina are more or less the same as in Gome. Another interesting relation is the detailed short steps in Kumina, similar to the Gome steps for men and women. Kple and Akom share the step pattern of Kumina as well as unpredictable trance movements that journey the inner self of the dancer or drummer when the higher energies descend on individual performers.

John Blacking (1973, 89) maintains that "Music is a synthesis of cognitive processes which are present in culture and in the human body." I perform African music frequently through recreation, rituals, education, and abstract experiments. I am interested in meaning creation and the cross-examination of the meanings embedded in coded messages handed down by ancestral practices of African music and dance. Blacking notes (1973, 89) that its form and effects "are generated by the social experiences of human bodies in different cultural environments. Because music is humanly organized sound, it expresses aspects of the experience of individuals in society."

Though these expressions within various societies differ in spirituality and function, a common denominator controls the organized sound, the ritual, and the outcome.

## Spi-ritual-ity

Oxygen, wind, hurricane—they all share common elemental traces as "air" in a variety of modes. So, too, does an African ritual share many forms of energies or "Gods, Aklama, Dzo" (Gavua 2000, 90) in different embodiments. Each possession is unique, even if it is the same person on separate occasions. It cannot be easily described as it is a ritual dance that delves deeply into spirituality; rather, we should try to appreciate it from an insider's perspective in order to gradually assimilate its essence, potency, and social function. Many modes of Kumina practice, including (but not limited to) recreational, educational, and ritual forms, can be found within existing structures and parishes in Jamaica. Turning to the functions of drums, Joseph Graessle Moore (1954, 129) notes that "drums [take] up a special beat invoking the principal gods and ancestors of Cumina."

This sounds familiar, as drumming and dancing are the foundational codes and mnemonics upon which specific African arts are based. Pelvic movements, as smooth as boneless hips (as in Kumina), make statements beyond the notion of "exotic" to the spirituality and well-being of the practitioners. Dances emphasize lineages, kinships, polarities in energies that control the ancestors' abodes, the living, the existing, and the future generations. African music inspires deep connections, transcending human DNA to the very iota of energy—with deities as the closest local links. To understand deeply embedded spi-ritual-lity in African music and dance is to transcend the current surface of the research. If we take the trance to be the "icing on the cake," to return to an earlier metaphor, then we need to extend our understanding beyond the icing into the actual cake. The cake contains elements that cannot be seen from the outside, such as nuts and berries, which represent lineages of the fore-ancestors, clans, inter- and intra-god links, and polarities such as positive and negative energetic fields.

"Cumina theology resembles in structure, religious aspects of West African and Congo culture" (Moore 1954, 180). Such realms are part of African metaphysics. The metaphysical is a great conduit for feeling Kumina and many other African ritual energies. These energies transmit through coded lineages that share a common source, a source full of healing, protection, and preservation. Ryan Masters (2008, 9), a freelance journalist who attended a Toronto performance of the African Dance Ensemble (ADE), noted that "Isaac Akrong seemed to have fallen into trance. A swift transformation." This transformation in mode occurred during a four-hour African performance. Masters' observation brings to light the same energies that have kept African performance practice alive for generations. As he concluded, after the show, "Akrong had transformed once again. Now he was back to his everyday normal self—quiet and perhaps even shy but also satisfied and serene" (Masters 2008, 9). I call this transformation process a conversation with the core-root that embodies the person at a specific feeling-in-time: the feel of the soul.

Twenty-first-century Western society is at risk of transforming many cultural practices, including African music and dance, to obscure some of the traces I am examining. In the world of tradition, Africans have strong links with Kumina. In the solid flow of African tradition, resemblances between music and dance forms are not uncommon. It is possible to trace paths within the elemental structures of an ethnicity that carries a tradition. With that given, insiders and outsiders may debate forever, but a knowledgeable insider knows exactly what s/he is talking about. To understand Kumina, one must really feel the rhythm, the energy, dust, sweat, and songs. Upon an inner call of the gods, one may visit the supernatural if one is capable of communicating at that level, translate at the ordinary level, transmit through codes, command each and every muscle to speak in the dance, and let the ululation rituals flow from the inner blood to the joy and "refreshness" of the human existence: life.

## Views of the Other—Which Other?

All persons are "others" sometimes. Who poses the research questions, and to whom? How does such questioning salute the traditions in which studies are conducted? Timothy Rice (1997, 105), in his treatment of ethnomusicological field methods, states that "the field emerges as the place where data are collected to test theories." These theories are often from Western constructs and may lack what appears to cultural insiders a certain "common sense" factor. Western theories may begin to be tested by puzzles in the African field experience. Rice acknowledges that the field "is a bounded place filled with insiders who share views about [their] music, [and] musical practices" (Rice 1997, 105). Which brings us to rightly interpreting field data according to insiders' perspectives, a key to "keeping it real." Postcolonial discourses or doctrines flourish under the camouflage of "free speech," which is not free for all. "Free speech" is avoided in traditional African practice. It breaks the kinship codes of the village, a taboo.

Kumina, in a broader sense, shares complex African nuances. Returning to Kumina in contemporary performance, people of the St. Thomas area of Jamaica, as well as other communities, have shared a similar generational understanding or application of educational and historical versions of Kumina. Kesi Asher, a reporter with the *Jamaica Gleaner*, notes in "Africa live in kumina" (Sunday, October 9, 2005) that "Kumina ceremonies are usually associated with wakes, entombments or memorial services, parties, weddings, functions, the healing of sick people, births and thanksgiving, among others." There are male and female leaders, kings and queens, with long training in spiritual and performance practices.

Bernice Henry, queen of the long-established Port Morant National and International Kumina Dancers who bring Kumina to schools and teach it at the Edna Manley College of the Visual and Performing Arts, "danced to the beat of the drums, moving only her waist in an amazing fashion," according to Asher. She performed "with a tin candle perfectly balanced on her head." But Asher notes, "To Bernice Henry, kumina is much more than just a dance, it is a religion." Kumina, in my view, is the tip of a larger iceberg of traditions, spanning physical and spiritual spaces in Africa and the Caribbean. The fluid nature of migration and trade and the interethnic syncretism of religions are evident in certain versions of these traditions, including Kumina.

### Feel the Vibrations of Africa

As I think about Kumina, subtle vibrations of rhythm run through my veins. I hear chants, the voices of performers, and see images that connect to deep rituals. African influences have shaped Kumina in the realm of people, work, life, lineage-kinship, and strong ties with similar polarities in the spiritual realm. Examining common links of Kumina practices with Ga, Ewe, Ashanti, and Dagomba traditions in Ghana is similar to tracing the roots and transformations within hip life music, a contemporary form similar to dancehall, hip hop, and other such genres and their roots that has surfaced in Ghana in the last ten to twelve years (driven by Reggie Rockstone). When we trace this deeply, it takes us to similar vocal connections in terms of call and response; however, in this case, synthesized music is used, just as hip hop has borrowed from sampled sounds, DJ record scratching, and the building of loops.

John Collins (2004, 57) underscores that "the African Beat revolves in time, it is quite reasonable to represent it figuratively by looping the previous linear notations into circles [ . . . ] the adowa, agbadza and gahu." Though I am not focusing on this contemporary art form here, I am bringing to light some of these commonalities, as they are quite fluid. The African traditional paradigms share a tone that seeks to tell our insiders' story from our innermost passionate point of view and not to sacrifice the criticism. We will still criticize our own art form in our own way, because a form like Kumina's core energy is a living practice wherever it is now, in both Africa and the diaspora.

## Increasing Awareness of Kumina and Gome

It would be useful if readers had the opportunity to immerse themselves in Kumina and Gome performances to understand the fluid commonalities that surface in these two repertoires. To unpack the entire ritual is to showcase the sacred—which does not sit well with the norms of the tradition; however, we can unpack and examine the salient traces, elements, and modes that relate these two practices. Training our ears and gearing our minds to Kumina or Gome should transcend terms like "world music" or "world dance." The African traditionalist tells and reflects on the ways of his or her people through passages in life. Sounds of a tradition in contemporary media such as Internet, television, CD, or radio may offer aesthetic exposure, but the most realistic experience of a people and culture comes through sitting in on African traditional practices in village settings.

## Conclusion: Pack the Drums

Yes, in the interim let us pack the Kumina and Gome drums. Tomorrow we shall converge at the community corner to share some of the lasting stories narrated through the unique lens of our twenty-first century. The positioning of Ghana and Jamaica in the events of British colonization established the basis by which syncretic modes shaped the cultural practices of a people over time and space. This initiative is to open up another perspective in the discussions of human experience that have shaped art, religion, kinship, and history. Jamaica and Ghana have been interesting symbols in the history of Africans in the Caribbean, or the diaspora. Considering where and what we are examining, and understanding the very foundations of who came from where through events that cannot be forgotten, we seek to tell our story for posterity. This keeps African culture and tradition with integrity, a road map for traditional kinship (Akrong, n.d.). It takes a community (Africa) to raise a child (Kumina), as narrated through a perspective here. It is good to have Kumina alive: traditional (African) archives begin with the oral tradition.

# HAITI

# 11

# Chimin Kwaze

## Crossing Paths, or Haitian Dancemaking in Port-au-Prince

CELIA WEISS BAMBARA

In 1999, Djenane St. Juste, the principal dancer and a choreographer for JAKA (Jen Artis Kanga Ayisen), appeared as the Vodou lwa or spirit Simbi Dlo wearing a white flowing skirt, cropped white shirt, and flowing gold head covering. She projected the waterlike qualities of Simbi Dlo by gliding toward the audience while keeping her gaze serene as her head covering fluttered in the wind. This improvisational dance theater introduction to a piece of Kongo choreography directed by Florencia Pierre was performed on an outdoor stage on Champs-Mars in downtown Port-au-Prince for a celebration of the International Day of the Woman. Drawing upon Vodou-based ideologies and the politics of the Haitian roots movement, JAKA's piece addresses women's sexuality and spirituality while encouraging participation in the revision of indigenist representations of Haitianness.

From the 1930s to the 1950s the ideological/artistic movement indigenism catalyzed the development of Haitian dance and established a notion of tradition. Over the years choreographers have revised aspects of indigenism. Current dancemakers are in constant dialogue with these notions at play in the set of Kreyol cultural practices that stemmed from the movement, staging aspects of Vodou-based dance that remake ideas of tradition.

In 1928 Jean Price-Mars published the indigenist tract *Ainsi parla l'oncle* (So spoke the uncle) that introduced the concept of folklore to Haiti. Indigenism encouraged the separation of Haitian practices of music, dance, and song from Vodou ceremony and their presentation on stage to produce a universal national culture. Indigenism was envisioned as a way to valorize Haitian cultural practices and history and to express a conception of

Figure 11.1. Djenane St. Juste appearing as Simbi Dlo, Port-au-Prince, 1999. By
Celia Weiss Bambara; used by permission.

Haitian modernity that countered American notions of race and Vodou as
well as Haitian class-based stigmatizations of the religion. The U.S. occupation (1915–1934) of Haiti brought with it an American binary, black-white,
conception of race. U.S. imperialism in Haiti was premised upon a "ready
made ideology" that fused notions of race with Vodou (Hurbon 1995). Haitians, who maintain a much more fluid system of concepts of race influenced by notions of class and practices such as religion, music, and dance,
were greatly affronted by American imperialism and its conceptions of race
(Bellegarde-Smith 1990; Trouillot 1994; McAlister 2002). Indigenism con-
figured a symbolic national body meant to express Haitian cultural practices
and an idea of race as a historical set of changing signifiers.

From the 1940s through the 1950s, Haitian dance became of interest to the Haitian government, the elite, intellectuals, and tourists. Notably, the Institute of Ethnology in Port-au-Prince promoted and documented Haitian dances under the tutelage of Jean Price-Mars. Following the folklorizing impetus of Price-Mars, Michel Lamartinière Honorat, a student at the Institute, published *Les Danses Folkloriques Haïtiennes* (1955), describing and codifying Haitian dances and their reproduction for the public. Anthropologist Kate Ramsey articulates that the systemization of Haitian dance occurred during the confluence of government-sponsored tourism initiatives and in the wake of the U.S. Marine occupation (Ramsey 1997, 357–358). As a result of the Haitian government's focus on expanding external interest in Haiti, dance became important to tourist presentations, in promoting the economy, and as a vehicle for expressing Haitian history. However, the indigenist idea of tradition, promoted by Price-Mars and furthered by Honorat, sought to arrange a notion of tradition as folklore in Haitian dance as well as control its reproduction. Honorat's stipulations included controlled improvisation, stylization, fusion, staging, and citation of Haitian dances, which he organized into categories of sacred and profane.

Indigenism, in general, separated Vodou practices from the spirits and promoted the copying of Vodou practice for the stage. As part of the separation of Vodou spirituality and folklore, Haitian dances were included in a new category of tradition, later promoted by the state. This category of tradition can be differentiated from Vodou community and family traditions in that it assumes the citation and copying of Vodou practices for implementation outside of ceremony. These two notions of tradition, Vodou and folklore, overlap in terms of spirituality and community, and in practice.

Since the 1940s, choreographers have pushed the barriers between tradition and contemporaneity in Haitian dance. In 1949, Jean-Léon Destiné introduced structured improvisation, staging, and theatricalization to Haitian dance as choreographer for the Troupe Folklorique Nationale, the national company formed that year. From the 1950s, when she was invited to Haiti (Wilcken 2002, 116), through the 1980s, Lavinia Williams introduced ballet technique, modern dance, choreography, and fusion to the national company and later to the National Arts School, ENARTS.

Jean-Claude Duvalier, the son of dictator François Duvalier, succeeded his father as the president of Haiti in 1971 at the age of nineteen. In 1982, Jean-Claude closed the national company and opened ENARTS (Interview with

Edwidge Duverger, August 18, 2005). The goal of the four-year, university level, dance conservatory at ENARTS was to produce professional dancers, choreographers, and teachers well versed in Haitian dance, contemporary dance, improvisation, and dance history. In addition, Jean-Claude Duvalier and his wife at that time, Michèle Bennett Duvalier, hoped to create a notion of Haitian contemporary identity through the arts (Interview with Edwidge Duverger, August 18, 2005). At ENARTS, Williams collaboratively constructed the curriculum and many dance pieces with Haitian choreographer and dancer Edwidge Duverger that were performed for state-sponsored events.

Currently, tangled concepts of tradition and contemporaneity exist in Haitian dance. This essay will focus on exploring the interwoven threads of tradition and contemporaneity between 1999 and 2003 in Port-au-Prince, considering the viewpoints of Viviane Gauthier, Florencia Pierre, and Nicole Lumarque, Haitian female choreographers from different generations. I gathered this material during this period through the process of dance study, collaboration, performance, and conversations with elders.

## Dancing on the Porch: *Lakay* Viviane, Talking Tradition

Viviane Gauthier has maintained one of the longest-standing dance schools in Port-au-Prince and has taught generations of dancers and choreographers. She created a studio, company, and training system that promoted an idea of tradition linked to the Haitian national identity espoused by indigenism. At thirty years of age, Gauthier viewed a dance presentation at the historic Théâtre de Verdure, built during the Estimé presidency (1946–1950) and the home of the national folkloric company, originally formed by Destiné. Gauthier, inspired by what she saw, set about learning Haitian dance and ballet. Since the 1940s, Haitian dance had merited critical acclaim as a nationalist art form, and by the 1950s, the government and individuals sought to systematize it. Gauthier entered an artistic milieu influenced by a nationalist notion of dance.

She studied with Haitian dance teachers André Germain, André Narcisse, and Louines Louinis, who maintained the national folkloric company after Destiné's departure in 1950. Notably, André Narcisse was the director of Troupe Macaya and had spent time in the United States on a government scholarship, studying with Syvilla Forte, a former dancer with Katherine

Dunham and teacher at her school (Interview with Jean-Leon Destiné, August 18, 2007). Gauthier also received lessons on the history and codification of dances from Michel Lamartinière Honorat. Of her studies with Honorat she says, "He knew how to give classes. Because, at that time, he was not a dance professor. But, he gave classes on the history of Haiti. Yes, he researched who dances which dances, which *neg* (black) knew how to dance them," (interview with Viviane Gauthier, July 17, 2003). In addition to these studies, she studied ballet with African American dancer Lavinia Williams. Gauthier, encouraged by Lavinia Williams, started a dance school. She opened her dance studio in 1963, and from this she drew her company in 1968. Viviane's dance school, École de Danse Viviane Gauthier, is based in her lakay (home) on Rue M near the Sacre Coeur in Port-au-Prince.

Gauthier's school promotes a notion of tradition, training her dance company and many members of the community to express the idea of national merit in performance. Her take on tradition is, arguably, quite similar to the government-sanctioned concept of tradition in Honorat's 1955 treatise. Specifically, Gauthier teaches the steps for Haitian dances that express Honorat's codifications of the dances. Gauthier articulates her notion of a base of Haitian tradition in its dances by comparing them with ballet and modern dance. In reply to a question about the dances to be presented at the then upcoming bicentennial, she states, "Haitians think if they are going to arrange le folklore they need to modernize it. Non, (she waves her finger). Before modernizing it, they need to know the base. All the dancers, they have just about a classical dance base. Non." (Interview with Viviane Gauthier, July 17, 2003).

Gauthier indicates limits to her ideas of acceptable fusions and alterations of Haitian steps and staging. She does not approve of the obvious mixing of ballet and modern with Haitian steps, but insists that all her dances be firmly rooted in the intention of the specific rite from which they are taken. In addition, Gauthier promotes folklore based on choreographic structures such as staged ceremonies or the presentation of a single dance. One good example of Gauthier's perspective on tradition in staging is her thoughts on Yanvalou Doba, danced for the lwa Damballa in the Rada rite. She states, "When I am going to make Yanvalou, we are going to dance Yanvalou Doba; you can't make a Yanvalou Doba and lift your leg. It is not possible." Yanvalou Doba is danced with extremely bent knees that organize the back almost parallel to the ground. For Viviane, the shape and perhaps intention of Yanvalou Doba is altered when movements from contemporary or ballet dance are fused with it.

Viviane does, however, revise aspects of indigenist ideas of controlled folklore in teaching *kultur physik* and adding thematic material to her choreographies. Kultur physik is a blend of modern, contemporary, ballet, and floor exercises adapted by various teachers to train the body to perform Haitian dance. Lavinia Williams is the originator of this technique, and current choreographers adapt aspects of kultur physik to their particular teaching style. This Haitian technique shapes the body, giving it greater flexibility, and allows movements to be clearer, bigger, and sometimes more stylized. In terms of thematic material, Viviane organizes her staged Haitian dance works around themes and stories like Bois Caiman, a historic Vodou ceremony in 1791 signifying resistance during slavery. These aspects of dancerly training and composition at Viviane's school do not negate her definite opinions of the ways in which Haitian dance should be taught and performed in accordance with indigenist principles. Kultur physik, however, revises the representation and staging of Haitian dance, and additional thematic material promotes notions of Haitian history and spirituality. Gauthier's complex concept of purity in Haitian dance echoes Honorat's systematizations while accepting stylizations of movement created by kultur physik.

## Marketing the Mouvement Rasin: Florencia Pierre and JAKA

As a student of Viviane Gauthier and a dancer for the national company, Florencia Pierre garnered training in indigenist ideas of tradition, kultur physik, and folkloric choreographic structures. Pierre, however, has revised this concept of tradition through fusion of movement and ideas of rootedness drawn from the Haitian *mouvement rasin* (roots movement).

Pierre was born to a lower-class family in Gonaïves and moved to Port-au-Prince at sixteen to study dance with Viviane Gauthier. She received her early dance training with Gauthier between 1972 and 1980. She continued her dance career, performing with the national company from 1980 through 1982, and with Viviane Gauthier between 1983 and 1987. In theater, she performed with Evans Paul's group, Konbit Pitit Kay, and in presentations directed by Jean-Pierre Berney and Hervé Denis. She also performed with the musical, dance, and theater groups Foula, Pyepoudre Cultural Center, The Voice of Harmony Group, and The Potomitan Troupe. She has toured with these various companies and with her own troupe, JAKA, in Haiti, Montreal, Louisiana, Paris, Seville, Barbados, Colombia, the Dominican Republic, and Guadeloupe. She has also appeared in films directed by Rassoul Labuchin and Jean Rouch. In 1986 she started her own dance company, Troupe JAKA (Jen Artis Kanga Ayisen), based on the peasant cooperative *konbit* model for labor. I began study with Florencia Pierre in 1997 and later performed and collaborated with JAKA between 1999 and 2003.

JAKA's class/caste composition is the result of Florencia's organizing the company around the concept of a konbit, thus granting its members access to Haitian dance training, food, and aid. The type of dance members practice and choreograph relates to their lived realities in Haiti's race/class system as predominantly lower and middle class, Vodou practicing and Catholic, darker-skinned Haitians. Florencia locates Haitian dance in the context of the Haitian mouvement rasin. For Florencia, rootedness draws upon a conception of tradition in Haitian dance that comes from Vodou ceremony. She bases her movements, rhythms, and stories in Vodou and community life in ways that make public her alliances with Vodou communities.

Florencia's choreographies will often cull and incorporate steps and stories directly from her religious community and daily life that may not exist in certain repertoires. She will draw upon gestures she sees in the street or in events in her life. Some of her choreographic work expands upon family relationships, Haitian life histories, specific Vodou ceremonies such as a *kanzo* (initiation ceremony), or relationships between the spirits. In addition, she makes fusional movement by melding contemporary steps with Vodou steps and inserting contemporary steps into her choreographies. For example, Florencia may add a Horton tilt, an improvised section, or adapt a yoga asana in a piece. These changes always adhere to the base or content of a specific rite. Her choreography stays grounded in traditional staging practices and choreographic structures.

While she has garnered success in many arenas, consistently obtaining rehearsal space remains difficult because of the many race, class, and religious stigmas that associate Haitian dance and Vodou. In addition, it has been difficult for her to have consistent access to contemporary dance in Port-au-Prince. In 1999, Florencia was rehearsing in friends' homes, in schoolyards, and in driveways. In 2001, she procured a small studio where she based her dance school and company. By 2003, she had lost her studio and was rehearsing on the concrete floor of a local grade school. In

Figure 11.2. Djenane St. Juste, Emmanuel Louis, and Celia Weiss Bambara in *Chimin Kwaze*, JAKA, Port-au-Prince, 2003. Still from a video by Joey Chau Huynh. Used by permission of Celia Weiss Bambara.

order to build her company and create new work, Florencia, her daughter Djenane St. Juste, and I worked on a collaborative, evening-long project, *Chimin Kwaze* (Crossing Paths), during the summer of 2003. Djenane St. Juste began dancing with her mother as a child and has danced for other touring companies in Haiti, including BFH and ARTCHO. This collaborative project engaged dancers from JAKA, BFH, Ayiti la, and Tamboula, as well as the mentorship of Nicole Lumarque and Emerante de Pradines. The dancers and choreographers from each company gave classes in their style of dance throughout the project as well as giving feedback, commentary, suggestions, and movement to each of the pieces.

The *Chimin Kwaze* project was meant to produce new fusions of Haitian dance with contemporary and other diasporic forms while building upon Florencia's idea of rootedness in Vodou. In the span of three months, we produced five pieces based on the rhythms Yanvalou, Yanvalou Mascawon, Nago, and Mahi. The work produced ran the gamut of ways of making contemporary Haitian dances, including fusion, re-staging of Vodou rites, new choreographic structures, and improvisation.

In our project-formulating discussions, Florencia, Djenane, and I decided that the pieces in the show would reflect the process of transformation, contact, travel, displacement, love, violence, and struggle in Haitian life. Florencia said during one such discussion, "I saw something today that gave me an idea for a piece. I saw a painting of a tree that seemed to move and grow. The first piece will be a dedication to Erzili showing trees that develop life." Djenane's response to this was that we begin the piece as statues in the audience that come to life and move onto the stage.

Florencia decided that in this way the show would open with improvisation illustrating the transformation of tradition that occurred in the process of making the show. Three dancers in the audience would move slowly onto the stage employing contemporary structured improvisation. Djenane St. Juste, Emmanuel Louis, and I were given a set of directions or structures with which we created movement that bridged and combined contemporary dance, Haitian physical theater, movement from ceremony, and postmodern styles of everyday gesture. As we were clothed in garments for the spirits by Florencia Pierre, Joseph Velcimé, and Pierre Richard, we began an improvised possession sequence that led into a movement theater–based exploration of the Haitian spirits Erzili Danto, Erzili Freda, and Agwe. Expressions of tradition and contemporaneity came about in the actual process

Figure 11.3. Dancers in Florencia Pierre and Djenane St. Juste's company JAKA's *Chimin Kwaze*, Port-au-Prince, 2003. Still from a video by Joey Chau Huynh. Used by permission of Celia Weiss Bambara.

of putting together all the choreographic, advisory, and dancerly voices. In a greater sense, *Chimin Kwaze* bridged differences of race, class, religion, and nationality in Haitian dancemaking in Port-au-Prince while experimenting with different choreographic, improvisational, and collaborative modes.

### In the Break: Nicole Lumarque's Cassé, Fusion, and Improvisation.

Nicole Lumarque directs Ballet Folklorique d'Haiti (BFH), one of the larger contemporary Haitian touring companies in Port-au-Prince. Lumarque's travels and access to contemporary, ballet, choreography, and yoga training have allowed her to develop innovations in Haitian dance. These changes include a practice of Haitian improvisation, a fusional dance technique, and a vision of using the *cassé* (break) to express contemporary identity. Lumarque studied Haitian dance with Viviane Gauthier and Florencia Pierre, among others. She trained as well at ENARTS and later became a student of yoga. In addition, Lumarque performed her own research on Haitian ceremonial dance, studying with elders and Vodou community members in *hounfor* (Vodou temples) throughout the country. BFH has performed nationally in Haiti and internationally. Lumarque, in her travels, has taught or collaborated with artists in locales including Senegal, Benin, Cuba, Asia, and Europe. Her company is based in a studio built into her home in Port-au-Prince.

Nicole Lumarque embraces notions of change in Haitian dance, engaging in practices of fusion and contemporary improvisation. Of her practice she states, "There is a difference between a fusion, a modernized Haitian rite, a technique, and a style. I have created my own technique that is a fusion of Haitian dance, modern, and yoga. . . . I based my choreography on Haitian rhythms" (Interview with Nicole Lumarque, July 20, 2003). Lumarque creates a distinction between her fusional technique and her choreography. She bases her choreography on the content of specific rites, while employing fusional movement that remains within the character of the ritual. She articulates, "If I am working with Yanvalou Mascawon, I do not place a step from another dance in it. But, I will create new steps that retain the character of the rite. The only time I will place a modern step in is during the break" (Interview with Nicole Lumarque, July 20, 2003). The break or cassé is a liminal space in which rhythmic change and spiritual possession occur in ceremony. Lumarque has adapted this rhythmic and spiritual change in

Haitian dance to be a space in which new movements, improvisation, and contemporary dance are employed.

Lumarque's concept of contemporary improvisation is also based on the content of Vodou tradition, yet permits artists the freedom to express their subjectivities. By engaging in this type of improvisation, dancers may create something that may not adhere to previously created movement, yet draws upon the thematic content and intention of a ritual. Ultimately, Lumarque's Haitian contemporary improvisation revises notions of tradition, drawing upon Haitian dance to create movement that expresses new Haitian identities. Lumarque's fusional works and contemporary improvisation rewrite Honorat's codified notion of Haitian dance. Specifically, Lumarque's conception of improvisation engages subjective interpretations of Haitian themes and movement premised on life experience.

### Concluding Notes: Crossing Paths

Haitian dancemaking in Port-au-Prince engages practices of improvisation, fusion, stylization, and contemporary dance. In the midst of changing concepts of tradition and contemporaneity, choreographers revise indigenist ideas of dance by creating works that express their subjectivities. In Haiti, dance practitioners Florencia Pierre and Nicole Lumarque create revolutionary dance works. Pierre revisits and revises indigenist notions of tradition by combining dance with personal history and roots movement ideologies, thus resituating dance in a diverse community. Lumarque bases her dances on specific Haitian rituals and has created a fusional technique, use of the break, and practice of Haitian contemporary improvisation that revise notions of tradition and race in Haitian dance. Lumarque's fusional technique allows for the shaping of dancerly bodies able to perform her fusional work, her conception of improvisation permits dancers to create movements expressing their subjective voices, and her use of the break facilitates a choreographic space in which she can express contemporary and fusional movements amid steps drawn from ceremony. Arguably, Lumarque and Pierre create change in different ways, yet both artists revise indigenist conceptions of tradition that limited the expression of subjectivity through controls on improvisation, stylization, and fusion in Vodou-based dances.

Other schools and choreographers that engage contemporary and fusional notions of Haitian dance include RMT, Jeanguy Saintus, Peniel Guerrier, Daniel Désir, Djenane St. Juste, Joseph Velcimé, and Emannuel Louis; however, each artist or company does this in the context of its vision and experience, choosing how to define Haitian identity through movement. Of note, Haitian dancer and choreographer Kettly Noël, who received her early training from Viviane Gauthier in Port-au-Prince, has currently established a contemporary African dance practice, school, festival, and company in Bamako, Mali. Nicole Lumarque has traveled to Senegal to participate in a forum organized by Germaine Acogny on contemporary practices in the black diaspora. In another vein, young Haitian choreographers engaging in fusions of ballet, contemporary dance, and Haitian dance are emerging in Canada and the United States.

Many transfigurations in Haitian dance have gone unnoticed as a result of Haiti's difficult political history and recent coup. The U.S.-sponsored coup d'état ending Jean-Bertrand Aristide's government in 2004 forced many artists and schools to close because of daily violence and insecurity; however, despite these incredible difficulties, BFH, RMT, JAKA, Viviane Gauthier's school, ENARTS, Tchaka, and many other companies are again producing work in Haiti. Other artists have immigrated to the United States since the coup; these include Peniel Guerrier, Cassandra Bissainthe, Edwidge Duverger, Joseph Velcimé, Jean-Marie Brignol, and Fan Fan. While Haiti is rebuilding, the artists in Haiti and abroad continue to create expressions of contemporary Haitian dance and identity in meaningful ways. Importantly, many artists recognize the tensions between the Vodou base of Haitian dance catalyzed by indigenist ideas of folklore, contemporary dancemaking practices, traditional notions of dance, and the small changes and fusions that have occurred since the 1940s. Somewhat divergent from experiments with Haitian tradition in dance, although not separate, is the strong presence of ballet schools in Haiti that stage European, American, and Haitian ballets, and Haiti's theater tradition, which seems to embrace more abstract movement and staging practices through physical renderings of events.

Fundamentally, these changes in Haitian dance motivate new considerations of what is termed traditional, folkloric, and contemporary in dance in the Caribbean and in the African diaspora. This glimpse into the viewpoints and methods of Viviane Gauthier, Florencia Pierre, and Nicole Lumarque indicates the ways in which artists have incorporated various aspects of contemporary dance, improvisation, other movement forms, and staging into their dancemaking practices, while basing their work on Haitian rites and themes. Arguably, Haitian dance needs to be seen in its own terms and not as a fixed set of practices that occur outside the scope of time or the international dance scene. Indeed, the fusions and changes made over the years need to be viewed in terms of artists' realities, visions, locations, and lineages. Certain Haitian dancemakers do embrace and base their work on Vodou practices and the original folkloric dances coined in the 1930s to the 1950s. Many artists, however, struggle to create new views of Haitian dance that are often not valorized because of notions of authenticity, race, and tradition. It might be useful to consider Haitian dance as a set of practices that express contemporary identities that in many instances change in pace with contemporary and modern-based creations in the United States, Europe, and Africa. Ultimately, the fusions in Haitian dance are changing, just as they are in the Vodou religion, in ways that need be recognized.

My sincerest thanks to Viviane Gauthier, Nicole Lumarque, and Florencia Pierre.

# DOMINICAN REPUBLIC

# 12

# Dance of the Dominican Misterios

MARTHA ELLEN DAVIS

Marisol is only ten years old, but already she has been chosen by higher powers as a *servidora* of Metresilí (the Dominican contraction of Maitresse Erzulie, as she is known in neighboring Haiti), the Vodú-spiritist *misterio* whose protector is Our Lady of Sorrows, Nuestra Señora de los Dolores. She must now serve her for life, attending to her altar, albeit in a modest corner of the family bedroom, and receiving and treating the public who appeal to Metresilí and other spiritual entities through her as a medium. They will come with physical and mental ailments and with problems in everyday life, imbalances in health and well-being that might be called dis-eases. Marisol will channel messages of healing procedures and herbal prescriptions from the wisdom of a higher intelligence beyond the humanly knowable. Whether or not it is her will, it is her destiny.

Her gift (*don*) was revealed to her through an illness that was untreatable, although her mother took her to "all the doctors." She got worse and worse. Finally, in desperation, her mother turned to Doña Iona, a highly recommended spiritual healer in Azua, who diagnosed Marisol's malady as a sign that she is a medium. So training will provide her healing. She thus became a disciple of this servidora. This is shamanism in modern life, not a relic of faraway times and places, but a universal human phenomenon, certainly a central part of the living tradition of Dominican culture, past and present.

Marisol must follow through with her training to manage her gift of mediumship until her "baptism" or initiation as a medium; otherwise, her uncontrolled powers of perception and reception can jeopardize her mental health and physical safety. If untrained, she can unexpectedly "receive" misterios and spirits of the dead, that is, be "possessed," even in the middle of the street, and be knocked to the ground. If untrained, she will not be able to distinguish between divine messages communicated through clairvoyance

Figure 12.1. The misterio Metresilí (Our Lady of Sorrows) being trained in public by San Miguel (St. Michael) possessing the patron of a vow-based saint's festival who is a medium. Azua. Photo by M. E. Davis; used by permission.

or revelation in dreams and her own imagination and normal perception. This will be confusing. She will not be able to block the entry of entities and messages when she wants peace of mind. And she will be susceptible to "intrusive spirits" or spirits of the dead—family members who do not want to leave their loved ones, strangers who wander the earth because they have not been properly dispatched to their final resting place, or *enviaciones*, spirits of the dead summoned to do evil, that is, witchcraft. They encumber the lives of the mortals to whom, through affinity or weakness, they adhere. Both the mortal and the intrusive spirit must be treated, the mortal with exorcism and the spirit with orders and prayers to send it on its way.

In these concepts, one can perceive a merger of generic Sub-Saharan African beliefs in the dead and the deities and European spiritism (or spiritualism). The latter is practiced in the urban elite and middle class, the former in rural and lower-class sectors, especially in the highly African-influenced south and southwest of the country, although African-influenced rituals have European and spiritual components as well. The training is done in phases: sometimes individually, sometimes collectively; sometimes in private, sometimes in public. During Doña Iona's annual festival, undertaken as her personal vow to the Virgin of Fátima (May 13th), Marisol takes, in public, another step in her training to gain control over her faculties as a medium. With Metresilí "mounted in her head" (*montada en cabeza*, possessing her), St. Michael (San Miguel), "in the head of" Doña Iona, "settles" (*afinca*) the misterio so Marisol gains control over it, rather than the misterio over her. As in figure 12.1, St. Michael does this using a prepared libation of blessed perfumed water with flower petals (*"un baño"*).

Meanwhile, Metresilí, wanting to do her will, to break loose and dance, moves in vertical jerks with arms stiffly extended—the right arm toward the front, the left toward the back—to the punctuated rhythm of the long-drums and the song (a "Salve con palos"): Los coros de San Miguel / son preciosos y son benditos; / Pero sólo los cantamos / todos los hijos de Cristo. (The versos of St. Michael / are beautiful and they are blessed; / But they are only sung / by all us children of Christ.) Chorus: Y esa es la verdad, / Ay, San Miguel / Esa la verdad / Ay, San Miguel / Y esa es la verdad, / Ay, San Miguel . . . (And that is the truth! / Oh, St. Michael / That is the truth! / Oh, St. Michael / That is the truth! / Oh, St. Michael . . . ) El que quiere ver a Dios, / que limpie su corazón; / Que "ellos" tienen para todos, / pero no para "El," por Dios. (Whoever wants to see God / must cleanse his heart; / "They" [the gods] have enough for everybody. / But certainly not for "him" [the Malignant One].)

## Dominican Vodú-Spiritism in the Context of the Afro-Americas

Dominican culture lies at the margins of Afro-America. Although components of Native American Taíno, Spanish, and West and Central African origins are ethnographically discernible in various cultural domains, Dominican national culture is best characterized by its hybrid, creole character. This is epitomized by Dominican Vodú-spiritism (see Davis 2007b), the devotion to the misterios. The term Vodú is not used by Dominican believers or practitioners, except those scholars of the subject who want to suggest that the Dominican phenomenon is a variant of Haitian Vodou. There really is no generic term; rather, the practice is referred to as "devotion to the misterios" or "devotion to *la veintiuna division*," in reference to the twenty-one *divisiones* or families of deities. The medium is called the servidor/a, or less elegantly and less respectfully, *caballo de misterios* (from the French *serviteur* and *cheval*), but may euphemistically refer to him/herself as an *espiritista*, even within a Voduist domain.

The phenomenon this writer terms Vodú-spiritism is a relatively minor component of Dominican folk Catholicism (which otherwise is largely Hispanic in nature) whose purpose is healing and which is characterized by spirit possession (Davis 1987). As in its counterparts, Dominican Vodú-spiritism entails two dimensions: the private consultation and the public ritual; dance is used only in the latter. The public rituals include saints' festivals sponsored by a Vodú medium and celebratory events of Vodú-spiritism called *maní* or *priyé*. Maní (peanut) refers to the four-part offering tray at these public celebrations, with roasted peanuts, corn, chopped coconut, sesame, and a boiled egg in the center. Priyé is from the Haitian term for the ritual prayer segment of a Vodou event. Such celebrations encompass festivals for a medium's patron saint's day, a vow for healing, or the completion of initiation of a new medium.

The creolized, nonliturgical Salve of saints' festivals of the east and the south is also the most common music used for public rituals of Dominican Vodú-spiritism. This musical subgenre exemplifies the hybrid nature of Dominican culture, as does the dance it accompanies.

In contrast with Salvador da Bahia, Brazil, said to be the most African city in the New World, the Dominican Republic has no spiritual centers known by their specific African-cultural ancestry. In contrast even with Haiti, rather hybrid itself, and other places in the Caribbean such as Carriacou and its Big Drum Dance, there are no culturally designated distinct ritual and dance components with names of African ethnic groups, no notion of "nations" at all. Unlike some other places in Afro-Latin America, there is no Dominican memory of an African past. In Haiti, the mystical site of Afrique Guinée, resting place of the ancestors, is recalled in the collective conscience. Among Dominicans, it has been obliterated by five centuries of cultural fusion born of social liaisons among various races and statuses, with no later huge influx of Africans, as was the case with Saint-Domingue (later Haiti) under the French. This collaboration was necessary for mutual survival during the Spanish colonial abandonment of the island following exhaustion of the gold. The cultural amnesia was later reinforced by the cultural policy of the elite, particularly in the twentieth century. They rewrote history so that all that remained in the popular concept of national culture was *hispanidad*, the imposed memory of Spanish heritage as presumably emblematic and superior.

The diversity of the Dominican ethnic heritage is reflected in the specific spatial placement of the pantheon of deities on the Vodú-spiritist altar. Placed above and on the main altar are the West African Rada and Legba families of deities—called the "white deities" because of their good works. The Guedé family of deities—called the "black deities" because they work on the earthly and subterranean plane and can do both good and evil—are placed on a lower altar, preferably on the floor or ground, to the side or in front of or underneath the main altar. The Petró family—comprising Central African plus creole deities and features—is more prominent in Haitian practice, but Dominican misterios can present themselves with Petró character (*en punto petró*) to take on difficult healing jobs, such as insanity or the exorcism of witchcraft.

It is only the Indian family of deities (*los indios, los indígenas*) whose ethnic origin is identified by the practitioners. Whether their presence in the pantheon really represents cultural continuity or simply Afro-Dominican affinity with another oppressed sector, is a matter of dispute. In the Dominican case, it is probably both, depending on the region. Continuities are probably present in the far western region, the epicenter of Taíno religious and political power at the time of the conquest. There, "Indios" are considered to inhabit springs and streams. In an altar room, throughout the country, the service for los indios is usually situated on the ground or floor in a corner.

### The Spiritual-Material Continuum

No real survey has ever been conducted of the range of manifestations of Dominican Vodú-spiritism as a component of Dominican folk religion and less of the associated music or dance genres and style, that is, the music and dance of the misterios. But, to begin, one could place ritual expressions in Dominican folk Catholicism dedicated to saints and misterios on a continuum from the "spiritual" to the "material." Such a continuum should take into account both the type of ritual and, within a given event, the components of ritual. The spiritist events of the urban elite are entirely or almost entirely "spiritual," while all other folk-Catholic events for the saints and the misterios of both Dominican Republic and Haiti have "spiritual" and "material" components. The "spiritual" component prefaces the "material" component. Dance is performed only in the latter.

On one end of the spiritual-material continuum, the beliefs and practices of the urban elite are entirely or almost entirely spiritual, based on European Kardec spiritism rather than African-derived Vodú. Kardec spiritism refers to the systematization in 1857 by Allan Kardec (the spiritual name of Hippolyte Rivail) of France, through his publication of the *Book of the Spirits*, which was translated from the French into many languages and distributed throughout North and Latin America, popularizing spiritism (or spiritualism) in the late nineteenth century. Their events are called "sessions" or "Horas Santas" (a home devotional prayer ritual) and do not use music or dance at all.

In these events, they summon their intellectual powers of clairvoyance rather than, or more than, physical "incorporation" or possession. However, unlike Kardec spiritism, the emphasis is not on contacting spirits of deceased family members (although they may appear), rather on receiving elevated spirits of prominent spiritual figures of the twentieth century— latter-day saints, as it were, such as the Venezuelan physician Dr. José Gregorio Hernández (d. 1919) or the saintly, nunlike Dominican healer of Sabana de la Mar, Señorita Elupina Cordero (d. 1939). Increasingly in such sessions during the course of the late twentieth century, spirit possession by deities has been accepted in some centers, but more in their manifestations as saints (their European personae) rather than as misterios (their African personae), or, if by misterios, in a spiritual expression (*punto*) thereof. At one time, such entities did not speak, but later in some centers they have begun to do so. Thus, in the last some sixty years there has been an evolution in extra-official folk-Catholic practices, even of the elite, reflecting an increasing African influence. But in the elite sector, still no music at all is used and hence there is no dance. Neither is there animal sacrifice.

Next on the spiritual-material continuum would come saints' festivals (called *velaciones*, *veladas*, *velorios de santo*, or *noches de vela*, depending on the region). These events, of individual or brotherhood sponsorship, traditionally do not include possession by misterios. The phenomenon can occur, but the possessing entity would be a spirit of the dead, namely a former sponsor who has come to enjoy his/her festival by dancing to the drums, or

Figure 12.2. General possession on the day of St. John the Baptist at La Agüita de Liborio sacred spring in La Maguana, Province of San Juan. Photo by M. E. Davis; used by permission.

to criticize the attentions shown the drummers by his/her heirs. The exception is the saint's festival whose organizer is a Vodú-spiritist medium.

A saint's festival of either type begins with a spiritual component, namely Catholic prayers, largely the rosary, followed by three sacred sung *Salve Regina* prayers or their equivalent. This is an obligation that must be fulfilled before either other *Salves* (in an area that does not use drumming) or the long-drums are permitted. When drumming is used, the first three drum pieces following the prayers are sacred. This is a time when the ancestors are recalled and, if a Vodú event, the sponsoring entities are invoked, sometimes through dance. So the prayers, the three sacred *Salves*, and the three sacred drum pieces together constitute the "spiritual" component of the event; then the less structured, longer, and more "material" component continues. In a saint's festival, this pattern is replicated three times throughout the night-long event. In a Vodú celebration that is not a saint's festival, a single trajectory moves from prayers to possession by the main mediums to general possession (fig. 12.2).

Figure 12.3. The first and most sacred drum piece, "Cautivos son," following the rosary and liturgical Salves at the Brotherhood of the Holy Spirit, Las Matas de Farfán. Photo by M. E. Davis; used by permission.

The initial sacred African-influenced component in a saint's festival can be seen in figure 12.3, the Sunday gathering of the Brotherhood of the Holy Spirit of Las Matas de Farfán in the Province of San Juan in the southwest. Following the rosary prayers and the three sacred *Salves*, the first drum piece is called "Cautivos Son" (Captives they are), presumably referring to the ancestors in Purgatory. The members, in a rhythmic walking step to the Palos del Espíritu Santo (Drums of the Holy Spirit), bearing banners color-encoded with the saints/misterios, trace a counterclockwise circle in front of the altar.

Their countenances reveal the transcendent state of mind in which a momentary connection is made with the late members of their brotherhood, their personal patron saints, and the Holy Spirit, patron of the brotherhood. In the two ensuing sacred drum dances and even the later pieces, members may "receive" the Holy Spirit or other misterios, but the deities manifest in a most subtle, dreamlike, and "spiritual" way.

The next stage in the spiritual-material continuum would be the individually sponsored saint's festival of a Vodú-spiritist medium, in which possession by misterios is a component. Beyond that on the continuum is the Vodú-spiritist celebratory event (maní, priyé), not for a patron saint, but rather to celebrate healing or initiation. Such events with possession are growing in frequency compared with those without spirit possession. All of them entail drumming and dance of the misterios. In such events, music is performed first to invoke the misterios, then to honor them and allow them to express themselves through dance. Mediums and others alike may dance without being in trance, as an invocation or simply in enjoyment. After all, these ceremonies are sacred rituals and public entertainment at the same time.

## Music of the Misterios

The music is the creole, nonliturgical *Salve*, accompanied by an ensemble of various types of drums and other percussion instruments—scrapers (*güiras*) and perhaps maracas, the ensemble varying regionally. In the central south and east, singers accompany themselves with polyrhythmically played hand drums (*panderos*), similar to tambourines without jingles, plus other small drums. Farther to the west, the long-drums (*palos*) are used; however, these are originally associated with Afro-Dominican religious brotherhoods of the Holy Spirit and are more traditionally played for saints' festivals, not allied with Vodú, and for the deceased members of such brotherhoods.

The Salve, the most ubiquitous genre of Dominican folk music (more so than the better-known folk merengue), is the musical setting of the *Salve Regina* prayer in Spanish (in English known as "Hail, Holy Queen"). Today's Dominican Salve comprises two subgenres. The traditional Salves are Hispanic a cappella settings of the sacred text, sung antiphonally at the altar of a family-sponsored saint's festival or in procession or pilgrimage. From this, a creole subgenre, the *Salve con versos*, developed as a musical and instrumental lingua franca for people of various African cultural origins in contact at work and on pilgrimage. Its structure is the common African call-and-response form. The Salve con versos replaces the sacred text, partially or entirely (regionally varying), with improvised quatrains and a fixed response. Its accompaniment ranges regionally from hand-clapping as percussion to an ensemble of polyrhythmic hand drums to the ensemble of the long drums.

## Dance of the Misterios: Two Manifestations of St. Michael

St. Michael was observed dancing at the final Friday of seven celebrated by the Afro-Dominican Brotherhood of the Holy Spirit between Easter and Pentecost in Santa María, Province of San Cristóbal, in front of the chapel as people awaited the Mass. He danced to Salves con palos. This is a different use of the palos than the lugubrious sacred rhythms of the brotherhood, associated with death rituals, although they can be danced by the living. These rhythms were played as an extension of the spiritual component represented by the Mass (as Salves are sung after the rosary at a saint's festival altar). Dancing with a female partner, St. Michael incarnated in Pichingolo, a servidor from Medina, San Cristóbal, who had come in pilgrimage from that rural site to the north.

In Cabral, Barahona, as throughout the southwest, the drums, as "noise-makers," are silent during Holy Week and the altar shrouded in black in commemoration of the death of Christ. With the stroke of midnight at the end of Good Friday, the drums can play again. "Mi Mae" lifts the mourning period with a miniature saint's festival on Easter Monday, in the midst of the post-Lenten carnival celebrated in that town. On the occasion observed, the rosary was prayed, three sacred Salve-like songs were sung, three sacred drum pieces were played, and then any drum piece could continue.

The second of the sacred drum pieces was intended to invoke St. Michael, the "protector" of the altar and of the medium: "San Miguel, te llamamos . . ." (St. Michael, we are calling you). And he did indeed descend, upon which the response switched to: "San Miguel, ya llegó . . ." (St. Michael has arrived). The medium pulled the kerchief from her head to receive the deity better, and her countenance changed as "he" took over her consciousness. "He" launched into energetically dancing counterclockwise around the center post. The piece finished with a synchronized final two beats. All was silent. St. Michael kneeled before the altar, raising "his" head; "he" said hoarsely: "Gracias a la Misericordia" (Thanks be to Mercy). Someone rang the little bell on the altar, signaling to St. Michael it was time to go. And he went, abruptly, causing the medium almost to fall over. Hanging onto people nearby, she pulled herself up, confused, as if awakening from a deep sleep. She placed both arms, crossed, on the center post in salutation, and did the same at the back wall. Then the festival and the general dancing, in couples and individually, continued.

## Style of Dance of the Misterios

Unlike its counterparts more true to African continuities, Dominican Vodú-spiritism has no specific rhythms for specific deities or families of deities. Music for a misterio is distinguished, rather, by its melody and text, such as the piece cited above, played to invoke St. Michael. In turn, each deity has his/her properties and gestures. Often, a dancer is not obviously in trance, but in a transcendent state (such as in the sacred first piece of the Brotherhood of the Holy Spirit in Las Matas de Farfán, mentioned previously and depicted in figure 12.3), which may or may not be trance. This would be a very elevated "spiritual" manifestation, in which the gestures and movements do not reveal which deity (or spirit of the dead) may be present; the individual him/herself, emerging from trance, may not recall either.

In a more material expression, St. Michael, the most ubiquitous of Dominican Vodú deities, uses a sword as his symbol (as the counterpart of the

Figure 12.4. San Miguel (St. Michael) possessing the sponsor of a Vodú festival, in a characteristic pose. San Felipe, Villa Mella. Photo by M. E. Davis, used by permission.

Haitian Ogun Ferraille, i.e., Ogun of Iron). When he dances (at least in the southern region), he gestures with his index finger pointed up, as in figure 12.4, suggesting, perhaps, the pointed sword.

He dances energetically, pivoting on an axis in one direction, then the other, abruptly alternating a bent waist with an erect posture, knees straight. Meanwhile, as observed in Santa María, a female partner simply marks time to his virtuosity, not unlike the gender roles of some genres of Dominican social dance, such as the son.

Looking at yet more "material" manifestations of Haitian influence, dancer and folk-dance instructor Manuela Féliz of the National School of Dance has conducted field observation among Haitian-Dominican sugar-cane settlements (*bateyes*) where the author has not: Haina and Batey Palavé (Province of San Cristóbal), Batey Bienvenido (San Pedro de Macorís), and Batey La Ceja (La Romana). She observes that the deity Metresilí uses the shoulders. (See her extended arms in figures 12.1 and 12.5.) Anaísa—a flirtatious and sensuous misterio, the counterpart of the Cuban Oshún—uses the torso and the waist, moving her midsection. Féliz further observes that the Petrós use their feet a lot and that Santa Marta la Dominadora (a creole deity of the Guedé family) undulates up and down, replicating the movement of the snake she holds and dominates. She also may fall to the floor and writhe like a snake. San Elías (St. Elijah), the head of the Guedé family, called Papá Guedé or El Barón del Cementerio (the Baron of the Cemetery), incarnates as a cadaver. He knocks the medium to the floor and "his" belly swells and "he" foams at the mouth. "He" is then covered with a small shroud topped with a crucifix, and four candles are placed at the corners of the body as at a wake, all amid raucous drumming. When "he" leaves, the medium simply gets up and resumes participation in the fiesta.

Very different forms of dance are found in the Haitian and Haitian-Dominican "gagá" society events. *Gagá* (the Dominican pronunciation of the Haitian *rara*), is a batey-based folk-religious society dedicated to a Petró deity and active during the Lenten season. It is mysterious within, but carnivalesque for the public. Gagá actually uses two styles of dance, one danced by the *mayores* and another by members of the society and the public.

The mayores are four leaders, all young men, dressed in skirts of multicolored scarves (each color representing a different deity) and sequined and mirrored fancy tunics, not unlike Morris dancers. Each twirls a baton. They are "born" just before dawn on Good Friday, shrouded in sheets like fetuses or pupae and carried into the *enramada* (roofed patio), one by one, by the "owner" (*dueño*) or head of the gagá. When each is deposited, he springs into life, with whirling, acrobatic movements in place, knees bent, then launches forth around the center post (in counterclockwise direction). He is joined by another, who emerges identically from his shroud and likewise springs to life, then another, then another. Finally the four are alternating whirling in place, then dancing around the center post, twirling their batons, to the beats of the drums and the hocketing tones of the single-note bamboo trumpet ensemble.

The gagá society then sets forth to make the rounds and show themselves off in their own batey community. On Holy Saturday and Easter Sunday, it visits other bateyes, going door to door to ask for money and rum; the mayores and groups of girls perform routines to encourage contributions. These routines, and the public dance in general, is lascivious in nature, because in the Lenten and Easter celebrations of death and life, the gagá celebrates human fertility, overtly stated in the off-color lyrics of their songs. Two or three, often young, girls, legs splayed and knees bent, adhere to each other, front to back, and wriggle up and down with forward and backward movement in simulation of copulation. In the dance of both the mayores, with their bulky multicolored skirts, and the girls and the public, the emphasis is on hip movement. This strikes a contrast with the spirituality and stiff formality of the semisacred Dominican drum dance, called a "dance of respect."

## Vodú-Spiritism in Modern Times

It is only since the death of dictator Trujillo in 1961 and a trend toward free and democratic expression that Vodú, still legally proscribed, can be practiced openly. The spiritism of the elite undoubtedly fell under the authorities' radar because they did not incorporate African-derived noisy elements such as drumming. The religious expressions that are overtly growing in visibility and popularity during the last fifty years are thus the "material" expressions, for several reasons: the legal proscription is now overlooked; the performance aspects of public rituals are attractive; a Haitian influence is burgeoning, given the "silent occupation" of the country; and finally because the misterios help mortals confront the problems and challenges of modern, transnational life.

As with any folk religion, however, much variation can be found by region, rural or urban location, social class, and ethnic composition, duly reflected in the dance. Regional variation stretches to emigrant Dominican populations in New York, Boston, Madrid, and other U.S. and European sites (see Sánchez-Carretero 2005). Variation according to social sector and region encompasses the Haitian-Dominican expressions of Vodou-Vodú. The growth of Vodú presence and popularity and its evolution mean that dance is undergoing change as well.

## Eclectic Music for Today's Dance of the Misterios

The Dominican creolization is such that other genres of music apart from the Salve, including even entirely secular dance genres, can accommodate spirit possession at Vodú-spiritist festivals or saints' festivals of mediums' sponsorship. It appears to be the ambience of the festival rather than the music, or perhaps it is the dance, that cues or invokes the deities. For example, during the 1990s at the altar of the late Félix Antonio Maríñez (Popa) of San Felipe, Villa Mella, the *congos* drums of the large Brotherhood of the Holy Spirit started to be played during the July 25th festival of St. James ("San" Santiago or Ogún Balenyó as a Vodú deity)—rather unprecedented because they were traditionally circumscribed to their own brotherhood rituals in which the only possession was occasionally by the spirit of the deceased at the brotherhood's numerous death rites.

Then, equally interesting, the next day, the 26th of July, for the festival day of St. Ann—the Vodú deity Anaísa, notorious for her flirtatiousness—a local son ensemble was contracted, bringing a pan-Hispanic Caribbean social dance genre significant in the Villa Mella area into the sacred arena. The music, performed live right outside the altar room, was enjoyed all afternoon by Anaísa "in the head" (*en cabeza*) of the medium, Félix Antonio, who, as the honored entity of the day, courted and flirted with male mortals, dancing with whomever "she" fancied, in the style of dance of the mortals. "She" was more dominant than the usual male-female power structure in the Dominican son couple (see Davis 2007a), however, in part because the fiesta was in her honor and also because of the towering size of the medium, dressed in the gold yellow of Anaísa, down to "her" matching pumps in men's size twelve.

Figure 12.5. Metresilí dances to nonliturgical Salves in the sponsor's folk chapel at a vow-based annual saint's festival of the brotherhood of St. John the Baptist, while the drums of the brotherhood play their signature *sarandunga* music for dancing outside. Fundación de Peravia, Baní. Photo by M. E. Davis, used by permission.

They also played arrangements of Salve-like compositions presumably by local mediums Félix Antonio and Enerolisa, the latter recently becoming well known because of the efforts of folk revivalist entrepreneur Roldán Marmol. They were then appropriated by commercial musician Kinito Méndez, whose most popular piece of this sort, played repeatedly by revivalist ensembles from Santo Domingo to New York as a new symbol of national identity, is "Yo soy Ogún Balenyó."

Parallel to the unprecedented incorporation of the congos of Villa Mella into the context of Vodú, is the incorporation of Vodú into an annual saint's festival of another Afro-Dominican religious brotherhood, that of San Juan Bautista (St. John the Baptist) and its *sarandunga* drumming. A second event in its annual cycle is the festival on the day of San Pedro (St. Peter), sponsored by a member of the brotherhood. In the past twenty or more years, it has been offered by the Vodú medium Hilda Peguero, of Fundación de Peravia, at her complex on the east bank of the Baní River. In the chapel

Figure 12.6. San Juan Bautista (St. John the Baptist) in a vow-based festival in his honor, possessing the sponsor and dancing to one of the musical genres of the event, a traditional northern-style merengue (perico ripiao) at Fundación de Peravia, Baní. Photo by M. E. Davis, used by permission.

where she conducts her healing, the sacred Salves in the morning, led by women, are replaced with nonliturgical Salves as the male musicians arrive (see figure 12.5.) Outside, under a mango tree, sarandunga is performed and danced.

Hilda supposedly takes possession in the altar with St. John, a phenomenon emphatically denied as possible by the late head of the brotherhood and some of its more traditional members: "¡San Juan no monta en cabeza!" (St. John does not possess people!). "He" then proceeds out to the sarandunga and dances to "his" music. At noon, Hilda's cousins arrive to perform social dance music, the folk merengue originally from the north called *perico ripiao*, at another location on the grounds. St. John, still possessing Hilda, comes over to dance to the merengue as well (see figure 12.6). It is a solo dance, unlike the mortal dancers in couples, with the musicians themselves as a sort of a dance partner for St. John.

Prior to the ample availability of live ensembles and recordings of Dominican compositions used for Vodú-spiritist events, records were used, and they still are. Previously, the favorite recordings, known throughout the Hispanic Caribbean, were those by Cuban musicians Celina and Reutilio (Celina González Zamora [b. 1928] and Reutilio Domínguez Terrero [1921–1971]), in *guaracha* and similar rhythms. Among them, the most famous is their composition "¡Qué viva Changó!" (Also known as "A Santa Barbara"), played in Vodú contexts in Santo Domingo even though the deity known as Changó is not part of their pantheon.

Other recordings, not specific to the milieu but appropriate for it, can also invoke and entertain the misterios. In Cabral, Barahona, the author was obliged to dance with St. Michael (Belié Belcán) to the recording of "Tabaco y ron" (tobacco and rum) sung by Fernando Villalona. The dance, led by St. Michael, was in a side-to-side guaracha-like step. The record was repeated ad nauseam since St. Michael was supposedly enamored of the writer. How could she say no to a misterio?

# 13

# How to Dance Son and the Style of a Dominican Sonero

XIOMARITA PÉREZ

TRANSLATED BY MARIA LARA SOTO

Being a teacher has forced me to take shelter in a method to implement a pedagogy, because not all people who know how to dance, know how to teach. The most important thing in learning to dance is that the future dancer must have the interest and willingness to learn to dance. Therefore, patience, empathy, and a friendly exchange with the instructor are basic to enable a collaboration of both parties to reach their goal.

The teaching of the first three sessions should be individualized. The participant must feel safe and at the same time feel confident in himself before he can dance with a partner. Every person has rhythm, but some have not discovered that they have it and can follow it. That is why we have dance schools: to help find that rhythm inside ourselves. The emotional aspect is also important, because if a person cannot focus on learning or if his mind is someplace else, he will not even know how to take advantage of the teaching. Sometimes this happens with politicians, businessmen, or adolescents who are forced to take classes in which they have no interest that their parents have obliged them to take.

When we walk, we keep up a rhythm, fast and smooth. When we dance, we do it in time to the music that is playing. The majority of popular music compositions are in the 4/4 tempo. Of the four beats, the first is the most intensely accented. If we observe an orchestra playing merengue or salsa or son, we will be aware of the instruments that always play and the other instruments that play only some of the time: the first are rhythmic instruments and the second are the melodic instruments. But for dancing, we are interested only in the rhythm instruments, because those are the ones that play the rhythm we dance to.

To learn to dance to a piece of music, we must first identify the instruments that mark the rhythm in order to follow them and anticipate them as we dance. The melody of a piece, including the artist's voice, always follows the rhythm, although it is not always played by the same instruments that mark the rhythm. Moreover, there are melody instruments that sometimes trace over or hide those instruments that set the rhythm. Some people are very sensitive to this, and it sets them to dancing in an instinctive manner, sometimes without paying attention to the melody or to the basic rhythm. At times they go off the beat or sense that they've somehow failed to catch it.

The steps are the way we move our feet and also our body, always being aware that, in anyone, dance and rhythm are carried by the feet and the melody in the body (though the flow of the melodic notes coincides with the rhythmic beats). In a general sense, to dance allows us to use the same steps we use to walk, but always governed by the rhythmic flow imposed by the music; that is why it varies according to what we are dancing. When we speak of the rhythm being borne by the feet, we are referring to stepping with emphasis, as we do when we count the beats with our fingers. It is similar to when soldiers are marching 1, 2, 3, and 4, counting each beat when the foot hits the ground. We never put out a foot two times in succession, except to make a catch-up step, which happens when one of the partners loses the rhythm and makes the step to catch up with the tune.

## The Son

The son is the most elegant and sensual urban folkloric dance in our country, the Dominican Republic, and the schools that teach it must use as a reference the soneros themselves, because they are the real essence of the dance. I don't consider myself a sonera; I consider myself a dancer of all the rhythms, which is why I respect and admire those who enjoy and love the son in a very special way, because this is a way of life. For them as for no others the source of pleasure and healthy life springs from the kind of partnership in which two dance partners become one. For this reason, I don't agree with holding dance competitions for this kind of dancer, but

Figure 13.1. Noelia Holguín, daughter of Xiomarita Pérez, and Gustavo Adolfo Fernández dancing the son at a lecture demonstration at the Son y Salsa conference, Centro León, Santiago de los Caballeros, April 2007. Photograph by Alejandra Aguilar; used by permission.

only with showcases or exhibitions of this dance, because each dancer, each couple, is unique.

The rhythmic instruments of the son are the conga and bongo drums, the clave sticks, and bass. The melodic instruments for son are the guitar, the tres, and others.

Characteristics of the man and the woman in the dance: The man is the one who leads the dance, and the woman follows him. They dance on the toes, contrary to the Cuban dancer. The man makes all the elaborate solo figures with the body and the feet, and the woman continues dancing, keeping the rhythm and moving with grace and elegance, showing she is a good accompanist who can speak in the same language as "a good sonera partner." The man makes the figures to the key rhythm instruments like the bongo, to which, on its accents, the dancer will make his solo moves and by-and-by fall back into the rhythm with his partner, while the woman continues with the basic step. The woman places her left hand on the man's neck in a position of surrender to the dance and to her partner. He can also mark the rhythm by resting his right hand on the woman's waist, giving light taps with his fingers. This makes the woman feel the dance more and want to dance more passionately. The man moves his waist in a rhythmic way with his steps, contrary to the danzón, where there is less movement of the waist and the steps are much bigger.

The son is a dance of partnership, but not just with any partner. For a sonero to dance son, he has to be sure that the woman is a dancer willing to be led, at least for the dance. It is important to note that in this dance one does not do turns or counterturns, nor let go of the hands. The dance expresses a bond not only between the dancer and his partner, but also between the dancer and the musicians. Every instrumental accent is felt in the feet and reflected in the hip movement. When the dancer places a foot down, the opposite hip is raised. What is it that gives beauty to this dance? It is the constant contrary movement of feet and hips, while the feet mark the rhythm with short steps and great elegance.

## Clothes

Two or three days before they dance, the partners already know what outfits they will wear. The man will dress with a jacket, a *chacabana* or *guayabera*, or a long-sleeve shirt with suspenders. Some, for more elegance, will put on a formal hat that naturally matches his outfit. Others will wear a handsome *boina* (a soft woolen cap with a small bill), and a guayabera with short sleeves for a more casual look. The majority of the time, the clothes are white and the accessories of another color combination: the ribbon of the hat, the pocket handkerchief, the tie are all the same color. The shoes are of two tones, brown and white or white and black.

The woman wears her best to dance the son. She wears a sparkly dress, most of the time in black. The hair is always well dressed, the shoes are high heels, and it is rare that a pants suit is worn. It is common to wear an ankle bracelet.

## Anecdotes

Once I was with my daughter at "Secreto Musical" with a North American who had come to the country to take dance classes. When I go with my students, I like them to observe me dancing, and this night I told a man who was walking with his partner that I wanted to dance with him and he agreed. A moment came when the woman stood up and came toward me, and you can imagine what my daughter and I thought: that she was going to attack me. The surprise was even greater when the lady took my left hand and put it around the neck of the gentleman and asked me to put my body close to his, and then she said, "That's the way you dance the son!"

The last time Compay Segundo, the late Cuban guitarist, came to the Dominican Republic, I went to the Monument of the Son at 3:30 in the afternoon to secure a place next to the dance floor and Compay. Meanwhile, I could listen to the music and watch the couples dancing, but since no one knew me as a dancer, no one invited me to dance. My girlfriend only laughed, because I wanted to dance. It was not until 8:00 at night that I began to dance because one person knew me. Later the dancing men rained on me. This confirms what was explained above: if a sonero doesn't see you dance, he will not invite you to the dance floor.

## Personality of the soneros

They don't get drunk. They have high self-esteem, without complexes. The sonero doesn't dance in the dark, because the purpose is to show that he is a great dancer. The sonero doesn't smoke. The sonero does not dance bachata. He is a loner. He is the macho one in control of the dance. He is true to his rhythm, so faithful that in all dance rhythms—the cha-cha-chá, the danzón, salsa, etc.—he dances in the son style. If his wife doesn't dance son, he will look for a dance "companion." Where there are soneros, there is decency and respect. He has a collection of hats, suspenders, handkerchiefs, and ties in different colors, all in matching sets. The son is a lifestyle, and only they know how to carry it off. When the soneros arrive at a son party, all the tables are reserved for them: they are the kings.

Many thanks to M. E. Davis for assistance with the translation.

# 14

# The Drums Are Calling My Name

NICOLÁS DUMIT ESTÉVEZ

Drum-proofing the Dominican night can become a challenge vaguely related to that of counting the sands of a desert or tallying with accuracy the exact number of hairs on one's head.

A tête-à-tête between a well-endowed vedette (a multitalented female performer who sings, dances, and/or acts) and a pale, sixty-pound boy is likely to be a one-sided affair; that of the scrawny boy hosting the encounter on the stage of his delusional imagination. At an early age I became aware of the weight that flesh held for the voyeuristic audiences who followed the contours of the women dancing on local TV, and I secretly craved a share of the attention generously dispensed to them. For this reason our black-and-white Sanyo screen at home served as the lab where I researched with meticulous detail the subjects of my interest.

I made sure to keep both eyes on every single one of the televised movements their bodies generated. To be more specific, the boobs and the rear ends held a particular fascination for those of us ensnared by their hypnotic jerks. With close-ups from time to time, the camera man gave each of these siliconed body parts just enough visibility to threaten viewers with the prospect of them emerging from the screen, right onto our dining room tables. *El Show del Mediodía*, a TV show at noon, and *El Show de Iris Chacón*, a variety show hosted by vedette Iris Chacón that ran from the '70s through the mid-'80s, were aired at the times most people in the urban centers of the Dominican Republic ate lunch or supper. It made sense then for spectators to mix their dishes of white rice with red beans and to coordinate chewing with the drumbeats coming from the TV speaker. The customary two pieces of meat the fortunate ones got as part of the midday meal could be cautiously saved for the sections of the spectacle where no serious contorting by the vedettes occurred, a measure to prevent choking that applied to the mashed green plantains of mangú and salami as well. It sure made sense to enjoy the fried ripe plantains or bananas that added a sweet touch to the tropical diet at the closing of the show when applause, live or prerecorded, showered the scantily dressed dancers with a torrent of thank-yous. Sweetness made for a good closure. No bitter ending.

Among many other things in life, I wanted to be a vedette. This was a worldly preoccupation that held very little in common with my spiritual pursuits, but one with a close relationship to my curiosity about the largest organ of the body: the skin. Iris Chacón, from the neighboring island of Puerto Rico had, as a matter of fact, devoted one hit parade song to the flesh: "Si tu boquita fuera" (if your mouth were), its lyrics detailing the sensual possibilities that the lips of a potential lover would hold for her in the event they were made of chocolate, mayo, rice with yam, or sugared bread. In my case, the sensual possibilities were few, yet La Chacón, like the rest of the vedettes who populated the islands of the Spanish-speaking Caribbean in the '70s, became the object of a quasi-obsessive pursuit on my part. Futile in some ways. For very obvious reasons, I was at a clear loss in terms of the voluptuous anatomy of the Borinqueña Iris, at a significant disadvantage competing for a stormy stage name with the Dominican Mayra el Ciclón del Caribe, the Cyclone of the Caribbean, and at odds with the sultry looks of the much more seasoned dancer and actress, Tongolele, born Yolanda Ivonne Móntez Farrington in the city of Spokane, Washington.

Nor did I yet have the skills to weave my ethnic background into the moist tropical rainforests of the Third World. There was little trace in my physique attesting to my African heritage, and even less to a Taíno background. The Spaniard in me, if there was any, would have appealed only to those on the island trying desperately to cling to their obscure European ancestry. If I were savvy enough, I could have tapped into the Middle East and brought to light my Lebanese descent to craft an exotic genealogy deeply rooted in belly dancing and thirsty deserts populated by Bedouins. Tongolele had successfully done so. She somehow had overcome her bland birthplace to become a global ethnic par excellence, and in her journey through imaginary jungles, she seemed to have drunk large cauldrons from the nectar of Ponce de León's Fountain of Youth. According to my family's folklore, when my grandmother was young she watched a grown-up Tongolele dance. The vedette never got old and escaped death by a hair in a Mexican B-movie called *Han matado a Tongolele* (Someone Has Killed Tongolele). It makes sense to keep the plot consistent all the way through.

The offspring of the '80s were tame enough to give audiences a subtle hint of the decline of an era. Off the top of my head, I can faintly recall the fierce Dominican Martha Vargas as the exception to the trend, shaking her anatomy as much as she possibly could while at the same time gasping for oxygen to prove that she was perfectly capable of carrying on two bodily tasks at once: dancing and singing. She was GOOD. *El Show del Mediodía* competed for an audience with *Fiesta*, the new noon TV show. Each of these programs had, of course, a vedette in their repertoire. *Fiesta* boasted Wanda, the goody-two-shoes girl whose mechanical movements were confined to her lower extremities, while its rival relied on the ratings that its "blue-eyed girl," the mulatta, La Mulatona, raised. The humongous Chacón breasts were rarely seen. Neither was the butt that made a name for the dancer. The new vedettes were a far cry from their well-oiled, pumped-up predecessors. If anything, their movements were more restrained. La Mulatona's main number was to dance to *los tres golpes*. These were three symbolic smacks on the face, executed on the skin of a drum, used by a male presenter to make an equal number of pointed comments on the rotten politics of the Dominican Republic. Iris had gradually waned from the screen, having become, along the way, a born-again Christian and eventually moving to Florida to work on a children's TV show. The movements of her younger sister Lourdes, who herself had emerged as a vedette, didn't produce the same reactions. My interest in the body had by then become clinical. I was a self-conscious teen trying to make his way into a reputable medical school. News from Tongolele would arrive sporadically. She was still kicking . . . and dancing. Anyhow, I lost interest in the subject, for the time being.

The beats can and do spread far beyond the coastline of Hispaniola and into New York City. On the island of Manhattan I corroborated the veracity of my opening statement about drum-proofing the Dominican night. Ten years after I'd left my Caribbean homeland for the United States, the drums, like audible smoke signals, were clearly calling my name. I responded to them by hunting for a pair of black-and-green striped Speedos in a winter storage trunk that also worked as a repository of tropical artifacts. The male vedette I brought to life, who later took the name Machete, made it to Dixon Place, the performance art space on New York City's Bowery, without a stage name. He danced under the red-lit sky in a performance I called *The Land*

Figures 14.1. and 14.2. Photographs shot by the audience with disposable cameras at *The Land Columbus Loved Best*; performance by Nicolás Dumit Estévez with percussionist Louie Gamboa at Dixon Place in New York in 2001. Used by permission of Nicolás Dumit Estévez.

*Columbus Loved Best.* He reversed the arrangement of La Chacón's body by swapping the excess from the back to the lower front. With no need for silicone breasts, he fashioned a velvet penis that he popped inside the Speedo at the beginning of the show. He sipped Hawaiian Punch from a plastic champagne goblet as though there was no tomorrow. In fact he was right. The percussionist he hired to watch him move would pack up before the end of the night. Machete ultimately drove himself to collapse, dizzy from the flashes of the disposable cameras that he distributed among the audience for the purpose of recording his act. At the end of the show he would leave the stage overdosed on the punch's food coloring, half wondering whether Tongolele was still in this world or dancing a heavenly rumba in the hereafter.

Written while in residency at The MacDowell Colony, Peterborough, New Hampshire.

# PUERTO RICO

# 15
# Contemporary Dance in Puerto Rico, or How to Speak of These Times

SUSAN HOMAR

Countries with a dance tradition and history allow, even invite, the isolation of periods or genres when one is writing about them. But countries with a recent development of professional dance and a history of theatrical dance that does not date back very far, such as Puerto Rico, demand a consideration of its beginnings. Everything is still very much interrelated. So, in order to reflect upon contemporary dance in Puerto Rico, a form that reacts to the established dance styles and institutions, one must briefly look at how it all started and the context against which it reacts and within which it flourishes.

Until the mid-twentieth century, Puerto Ricans training in theatrical dance were starting out with local teachers, some of whom had trained abroad, and performing in self-produced events or single dance performances sponsored by groups dedicated to classical music that were also promoting the development of academic and classical dance. Meanwhile, dancers like Anna Pavlova and Tamara Toumanova, and companies such as Ballets Russes and Spanish dance groups, classical and flamenco, visited the island periodically from the nineteenth century on, inspiring young dancers.

Professional dance began to develop in the middle of the twentieth century under the aegis of Ana García and Gilda Navarra, sisters who initially trained in San Juan and later in New York and Spain, respectively, and performed professionally: García with Balanchine's Ballet Society and Ballet de Alicia Alonso, Navarra with the Pilar López and José Greco companies. In 1951, García and Navarra returned to Puerto Rico to open a school, and in 1954 they started Ballets de San Juan (BSJ), a company that still exists. Its original repertory had classical and neoclassical ballets; classical Spanish, flamenco, and Spanish-inspired pieces; and a genre based on Puerto Rican stories, legends, and topics that usually brought together young Puerto Rican choreographers, composers, set and costume designers, and sometimes librettists (surely inspired by the Eugene Loring and Agnes de Mille Americana pieces García and Navarra came to know in New York).

While Spanish dances disappeared from BSJ's repertory when Navarra left in 1960 and interest in them waned in Puerto Rico in the '60s, ballet has continued to reign on the island while modern dance has not taken hold, although a couple of teachers and choreographers cultivated its different techniques over the years. The only one that has been somewhat more accepted and practiced has been a derivative of the Horton technique, but always as part of a more diverse vocabulary. However, what did strike a chord in San Juan at the end of the '70s was postmodern or "experimental" dance, as its Puerto Rican practitioners prefer to call it, and, more recently, contemporary dance (the latter based on ballet training).

So how did dance in Puerto Rico evolve from ballet to experimental, without the modern dance transition? Is it, in any case, an obligatory stepping stone? Actually, a transition of sorts occurred, although it was not through modern dance itself. When Navarra left BSJ, she retrained in pantomime under Etienne Decroux and Jacques Lecoq, in New York and Paris, a professional decision she has always attributed to Mexican American modern dance master José Limón, in whom she saw another way to use the body. Once she returned, Navarra created a pantomime curriculum at the University of Puerto Rico's (UPR) Drama Department. In 1971, she founded Taller de Histriones (Concepción 2002b), whose fourteen pieces (most choreographed by Navarra after developing lengthy improvisations with the company in a workshop setting) could be characterized as expressionist dance-theater and were an important evolutionary stage in Puerto Rico's dance scene. Taller de Histriones closed in 1985.

In the late '70s, a crop of Puerto Ricans studying dance and art in New York returned to the island and, with three local experimental artists, started Pisotón, a dance and theater group grounded in postmodern aesthetics (Banes 1987). These artists were Viveca Vázquez, Awilda Sterling-Duprey, Petra Bravo, Gloria Llompart, Jorge Arce, and Maritza Pérez. San Juan was a city shaped by modernist tastes and values; Pisotón stomped in true to its name (which suggests that it was, indeed, stepping on the establishment's

toes) and took the audience to new places. Its work spawned new generations of dancers and choreographers, even of dance writers, and changed
San Juan's dance spectrum (which by then included two more ballet companies, Ballet Concierto and the San Juan Municipal Ballet).

Staid ballet companies invited some of Pisotón's members to choreograph
(principally Bravo, a Cuban who trained under, and danced with, the Ballet Nacional de Cuba, and later studied modern dance), while ballet dancers incorporated experimental moves and issues into their choreographies.
Pisotón lasted about five years, but its influence was long lasting. According
to Sterling-Duprey, it gave them the liberty and enthusiasm to develop their
personal projects, as well as the collective ones, and pushed dance into unexplored territory in the Puerto Rican dance spectrum.

Most recently, some of the island's best ballet dancers came together to
start a contemporary dance company, the first on the island, called Andanza
(a word meaning random or adventurous strolling). Since 2000, they have
been performing regularly, they have danced abroad, and they have a vibrant school and several community outreach projects.

## Where Do They Come From, What Do They Want to Do?

The initial tendency toward formalism among the New York postmodernist
dancers provided an example, techniques, and especially questions, but it
did not satisfy the Puerto Rican dancers' concerns. Formalist ideas regarding dance and performance were fundamental, but it was just as important
for them to express political, ideological, and personal issues that directly
grappled with gender and identity in ways they felt neither ballet nor modern dance offered.

Viveca Vázquez has often explained that the unrest of the 1960s as much
as the challenges and changes of the times—the experimentalists' own as
well as Puerto Rico's—required new forms of expression. She establishes an
analogy between the experimentalists' desire to develop a different movement idiom and general aesthetic to address the context within which they
were speaking and dancing and the *nueva trova*'s acknowledgment and appropriation of traditions in music, rhythm, instrumentation, and poetry to
better speak to and about their times. (Nueva trova is a Latin American
popular music form that started in the '60s in Cuba and other countries
and rapidly spread among progressive singers and composers.) This did not

mean, however, that they all wanted to merge into a homogeneous group. Their backgrounds were as diverse as their interests and, even though they have performed with one another during and after the Pisotón years, each has maintained a personal profile.

Vázquez has been the most prolific and consistent of them all, and probably the most ambitious. An attentive and consistent spectator can discern the movement, choreographic, and conceptual questions she has asked herself while moving from one piece to another, from one period to another. She formed a company, Taller de Otra Cosa (Something Else Workshop) and under this umbrella produced her own work, that of her colleagues, and, especially, a very important festival called Rompeforma: Maratón de Baile, Performance y Visuales (Breakform: Dance, Performance and Visuals Marathon), co-organized with Merián Soto and coproduced with Pepatián, that presented five editions between 1989 and 1996.

Rompeforma was a key event in the development of the contemporary dance scene in Puerto Rico and, as a presenter of multidisciplinary pieces by Puerto Rican, Latin American, and U.S.-based Latino experimental artists, it also cultivated supportive sponsors and audiences and therefore served as a model for other festivals. Participants included Guillermo Gómez-Peña, Coco Fusco, Pepón Osorio, Patricia Regalado, Dhara Rivera, Rafael Trelles, Awilda Sterling-Duprey, Nelson Rivera, Antonio Martorell, Luis Eduardo Araneda, Patricia Hoffbauer, Javier Cardona, Eduardo Alegría, Rosa Luisa Márquez, Karen Langevin, Juan del Hierro, Ivette Román, Antonio Pantojas, David Zambrano, Teresa Hernández, Arthur Aviles, George Emilio Sanchez, Elia Arce, Miguel Villafañe, and others, with support from the Institute of Puerto Rican Culture, the Rockefeller Foundation, the National Endowment for the Arts, and the University of Puerto Rico. In 1996, Rompeforma also produced a retrospective of Petra Bravo's work called *Retropetractiva*.

While teaching dance at the UPR Drama Department, Vázquez formed her group with colleagues and her best students, some of whom have become performers and choreographers in their own right: Teresa Hernández, who does dance-theater, Javier Cardona, Alejandra Martorell, and Eduardo Alegría, among many others. Vázquez, however, has not been creating as much in recent years because of her position in the institution's Humanities Department, where she teaches general education courses, but these courses have generated some interesting pieces for her students: *Plagio* (*Plagiarism* 2002, based on Augustine's *Confessions*), *MaRoma* (2006, based on Virgil's

*Aeneid* and a Passolini film; Vázquez's title is a play on words that refers to tumbling), and a work based on one of the cantos in Homer's *Iliad*, presented in 2005 at the University of Puerto Rico as part of a twenty-four-hour "marathon" in which each canto was read or performed.

Stylistically, Viveca Vázquez creates strange and bizarre movements in choreographic phrases that suggest fragmentation, contrast, and multiplicity (see *Riversa* 1997). Her work is physically, conceptually, and choreographically risky, questioning dance while affirming itself as such. One of her most eloquent interrogations is carried out through her oppositional strategies: weird, eccentric movements are picked apart into their smallest and most nuanced elements while body sections are isolated or contrasted (arms from legs, head from torso), or as energy, rhythms, and effects are sharply juxtaposed (speed and calm, compression and dispersion, affirmation and challenge of gravity, large and small, balance and off-balance, control and collapse, form and content, multiplicity and ellipsis).

This style generates a sense of urgency and strangeness reinforced by the titles of her pieces. Most are clever wordplays (¡*Uy!* [*Scary!*] and *Maladjusted* of 2002, *Kan't Translate—Tradúcelo, Mast-urbana, Mascando inglés* [Chewing English or Spitting Out English of 1984]), difficult, if not impossible, to translate (in this, as in many other aspects, Vázquez's work is part of a tendency in Puerto Rican contemporary literature and art.) These decomposed, dis-mantled, dis-ordered titles underscore Vázquez's aesthetic of fragmentation, which is also present in her musical collages, voice-overs, props, program notes, and extravagant costumes (in color, design, and outright discordance, like a stiff pink tulle tutu over a T-shirt for a melancholic female solo called "Happy birthday, sweetie"). These elements are not organized hierarchically nor do they achieve synthesis; instead, they generate a proliferation of signification, produced by a dense syntax that forces the audience to look at one thing while overlooking another and to compose their own interpretations, even different ones at different showings.

Vázquez repeatedly returns to two topics: sexual politics and nation formation. Her approach to gender is thematic and formal, referential and expressive. Judith Butler explains that gender is socially constructed through a performative practice within which resistance is possible through cultural strategies that generate "discontinuity or subversive dissonance" (Butler 1990, 1993), a theorization that helps to understand Vázquez's strategies. For example, male and female dancers execute the same steps, with the same

Figure 15.1. Viveca Vázquez and Taller de Otra Cosa. *Mascando inglés* (Chewing English) (1984). Dancers: Viveca Vázquez, Alejandra Martorell, Eduardo Alegría, and Teresa Hernández. Photo by Miguel Villafañe; used by permission.

tempo and energy, sometimes in unison, others alternately, questioning and subverting conventional Puerto Rican choreographic patterns and thus highlighting the dissonance that treats gender as something cultural and shifting, not intrinsic or essential. By not stating this directly but constructing it choreographically, this dissonance also generates multiple meanings, some overtly at odds with one another, and multiple identities, communicated expressively through the pieces' nonlineal narratives. By choreographing sequences in which feminine and heterosexual "behaviors," gestures, or attitudes are performed by men and women, by hetero and same sex couples, her pieces illustrate how gender is not a fixed category. Thus Vázquez constructs gender as a fiction and alerts us about sliding back into repetition and confirmation of the norm.

Nation formation has been the major topic of Puerto Rican art for many decades, perhaps even centuries, because of the country's colonial status under Spain and later the United States. This topic, when invoked as a moral imperative, as it often has been, demands sameness; difference is made invisible, and an essentialist identity is thus reinforced. As Jossianna Arroyo has stated, "in Puerto Rican society race, gender, and sexuality are discursive orders organized through 'invisibility' and silence," to the point that for these performers to tackle them is to deal with stigmatized topics that appear "absent." Furthermore, she adds: "Ideas of 'whiteness' and of a harmonious multiracial or democratic society are connected, then, to an intellectual/ cultural discourse of [a] Puerto Rican harmonious 'nationality'" (Arroyo 2002, 155). The past decades, however, have seen a change; perspectives in the arts have diversified as artists struggle to represent the nation differently, and more inclusively. Vázquez has contributed to this change, spearheaded by literature, the visual arts, and artists from other disciplines.

In exploring and welcoming dissonance, contradiction, the anxiety of misunderstanding, even a multiplicity of utopias, Vázquez's choreography offers a different focus, and she has put it forth without actually *saying* it. Her work does not contain linear stories, clues, anecdotes, or events that accumulate and finally reach a crescendo and closure. On the contrary, her uncomfortably open endings underscore what is missing, up for grabs, or left unsaid. Instead of arriving at conclusions for the audience, she invites spectators, forces them even, to analyze an ongoing, unpredictable, and incomplete present. Stylistically, repetitions occur that are never identical, so that, by introducing new references, alternate interpretations are stimulated concerning, for example, a fragmented nation whose symbolic energy does not aspire to an impossible unanimity (as in *En-tendido* [*Under-stood*, 1988], *Mascando Inglés*, and *Tribu-to* [a play on words referring to a tribute and to a tribe, a family]). Thus, she makes power structures relative, de-centering their regulatory force.

Awilda Sterling-Duprey, on the other hand, has brought popular, folk, and Afro-Caribbean dance and contexts to her choreographies. She incorporates music and steps from these dance traditions, then unpacks and recombines them with nonreferential abstract or everyday movements. In some pieces, like her semi-autobiographical *Pieza de balcón* (*Balcony Piece*), the thematic and stylistic references help her tell a story, *her* story and history retold. In others, the contrasted or broken-down movements inscribe a different story, full of dissension and discordance, creating challenging and often subversive readings.

Sterling-Duprey's choreography uses rhythm strikingly, often shifting the music's accents through the use of a bodily stillness that suggests a serene atmosphere and at the same time an uproar just beneath the surface. The deployment of the body in space as well as its movements come about slowly, letting rhythms reverberate gradually while making the spectator adjust to her time frame and her terms. This plays with anticipations, often proving them wrong, and draws the audience into the choreographer's unhurried and deliberate use of the body, paying attention to each body part independently as it is presented. Details are minute, but the rhythm with which they are presented helps us remember and incorporate them into the whole.

Presently, Sterling-Duprey continues to rely on improvisation to discover and compose her pieces, but she is also working with more Afro-Caribbean and Yoruba elements in an effort to understand her Caribbean identity and cultural context and to develop new vocabularies that can enrich her movement concepts. Working with more concrete referents that come from the deities, the music, and the movement phrases, she searches for the space *between* this vocabulary and her usual abstract style and idiom in order to determine what to use and where it can take her (as she explores in her 2007 production, *Introspectiva*, a play on words combining "introspection" and "retrospective," describing the combination of new and old pieces presented).

Sterling-Duprey's strong foundations in Afro-Caribbean and popular culture were enriched by her early performances with the marginalized and idiosyncratic black Puerto Rican dancer, choreographer, and singer Sylvia del Villard, who studied African and African American dances and culture as a student at Fisk University in Nashville, Tennessee (probably in the late '50s). When del Villard returned to Puerto Rico, she choreographed evening-length pieces for her company that included poetry, song, and dances combining Afro-Caribbean and modern dance elements. She did this in the early to mid-'60s, when the island was still wary of acknowledging its African roots and preferred to emphasize its Hispanic past.

Petra Bravo, a gifted teacher, has created work that explores many different formal and thematic aspects of dance and culture. While working with ballet dancers, she has favored a more contemporary idiom in mostly nonreferential, abstract, nonthematic, movement-focused pieces, basically offering the dancers the opportunity to use their bodies and technique in new ways. These pieces can sometimes be considered modern ballet, as a grounded energy or parallel placement of the legs and feet accompanies the use of balletic steps. While performing her own pieces and choreographing for experimental dancers and students, on the other hand, she has often relied on everyday movements to reflect gender and ideological issues.

The second generation of experimental dancers and choreographers—

Eduardo Alegría, Javier Cardona, Teresa Hernández, and Alejandra Martorell, among others—have worked with most of these choreographers, if not all of them. Some received their early dance training from Viveca Vázquez and performed with her consistently over the years, traveling back and forth from New York and participating in workshops or performing with groups elsewhere, especially in New York and Latin America. Cardona and Hernández also trained as actors, so this experience and these resources play important roles in their work.

Javier Cardona's best known piece is *You Don't Look Like* (1996), a solo in which he questions and parodies social constructions of race, gender, and sexualities in Puerto Rico and the Caribbean. With mirrors, photographs, and costumes, as well as a verbal text, Cardona considers the all-too-common stereotypes of a black savage, an Afro-Caribbean clubby rumba dancer, a black *jíbaro* or peasant, a basketball player, a rap singer, a black maid, a Santería priestess, and, finally, a blacker than black blackfaced actor with an afro wig, in order to understand, critique, and redefine from within historical and contemporary representations of the black body. Cardona's stretched-out, elegant, pliant body in motion actively contradicts the labels piled upon it as well as any expectations of the "essences" of a male black body (see Arroyo 2002, 153–171, for an analysis of the piece that unfortunately excludes its movement text almost entirely).

With *Ah, mén* (2004), Cardona again looks into gender issues by exploring the male stereotypes that condition masculine and "non-masculine" behavior and movement. With a cast of five men, he presents different segments in which conventional situations concerning friendship, affection, and desire are recontextualized through cross-dressing, dancing in couples, humor, text, and the expression of emotions that evolve from aggression to tenderness.

Teresa Hernández has dedicated most of her creative work to creating characters, mostly in solo pieces that home in on gender and ideological topics. Her texts are both spoken and danced, one intensifying the perspective of the other. Some characters are more straightforward and their movement text is basically supportive, like a very mundane Spanish nun who critiques the difficulties of everyday life, or a government employee who complements her meager salary by selling jewelry from the back of her car. Others parody the spoken text, as in the case of her cultural commentator Isabella, accompanied by her sidekick Fernando (as in the king and queen of Spain when Columbus was setting out for America). Isabella pokes fun at the likes of herself through a postmodern babble while her jolty, off-kilter dance gives away the commentator's total lack of understanding of what she is saying and the discomfort her role produces, reminding the audience that Isabella, who turns into the character on stage, right in front of us, is pure theatrics.

Other characters say one thing while insinuating another, so that when they dance, this nonverbal expression presents a contrasting or an illuminating discourse, as is the case with one of her characters in a full-evening "play" that ferociously critiques the nostalgia of the many dance and theater pieces that purportedly narrate an essentialist Puerto Rican nationhood. This character tells how her voice has been surgically altered through two "interventions" (the Spanish and the American colonizations of Puerto Rico?), in order to eliminate the local voice and assume a more "global" one (Spanish vs. English?); she then dances when she is supposed to be singing. Her dance, mostly on the floor and full of spastic twitches and abrupt changes, emphasizes hybridity as a form of resistance. While the text turns somewhat platitudinous, the dance opens up avenues of expression and critique.

Hernández's thirst for a community that can nourish creation and creativity fuels her late 2006 piece, *Nada que ver* (meaning "nothing to see" as well as "neither here nor there" or "quite another"), in which she reviews her past work and the sources—technical, creative, and scholarly—she has sought to understand and foster it. Structurally, it consolidates a pattern: pieces that start out with verbal texts, establishing a character and a context, culminate with a danced text. The piece suggests an ending, that of exhaustion, while acknowledging the urgency of creative expression.

Jesús Miranda is another contemporary choreographer who trained, as so many dancers do today, in many forms: folk dance, ballet, modern dance (the Lester Horton technique at the Alvin Ailey school as well as with Julio Rivera, a U.S.-based Puerto Rican dancer, choreographer, and teacher who trained with Alvin Ailey and Joyce Trisler and later directed his own company, Contemporary Motions). He has danced professionally with Rivera in the United States as well as with Ballet Concierto de Puerto Rico, Andanza, the contemporary dance company, and independently. His first choreographies were set on ballet dancers and were balletic in nature, but he turned to a more contemporary style that makes full use of the floor alongside slides, bends, stretches, and lifts. He choreographs solos as well as for groups of all sizes; his use of large groups is strikingly graceful.

Miranda's pieces are very clear, his steps precise, with well-developed phrases whose energies and direction extend or contrast with the previous ones and are attuned to each body's possibilities. He is very sensitive to his dancers' skills and talents, always extending these but only insofar as the patterns make sense, not for effect. The dancers, one or a large group, always look good in his pieces, whether executing steps in unison or each one a different step or sequence.

Miranda has also created pieces with Puerto Rican themes, but, contrary to the usual formula, the emotions or impressions the landscapes or places provoke in him and in contemporary culture are re-created through dance. Except for symbols used in the sets, for example, there are no literal references in dances like *Clear Cavern*, 1988, reminiscent of caves in the karstic rock formations along the island's north coast; *Portal to El Yunque*, 1991, relating to the Puerto Rican rain forest; or *Mabokadama*, 1996, inspired by a Taíno Indian ceremonial center.

Other choreographers have contributed to the experimental and contemporary dance scene, among them Oscar Mestey, a painter who also trained in folk, modern, and jazz dance forms, and Myrna Renaud, who trained in modern dance and brings bomba, Santería, and popular dance references to her pieces. Mestey is aesthetically very close to the chance strategies and sound and movement style of Merce Cunningham and John Cage, but as an early member of Taller de Histriones, he choreographed a piece for that company called *Petroglyphs*, which refers to the rock carvings left by our Taíno Indians. In my recollection, the style was closer to modern dance idioms in which the solar plexus, the contraction, and a strong gravitational pull predominated. He later choreographed for ballet and experimental dancers alike, as well as for himself, with movement sequences pared down to the essence. Mestey has also done set and costume designs for dance pieces.

Although all these choreographers do not fit under the "experimental dance" umbrella, they have undoubtedly opened up a space for themselves and developed an appreciative audience that learns and grows with them. The frequency of their presentations, the festivals and seasons they organized, both local and international, as well as the alternatives they offered in the '80s and '90s are sorely missed.

## What Is Happening Now

Although the experimental dance scene has been less active than it was during its first two decades, pleasant surprises promise continued creativity. Karen Langevin, a choreographer and one of Vázquez's long-term dancers, recently presented an unusual piece called *Atlas consentido* (*Nurtured Atlas* and also *Meaningful Atlas*, 2006), an atlas of the body within, bones and all, and of the world beyond, on which she collaborated with Alejandra Martorell and Eduardo Alegría, as well as with Lydia Platón and Yamil Collazo. Under Langevin's conceptual umbrella, each one contributed with improvisations, music, video, or lyrics to speak about how art produces well-being by resisting, through beauty and laughter, the triviality, pettiness, and pessimism of our times. Langevin's long and improvisational solo, as well as her dances with others, made extensive use of the off-balance, the brink she challenged and recovered from, an apt analogy for the piece's all-encompassing nurturing and meaningfulness.

On the other hand, the contemporary dance company Andanza has been a major force on the scene since 2000. It is the dream-come-true of Artistic Director Lolita Villanúa, who trained and performed as a ballet dancer in Puerto Rico and the United States and was a member of the excellent Grupo Corpo of Brazil for several years. She has developed this project with two colleagues, María Teresa Robles, former principal dancer of Ballet Concierto de Puerto Rico, and Carlos Iván Santos, also a former principal dancer of Ballet Concierto and a Boston Ballet soloist for many years. At this point in time, Andanza brings together a group of ten dancers who are some of the best on the island. Although they come from different backgrounds and certainly keep their personalities, it is interesting to see how rapidly they assimilate into the company's style.

This style is based on different techniques and forms, including ballet, modern, experimental and postmodern, even some jazz. Andanza's basic maintenance training is ballet, although they also take modern dance classes with different teachers to study their idioms and approaches. Theirs is a highly charged style that covers a lot of space, with complex and fast sequences, usually full of extensions, slides, lunges, partnering, and lifts. The dancers are generally in flat shoes, sometimes bare feet, never a toe shoe or dance slipper in sight, and the body tends to be in the parallel placement. Music is regularly commissioned, and live music is used as often as pos-

Figure 15.2. *Lienzos* (Canvases) (2003) performed by Andanza, choreography by Lolita Villanúa. Photo by Robert Villanúa; used by permission.

sible, an unusual occurrence in the Puerto Rican dance scene, while collaborations with visual artists, fashion designers, and other colleagues are cultivated (as in the early Ballets de San Juan days).

Since the beginning, the company has had a connection to Brazilian dance through invited choreographers and dancers, whose pieces greatly enrich the repertory. Andanza's most ambitious piece, for example, is choreographed by Antonio Gomes, a Switzerland-based choreographer, whose *Death and Life* (2003), set to Mozart's *Requiem* and Philip Glass's *Concerto for Violin and Orchestra*, represents the company's aspirations and capacity, which go far beyond those envisioned by more established companies. "Death," the first part, includes ten dancers, ten actors (or alter egos to the dancers), a full choir, the *Requiem*'s four soloists, and a full orchestra. The second part, "Life," is true to the Glass score, minimalist and spare, with ten dancers and a violinist on stage.

Themes of elation or despair, conviviality or separation, individuality or community characterize Andanza's pieces, with some clearly related to contemporary island issues. They are seldom narrative or linear; rather, they tend to insinuate and suggest through their atmosphere. However, a few years ago the Casals Festival (a Puerto Rican institution, founded by cellist Pablo Casals in 1957, that included dance in its first editions) commissioned Andanza to do Stravinsky's *The Soldier's Tale* (2003), choreographed by Michael Uthoff. The company also performed a danced version of Rosa Luisa Márquez and Antonio Martorell's *Family Portrait* (2002), a theater piece in which scenes of family life are told and photographed, only to affirm their theatricality at the end when the performers tear off the elaborate paper costumes designed in collaboration with the audience before the performance.

While the company's style is still in flux, there is always a contagious atmosphere of joy and, even after several years, of accomplishment. The audience received them enthusiastically at their first season, has grown to admire their quality and professionalism, and supports their presentations and community projects.

## What's Next

While dance is funded mostly by the government, the Institute of Puerto Rican Culture, the state arts agency, does not have a dance department (as it has for most other arts), and dance is placed in the theater department, where its relevance is often questioned by those who want to see all funds go to drama. This has not helped to further development and professionalization of dance.

Contemporary and experimental dance is still a work in progress in today's Puerto Rico. Funds have been coming up short, options have diminished, and very few opportunities exist to see a variety of classic and new dance expressions from abroad, as we lack the producers, venues, and festivals that include dance. This does not help to develop dancers and choreographers, nor does it contribute to the development of a knowledgeable and discerning audience. We do not lack young dancers and aspiring choreographers, however, some of whom are turning not only to the United States, but also to Europe and Latin America for further training and to New York for performance opportunities. Andanza's achievements, as well as recent presentations such as Langevin's *Atlas consentido* and Hernández's *Nada que ver* infuse the dance scene with optimism.

# DOMINICA

# 16

# Bele and Quadrille

## African and European Dimensions in the Traditional Dances of Dominica, West Indies

JANET WASON

"This quadrille came out in, we dancing that after slavery. My quadrille is after slavery. That is the first dance after slavery. . . . That came out in the root in Africa, our quadrille. . . . It's an old woman and an old man open the quadrille after slavery," said a dance practitioner in Woodford Hill, Dominica in 1986. (Wason 1987, 80).

In the Commonwealth of Dominica, two dance genres reflect the island's creole heritage. One, which comprises the bele—bele pitjé, bele soté, bele djouba, and related dances such as the rikitik—carries the hallmarks of its African forebears. The other, which includes group dances such as the quadrille and lancers, and couple dances such as the mazouk and the heel and toe polka, is clearly a descendant of nineteenth-century European ballroom dance. As with other dances in the Afro-Caribbean diaspora, each genre has to a greater or lesser extent absorbed elements of the other.

Once entwined in the daily fabric of life, whether as recreation or communal outlet, by the latter part of the twentieth century the dances were performed mainly at cultural events, national holidays, and religious (Catholic) feast days. Various factors have kept the traditional dances alive as part of the cultural heritage. Arguably, the most important one is the National Day competitions. In the series of competitions, the island's seven districts compete in the various dance categories as well as in other folk arts such as patwa story and jing-ping music. Winners then perform at the Cultural Gala, held every year on November 3rd as a showcase for the performing arts. The competitions were started in 1965 by then-prime minister Edward LeBlanc.

LeBlanc was able to build on earlier work by people such as folklorist Mabel "Cissie" Caudeiron, who, as early as the 1940s, arranged performances of the Kwéyòl African-based arts. As a proponent of creole nationalism, LeBlanc used the competitions as a means to preserve national heritage and foster national identity. This initiative paralleled activities in other islands, such as Trinidad's Best Village competitions.

In July 1986, I arrived in Dominica on a project to research and record the country's traditional dances. Funded by the Agence de Coopération Culturelle et Technique (ACCT, an international body serving Francophone nations) and administered through the Ministry of Community Development's Cultural Division, the project continued the government's mandate to preserve and promote the country's cultural heritage. The project lasted six months and comprised newspaper research, interviews, participant observation, and videotaping sessions. With the assistance of local cultural experts and Kwéyòl speakers, I was able to engage in numerous interviews and dance sessions with dancers, musicians, and community members. Particularly memorable were the group gatherings when elderly practitioners talked about dance in pre-1965 days. The project culminated with two day-long videotaping sessions. With the aid of a local media company, we were able to capture fourteen different dances, examples of most of the Dominican repertoire. Six different groups performed, representing a variety of styles from the north and south of the island. The resulting videotapes are accompanied by a report describing the dances and recording some of the choreographies; these reside both with the government and with ACCT. Researching the dances of the indigenous people (descendants of the early Caribs still living in Dominica) lay outside the scope of my project. Daryl Phillip and Gary Smith's book, *The Heritage Dances of Dominica* (1998), discusses their dance forms.

For me, a recent graduate in dance history, the opportunity to immerse myself in these dances was a dream come true. The Dominicans I encountered danced these forms with vitality, verve, and skill, and shared their knowledge generously. They saw the dances as expressions of their dual heritages, acknowledging the central role of their African roots in shaping their island culture. Dominican historian Lennox Honychurch (1984, 60) noted that "the African rhythm and tempo were added to the dances of European origin. . . . Probably the earliest dance, the root, and the one that seems to have survived stronger than the rest is the 'Bele.' The African influence appears to be untouched by other dance or music forms." Given their importance to national identity, what are some ways in which the dances express Dominica's dual heritage? Taking the bele and quadrille as representative, I shall use observations and quotations found in my report to describe the dances as I encountered them in 1986. I shall also discuss selected aspects that may be considered to have European or African movement qualities. In doing so, my goal is to deepen understanding of this rich dance culture. (I delivered an earlier version of this chapter as part of a video presentation at the 2006 World Dance Alliance Global Assembly in Toronto.)

## The Land, the People: A Brief Overview

The island of Dominica lies at the center of the chain of Caribbean islands. It is sandwiched between the French overseas departments of Guadeloupe to the north and Martinique to the south. English is the official language, but when I worked there in 1986, some people, mainly older people, spoke only Creole or Kwéyòl, a language based on French words and African sentence structure. Although Dominica was British for more than 200 years until its independence in 1978, the first European settlers were from the French islands, and that French influence has remained strong. Agriculture—mainly bananas and coconuts—is the chief economic mainstay. The country's motto is "Après Bondie, C'est La Ter—After God, the Land," and in 1986, everyone, even urban dwellers, had some tie to the land (Honychurch 1991, 18).

Slightly less than 300 square miles in area, Dominica is the most mountainous island in the Caribbean. That landscape determined settlement patterns, which in turn had a profound effect on the culture. Because the island is mountainous, most settlements of any size are along the coast. The island was completely linked by roads only in the 1960s. Most interactions between the villages and the towns of Roseau and Portsmouth could be accomplished only by long journeys by foot or by sea. Villages were isolated and virtually self-reliant. Jocelyne Guilbault (1998a, 840) suggests that because of this, five distinct musical cultures developed. My observations in 1986 identified obvious choreographic and stylistic differences between dances from the north and south of the island, but further investigation may well have uncovered comparable distinct dance cultures, though now in the twenty-first century perhaps blurred by time.

The rugged interior also presented a barrier to other methods of communication. For example, at the end of 1986, much of the east coast was still without electric lines or telephone service, though villagers were by no means behind the times, because gasoline generators and batteries provided power for radio and television. Nevertheless, the quadrille and other dances formed a part of people's entertainment until well into the twentieth century. For example, in Riviere Cyrique, on the east coast, some villagers were still dancing the traditional forms as recreation when the National Day competitions started in 1965 (Wason 1987, 17).

Mountainous and heavily forested, Dominica was thought unsuitable for the large sugar plantations found in islands such as Barbados and Jamaica. Although it changed hands a number of times in the years after Columbus landed on the island in 1493, by 1750 the island provided a livelihood for poorer whites from France. It offered an opportunity, as well, for free people of color (people of African descent or mixed race who were not enslaved) from neighboring Martinique and Guadeloupe to own land. These groups established small holdings requiring a minimum of slave labor. Up to this point, few slaves came directly from Africa; most were trans-shipped from other islands or were creole, meaning born in the West Indies (Honychurch 1984, 38). This changed in 1763 when the British gained Dominica as part of the Treaty of Paris. For the British landowners the focus of the economy became large agricultural plantations, including sugar, and that required more slave labor.

Even after the British abolished their slave trade in 1807, Dominica still saw at least two more influxes of Africans. In 1834, Africans (probably from Sierra Leone) were brought over as indentured laborers. In 1838, a boatload of Africans who had been liberated from the foreign slave trade by the British Navy landed in Dominica. These people settled primarily in the north of the island, in areas such as Woodford Hill. According to Lennox Honychurch in "Africa and Dominica" on his Web site, the local villagers distinguished these new arrivals by the epithet "Africans." One elderly bele practitioner from Woodford Hill recalled how, as a child, she had been exhorted to dance like an African. It is possible that elements of the bele of Woodford Hill stem from that period, though certainly eighteenth-century observers, such as the painter Agostino Brunias, recorded dances with features reminiscent of the twentieth-century bele.

Originally, creolization meant simply the adaptive effects of living in a new environment. Today, the more common meaning, as defined by the

"Encyclopedia of Cajun Culture," is a "coming together of diverse cultural traits or elements . . . to form new traits or elements." At this point, I'd like to offer a few thoughts on how the coming together of dance elements might have occurred, Dominica style. In their 1988 article, Szwed and Marks describe the process by which enslaved Africans in the American south adopted European dance forms and their reasons for doing so. A similar process may have been going on in some situations in Dominica. In addition, because the holdings were smaller, a closer relationship likely would have existed between owner and slave, with a consequent transference of customs back and forth (Honychurch 1984, 39).

As well, in the eighteenth century, free people of color, who could also be slave owners, aligned themselves with their French heritage, adopting European customs as much as they were able. They formed the basis of the class known in the nineteenth century as the mulatto elite. According to Mitchell (2005, 2), "at every level of society, free people of color interacted with enslaved and white people of comparable status." In an interview for the project, Honychurch explained that class boundaries in Dominican society were loose, with a flow of members between one stratum and another, allowing mingling of dances and movement styles.

> You have the urban mulatto like people in Roseau . . . [who] would be having their balls. . . . And parallel to that, you get the little houses in the villages or the schoolrooms . . . with their Quadrilles and Lancers. . . . but it did not mean that the mulatto elite would not hear of a dance going on in Massacre and ride from Roseau to Massacre. . . . And although they would get . . . respectful positions in the dance, they would dance with the fishwife . . . so there was a lot of intermingling which meant that naturally the influences interplayed. (Wason 1987, 16)

## The Dances: Bele

Bele forms part of Dominica's oral tradition; its origins are thus difficult to pinpoint. Dominicans I interviewed in 1986 can trace the bele back to the turn of the twentieth century, and it is likely that the form is much older. Franco (1999, iii) suggests that the bele originated in the French colonies of Saint-Domingue (Haiti), Martinique, and Guadeloupe, then was carried to other Caribbean islands as territories changed hands during the eighteenth century. Phillip and Smith (1998, 22) mention an elderly source who "stated that elders in his family had always told their children that the nèg mawon originated bélé." Dominica had settlements of Maroons or escaped slaves as early as the 1760s (Honychurch 1984, 70).

The two basic dance types of bele are distinguished by tempo; the bele pitjé is slower than the bele soté, and the faster tempo is also known as the bele djouba in certain areas. There are other dances that people called "play on the bele" or "bele play," because they are sequences devised for amusement, accompanied by the bele drum. Some others in the 1986 repertoire were the rikitik (Woodford Hill), the ophelia (Paix Bouche), and saywa zozyo (Laplaine). Honychurch lists a variety of dances, including the priorité, rickety, and contredanse, that most likely fall into the category of bele play.

As described by one practitioner, a typical bele event starts with the drum, the tanmbou bele, made from a hollowed tree trunk or a small rum barrel with a goatskin stretched over it. There is just the one drum, held between the legs of the seated drummer, who plays it with his hands. Sometimes another player kneels beside the drum, beating a steady pulse on it with one hand. In some areas, such as Grand Bay in the south, the drum is accompanied by a ting-ting or triangle, which can be an actual triangle or a length of metal pipe. Under a tree in some open space, the drummer starts playing, and people start gathering. The dancing space is circular, circumscribed by the spectators, who can become participants. A woman with a strong voice, the *chantwelle*, sings out the call, and the chorus, or *lavwe*, responds; the dancers join in. Usually a man, or *kavalyé*, starts the dancing, selecting a woman, or *danm*, from the crowd to dance with him. The dancers first dance one at a time, then together. Franco suggests that the inclusion of a dancing couple, a formation alien to West African dance, has its roots in the minuet and other eighteenth-century couple dances (1999, 38). Because of the performance criteria, bele for competitions and festivals is choreographed in a set sequence of dancers entering together, kavalyé dances, danm (woman) dances; then they dance together.

Although the event allows the entire community to participate, whether as singers or spectators, successful performance of the bele requires special skills. Informants refer to themselves as having a "talent" for dancing or singing and become identified as such. Often the skills are handed down

Figure 16.1. Woodford Hill Bele Group performing bele at Heritage Day in La Plaine, October 26, 1986. Dancers: Octavia Laville and Johnny Skerrit; Chantwel: Magdalena Andrew. By Janet Wason; used by permission.

through the generations, so that frequently bele practitioners in a village come from one extended family, as in the Bioche and Woodford Hill bele groups. (Wason 1987, 24).

In bele the emphasis is on rhythm, shown in the feet slapping the earth, in the drum rhythms, in the relationship between dancer and drummer. The rhythm is in duple meter, and a bele step occurs in a unit of four beats or counts. Many of the steps appear islandwide, under different names, or with no name at all, albeit with different weight emphases and variations peculiar to each dancer. The stationary step known as the *pitjé* in the south is performed in different communities across the island, and by both men and women. With the weight poised over the balls of the feet, the dancer thrusts the ball of the right foot into the ground (counts 1, 2), steps in place with the left foot (count 3), steps right foot beside the left, at the same time releasing the left foot, ready to repeat the step unit (count 4). Traveling steps are performed with a spring; younger dancers often appear to bounce off the ground. The steps can also cover a fair amount of space, a modification introduced when the dance was transferred to the proscenium stage.

The *gwiji* appears islandwide under that name, both in the bele and also in the quadrille. Known also as a "Congo step" (Phillip and Smith 1998, 54), the gwiji is a traveling step, used by both men and women, either when dancing together in waltz position, or separately, as when spinning. In it, the dancer moves by alternately stepping on the weight-bearing leg and pushing off with the free foot; the step does not change weight.

The torso is relaxed and quiet, with no separate movement in the shoulder or ribcage. The back is kept straight, usually with a slight forward inclination. The degree of pelvic motion varies, depending on the nature of the dance step and on the inclination of the dancer. Arms for the most part act as a counterbalance—men can dance with arms outstretched or placed on the hips to draw attention to their footwork; women can spread their skirts wide with both hands in a gesture reminiscent of eighteenth-century deportment, or loop one section up over a hip, arm akimbo, shaking or flicking the rest of the skirt with the other. What differentiates the bele from African dancing, in my opinion, is that the rhythm is expressed through the footwork, for the most part, rather than through the total body, again suggesting the influence of eighteenth-century European dance characterized by a quiet body but intricate footwork.

In a practice similar to that in the Congo (Crowell 2002, 12) and to the bomba of Puerto Rico, the dancer dictates the drummer's rhythm. The change from one rhythm to another, from one step to another, is marked by a movement called a "cut." One dancer remembered, "Papa tell me as long as you dancing bele and you not making cut, you not dancing bele yet. . . . You must make cut for you to dance bele." The cut is an accent movement. Men's cuts include karate-like kicks, sudden stops with the legs wide apart, dropping the weight suddenly so that the knees bend as the heels release from the ground, or jumping in front of the drum with legs together and arms stretched wide. Women's cuts involve flicking or shaking the skirt with a fair amount of force, almost hurling themselves at the drum before resuming the dance (for a discussion of the "cut" in West African dance, see Thompson 1974, 18–22).

Bele songs are always sung in Kwéyòl, reflecting current events, whether personal or political. One informant recalled that in Grand Bay, bele songs used to be *mépwi*: "harsh words" or "quarrel" songs. All aspects of a quarrel could be put in a song which acted as a safety valve. In one instance, the late Ma Tou-Tou, the village's grande dame, had a philandering husband named Anayé. Whenever he returned from visiting his girlfriend, La-La, Ma Tou-Tou would beat her drum and sing "Anayé óti La-La, way" (Anayé, where is La-La, wai) (Wason 1987, 41). Because it became the custom to take old songs, whether quarrel, rude, or sexually explicit, and change the words while retaining the chorus, that phrase could still be heard in songs in 1986. Many of the newer songs talk about Dominican heritage and culture, natural resources, or current political events.

Participants in the bele had been, and still were in 1986, villagers who worked the land and fished for a living. Class or occupation defined the choice of recreational dance to a large extent, but there was also the question of inclination. Many people who shared the same lifestyle as bele practitioners preferred the quadrille, perhaps for religious reasons or because it was associated with a "better" way of life. As an African-based dance, the bele carried the stigma of slavery and was considered suitable only for peasants and lower classes (see also Phillip and Smith 1998, 131). As well, the liberal use of rum, suggestive pelvic movements, and the display of petticoats and legs by the female dancers gave rise to the attitude, still prevalent at the time in some circles, that bele practitioners were drunkards capable of anything.

Although Stubbs suggests that in the past bele might have been connected with an African ancestral belief system (1973, 11), as described by Dominicans in 1986, it is a pastime, a mating, or a competitive dance. I found no mention of African spiritual traditions when I was there (see also Franco 1999, 21). Guilbault (1998a, 840) states that "Roman Catholicism had taught [Dominicans] to believe that African-derived traditions were 'uncultured,' 'demonic,' and 'evil'"; however, according to one cultural expert, the Catholic Church had always tolerated traditional dance forms (Wason 1987, 42). Indeed, bele is particularly associated with two Catholic feast days, Fete la Saint Pierre (Fisherman's Feast) and Fete St. Isidore (Workers' Holiday), which are always initiated with a mass. Since many elements of Afro-Caribbean ritual—drumming, dancing, the use of rum—still exist in the bele, it is likely that the Church allowed Dominicans to retain the form of the dance while eradicating the traditional meaning.

Certainly, bele's communal nature could be used to the Church's advantage. People in Castle Bruce related how, on moonlit nights, the parish priest organized a bele group to dig the foundations for the new church. Attracted by the sound of the drum, the villagers took turns digging and dancing.

With the aid of a few bottles of rum, they danced and worked late into the night. During the dark of the moon, the priest organized a prayer group after the main work was accomplished (Wason 1987, 43).

Although no trace of African spiritual traditions associated with the bele appeared, other conversations hinted that communication with the spirit world is part of it. For example, with dancing and singing and drinking rum putting the heat in people, they would stay out until midnight to see if *adjables* ("La Diablesse," who appears in the guise of a beautiful woman, but with a donkey's leg hidden beneath her skirts) would come. One elderly female drummer (drummers I encountered were mostly men), could tell when the spirit had arrived because her hands got very light and she could feel someone drumming along with her (Wason 1987, 43).

## The Quadrille

The quadrille belongs to the category of dances Dominicans call the "jing-ping" dances, which, as recorded in 1986, included the lancers, three types of flirtations, the waltz au vien, the heel and toe polka, four types of mazouk, and the sotis. I have been unable to find a European counterpart for the flirtations, a mixer-type circle dance; for the others, the dance names and choreography indicate that these are descendants of elite social dances created in the first half of the nineteenth century: the quadrille, lancers, waltz, polka, mazurka, and schottische. In order to place the quadrille in context, I would like to give a brief overview of social dance in the nineteenth century. For an in-depth exploration of all aspects of dance at that time, please see *From the Ballroom to Hell* by Elizabeth Aldrich (1991).

The dances were first seen in aristocratic European ballrooms, especially those of Paris and London. For example, the scandalously intimate form of the waltz, with its revolutionary, face-to-face close hold (prior to that, couples danced side by side) appeared in London around 1812 (Richardson 1960, 63). The polka became the rage in Paris in 1843 and was brought to London a year later. The quadrille, as described below, was first danced in Paris in the early years of the century before being introduced to London society in 1815 by Lady Jersey, one of the patronesses of Almack's, the exclusive London assembly rooms.

The contents of instructional dance manuals published in the late 1800s indicate that the dances remained popular throughout the century, although in a simpler form. They also show that a knowledge of dancing was still considered a mark of good breeding. In *Everybody's Guide to Ball-Room Dancing*, the British dance teacher, William Lamb (1898?, 8), wrote, "dancing is now so universal a recreation, and forms such an important feature in all domestic circles, that no one can well enter into society without possessing a knowledge of it." The association of quadrille dancing (as opposed to the bele) with a higher social status was still evident in Dominica in 1986.

Just as the latest fashions in dress spread from the centers of Paris and London, so, too, did the dances. As subjects of the British Empire, nineteenth-century Dominicans participated in colonial social life. Contemporary accounts in *The Dominican* mention balls given for visiting naval fleets, New Year's balls given by the governor of the time, and, in 1889, a costume ball where the dancing lasted all night (7 March 1889, 3). *The Dominican* was a liberal newspaper supported by the colored families (Borome 1969, 27; Honychurch 1984, 98). Another article proudly notes the publication of "The Roseau Polka," a "production . . . from the pen of our gifted young countryman, Mr Wilfred Kenneth Hamilton, who is at present pursuing his studies at a high class Grammar School in the Mother Country, and where his musical talents have been so much developed, that he has ventured on authorship" (14 March 1895, 2). Informants told me that quadrilles, lancers, and mazurkas were among the dances enjoyed in Roseau until after the First World War.

Like the waltz, the quadrille was a new dance for a new century. During the eighteenth century, the popular group dance had been the contredanse, the French adaptation of the lively English country dances of the previous century. Indeed, they called the longways formation the *contredanse anglaise* to distinguish it from the *contredanse française*, or square formation for two or four couples. The quadrille was compiled in the first decade of the nineteenth century from four of the most popular contredanses: Le Pantalon, L'Été, La Poule, and La Trenis, later replaced by La Pastourelle; a fifth figure, called simply "the Finale," was added a few years later. Each dance, or figure, as they were called, is composed of patterns with names such as *chaine anglaise*, *chaine des dames*, and *tour de deux mains*. Since the quadrille was formed from a selection of contredanses, any number of versions conceivably could exist. For example, the lancers, which rivaled the quadrille in popularity from mid-century on, was called the "lancers quadrille" when it first appeared around 1817 (Richardson 1960, 71). In reality, all references to the "quadrille" meant the original version, also known as the "First Set."

The dance is for four couples arranged in an inward-facing square. Hierarchy is built into the dance in that the head couple has their backs to the musicians, with the second couple positioned opposite. The third and fourth couples complete the sides of the square. Each dance figure is done twice, with the first two couples performing the various patterns while the other two couples wait their turn (in Dominica, these dancers are moving in place in time to the music) to repeat the dance. When the quadrille was first introduced in Europe, the steps used were various and intricate, including coupé, chassé, glissade, and assemblé. By the middle of the century, however, dancers "walked through" the various figures in time to the music. Although it was important to perform the dance accurately and gracefully, the emphasis was on social interaction. As the anonymous author of the *Canadian Ten Cent Ball-Room Companion Guide to Dancing* wrote, "the quadrille, though generally considered the slowest of dances, is, perhaps, about the pleasantest and most sociable ever contrived" (1871, 15).

Overall, the Dominica quadrille adheres to the structure of the nineteenth-century quadrille, with the rolling-hip dance style and syncopated accompaniment adding a distinctly Caribbean flavor. As in the early nineteenth-century version, this quadrille consists of four sections, which in most areas are called pieces or, in Kwéyòl, *fidji* (as in *pwemyé fidji, dézyem fidji,* and so on). In 1986, versions of the quadrille were numerous, with each village having its own particular variation (many of the choreographies are published in *The Heritage Dances of Dominica*); however, despite individual differences, a common structure prevails islandwide in that each piece or fidji is built around the same pattern. For example, in the first piece, couples cross over and back again; in the second, the kavalyé and opposite danm dance together, either in a circle inside the square or exchanging places across the set and back.

The fourth piece always contains the pattern called the "malengé," considered the highlight of the quadrille because it offers dancers, especially the kavalyé, an opportunity to show their individual qualities. In it, a kavalyé dances with two danm, leading them around the inside of the square, before handing them over, usually with a spin, to the opposite gentleman. Except for the third, which is known as "alma de," all pieces contain the relevant elements of the corresponding nineteenth-century figure. Interestingly, the Pe-

Figure 16.2. Tete Morne Cultural Group performing the malengé in the quadrille with leader Vernice Joseph St. Luce on the accordion; note the female drummer. December 14, 1986, taken at videotaping session on the road. By Janet Wason; used by permission.

tite Savanne version retains names resembling the original European names for each of the pieces: *pastouwel* (first piece), *lapoul* (second piece), *l'été* (third piece), *latrinitez* (fourth piece). In Woodford Hill the first three pieces are called *quadrille koupé*, *quadrille sek*, and *quadrille baloté*. The fourth piece is called the fourth figure, a name that occurs in other communities in the north, such as Paix Bouche.

The most obvious differences are between the quadrilles of the north and south, with the imaginary dividing line running through the top quarter of the island (from Dublanc across to Marigot). Reduced to their essence, the dances of the southern areas can be regarded as geometric structures, adhering to the principle that only opposite couples dance together. In contrast, the northern versions seem ornamented, with patterns like the ladies' chain repeated more than once, giving the impression of continuous circling. In addition, this version seems even more communal, since patterns in which all dancers participate are inserted between "regular" patterns in which only opposite couples dance. One example is the roundabout—here all four kavalyé progress counterclockwise around the set, turning each danm un-

Figure 16.3. Petite Savanne Cultural Group performing the malengé in the quadrille at an indoor videotaping session, Nov. 29, 1986. By Janet Wason; used by permission.

til they regain their own partners. There was lots of controversy over who danced the "real" quadrille, with some saying that northerners were really dancing the flirtations instead; however, an informant who traveled to both neighboring French islands stated that the quadrille of the north is the same as the one danced in Guadeloupe, while that of the south is danced as in Martinique (Wason 1987, 54; see also Bilby and Marks 1999).

In general, for both men and women, the posture is upright, but the loosely flexed knees and slightly curved spine establish a connection to the earth that contrasts with the European ideal of a pulled up or erect stance. Posture and movement style can differ, however, depending on the amount of European or African influence in a community. Some Dominicans hold their bodies upright and dance with the light quality associated with a European style of dancing—but with lots of hip movement, of course. Others show a more African configuration, adding a slight forward bend at the hips, a bent neck so the gaze is often focused on the ground, and a weighted feeling to their steps. The footwork includes walking in time to the music and variations such as a sequence of three steps and a touch, used in the pattern called the *balansé*. For fast-moving patterns such as the ladies' chain, traveling steps such as a step-touch-step sequence, divided between two beats of music, are used, as well as the *gwiji* (the bele Congo step), used most often when partners are dancing in waltz hold.

Prior to 1965, the quadrille was part of people's recreation and social interaction. In some areas, groups of friends would hold a dance at one of their homes on a rotational basis every Friday night. In places like Grand Bay, where dance halls opened in the mid-1930s, for a penny a dance from each gentleman, the musicians would play all evening. On certain occasions, dedicated dancers traveled to far-flung villages in search of entertainment. One gentleman from Paix Bouche recalled taking a boat from Dublanc to dance in Grand Bay (Wason 1987, 17). With the advent of annual competitions, the emphasis has shifted to the performance aspect of the dance, with dancers concentrating on structural elements such as footwork and floor patterns.

The quadrille and related dances are accompanied by a four-piece ensemble known as a jing-ping band. This reinterpretation of a European dance band is very much inspired by African percussion ensembles. The accordion is the single melody instrument. The other three provide rhythm: the tanmbou bas, a large flat drum, sets the tempo and carries the rhythm; the gwaj, a seed-filled container, augments the rhythm; the boom-boom, a long straight tube of bamboo or latterly PVC, is blown with a syncopated rhythm. Dance tunes consist of a few phrases of music, repeated as many times as required. The accordion player avoids monotony by improvising around the melody line, as do the other bandsmen who vary the rhythmic accompaniment. Nineteenth-century quadrilles were accompanied by tunes based on popular songs of the day, and so, too, was the Dominica quadrille. Though the practice was frowned upon by traditionalists, some musicians had begun to add variety to the long malengé section by incorporating hit songs and carnival road marches. Opinions differ about which instrument is more important for the dancers. I was told by an informant in Portsmouth that the drum cues the dancers: "The accordionist plays the song agreed . . . but the boss-man of the Quadrille is the drummer because he is the one who has to keep looking at the dancers" (Wason 1987, 75).

## Dimensions II: Aesthetic Considerations

In viewing African and African diasporic dance forms, scholars such as Robert Farris Thompson (1966) and Brenda Dixon Gottschild (1996, 2002), to name only two, have identified various common traits and aesthetic considerations. I will apply a few of their ideas in the following discussion.

Dominican dancers evince polyrhythmic and polycentric movement characteristics (see Dixon Gottschild 2002, 5) to varying degrees. The typical bele posture is upright with a slight forward inclination. The knees are flexed with the weight solidly balanced over the feet. The degree of flexion at the hips varies according to gender, region, or emotional intensity. In general, men bend farther forward from the hips than do women; dancers from Grand Bay remain mostly erect with only a slight degree of forward bend, while dancers from Woodford Hill in the north vary their posture by dancing erect or low to the ground. An individual may not move her or his body polyrhythmically, but I suggest that a woman manipulating her skirt, a European dress style, in the bele is expressing polyrhythm. In some ways, the quadrille seems to present more opportunity to display these characteristics, although subtly, for dancers can shake their hips and shoulders and bob heads, whether dancing in place or traveling through the figures. Women employ the rolling hip movement known as *woulé*, with the accepted degree of woulé varying from community to community. Above all, contrary to the practice in the European quadrille, the entire set is always moving, even when the dancers are standing in place, filling the whole with visible rhythms.

The qualities behind Thompson's idea of "aesthetic of the cool" are balance, collectedness. Dixon Gottschild explains it as an attitude that combines vitality with composure. To exhibit the cool involves dancing and presenting the self with clarity and lucidity. It is the calm, masklike face over the vigorous body. Octavia Laville, as a sixty-four-year old bele dancer, alluded to this when she said, "I never smile. I always vex because my father them used to teach me to dance; they call that African dance" (Wason 1987, 35). In contrast, the ideal expression in the quadrille, particularly in performance, is one of enjoyment and flirtation, befitting its purpose of recreation and courtship. A dancer from Woodford Hill explained: "Marigot people dancing you will say 'well, you and I going to sleep in bed now, you is my wife, I is your husband.' You see? They laughing for each other and they holding each other on the stage. . . . That is how you should dance. You can't vex . . ." (Wason 1987, 72).

African dances are usually done in the open air, and the dancing space is circular, circumscribed by the spectators surrounding the performers; the same thing happens in Dominica, unless the performance happens on stage. The circle can shift and an onlooker can become a performer; often more than one performance is going on. In Dominica, this happens most frequently in the bele, but a perfect example of this can be seen in a quadrille we filmed in 1986. One of the men among the resting couples seems to become part of the pattern as he indulges his joy of the dance. To European-trained eyes, used to the proscenium stage and a single focus, the scene might look chaotic, but he is merely expressing his communal feeling African-style. On top of this, he was probably expressing "vri," as described below.

Within the set form, no dancer dances like another. This is certainly true of the bele, where appropriate steps and movements are tacitly understood and where deviations from the norm are hotly debated. For example, in the 1986 Independence Day competitions, one young dancer included moonwalking (à la Michael Jackson) in his bele performance, causing great controversy and leaving some members of the audience crying, "Break dance, not bele!" Hand in hand with the aspect of improvisation goes the idea of personal expressivity. In Dominica they call this idea "vri," or "making style." In the quadrille, the kavalyé is expected to be flamboyant, which men do primarily by devising fancy steps. The danm's way of making style is less obvious, having more to do with the way she presents herself and relates to her partner than with any specific step.

In statements alluding to the element of "marathoning," or dancing beyond natural capabilities (Dixon Gottschild 2002, 8), bele practitioners reported that they could dance all night and feel good while doing so, even though they were exhausted afterward (Wason 1987, 44). The jing-ping dances also exhibited this characteristic, for the quadrille originally formed part of the quadrille set, which comprised seven (some say five) different group and couple dances. The sequence of dances varied a little depending on the area, but the main intent was to give all a chance to participate. For example, in Paix Bouche in the north, the set began with the quadrille and fourth figure, and ended with a selection of other dances, such as the mazouk. Eight people at a time would perform the set, retiring to refresh themselves while another group of eight took their turn on the dance floor. In 1965 the set was broken into separate sections for exhibiting at the National Day competitions (Wason 1987, 47).

## Conclusion

In 1988, Rex Nettleford, founder of the National Dance Theatre of Jamaica, wrote, "The African presence is yet to be universally acknowledged as central to the Caribbean ethos. The disparate entities have indeed been creolized over time into native born and native bred entities that are no longer clones of their separate origins. . . . Much that became "West Indian" or "Caribbean" was actually forged in the crucible of African experience in the Americas. The Africanization of the European was no less important to the creolization process than the Europeanization of the African."

The underlying ideas in that quotation, of disparate African and European elements meeting, borrowing, adapting, and mutating into a new form, certainly hold true when applied to the traditional dance forms of Dominica. While retaining the structure of elite ballroom dances of nineteenth-century England and France, the quadrille is layered with African rhythms and movement sensibilities. In encompassing certain elements of European movement, the bele embodies an African adaptation to the new life in the Caribbean. The bele embodied African values and remained associated with the lower echelons of society; however, by 1986, the renaissance of African values was under way. Youth were encouraged to embrace the dance as an expression of their national identity and African heritage. In Dominica, each dance form is acknowledged as a part of the national creole heritage, taking on a new role as a hallmark of national identity.

# ST. LUCIA

# 17

# Helen, Heaven, and I

## In Search of a Dialogue

TANIA ISAAC

## Introduction

So here I am at the intersection of modern dance and . . . I am a kinesiophile; I crave movement information, and I am compelled to see how it all fits together. As a West Indian straddling aesthetic worlds, my process focuses on investigating the visceral communication inherent in the Caribbean dance form, both in the culture and as it exists in my own body. While I do not choreograph "traditional" Caribbean dances, my experience with tradition allows my work to reflect this cultural form rather than conform to an existing movement vocabulary. My experience with movement is closely tied to my love of language, prose, and poetry. The rhythm of language and how it translates or moves through the body are fundamental in my approach to choreography. I revel in the idea of complete abandon. For me this translates as allowing movement to exist without pretense, and at times without conscious thought, while maintaining very specific structures. It requires finding freedom in a disciplined, sinuous muscularity and demands that every moment exist with an ease and flow and complete conviction.

I make dances because, for me, movement, above all else, is where I can communicate the complexity of human experience. I want to tangle up the body and the intellect and make thinking inseparable from feeling. I am inspired by histories, how they unfold, the way they are recorded across cultures, and whose point of view is being told. I am inspired by how experiences repeat and are similar across generations, societies, and eras—and

Figure 17.1. Tania Isaac. Image by Belkowitz Photography. Used by permission of Tania Isaac.

intrigued by what is being recorded as history in our time. I look at literature and how it is represented in written and oral traditions and seize the
opportunity to tell stories. At the heart of it all, I am driven by the idea that
we are all searching for a place to belong, all wrestling with our purpose,
trying to find peace and places where we feel safe, supported, and sheltered.
I cannot separate my culture from my art, my art from my life, my life from
my social beliefs, my beliefs from my experience. I am West Indian, raised
middle class by virtue of education, with parents who were and still are avid
consumers of art and literature. Along with strong opinions and a strong
desire to share them comes an equally strong desire to hear others' opinions
and to facilitate a space that encourages social dialogue.

I make narratives that hover somewhere between the literal and the abstract. I aim to tell stories of people, societies, situations; of the compelling
and the absurd in us as we negotiate our lives. At the core are the following
ideas: that individuals can potentially shape their society in as much as they
can follow the conviction of their ideals and that human beings have the
power to affect each other deeply in thought, action, and intention.

## Helen

St. Lucia, "the fairest isle of all the earth," according to its national anthem,
with lyrics by Charles Jesse, is nestled in the lower curve of the Caribbean
chain. Twenty-one miles south of Martinique and twenty-six miles northeast of St. Vincent, she is part of an archipelago that stretches for more than
two thousand miles from Cuba to the northern coast of South America. Existing right at the point where hurricanes turn north or south, she tends to
be protected by whimsy and geography from some of the worst that comes
at her from the ocean. Iouanalao or Hewanorra (Land of the Iguana), two
European transliterations of the Kalinago name by which she was once also
known, is the second largest of the Windward Islands, 27 miles long and 14
miles wide, covering an area of about 238 square miles. Her population of
166,838 (2006) is predominantly of African and mixed African-European
descent, with very small East Indian and European minorities. Seventy percent of St. Lucians are Roman Catholic.

Originally settled by Arawak/Taino and then Carib/Kalinago Indians between 200 and 1000 AD, the island is believed to have been discovered by

Europeans in either 1499 or 1502. St. Lucia, nicknamed "Fair Helen" for the incendiary beauty Helen of Troy, changed hands between the French and British fourteen times before finally being ceded to Britain in 1814 after a series of enormously destructive battles. St. Lucia, Helen, Iouanalao, Hewanorra, became independent of Britain in 1979 and is currently part of the British Commonwealth. And maybe, like her many names, she wears many identities. The island's first enduring settlements and towns were French, beginning with Soufriere in 1746, and despite the long British rule, the culture is steeped in a French African aesthetic. The result of this experience is a visceral creole culture lightly cloaked in the more austere posture of a British isle. As her offspring and the carriers of the history in her soil, we shift, we mask, we wear second, third, and fourth skins that all seem to fit.

## Dance and Culture

win'(pronounced wine): rotation of pelvis
fete: party
making mas: creating band themes and costumes for Carnival
playing mas: participating in Carnival bands

"Helen" is considered part of the Francophone Caribbean. The official language is English, but the language of living is Kwéyòl (Creole), both formal and vernacular. It is the kind of tension, of duality, that breeds intellect and art and internal conflict.

As a relatively young and very small nation, we are in the process of carving out an identity, creating priority and trying to have a voice in a newer world where smaller voices are no longer heard. Our tiny land mass is proud of having produced two Nobel laureates: Sir Arthur Lewis, Economics (1979), and Derek Walcott, Literature (1992). We hover between the desire to keep turning inward, finding what is most valuable, and the impulse to keep looking outward to show what we believe draws others to us. This is the twenty-first century, island nations are beholden, cultures and traditions are often held hostage, and it is the nature of society to evolve, change, and shed. Yet even as I acknowledge this, I am romantic and nostalgic for what I remember, maybe even more than for what I know.

So, more to the point, when did you start dancing?

The cliché is that I remember the moment when I realized that so much more was possible than I imagined, and yet I don't remember ever not dancing or when it became more important than anything else. Maybe I can be absurd and say that since my home is a volcanic island, molten flow is always just below the surface, and it is in the nature of the soil to want to shift and heave. However it came to pass, this meld of societies, traditions, and histories is a moving culture. There is a rhythm and style and pattern in work, in play, in music. We duck and weave in language, speaking in allusions and references, describing but not saying, continuously implying. We fill in sentences with eyes and gestures and sounds that could almost be inconsequential except for the absolute weight they carry. Conversations are physical as well as verbal. Movement language is playful in its physical manifestations, dipping, skimming the surfaces, balancing carefully held tensions and total abandon.

The contradictions play out within many spheres of society. Embedded in the culture are patterns of separation between classes that are the entrenched remnants of the historic lack of value placed on the very central African presence in the "New World." We argue over what is sophistication, what is classical, what is valuable, what is creole and what is not, what is African, tribal, or European, civilized, modern. What is vulgar or not. We keep insisting that the ideas form opposing ends of a spectrum, not only of movement, but also of value, rather than allowing them equal agency in their respective manifestations. To wine or not to wine is the question, and if we do wine, how far do we go?

In my Helen, my Heaven, there are the upper and lower worlds that never catch sight of each other and for whom the opposing group exists only in imagination, in legend, in fear or envy or a conflicting combination of all. In the middle class, I remember nothing innately or overtly forbidden, but an unspoken understanding was that there were ways of being; people of a certain class or breeding or often color were not expected to behave in certain ways. It still seems to hold true. For me, in Helen, there has always been the call to let go—to get up, rise, like we don't care, as the mighty Ashanti, multiple Calypso King of St. Lucia suggested—to find out what is on the other side of that invisible line in the pure white crystal sand. When we speak of St. Lucia and the plurality of culture, I find that reflected in who I am. So, for me, my island is manifested in four forms.

Helen is the face we meet. She is vain, self-absorbed, self-assured. She is full figured but slender. She is cautious; her affection is fickle. She is the organizer, the planner; she will always put herself first. She is skeptical, cynical, and not easily impressed. Her energy is contained, her movement precise, quick, and fluid. Her posture is erect, upright with just a hint of sway. She is the creole idol, a modest *kwadril* (quadrille), precise and patterned, beautifully presented and giving nothing away. But she drinks her tea with a splash of rum. She is business.

Iouanalao is aggressive, defensive, quick to take offense and to act on a perceived insult. She is wiry and muscled, incredibly smart. She leaps, spins, charges, but teases with an open smile when she does smile. She does not believe in artifice. Her energy is wild, barely restrained; she can be intimidating. Her limbs move like lightning from the center; she wines all the way to the ground. She is unpredictable; she is *debòt*, masquerade, and *jwè*. She drinks her rum with no ice.

Hewanorra is gentle, grounded, slow to offend, an open face and smile. She is a little heavier, her hips roll slowly, and her legs are stout. Her energy pours softly out from the center and is mesmerizing. She is the peacemaker, the caretaker. She moves like old reggae and calypso, swaying, her wine stays upright, her spine undulates slowly. She is the memory of soft sweet singing, country music, and creole Christmas. As she smiles easily and walks through the room, her half-lidded gaze takes the measure of everyone she meets. She will charm her way slowly through anything. She drinks rum in sweet coffee and *ti poche* ("little punch" of honey, rum, and lime, also rumored to have medicinal qualities).

St. Lucia is the flower child. She is stylish, creative, artistic, articulate, willful, and a little self-indulgent. She is the consummate flirt. She is smart when she needs to be, but prefers to have others take care of things. Her energy radiates, is internal, and spills over. She is dancehall reggae, soca, and new calypso. She dips and bends, shows a little leg or hip or chest; she is elusive. She steps briskly with a barely noticeable wiggle. She likes shandy and mixed drinks; her rum comes with Coca-Cola.

St. Lucia is the name we call them all. Helen is their face, beautiful, untouchable. Helen protects the others, and you need to earn her trust before she lets you get close enough to see them. At a given moment, she is any and all. We are all multiples, indefinable, shifters. The dances and the carriage of our bodies show who we are, how we think, our politics and personality, our sense of agency. In a moving culture, when we talk about dance, we talk about currency. We talk about class, economics, and the great colonial divide. We talk about the body, the spirit, the music, because, for many of us, to dance is heaven on earth.

## In Heaven: Dances and Divination

"Diaspora is . . . articulated through the experience of temporal and spatial disruption." When Sean Lokaisingh-Meighoo in "The diasporic mo(ve)ment" (1997) speaks of temporal and spatial disruption, for me there is also the implication that it is in our nature to draw seams together, and however appropriate or not, to try to create a linear history from situations inherently fractured and fraught with human irrationalities. The story of the new world is violent: continuous genocide, displacements, subterfuge, theft, and machinations of power, and when the dust settled for a time, on all sides people were left trying to figure out how to survive till the next upheaval. Each was isolated from the familiar and trying desperately to re-create home, inasmuch as circumstances would allow. Europeans (of both elite and criminal classes) and indentured laborers from China and India had more liberties than did Africans, but on this mountainous island the influence of Africa became predominant, by virtue of sheer numbers, despite the imbalance of actual power. In the end, each group, although separate, was trying to use every available resource to makesomething that most resembled what they remembered. But memory is not accurate and what they were searching for was a haven, a heaven of some kind, a place to be.

Dances: It is difficult to trace some of the historic folk practices that have come to define our current traditions. It is impossible to chronicle an entire history of movement here. There are dances that I know only by name, dances I have heard of, unnamed dances I have seen but no longer know how to find, and dances/practices that no longer exist. In some rural enclaves, ritual practices such as the *kélé*, with purportedly distinct ties to African (Yoruba) ritual, language, music, and dance may—or may not—continue. Crowley (1957, 8) notes,

> A prominent family in Resina claim to be of the "Caplawu" nation, and perform a kélé or sacrifice at the New Year or the anniversary of the death of a recent ancestor. This kélé consists of songs to drum

accompaniment and ritual prayers in an "African" language as yet unstudied. Aboriginal celts or "thunder stones" are given offerings of oil, as are the tools and personal belongings of the deceased. Then a specially-raised virgin ram is sacrificed by one stroke of the cutlass, and the fresh blood drunk by the family participants, after which the meat and other food are served to all present. The rest of the day and night is spent in secular dancing.

My practice as a child was the tradition at that time, but a legacy from my family has been a continuous effort to create a lens that compresses time, distilling from the past an essence of the way the present is constructed. So I start, as far as I can trace, with some of what defines Iouanalao/Hewanorra. Many of these dances I have never done, some I have never seen, but all I know and understand intrinsically because I have seen manifestations of them all my life. Most of these dances are not currently widely practiced but remain significant in that they constitute the basis of an underlying performance aesthetic. Here, they create a historical context for framing my main influences and experiences in contemporary social practices.

## Folk: Traditional/Historical/Limited Practice

"The most striking characteristic of St. Lucian musical life is the frequency and importance of 'fete' or *plezi*. Every weekend sees a dance in each village and the kinds of dances change with the season, the local area and the age of the participants," noted Daniel J. Crowley in 1957 (5). Jocelyne Guilbault describes St. Lucian jwé or play as a form of rural St. Lucian folk music associated with beach parties, wakes, débòt dances, and full moon gatherings. "They provide a source of entertainment, an opportunity to demonstrate verbal and dramatic skills, and a chance to make public commentaries in ways that would otherwise be impossible. Participants laugh at social conventions, criticize laws, and gossip. To minimize the possibility of offending anyone, participants perform all *jwé* with spontaneity and high spirits" (Guilbaut 1998c, 943). Of the dance she says, "*Jwé danse* include four play-song-dances: *débòt, yonbòt, jwé pòté* and *solo*. Except for solo (danced by a couple who undulate their hips and sway their pelvises forward and backward), *jwé danse* are performed in a circle and include the famous *blòtjé*, a movement consisting of thrusting the pelvis forward and 'doing a *touché*' (making contact) with the neighboring dancer" (1998c, 943).

The *gèm* (game song) also involves dance, with a leader who "plays with language by punning or using ambiguous phrases or metaphors. By adding some personal touch to the choreographed movements while following the rules of the game, other participants demonstrate their agility, imagination, and playfulness" (Guilbaut 1998c, 943).

Guilbaut adds, "Not everyone likes to be associated with jwé. Many educated people, and those from the higher social class, criticize such activities for their sexual overtones and the singers for singing whatever they please. Most of these critics, though embarrassed to take part, recognize the value of jwé. Yet like everyone else in the country, they daily use jwé strategies, metaphors and *lang déviwé* (saying the opposite of what is meant), verbal teasing, and other typical text-building techniques of jwé lyrics" (1998c, 943–944).

From Crowley's article, "Song and Dance in St. Lucia" (1957, 7): "The *kont* is intricate and acrobatic with the men leaping and doing crossover steps, then spinning around to stop at the drum with an upraised foot. Women are less energetic, sometimes merely standing and moving their hips while holding the edges of their skirts delicately in their fingers."

While I use the above historical examples to set a context, my main influences have been in following the contemporary social practices, the traditional folk forms more widely known today, including kwadril and masquerade, and the contemporary carnival forms, including calypso and soca.

## Dance: Kwadril

St. Lucian kwadril is universally agreed to have evolved from eighteenth-century European dances that became gradually popularized and then heavily imbued with African aesthetics. The dances are precisely patterned and timed, with some limited space for improvisation. I like to think of the music as a creole re-creation of a small orchestra. Guilbault seems to give an accurate description: "The most typical kwadril ensemble includes a violin, a banjo (the locally made *skroud* or *bwa pòyé*), the locally made cuatro . . . , a guitar (which plays the bass), and a chakchak (rattle). Whenever possible, the ensemble includes a mandolin, and occasionally bones (zo). Through syncopation and the chakchak's rhythmic effects, the performance strongly emphasizes rhythmic improvisation, especially in the unpredictable sequence of melodic patterns" (1998c, 945).

The kwadril is divided into couples formations known as figures (*fidji*) and waltzes. The *pwèmyè fidji, dèzyèm fidji, twazyèm fidji, latwiyèm fidji* (first, second, third, and fourth figures), performed by four couples on a four-sided figure, are a series of increasingly complex musical and pattern variations. The basic dance follows a pattern with two slower steps, followed by a quick series of three steps that dip and hesitate. In the opening of the dances, these three steps serve as a chance to acknowledge, incline your head, and gaze at your partner. The music and movement have a flirtation of their own; the dancers slide just a little around the music, never missing the rhythm, but always almost ahead of or behind it.

The four figures tend to be bookended by waltzes of two kinds. The first of these waltzes is the upright glide across the floor that we know (1,2,3; 1,2,3), but in the second waltz, the lead foot slides forward and out in a half circle on the first count with the second foot interrupting and shuffling sideways. The female maintains this precise movement and rhythm as a base, while the male is free to improvise, shuffling, sliding, dipping, stepping. Some popular improvisation includes heel clicks, the wiping of the brow by the woman, the dip of the leg off the edge of the stage (when performing onstage) or off the dance floor, the pause to wipe the scuff off a boot, the shuffle across the floor on one foot with the toe of the other tracing patterns in multiple directions. The challenge for this waltz is to "almost" miss the end of the measure rhythmically, and to catch the beat at the very last moment.

Other dances, such as the *lakonmèt* (mazurka), schottische, and polka, follow different phrasing and can be performed by individual couples. The lakonmèt, also called the mazouk, is especially popular and the only closed couple dance that originated in Saint Lucia. The *gwa won* (big round) is an open dance where participants change partners as they follow an inside and outside circle. There are marked similarities to the dances of the French Caribbean because of proximity and shared cultural history. In most cases, however, there are also marked differences in the tone or instrumentation and in the style of execution even when the time signature is the same.

The kwadril and lakonmèt were traditionally private dances or took place at parties hosted by individuals or in a banquet hall, but are now performed primarily onstage and in competition, especially in schools. The secondary school (aged 11–16) and preschool (aged 2–5) quadrille competitions are among the most popular. As folk tradition continues to become a form of cultural currency, these dances remain important as historic re-creations, for as times have changed, they do not enjoy the same social prestige they once did. The history of kwadril was also once closely associated with colonial power, and the dance was shunned for a while about the time of independence.

As Jocelyne Guilbaut (1998c, 944) notes, a successful performance brings respect and prestige for all participants who dance the correct steps, which are traditionally said to "demonstrate control over behavior, manner, and skills" and symbolize "a set of special values linked with a higher social class."

Movement Characteristics: Helen: The basic movement is confined and comes traditionally from the idea of corsets, petticoats, headdresses, jewels, umbrellas, tight shoes and waistcoats and fans. The carriage is held upright with the torso suspended from the chest and shoulders in a continual inhale, hovering gently over the hips, legs, and feet. The feet always land toes first, pressing toward the floor, but always catching the weight before the heels land. The torso turns as one piece; the head inclines gently. The roles are very traditional. The men lead and guide. The women follow and hold the line; they are delicate and hold their skirts. The tone itself has evolved over time, with the hips twisting a little more, the weight sinking a little lower, more direct eye contact rather than a demure gaze, more obvious flirtation. However much the style shifts, the use of weight-shift and its relationship to music remain the same. It is play.

## Masquerade

"On the next day, all the masked egwugwu of Umofia assembled in the marketplace. They came from all the quarters of the clan and even from the neighbouring villages. The dreaded Otakagu came from Imo, and Ekwensu, dangling a white cock, arrived from Uli. It was a terrible gathering. The eerie voices of countless spirits, the bells that clattered behind some of them, and the clash of machetes as they ran forward and backward and saluted one another, sent tremors of fear into every heart," says Chinua Achebe in *Things*

*Fall Apart* (1985 [1959], 149) (In the glossary to this novel, Achebe defines *egwugwu* as "a masquerader who impersonates one of the ancestral spirits of the village.")

Comparatively, in "Song and Dance in St. Lucia," Crowley (1957, 10) observes that "Bands of masquers roam the streets playing music, dancing and acting out skits. Some wear *pai banane* or dry banana leaves tied around them from neck to knees so that they look like animated corn shucks." In this light masquerade can be seen as an evolution of African tradition removed from its original context and existing in an altered form and function. Achebe (1985, 64) further describes the egwugwu's body as being one of "smoked raffia."

The leaves of the raffia palm were often used to create the African masqueraders' costumes, similar to the idea of pai banane mentioned by Crowley. The masquerade characters in St. Lucia also bear a marked similarity in intent to their African precursors: mysterious intimidating figures representing something otherworldly. They require us to suspend our knowledge of their origin and accept the artifice as a super-reality. They become concrete in our experience because we choose to accept them as beyond what we know and existing on their own terms.

The first sound of masquerade is a cacophonic blast to virgin ears. Between the whistles and the multiple drumbeats, it takes a while to find the melodic line and the base rhythm. The movement and costumes take on a similar carnivalesque role, with fabric, masks, sometimes highly exaggerated female figures, and fast-paced dancing. It is usually improvisation based on a few key movements, but it can also be more highly choreographed. In direct contrast to the quadrille, it attempts to create as many hypermobile parts as possible at one time. Main characters such as Pai Banane and Papa Djab (father devil) have consistent costumes and roles and sometimes enact skits based on human foibles. Other characters simply take on other supporting or individual roles, wearing horns, headdresses, and assorted clothing to create their own personas. These skits are more historically tied to festival holidays such as Christmas, Easter, or New Year, but many can also be performed at community or folk events throughout the year. I still have a lingering wariness of "Toes," a devil figure and his band who traveled the streets during the Christmas/New Year holidays chanting: "Djab la kaye manje a ti mamay; yon, de, twa ti mamay" (The devil is going to eat a child, 1,2,3 children . . . ).

Movement Characteristics: Iouanalao: The torso is bent over and the knees alternately pulled up high into the chest. The dancer leaps off the ground and spins, moving the costume wildly. The arms wave, the head bobs and jerks, the pelvis thrusts in any and all directions. This is the wine: The wine that moves with the sacroiliac joint taking on the characteristics of a ball-and-socket connection like the shoulder or femur, rolling the sacrum—the tail bone—forward, around, and back as though suspended independently from the spine. The wine that suspends from the abdominal walls, rotating the entire pelvis. The wine that moves the ribcage around, using the shoulders for additional articulation. The shake of the rump. The focus is on the center of the body, curving under and forward, instead of on the arch backward. It is aggressive, even when it shifts to small gestures; a hand may flick, or all other movement may stop while the pelvis rotates or thrusts forward with a scoot of both feet across the ground. Even then it is a challenge: dare to come closer and see what happens. Like the quadrille, it is marked by careful attention to the musical rhythm and tone, and because of its improvisatory nature, by the dynamics of the unfolding drama the character is creating. The aim is to be unpredictable, to draw your audience in and then surprise them. It is an acceptance, a willingness, for you both to be transported. And to play.

## Carnival, Calypso, and Soca: Contemporary Social Dance

Hell broke loose for a while throughout the soca-speaking Caribbean when the calypsonian David Rudder of Trinidad first released "High Mas High Mas I," a current classic, conflating Carnival mas (masquerade) with a kind of Lord's Prayer of Carnival. To be so explicit was to violate the rule that our personalities, our skins, were never to know of each other and that each realm was to remain inviolate. We took our church selves to mass/service, our folk selves to festivals, our carnival selves to the streets, and spread the rest out over whatever social worlds we had to navigate. The dances are part of the cultural strata that reflect our ambivalence and play with what is acceptable and not.

The strong Caribbean tradition of Carnival is credited to Catholicism and often to the French. This period of celebration and partying had its origin in the need to use up all remaining meat and animal products such as eggs and butter before Ash Wednesday, when Lent's forty days of fast-ing and sacrifice begin. (Carnival in St. Lucia is now, however, in July.) It has been widely accepted that the antecedents of calypso were created as a means of internal communication among slaves through song, since they were not allowed to speak frankly. Roaring Lion (Rafael de Leon), a famed calypsonian, contradicts this premise in his 1986 book *Calypso from France to Trinidad, 800 Years of History*, suggesting instead that calypso descended from the music of the medieval French troubadours.

The history of Carnival in the Caribbean is a reflection of the history of the region, with long political and social battles over who had the right to congregate or to participate. Although its manifestation is different on almost every island, the current Carnival is inseparable from what defines us as Caribbean in all its historical veils. The first calypsos were slower measured rhythms, equally known for social commentary and sexual allusion. In calypso, in creating costumes, in bands "making mas," we comment without constraint on current events. We make remarks on history, on personal views, personal agendas, and sometimes just on personal ways of being.

This is the realm of both Hewanorra and St. Lucia.

Movement Characteristics: Hewanorra: Slow sway, the knees alternately slide past each other, rocking the pelvis gently; the ribs respond. The arms often suspend half-open to the sides. The upper chest pulses gently, ripples through the neck, releasing the head at the top as it falls mesmerizingly back and sometimes forward. When the music is particularly sweet or the words come at you just "so," you raise a hand (and sometimes two) to acknowledge it. You lean or press against your partner if you decide to have one, rocking together easily, deciding when or if the dance might become something a little different. The wine is often slow and controlled.

Soca is the party music, born out of a high speed, percussive style of delivery. It is associated with the road march, the wine, what Lucians call *lydèyè* (commotion), the street fete.

Movement Characteristics: St. Lucia: You need space. There is no limit to what the movement could become. You wine, you jump, throw arms up in the air, let your arms dangle loosely at your sides while you jump or shuffle from side to side. You and your partner alternate between harmony and competition. You are waiting to be excited or to be tempted to lose a little more control. You fall sideways, bump and jostle each other. And sometimes you slow down and contemplate why the rhythm and the music feel so good. You rock again, that old calypso sway, you wine that masquerade, you dip

and pull back and balance lightly on heels, ready to move in any direction—
and you learned to do that from a quadrille. Whether you acknowledge or
define it, you are a repository of information, you contain a history of possibilities and you get to choose the mode of expression.

## Ol' Mas

Ol' Mas is an element of Carnival often overshadowed by larger, more elaborate costumes and the parade of the thematically costumed bands of cel-
ebrants. In this tradition, you are not required to be part of a band. The
masquerader creates an individual independent costume that represents a
personal platform. The homemade construction can be a satirical comment
on any political or social event or simply an opportunity to air your views.
It is the consummate Caribbean paradox: it must be well considered, well
crafted, well planned, but cannot take itself too seriously. There is no particular movement associated with Ol' Mas. Most shuffle through the streets
relatively slowly so you can get a good look at their costume, appreciate the
complexity of the design, or joke and read the signs they carry, with the
requisite puns that identify their topics.

Ol' Mas is the synthesis of personalities: the brain of Helen, the daring
of Iouanalao, the subtlety of Hewanorra, and the creative laughter of Lucia. With all the physical information that shapes how my body interprets
ideas, it is with this frame that the ideas are generated. For me, Ol' Mas is
an expression of possibilities, of the permission to participate actively, to
make your own voice, to not be too concerned about the "right" look, but
about the best way to shape dialogue, to question, to take yourself seriously
enough to be heard, but to remember that life is always a little larger than
you and to keep perspective. It is a confirmation that in the end we cannot
be other than ourselves, and that we do not have to choose between our
multiples. Our parts and experiences serve us well, can co-exist, and do not
have to be sacrificed into one correct way of being.

## And I

I was raised with strong ideas of social responsibility and accountability,
with strong opinions on class and culture. I was chafing, wanting to be free
of limitations on movement. What I find in quadrille, in calypso, in soca,

in masquerade is not a series of steps or moves, but a way of looking at the body. What I find is true postmodernism, with permission to really move from center, access to every moment, every motion, nuance, tension. I look to each moment of being lost in the music or in the silences, lost in a spirit, lost in a world of color, sensation, texture, smell. Infusion not fusion. This translates as an invitation and permission to use anything you deem necessary to communicate the essential idea.

Carrying a lifelong love of literature and a wealth of cultural information, I have begun a continually evolving exploration of music, language, and movement, at the intersection of the traditional and postmodern, looking not only at how they are manifested physically, but also at their underlying bodily or physical and aesthetic philosophies. The mobile center and elastic reach of limbs that snap or ease back into place, a sense of flight, of fancy, of abandon without losing control. My gaze and the impulse for creating movement come not from attempting to make linear shapes from an organic form, but from allowing all of my movement history to exist simultaneously, consciously and unconsciously infusing the linear with a unique organic undercurrent and clarity.

This is my journey of reconciling myself to my body, my history. To let my weight sit easily and be prepared to move in any direction. To know that it has to matter first and that, for me, it has to bubble up and pour out. Fall and recover. Weightless. Circular. Groaning. Creaking. Alternately pushing and sliding through. Accepting of sensual body without the intrusion of sex. What I find in this culture inextricably tied to the way I see the world is the capacity to be limitless while remaining connected and essential. I am interested in intent and initiation.

Where is movement generated? Initiated?

What is its history?

How is it supported by music? Or not?

How is it supported by its associated verbal language?

How does it create impact?

How is it functional? Whimsical?

What is its philosophical relationship to the body? To performance? To the society in which it exists?

I keep finding more questions, and the answers keep changing.

# BARBADOS

# 18

# Dance in Barbados

## Reclaiming, Preserving, and Creating National Identities

SUSAN HAREWOOD AND JOHN HUNTE

As the first volume of *Caribbean Dance* demonstrated, dance is an extremely fruitful site at which to explore the dynamic ways in which Caribbean identities are constructed. The essays in the earlier book, together with this present collection, clearly show that this cluster of islands and territories, famously described as "a musical region" (Bilby 1985), can just as easily be described as "a dance region." In this chapter our interest is in providing a broad overview of social and concert dance practices in Barbados. Very little has been written on dance in Barbados; thus we offer this chapter as a contribution to the tiny body of literature that currently exists and as an invitation for more work. As we make clear in the following pages, Barbadian dance practices reveal a great deal about the complex processes through which Barbadians construct their identities.

We begin by exploring the faint traces of traditional dances in Barbados. This examination permits us to consider the ways in which reclamation and preservation of those traditional dances were an important part of the contribution of dance performance to nation-building projects in Barbados in the 1970s and 1980s, though constructing new forms of movement, drawing particularly on the Martha Graham modern school, was also important. We show that the desire to reclaim, preserve, and create continues in dance practices today and that the present landscape of dance in Barbados is characterized by dance companies that have clear identities and draw on different sources to construct Barbadian styles of movement while also making strategic interconnections. These interconnections, we argue, make clear the multifaceted and dialogic nature of Barbadian national *identities,* as opposed to a singular Barbadian identity. In our research we found that an overriding discourse that shapes and directs the Barbadian body in motion is a discourse of "decency." Questions as to what is decent and what is indecent are never far from the dancing body on the stage, in the dancehall, or in the street. We show that this binary of decent/indecent is deployed as a means of social control, but is also a rallying point around which Barbadians offer various forms of self-assertion.

## Dance Traditions

Only traces remain of the dances performed during the slave period. In many instances those traces exist only in the very limited literature available on early aesthetic practices in Barbados. Jerome Handler and Charlotte Frisbie's extremely important examination of the music practices of the slaves also demonstrates the significance of dances in the social and political life of slaves in Barbados. Handler and Frisbie describe the weekend and holiday dances as "perhaps one of the most important organized social diversions for slaves throughout most of the slave period" (1972, 13).

Drawing from the writings of travelers to Barbados and colonial officials, we find that slaves frequently held dances on their few days off; these days off included special holidays such as Harvest Home, which marked the end of the harvest of the sugar crop. The dances were large group events where slaves would gather in a large circle; though everyone would move to the music, those who wished to dance entered the circle created by the crowd. Army doctor George Pinckard's 1796 description is the most often quoted as it is the most detailed account of the dances:

> Forming a ring in the centre of the throng (the slaves) dance to the sound of their beloved music. The dance consists of stamping of the feet, twistings of the body, and a number of strange indecent attitudes. It is a severe body exertion, for the limbs have little to do in it. The head is held erect, or occasionally, inclined a little forward—the hands nearly meet before—the elbows are fixed, pointing from the sides—and the lower extremities being held rigid, the whole person is moved without lifting the feet from the ground. Making the head and limbs fixed pointes, they writhe and turn the body on its own axis, slowly advancing toward each other, or retreating to the outer parts of the ring. Their approaches, with the figure of the dance and the attitudes

and inflexions in which they are made are highly indecent: but of this they seem to be wholly unconscious for the gravity—I might say the solemnity of countenance . . . is peculiarly striking . . . not a smile—not a significant glance, nor an immodest look escapes from either sex. (Pinckard, quoted in Handler and Frisbie 1972, 30–31).

Pinckard's description is perhaps notable for its detail and its relatively restrained assessment of the slaves' dances. It is easy to read the way in which Pinckard sexualizes the dances so as to provide himself with the moral high ground from which to judge the dancers; however, when compared with other observers, in this description at least, Pinckard can be described as practically reticent in his critique. Other observers held fast to the racialized myths of imperialism that pitted "African savagery" against "European civilization," describing the dances as frenzied examples of black idolatry. These racial biases in the observers, of course, together with the fact that there is no record of the slaves' own understandings of their dances, make it practically impossible to glean the meaning of those dances to those who participated.

Handler and Frisbie limit their analysis to the significance of the dances for the plantation system. Drawing on Frederick Douglas' interpretation of the U.S. slave system, they suggest that music and dance would have been like a pressure valve, providing enough release from the everyday brutality of slavery to allow the system to continue. However, we would argue that one might also view the dances as opportunities not only to accommodate the slavery system, but also to resist it. The dances provided opportunities for the slaves, through the embodied movements of dance, to articulate their own histories and identities in a way that would remain strategically cloaked to slave masters, and, so many years later, to us. Yet we are tempted to consider the possible parody involved in a dance such as the Treadmill Dance, based on one of the punishments inflicted on the slaves (Spencer 1974). At a more material level, the dances also gave the slaves opportunities to come together and plot rebellion.

Few descriptions remain of the actual movements of the dances. In the post-emancipation period, Charles Day in 1852 provided a description of one of the most consistently mentioned traditional dances of Barbados: the Jo and Johnnie or Joan and Johnny. It is not fully clear from his description whether the Jo and Johnnie was the dance event or the specific dance he described:

The object of the dance was to show the paces of the ladies to the admiring beaux, and a couple of dark beauties paid their "quaater-dollah"
each and commenced. The first movement was an *en avant* by both,
the feet close together toeing and heeling it very gently, the *retirez* the
same; then the feet were straddled in a somewhat indecorous manner for ladies, moving along and round *a la fandango* . . . the ladies
turned down the outer ankles as near the earth as possible meanwhile
advancing and retiring together, and they "sleuing round" each other
hold their frocks, *a la minuet de la cour'* with their heads looking down
at their feet. . . . These were the grand postures of the dance—an indis-
pensable requisite of which also seemed to be a solemn cast of countenance, occasionally varied by a sentimental inclination of the head,
as doleful in face, however, as if the parties were to be hanged the next
minute. (Day 1852, 47–48)

Notice that Day, like Pinckard before him, hints at moral censure with
his reference to "indecorous manner." Note too the solemn countenance of
the dancers in both the Jo and Johnny and the Pinckard description. There
seems more than a little correspondence between this solemnity and what
Brenda Dixon Gottschild (1996) has called the aesthetics of the cool—the
ability to balance the conflict between the solemn face and the energy of the
moving body. Similar "masks of cool" are found in the social dance form
"wukking up," which we discuss later in this chapter.

Laura Wilson Bergan (1979) found other descriptions of traditional Barbadian dances in the records of the Commonwealth Caribbean Resource
Centre (COMCARC), including the Chiggoe-Toe (Chiggoe foot) Dance,
the Donkey Man, the Four-Cent Fassy, the Four-Knee Polka or Belly to
Belly, and the Four Points of the Mill. Unfortunately, the COMCARC records are not readily available. COMCARC, established in 1972, was one of
a number of efforts emerging in the period of Barbados' independence in
1966 to document, preserve, create, and ascribe value to Barbadian cultural
practices.

It is difficult to say definitively why most of the traditional dances of
Barbados have disappeared. Discussions of social dance practices with older
Barbadians suggest that, for some communities, dance was caught up in the
demarcation of what was deemed decent and what indecent and how that
demarcation affected any hope that the poor might have for social advance-

ment. Both George Pinckard's and Charles Day's descriptions show the ways in which "indecent" was deployed as a means of defining blacks as morally inferior. Such a definition was important in the processes of validating white supremacist ideologies and justifying the injustices of colonial rule.

"Decency" was defined in rather narrow ways that gave European and European-derived cultural practices privilege over African and African-derived cultural practices. It was presented as a major qualification for social advancement. It seems possible that, in the long post-emancipation period (and we call it long because the Moyne Commission found that more than one hundred years after slavery not enough had changed in the living conditions for the vast majority of Caribbean people), when black Barbadians adopted a variety of micro- and macro-level strategies for winning their full rights as workers and citizens that "decency" was a primary qualification for receiving those rights. Thus some of those interviewed pointed out that decent, church-going people avoided dances and dancing. In addition to this, island authorities banned Sunday markets and dances, and this seemed to have limited opportunities for people to engage in their dance practices.

Nevertheless, some dance practices have survived. The survival of the Donkey Man, mentioned by Bergan, along with the Maypole and the Landship can be linked, in part, to the same impulse to document, preserve, create, and ascribe value to Barbadian cultural practices that led to the establishment of COMCARC. These nationalist efforts are characterized by the fact that they issued from multiple sources—public and private, internal and external—and that they often purported to teach Barbadians the true essence of Bajan culture. We are not suggesting, however, that these cultural practices, especially the Landship, have survived only because of the offices of archivist, cultural activists, and academics. Certainly their survival must be attributed, first and foremost, to the cultural practitioners who continued creating their art in the face of hostility.

## Toward an Independent Spirit

In his "Report on cultural formation in Barbados with proposals for a plan for national cultural development," Edward Kamau Brathwaite states that, until the advent of the Barbados Dance Theatre Company, "the main dance activities in Barbados centered around the teaching of classical ballet, on the one hand, and night club 'limbo' dancing, geared mainly to the tourist trade, on the other" (1979, 26). (Though we recognize the significant impacts of performances for tourists on dance practices in Barbados, space limitations prevent us from exploring this issue in this article.) His point may be overstated (our discussion thus far points to social dance activities); nevertheless, it can draw attention to the fact that a cultural policy plan was being developed in 1979, and this concentration on cultural policy reflected a strong desire in many quarters to use the arts for developmental and nation-building purposes. As we show in the following section, dance practitioners were very much involved in these nationalist enterprises.

The cultural policy plan should be understood as part of changes at the national and international level that resulted in the development of similar policies around the globe (see Harewood 2008). Barbados gained independence in 1966. Like many other newly sovereign states, Barbados joined the United Nations system. The rapid change in UN membership led to a change in focus, particularly in UNESCO. Whereas formerly, economic development plans had viewed the cultures of the so-called Third World as hindrances to their development, the representatives of the new nation-states called for culturally appropriate economic development strategies. UNESCO sponsored a series of Intergovernmental Conferences on the Administrative and Financial Aspects of Cultural Policies across the globe, and those conferences reached the Caribbean and Latin America in 1978. Barbados' own cultural policy institutions reflected this international concern with culture and development. In 1976 Barbados established a Cultural Division and a full Ministry of Culture in 1978. Brathwaite's report was funded by UNESCO and the new Ministry of Culture.

Cultural practitioners in Barbados often observe that the presence of a policy plan does not necessarily mean that a direct transformation of the cultural environment will occur in the ways specifically suggested in the plan. This is a fair comment; nevertheless, what Brathwaite's report signifies is a national and international discourse about the importance of artistic practices in both the pursuit of economic development and the creation of national unity and national identities.

In the 1970s a number of dance companies were established: Rontana Movement in 1971, Foundation Dance Movement in 1972, Yoruba Foundation in 1974 (emerging from another cultural organization, Black Night, formed in the late 1960s), Country Theatre Workshop in 1976, Tyrona Dancers in 1976, George Springer Group in 1977, and Pinelands Creative

Workshop in 1978. Many of these expressed an interest in creating a Barbadian style of movement. The conceptualization of what that Barbadian style might contain was understood differently by the different groups; nevertheless, in their constitutions they often wrote in terms of expressing, through dance, a Barbadian national identity. In addition, some groups, perhaps because in most instances they dealt directly with children and youth, also stated interest in ensuring that their dancers were good citizens with strong social consciences. Furthermore, the 1970s and 1980s were a period during which the extant traditional dance practices were often preserved and/or redeployed as part of the choreography for concert dances. Thus the 1970s and 1980s can be understood as a period in which dance practitioners (and other artists) seemed deeply invested in the nationalist project.

The Barbados Dance Theatre Company (BDTC) and the Barbados Dance Centre, its school, were part of these processes. The BDTC was established in 1968 by Mary Stevens, an American. Given that Stevens had studied under Martha Graham, the company was founded on the Martha Graham technique. Stevens did not believe it necessary to specifically develop a Barbadian or Caribbean dance style. "In dance, Mary took the view that dances we did were interpreted and performed by West Indians and, in some instances, created by West Indians, and that made them West Indian. The implication was they did not have to deal exclusively with the commonly held ideas of West Indian folk themes or be restricted to traditional West Indian musical patterns" (Bourne 1989).

We find use of the word "restricted" here interesting. Standing on its own, it could simply mean the BDTC was committed to pulling from a variety of sources; however, when we look across the discussion of Caribbean artistic forms, "restricted" is a word more often applied to African-derived forms. It is assumed that European forms deal with universal themes and that non-European forms are limited in some way. We offer that this is a thread that persists in national dance development.

By 1971 the new director, Virginia Seeley, a Barbadian who had studied and worked in Canada, was more actively drawing on the Barbadian archive. Seeley encouraged dancers and choreographers to research Barbadian traditions. Subsequent directors and choreographers would make their own decisions as to how they would create a Barbadian dance movement or whether they believed that constructing such a style was relevant to their artistic vision at all. Nevertheless, some felt by the late 1970s that the BDTC was not reflecting the cultural interests of Barbadians (Richards 1989). There was a sense in some quarters that BDTC was mostly made up of, and mostly reflected, the interests of the Barbadian middle class. There was some resentment, too, that the BDTC was the only dance company receiving government subvention until the 1980s.

Additionally, there were those who questioned whether modern dance was Barbadian enough. For example, a director of one of the folk dance companies stated, "Folk is more a part of us than say the modern dance and the audience that comes to our shows prefer Folk dancing because some of them cannot really understand, say, a theme behind modern dance" (Cave 1980, 17).

Embedded in this and similar statements are questions about the legitimate sources from which Barbadians can and should construct their national identity. As with many issues revolving around nationalism, there can be a tendency to seek out a single "authentic" source, one "true wellspring" from which the unified nation can emerge. The very presence of these multiple and competing discourses, however, should perhaps suggest the multiplicity of sources from which a nation can dynamically construct its identities rather than a single identity. While BDTC and Rontana worked with the modern style and drew on differing levels of folk at different points in their histories, Country Theatre Workshop and Tyrona were more committed to the folk dance traditions. Yoruba offered yet another expression, drawing on folk and very specifically seeking to explore Barbados' African cultural heritage.

Yoruba was involved in a broad range of cultural activities, including writers' workshops, theater, lectures, art exhibitions, drumming, and dance. In all these areas, they were concerned with reviving folk expressions and reintegrating African heritage. They brought in African dance instructors from Nigeria to teach their dancers African movement, and the director of Yoruba, Elombe Mottley, placed a great deal of emphasis on researching Barbadian folk traditions. Mottley's investigation of folk traditions has been important to the preservation and resuscitation of certain dance practices in Barbados. For instance, the leading proponent of stilt walking and stilt dancing in Barbados, Ife Wilkinson, learned the art at Yoruba. Mottley has been a leading figure in both the growing appreciation of Barbadians for the Landship and the ways in which Landship movements have become a standard part of the repertoire for a number of Barbadian dance companies.

The Landship is a particularly Barbadian social organization. Mottley (2003, 228) calls it "a crucible of African dance retention." It was established in the nineteenth century and became very popular during the first half of the twentieth century. Members of the Landship traditionally organized themselves into community-based organizations named after British ships; although, these days, only one united ship exists, called *The Barbados Landship*. The ships were (and the united ship continues to be) Friendly Societies, and members dress in British naval uniforms and go on parade. The parades consist of dance movements to the music of the *tuk* band, which developed along with the Landship. Tuk (sometimes tuck, or took) is generally identified as a traditionally Barbadian music. The instrument configuration can be found in many societies—a bass drum, sometimes called the bum-drum, a snare drum called the kittle, penny whistle, and steel or triangle—and scholars such as Curwen Best (2001, 52) argue that the music symbolizes the continuation of African musical expression in the "New World."

In the past, Landship societies have been ridiculed as ludicrous copies of the British Navy and dismissed as the sad mimicry of colonized minds. Recent research, however, highlights their importance as economic organizations for lower-income Barbadians. Further, other scholars argue that, rather than mimicking the British Navy, the Landship parodies the Navy and its British authority. These writers contend that the dance maneuvers are actually African dance retentions hidden behind masquerade costumes of British Naval uniforms in order to protect those retentions from the hostile gaze of imperial power (see Marshall 1990; Burrowes 2005).

In some ways it should be recognized that these artistic contestations over legitimate sources from which Barbadians should craft their national identities were, for the most part, coming from nongovernmental organizations. Nationalism research often focuses on the ways in which national identities are imposed from above; however, the dance companies' interests and commitments to fashioning national identities from the sources they viewed as important show the multiple ways in which people sought to participate in the processes of nation building. Nevertheless, one should not lose sight of the government's central role in nation building and the ways in which the political elite could assign value (Frow 1995) to certain practices and not others. Subsidizing the BDTC certainly seemed to suggest that the government was particularly supportive of their vision of Barbadian identity, and

Figures 18.1. and 18.2. The Barbados Landship Association performing at the Oistins Fish Festival in Barbados in 2008. By Susan Harewood; used by permission.

this impression of support was reinforced, perhaps, by the number of times the BDTC was selected to represent Barbados at international events.

In 1984 the National Cultural Foundation was established with a mandate to facilitate the development of all Barbadian cultural arts, including dance. This led to a concerted effort to hold workshops for concert dance as well as masquerade dance practices such as stilt dancing. The NCF was also required to administer Barbados' cultural festivals, including the ESSO Dance Festival that rose and fell in the 1980s, but also the two major national festivals: the National Independence Festival of Creative Arts (NIFCA) and Crop Over. NIFCA was established in 1973 as a cultural festival to mark the anniversary of Barbados' independence. Crop Over, a type of resurfacing of the old Harvest Home plantation holiday, was originally proposed by Yoruba, but did not get much support at the time. It was later adopted by the government and tourism officials as a means of boosting tourist arrivals in the slow summer months; later it became a cornerstone of the government's cultural developmental policy and is now Barbados' premier cultural festival. Dance practices within the contexts of both NIFCA and the Crop Over Festival demonstrate the creativity of the dancers and choreographers as well as government's role in shaping taste.

NIFCA has become one of the primary ways of indicating success in dance. Whereas NIFCA has the format of an arts festival, it is very much a competition, and competitions can be deeply involved in the regulatory processes of state (Guilbault 2002). Originally many of the participants came from community organizations; these days, participation by school groups under the direction of their teachers is extremely high. The didactic nature of the festival is most apparent in some of the drama presentations, where a schoolchild can often be heard delivering a moralizing message on good citizenship that one might surmise has been placed in his or her mouth by a teacher-author or parent-author. Such direct moral messages are less apparent in dance; nevertheless, given the limited dance calendar, medals (for the amateurs) and monetary prizes (for the professionals) are important ways of indicating mastery of a craft. And success at NIFCA can lead to more success at NIFCA, as winning choreographers might find that they are invited to choreograph more NIFCA entries in subsequent years. Additionally, participation in and success at NIFCA can draw dancers and choreographers to the attention of National Cultural Foundation administrators; and these administrators are often the ones who decide or advise who gets to represent Barbados at the international level.

NIFCA celebrates all the arts, so dance shares that space with many other disciplines. In some ways the same can be said for Crop Over, as far as concert dance is concerned. In the early days of Crop Over, dance was a major feature of Cohobblopot. A cohobblopot or cohobbleopot is "a stew comprised of a variety of ingredients" (Collymore 1970, 25). The word was adopted to name the penultimate event of the Crop Over Festival and is used to signify the variety of performances within the show, with artistic directors such as Anna Admira, Heather Forde, and Danny Hinds attempting to showcase the range of dance forms performed in Barbados. Cohobblopot has since become much more of a national party event in which concert dance is often merely a background addition to the stage presentation of calypsonians and soca artists. Dance also shares the stage with folk music in Crop Over folk concerts.

Though concert dance, therefore, shares the stage, social dance is center stage during Crop Over in dancehalls, parties, calypso, and soca events, and at the culmination of Crop Over: Kadooment Day, the carnival-like street parade of masquerade bands that concludes Crop Over. The main, if not only, social dance form on display in these environments is wukking up. Wukking up is defined in the *Caribbean Dictionary of English* as "dancing suggestively or erotically, with vigorous gyrations of the waist and hips." In this definition, which draws attention to the erotic nature of wukking up, one can begin to get a suggestion of the type of debates that revolve around wukking up. Many of these debates have to do with the same delineations of decency and indecency we noted earlier.

Wukking up is a dance activity focused primarily on coordinating rotary, percussive, and vibratory actions in the hip and pelvic region of the dancing body. In Barbados this dance is seen typically at calypso and soca music events. Wukking up requires pelvic and leg coordination to give the pelvic girdle relatively free mobility to move to the rhythm of the music. Public attitudes to wukking up display a great deal of ambivalence. On the one hand, wukking up has often been described as vulgar and subject to a long history of prohibitions. In the binary division of the society to which we made reference earlier, the expectation is that decent churchgoing people did not and do not wuk up; it is left to indecent rum shop-going saga boys and loose women. On the other hand, wukking up has also been identified as a source of pride and a distinctive feature of Bajan culture. Acclaimed writer Austin "Tom" Clarke (1994) states that Bajans are "a wukking-up people, a wukking-up country, a wukking-up tribe o' people. Even if tha' tribe contain black people and Bajan white people, we is still a wukking-up people." Columnist Al Gilkes (1994) claims that even though many cultures move their hips, only Bajans wuk up.

Both these comments were made in 1994, a significant year in this debate over the black dancing body and decency that has lasted more than three hundred years. In 1994 top NCF administrators publicized their intent to put restraints on the amount of wukking up taking place on Kadooment Day. The debate raged in the media, but calypsonians' hilarious representation of the NCF officials as the "wuk-up police" caused those officials to beat a hasty retreat (Harewood 2006). Nevertheless the issue of how to understand, accept, or reject wukking up is a perennial one, particularly as many Bajan youths have totally rejected the ways in which the binary decent/indecent has been used as a means of social ordering. Many of them use wukking up and dancehall dance styles as a way to articulate their own ideas of freedom within the nation-state. This has complicated the decent/indecent binary somewhat (though the major features of its structure remain). One could argue that three groups are now engaged in this debate: the decent churchgoing people who do not wuk up; the youth who, if we are to believe the discourse, have lost themselves down the path of indecency and wukking up; and a third group loyal to the break with colonial traditions that wukking up provides, but who believe that young people are excessive in their wukking up. This third group is caught in the desire for decent wukking up.

Interestingly enough, it seems as if youths' insistence that wukking up take center stage has resulted in a concomitant rise in ballroom dancing, Latin dance, and line dancing. In some ways ballroom dancing has long been an important signifier of respectability in the traditional renderings of Barbados. It faced a backlash in the early post-independence years, when dancing ballroom was seen as a rejection of Barbadiana. This backlash was most clearly represented when Wayne "Poonka" Willock sang the calypso "Ballroom":

Ballroom could brek yuh back
Or give yuh heart attack

Bajans come back to calypso
Ballroom will mek yuh lose yuh natural rhythm
Ballroom is cultural penetration

(lyrics by Anthony "Mighty Gabby" Carter, 1983)

In some ways, therefore, the "return" to ballroom can be seen as part of the continuing contestation over decent and indecent. Certainly it should be noted that many ballroom and line dancing classes are offered by church-affiliated groups; however, we believe it to be more complex than this. It should be noted that an array of ballroom dance schools exist whose membership rosters reveal a complex range of differences in class, denominational affiliation, gender, and age. In addition, ballroom social dances have been and continue to be centrally important dance practices in the "grand dances" held each weekend by working-class Barbadians. Observing this ballroom activity, we believe it feasible that its heritage is not an exclusively European heritage. This would be a fruitful area for further study.

## Dance Identities and Interconnections

The complexity that is part of the ballroom/wukking up dynamic, or even just the possible differentiation within ballroom in Barbados, gives some indication of the continuing ways in which dance practices in Barbados reveal interrelated artistic, political, and economic agendas. If the 1970s and 1980s were characterized by focus on culture and development, the mid-1990s ushered in an era that characterized artistic practices as cultural industries that should generate revenue. The impact of this has been much more apparent in music than in dance: it is still difficult to eke out a livelihood from dance. Recent policy documents, however, have drawn dance into the ambit of other national generators of revenue.

Additionally, it would seem that the government is interested in developing times for dance performance in the same way that calypso received attention beginning in the 1980s. Thus in 2006 the government established the Community Indepen-Dance Festival and in 2007 the Crop Over Dance Circle. The Indepen-Dance Festival harkens back to the idea of cultural development as it focuses on amateurs and youth and is coordinated by the Ministry of Social Transformation, the Community Development Department, the Community Independence Celebrations Secretariat, the Commission for Pan-African Affairs, the National Cultural Foundation, and the Division of Youth Affairs. The Crop Over Dance Circle focuses on the more experienced and professional dancers and companies.

The inaugural Dance Circle brought together nine local dance companies and one visiting dance company from Jamaica. The styles of dance performed by these companies demonstrated, to some extent, continuation of interest in different styles to which we referred earlier, including folk/community, modern, ballet, and, a relatively new expression for Barbados, liturgical dance.

Community-based groups tend to align themselves with working-class interests, placing emphasis on their point of origin or location. Thus Pinelands Creative Workshop (PCW), established, with so many other companies, in the 1970s, continues to go strong. Pinelands is a broad-level community organization that focuses on the personal and community-level development of the people of the Pine community. During the early 1970s the people of the Pine were forced to contend with a number of negative stereotypes. Given our attention to the ways in which notions of decency have been used as a means of social control, we do not think we would be belaboring the point if we pointed out that the people of the Pine were stereotyped as indecent people. PCW was, therefore, one of the ways in which community leaders sought to challenge the stereotypes and also provide members of the Pine community with a larger number of education, business, sports, and creative options.

The Israel Lovell Foundation (ILF), established in the late 1990s, had a similar focus for the Ivy community, and Dancing Africa had the same focus for the Passage Road community and beyond. These groups fill the niche of dance expression left by the demise of Yoruba. Dancing Africa, in particular, provides alternatives for dancers dissatisfied with what is often identified as the Euro-centric tone of dance classes at BDTC, ballet schools, and modern dance groups. Dancing Africa came into its own after members split from Dance National Afrique in the late 1980s. Dancing Africa was for a long time located at the Passage Road Pavilion near Baxter's Road. It represented and attracted several dance enthusiasts interested in presenting versions of African and Caribbean expressions of dance.

The Barbados Dance Theatre also continues to go strong, and other companies have grown out of the early training provided by the BDTC. For example, Sheron Trotman gained her initial training with BDTC, pursued further training overseas, and in the 1990s opened her own company, Dance Strides. Additionally, Louise Woodvine, who trained in ballet and was also a company member of BDTC , opened her own Louise Woodvine Dance Academy, a ballet and jazz school. An important feature of the Louise Woodvine Dance Academy, one of two ballet schools in Barbados, is the use of the Royal Academy of Dancing ballet syllabus. Each school, then as now, would have their teachers certified to teach this curriculum and present students to be examined by an overseas examiner each year.

Liturgical dance groups represent an emerging phenomenon in Barbados. In Barbadian churches there have been traditions of movement that seem to resonate with our earlier discussion of the mapping of decency and indecency, or perhaps reputable and disreputable. Thus within the established churches, such as the Anglican Church, the notion formerly existed that church people, decent people, did not dance. The folk-Christian churches, which, during the colonial period at least, would not have had as much social status as those churches associated more closely with the state, have always had a tradition of movement. Nevertheless, more recently, dancing as a mode of evangelism has found a home in a variety of Christian denominations. Since the 1980s what passed as a church group extracurricular activity slowly became more integrated into church services. Some of the earliest liturgical dancers in Barbados were from the Roman Catholic churches, and by the 1990s this form of expression had spread also to Anglican, Methodist, and Moravian churches. Eventually the African Methodist Episcopal, Pentecostal, and evangelical churches took the lead. The Apostolic Teaching Centre, Abundant Life Assembly, and People's Cathedral developed arts and dance ministries attracting a significant wave of dance enthusiasts.

Then along came Gospelfest, a festival of Christian music, drama, and dance established in 1993. Originally conceived as a way to boost niche tourist arrivals (in this case, Christian tourists), the festival has kept this focus while also seeking to encourage local and regional gospel artists. As Gospelfest took off, the Gospelfest Dancers looked to Jamaican-born Marcia Weekes to lead them. Through her affiliation with Jamaican dance minister Pat Noble, Weekes opened an affiliate of Pat Noble's Ministry Praise Academy of Dance in Barbados in 2001. Valerie Kirton also has a liturgical dance company. Kirton used to run a secular dance company in Sargeant Village. When she converted, she changed the name of her company to Psalm 150 and changed the focus of their repertoire to evangelical works.

Even though these different companies have quite clear artistic foci, it would be a mistake to assume that they remain sealed within these categories. Quite a bit of intercompany exchange occurs, mostly in an effort to increase training opportunities for individual dancers. Thus, for example, as a result of the bond of professionalism and through their years of dancing together at BDTC, Louise Woodvine and Sheron Trotman, in the development of their school system, strategically set out to support each other in their endeavors, lending and borrowing costumes, ideas, and even students and talent on occasion. This has extended to classes; students in Woodvine's school who wanted to develop their skills in modern dance were sent to Trotman's Dance Strides to train. Similarly, Trotman would send students she felt could benefit from ballet training to Louise Woodvine Dance Academy. The result has been a group of dancers richer for their varied training in technical and performing arts skills.

In recognizing the need for advanced technical training for her young people in Dancing Africa, Jennifer Sealy developed a relationship with Adonia Evelyn of Dance Place ballet school to take the more gifted children into the ballet school's curriculum. Dancing Africa, with its repertoire of West African, Caribbean, and regional theme–inspired dances, has also benefited from inviting various experienced and trained teacher/choreographers to work with the group in the past.

The interconnections also take place at the regional level. In recent times, the Israel Lovell Foundation has brought in a Trinidadian professional teacher/choreographer as well as a Canadian-trained modern contemporary dance artist with knowledge of Trinidad and Tobago traditional dance to work with their group. Similarly, Pinelands has had a long-standing relationship of cultural exchange with Malik, a group from Laventille, Trinidad. These regional connections are nothing new for dance in Barbados, or throughout the region for that matter. For example, the BDTC has always had a strong relationship with the National Dance Theatre Company of Jamaica. These connections highlight just how much the Caribbean experience is always a transnational experience.

## Conclusion

Dance in Barbados, therefore, seems poised on the brink of a second renaissance. The immediate post-independence period saw a blossoming of dance companies, and it appears that the government is interested in providing more opportunities for further dance development. Considering the role of the government in the promotion of dance, however, one should recognize that dance in Barbados has often developed in the face of government neglect and, particularly during the colonial period, government hostility. Barbadian dance reclamation, preservation, and creation, therefore, have largely been in the hands of private individuals and nongovernmental organizations. These individuals and organizations have, through dance, articulated different notions of Barbadian identity and the sources—European, modern American, traditional and contemporary Caribbean, and African—from which Barbadian movement and Barbadian identities should be constituted. The dancers and choreographers have relied upon sources of inspiration that have not only moved backward and forward through history, but also crisscrossed the region and the wider world and, though perhaps with more limited success, the boundaries of class.

Thus dance practices in Barbados seem to offer an indication of the processes and challenges involved in identity construction. One of the challenges dance in Barbados has consistently had to confront is the colonial leer and the ready labeling of the black dancing body as "indecent." The persistence of this label and its quick application, whether during the slave period or in the contemporary period, shows the persistence of colonial understandings about the Caribbean. The tenacity of those ways of knowing the Caribbean and its inhabitants should compel us to be ever vigilant about the language we use to describe ourselves and should inspire us to produce new knowledge about the Caribbean. Dance is an ideal space for that knowledge production.

# CARRIACOU

# 19

# Big Drum Dance of Carriacou

ANNETTE C. MACDONALD

The first time I traveled to Carriacou was in July 1966 to do field research on the Big Drum Dance for my master's degree thesis (in physical education, with emphasis on dance anthropology) at the University of California, Berkeley. M.G. Smith, a professor from Jamaica, told me that in all the islands of the Caribbean, the Big Drum in Carriacou was the oldest dance complex that still existed. I decided that this was definitely worth investigating. I was accompanied by my friend Mary Joyce, who was interested in the children's dance she might find on the island.

We flew to Grenada, then took a schooner ferry boat across the strait called Kick 'em Jenny, and were met at the dock by Mr. Redhead, the District Officer of Carriacou, to whom I had sent a letter. He told us where to go and whom to visit regarding the Big Drum. He said that he had heard the people had decided not to have the Big Drum that year for the annual regatta, but that we should try to find out. We then met two sisters at the Madonna House, a Catholic apostolate that performed nursing, teaching, and other services on the island. They suggested people to visit to obtain information about the Big Drum, and we also discussed the relation of the Big Drum ancestral cult to Christianity on the island. They were fascinated that I was so interested in the Carriacou culture.

We hailed a taxi (almost all the cars were taxis) and went to visit Harveyvale Primary School, where we met two young teachers, Elveta Gabriel and Ethlyn Alexander. They told us they had been dancers performing two Big Drum dances, hallecord and gwa bele, for Queen Elizabeth's visit to Grenada in the winter of 1966. The children at the school had already been dismissed, but were still playing outside on the playground, so the teachers called them back into the classroom. The teachers beat the rhythms on the wooden desk and asked the children to perform five of the Big Drum dances they had taught them.

The next day Mr. Redhead told us to go to a store and buy a present for Mae Adams, the wife of the master drummer, Sugar Adams, and deliver it to her. He said that if Mae said there were no plans for a Big Drum that I should offer them money to have it. So we bought a nice straw hat, then took a taxi to her house on the hill to meet her. She was pleased to receive the hat and told us there was no Big Drum planned. I gave her thirty-five dollars, and she agreed to plan it for the following evening.

At sundown, July 30, 1966, the Big Drum Dance was held in the yard of the master drummer, Sugar Adams. We had a Super 8 movie camera and a tape recorder. One of the Madonna House sisters, Marite Langois, held a lantern up in the darkness, and two children held three large flashlights on the dancers. I spoke into the tape recorder, describing all the dances. It was a wonderful evening.

I traveled to Carriacou three more times, in 1977 to reshoot some of the Big Drum dances in daylight, in 1996 to see a Big Drum performance for the annual regatta and connect with my friends Winston Fleary and Lucian Duncan, and in March 2007 to interview Winston Fleary. This chapter reflects two knowledgeable Carriacouans speaking and writing about the Big Drum today. It centers around information gathered from the interview with folklorist/Big Drum director Winston Fleary and from the book by school principal, folklorist, and author Christine David, *Folk Traditions of Carriacou and Petite Martinique*, published in 2004. Also very helpful was consultation given by Dr. Donald Hill, professor of anthropology at State University of New York, Oneonta, and the work of ethnomusicologists Lorna McDaniel, Alan Lomax, and Andrew Pearse.

Carriacou, seven and a half miles wide and two and a half miles long, is the largest of the Grenadine Islands and lies twenty-six miles north of Grenada. It does not have mountains or rivers, just lovely hills, valleys, and plains. Carriacou was originally inhabited by Native Americans who came from South America. It was alternately colonized by the French and British between 1650 and 1783 when Britain gained full control. In 1967 Grenada, Carriacou, and Petite Martinique, under the Right Honorable Herbert Augustus Blaize, became an "associated state," with Britain retaining authority over foreign policy. On February 7, 1974, full independence was achieved under Sir Eric Matthew Gairy.

Figure 19.1. Dancer Matilda Noel and drummer (standing) Caddie Lazarus John at a Big Drum in Carriacou in 1966. By Annette Macdonald; used by permission.

The folk culture in Carriacou is a blend of African, French, and British influences. The core of the folk religion is the Big Drum or Nation Dance ritual. Many people practice a dual religion, Catholic or Anglican and the Big Drum. Most of the 6,000 people in Carriacou are of West African descent, and some have French, Scottish, Irish, English, East Indian, or American Indian ancestors also. The Big Drum is a synthesis of many African and a few European traditions.

One purpose of the Big Drum is to communicate with and give pleasure by honoring the dead ancestors. The drumbeats, songs, and dances serve to perpetuate the link between ancestors and descendants, to respect the dead, and give pleasure to the living. A typical Big Drum is associated with a Stone (tombstone) Feast, the climax of funeral rites. The two necessary elements to a Stone Feast are the setting of the tombstone and a prayer meeting or a Big Drum dance. Until the ancestor is properly entombed, its spirit might trouble relatives in a dream by making frequent demands for prayer meetings, masses, or Big Drum celebrations. If these are not properly carried out, the Big Drum or "Beg Pardons" must be held during which the living must ask forgiveness from the dead for specific transgressions, as we see in this Cromanti "Beg Pardon" song, which begins: "Feh no aye contray, Nenen pardone mwe; Nenen si mwe merite, Nenen pini mi mwe." (If I have not done anything contrary [wrong], Godmother still forgive; should I deserve punishment, overlook my sins.)

The traditional African Big Drum dance ritual serves as the social glue that binds the community together at several annual gatherings called maroons. The Big Drum is also performed to restore good health, to celebrate at prewedding ceremonies, the opening of a shop, or a boat launching, for honored guests such as the Queen of England, and for tourists at festivals such as the Carriacou Regatta.

In an interview in Carriacou on March 23, 2007, with Winston Fleary, director of the Big Drum Nation Dance Company, Fleary said that the origin of the Big Drum dates back to 1650, when a group of freed slaves came to Carriacou from the island of Marie-Galante (near Guadeloupe). Another story by Fleary of the arrival of Big Drum on Carriacou says it arrived via nearby Union island, brought by Congo people who had mutinied on a slave ship off the coast of Union. They came to Carriacou as free people.

I asked Fleary if he got this information from an elder such as master drummer Sugar Adams, and he responded,

> Yes, I got an oral history from Sugar Adams. Adams spoke of his relatives who were Maroons (runaway slaves) in Jamaica in 1739. They were led by Cromanti Cudjoe, a master drummer, and they fought against the British. The English captured the drummers, although they [the British] lost the war, and sent them to Grenada. Cromanti Cudjoe reorganized the drummers and they were called the "Big Drum Nation" when they eventually came to Carriacou. Those Maroons were free slaves and they were from the Akan people in Ghana. I am descended from them and Sugar Adams is also descended from them. He learned the drums from Cudjoe. Cudjoe learned the drums from his forefather Cudjoe, who learned from his father in Jamaica, who

learned from the Akan people. It came directly from Ghana. The complexity of the drumming such as the tempo is still carried on today.

Fleary went on to say that slaves from Haiti and Jamaica came to Carriacou, and they were known to have their drums. They interacted, traded, and learned each other's language. They had ways to communicate that the slave masters didn't know about, something they spoke without opening their mouths. By 1783 the drums were banned in Barbados, Trinidad, and the entire Caribbean because the slaves were revolting and were using their drums to communicate. The enslaved people on Carriacou were left alone because of the island's geographic isolation from other islands. The extremely rough strait, Kick 'em Jenny, prevented many ships from crossing the sea. The planters of the time were mostly Methodists, and they gave the slaves some liberty to work for themselves so they would contribute more to plantation life. That worked, and the wives of several estates would patronize the African dance season, the Big Drum.

According to Fleary,

Madame Dumfries of the Dumfries estate was a strong patron of the dance. She added the petticoat to the costume of the ladies. They had big skirts over petticoats; she costumed them, which was a French influence. The slaves gathered in the yard in the moonlight and they beat their drums and danced so when she saw it she thought it was very colorful and the choreography was very stunning and natural. So she felt that their expressions should be highlighted. When she had visitors she showed off her slaves so the visitors could see they had talent. They not only worked, they had talent!

Bogles was the first Carriacou African village to have a community gathering called a maroon and the first settlement of the Big Drum. Today the maroon in Bogles is still a tradition and is held on the first Friday in May. Fleary says,

It's one nation which includes Union and Petite Martinique. But it proliferates in Carriacou. The word maroon is misleading. It's not pay at the gate and watch, that is too commercialized. That's not it, that's just a word to attract people. The maroon is a gathering of the people coming together to do something—cooking, building a house, or clearing a field voluntarily. Most importantly the people come together to unite the community, bring the religions together, recognize the ancestors, and give thanks. It's a community feast, not for money making. The community brings things and they share them! What is happening now in Carriacou is just fundraising and I take no part in that. Whenever I take part they have to do it my way, recognizing the ancestors and calling their names so that the children will know their history.

Christine David writes about the maroon feast: "Maroons are held annually for different purposes: (1) a response to a dream, (2) a traditional thanksgiving sacrifice for a successful harvest of garden crops, (3) a plea for rains during the dry season and for a bountiful rainy season to plant the new crops, (4) to honor the ancestral spirits of their fore parents." (David 2004, 110) David writes that most people immensely enjoy the saraca (a communal food cooking ritual) and the Big Drum dances that follow.

The Big Drum ritual begins with a warm-up of gwa bele songs accompanied by the appropriate drumming. The chorus sings in patois: "Ti way uwanga. La zur mete ba mwe Ti way," and the lead singer sings, "Za Beausejour . . ." (Chorus: Take out the evil you had inflicted on me. Lead singer: Please do me the good favor . . .) The gwa bele dance has strong pelvic and chest expressions.

Three drums are used in the Big Drum. The bulas are always played in groups of two, placed on either side of the third drum, the cot, played by the lead drummer. The chantwel (lead singer) introduces the song, and the other singers respond by chanting the chorus. The bulas respond to the vocal introduction by producing the basic beat; then the cot drummer introduces more complex rhythms. The chantwel sings "Cromanti Cudjoe" in patois, originally a dialect of French influenced by West African languages. The Carriacouans consider Cromanti the first nation, the most important on the island. The songs are called "beg pardons" and their purpose is to let the ancestors know the dance has started and to "wake up."

Winston Fleary sang this song during his interview and explained the patois: "Cromanti Cudjoe, let us go. You are telling the crowd to go and get him to come to the feast. You have to call him. And we say, 'Sing nation, oh nation, sing a song, oh nation, sing nation for drummer Cudjoe, Cromanti Cudjoe, weep, sing and wake him up.'" Fleary mentioned again that Cromanti Cudjoe (the legendary Maroon leader) came from Africa to Jamaica by way of the slave port in Ghana and his descendants to Carriacou, and it is Cudjoe who said to the people, "You are not tribes, you are nations."

Following the Cromanti song comes the "free ring." Two overlapped towels in the formation of a cross are placed in the center of the dancing space called the ring. The four ends of the towels symbolize the path of entry and departure for the ancestral spirits, the north, south, east, west points of the universe. The oldoe (a hoe struck with a piece of iron) is beaten, asking the ancestors to come and join the dance. The ring is kept free for the spirits to enter. The arrival of the ancestors is signaled by the quickening beat of the cot drum, the lively singing, and the shaking of the shac-shac (maracas). No one is allowed to dance while the spirits are in the ring. Tales are told of people who carelessly danced in a free ring and were met with bad luck.

Next the sponsors of the fete enter to do a Cromanti beg pardon dance starting with a libation. The man walks around the ring sprinkling rum, and his wife follows him sprinkling water over the rum, completing the ritual called "wetting the ring" to bless the yard and thank the ancestors.

Then the other nation dances follow. Each nation of Carriacou is expected to be present; nation dances are named for specific West African tribal groups from which most Carriacouans claim descent. The nation designation is inherited patrilineally. African nation dances include Ibo, Chamba, Moko, Manding, Congo, Temne, Hausa, and Arada. Christine David describes some of these dances:

> The Ibo and Manding songs and dances are categorized as "Beg Pardon" dances done on occasions when people thought they had offended their gods and therefore needed to make restitution for reconciliation and pardon. The dancer crouching with open palms demonstrates a submission. Another purpose for the dance is to give thanks for a successful harvest of crops from the land. The dance posture depicts earth worship for fertility of the soil. With outstretched arms the dancer threads the earth gently as if beckoning the ancestors to reciprocate. Then with crocked knees and a very low crouch symbolizing submission, the dancer kicks back as if searching in the dust, swinging her body in excitement in anticipation of communication. At the end she rises gently like air still paying reverence to the earth and to the ancestral spirits. The grounded bird image is revealed as the dancer moves clumsily like a duck, wabbling, unable to fly. The Arada dance is used for healing of the sick and casting out evil spirits. Because of the writhing movements it is referred to as the "snake dance." It's also done to bless those who sow the seeds of food crops. The Congo is referred

to as the "thunder and rain" dance. It is often done as a group dance in a circle formation. The dancers bend at the waist doing a shuffling rhythm with their feet, an African dance form imitating servitude.

The Banda uses imagery of the grounded bird. The movement also depicts earth worship. The dancers dramatize a scene of the fowl feeding from the earth, lifting up its head to swallow, making an intervention between heaven and earth. (David 2004, 82–84).

To replace a dancer before the session ends, the new dancer enters the ring. Both dancers link their right arms and move in rhythm with the drumbeat and song, wheeling counterclockwise. Then they link their left arms and wheel clockwise. With the new dancer being introduced and the first one dismissed, the last dancer moves out of the dancing arena as the second one begins a new dance.

When the nation dances are finished, the "old creole" or secular dances are done, most by couples. These dances serve the purpose of entertainment rather than ritual. The old creole dances are bongo, hallecord (noted for the spinning motion of the dancer, called the "wheel"), kalinda, juba, gwa bele, and the bele kawe. In bongo the dancer jumps and sways and sometimes is a part of a death ritual. It was believed that the bongo afforded the deceased easy transition from earth to heaven. Kalinda is a stick fight drama, a dance for two people that depicts a mock combat. David writes, "The dancers body language, feinting attack, depicts defenses against an opponent. The stick is moved to the side of the head to defend the part of the body aimed at by the enemy. There is exaggerated leg gesture. The moves are unpredictable" (2004, 84).

The gwa bele is performed by two couples. The steps, such as the side leap, the arm swing, and couple circle, plus the meeting and parting of partners, are reminiscent of the European quadrille, also a part of Carriacou's dance culture. The bele kawe (carré) is also known as the hen dance. To quote David:

> Usually two female dancers are taken into the ring by a male dancer who introduces them to the audience. It is referred to as the dance of the King's wives, the dance of royalties. The two women represent the Queen and second wife of the King. The man who takes them into the ring is the King. The dance is choreographed to depict dignity, pride, rivalry and challenge. The women vie for attention of their

spouse with mincing steps, basically in side and forward movements. The Bele Carre as the "Hen Dance" is two women representing two hens vying over a favorite cock. As birds they swoop and glide, each believing herself to be the hen and the other the guinea fowl whose character is questionable. Flight imagery is portrayed in their posture and extended skirts, as they soar and swoop in circular motion. (David 2004, 82–83)

David also mentions a third category of secular dance called "Frivolous Dances." These are flirtatious dances done later in the evening to evoke fun and laughter among dancers and spectators. The names are chiffone, pike, and cherrup. She describes the pike: "It is done by male and female couples. They imitate a cock and poulet mating scene. The male pursues and the female retreats. The basic movement can be referred to as 'The Shove Along' or the Carriacou jig. The dancers use their individual style based on creativity, a combination of jigs and wheels, hip movements, and arm swings. It is similar to the Cherrup but more flirtatious" (2004, 84). Historically, these creole dances developed through the process of acculturation between the enslaved Africans and the Europeans.

In past years the Big Drum has served as an important religious ritualistic tie with Africa for the people of Carriacou. May Fortune, dancer and highly respected elder, stated before she died, "You dance to give thanks for your life!" Winston Fleary said, "What happens today is different; it's just a little lessening of interest in Carriacou through the influence of Western people. Interest is waning among the young people. But I went over to Union Island to join them on the day of their maroon a few years back and the Union people were so glad to see me! So those old ones who knew it came out and the younger ones picked it up because they are so focused."

I asked Winston if he still has his Big Drum troupe in Carriacou, and he replied, "Yes, many singers and dancers between the ages of 5 to 95. They learned when they were children and some of them are the children of the drummers, dancers, and singers, so they saw it when they were very young and they really have been seeing and doing it most of their lives." Although adherence to the ancestor cult religion is dwindling, the Big Drum continues as a vital social force in the community and serves as a symbol of Carriacou national pride.

# TRINIDAD AND TOBAGO

# 20

# Tradition Reaffirming Itself in New Forms

## An Overview of Trinidad and Tobago Folk Dances

HAZEL FRANCO

An underlying African presence coupled with the influence of Spanish, French, and British cultures accounts for the aesthetic attributes of the folk dances of Trinidad and Tobago and the wider Caribbean. The evidence is in the style, manner, movement, and body articulation of the region. What are considered folk dances are dances that originate with ordinary people who were driven to move, to sing. There are dances specific to religious or spiritual worship, including funerary dances such as the bongo and limbo, nation dances, and Orisha worship; dances for social events such as the traditional wedding, celebrated on Tobago with the jig and reel, and work dances that show the nuances of the predominant life skill peculiar to a village or community. Choreographed movements designed for the stage as work dances can be associated with fishing, the growing of crops, and harvesting.

They may grow out of work movements that are themselves a kind of dance. Spending my early impressionable years in a village, on a cocoa estate in Tortuga, I remember the process beginning the transformation of cocoa beans to chocolate. The cocoa pod is picked when it is ripened and spread out for a number of days in an open space or cocoa house for the beans to "sweat." After this sweating process, it is cleaned and left to dry in the sun. The women of the village then proceed to "dance" the cocoa seeds to remove the shell encasing the bean: with the feet flat they do a shuffling step, alternating right and left, backward and forward. This is done for hours until the goal of cleaning the cocoa bean is accomplished.

In this way dance is everywhere in Trinidad and Tobago. In this chapter I will introduce the islands and then discuss religion, ritual, and dance among Trinidadians of African descent, Trinidad's Carnival and its historic dances, other historic folkloric forms, the legacy of Beryl McBurnie and her Little Carib Dance Theatre, my own experience with dance and Cyril St. Lewis's Humming Bird Dance Theatre Company, the changes brought by independence and their impact on folk dance, and the continuing era of innovation with the emergence of the Astor Johnson Repertory Dance Company.

## Introduction

The twin island state of Trinidad and Tobago is at the southern tip of the archipelago of islands situated between North and South America, bordered by the Caribbean Sea and the Atlantic Ocean. The Amerindians already inhabited our country when Christopher Columbus claimed it in 1498. He sighted land with three hills protruding high in the sky and named this land the Trinity: Trinidad. This celebratory time for the Spanish government was to be remembered as full of disease and slavery in the destruction of the Amerindian peoples and the beginning of a new life for European conquerors and their slaves.

For three hundred years the Spaniards claimed the land described by the late Dr. Eric Williams as "poor, underdeveloped, a showpiece of metropolitan incompetence and indifference" (1993, 27). Luring French plantation owners to the lightly populated island of Trinidad with the promise of freedom to own plots of land accounts for the cultural changes in social behavior, dress, and style that took root and flourished and left an indelible legacy dating back to November 20, 1783, when the king of Spain issued the famous Cedula of Population. The plan was to transfer as many Catholic planters as possible and their African slaves from the French-colonized islands of Martinique, Guadeloupe, Dominica, St. Lucia, St. Vincent, and Grenada. In 1797 the British captured Trinidad and became well entrenched in conducting the affairs of the island; the Spanish officially ceded Trinidad to them in 1802.

The British were debating the profitability of slavery in and out of Parliament. The result was the eventual abolition of slavery by 1838 and the introduction of indentured labor, primarily from India. Although plantation owners sought indentured workers from China and elsewhere to fill the void in sugarcane harvesting after emancipation of the slaves, it was when they turned to India that they found a large, continuing source of labor, beginning in 1845. The Indians tried to maintain their cultural and religious forms; music and dance played a very important role in preserving and perpetuating their cultural heritage.

Tobago was a different story. In the seventeenth and eighteenth centuries, Tobago changed colonial hands so often that the island was described as no man's land. Britain claimed the land, only to have France come and lay claim to it. Holland also had its time as colonizer of the island. So too, at times, did the Duke of Courland in what is now Latvia claim it on the basis of a grant from the King of England. This continuous changing of power meant that no real development of Tobago occurred, much like the situation in Trinidad under the Spanish during the same period (approximately three hundred years). What little sign of economic growth existed in Tobago was attributed to the efforts of the French government and allowed for migration from other French colonies, particularly Grenada. By 1790 Tobago was predominantly of African population and fundamentally a slave society. The sugar industry flourished on the island under French occupation until the British reacquired it in 1803. Tobago, under British rule, joined Trinidad as a British Crown Colony in 1888. This history leaves no doubt in my mind that the infiltration of the colonials, the enslaving of the Africans, and the pilfering of resources in the region has to a great extent shaped the cultural tapestry of the islands of Trinidad and Tobago.

This colorful history provides the backdrop for the detailed account of the ways in which colonial influences as well as political and class structures played an important role in the evolution of cultural forms. From colonialism and slavery, folk forms developed, rooted in the African and colonial experiences that defined ritual practices and social behavior. By the 1930s the movement of this rich, raw folk material to the theatrical stage was seen as significant for our dance history. It was the first time that most people of the upper class witnessed the folk dances and music that were a common feature among the villages. Although this move was met with great apprehension, it was the beginning of major changes that would inform the acceptance of folk culture as art.

With the local political directorate finally freeing the people from colonial powers, gaining independence in 1962 meant a new focus on and commitment to identifying ourselves through our music, dance, food, and sense of style. The 1970s, with the black power movement, was a pivotal point in the nation's history that helped solidify our national identity. People of African ancestry saw an opportunity to reconnect with their African heritage, and so the dances reflected the African aesthetic found in religious ritual practices, festivals, and community celebrations. The folk dance traditions that were a major part of life in the villages have now manifested themselves in new forms, a testament to the ingenuity of the formerly enslaved African in embracing European culture, modifying it, and creating distinct dance forms unique to the islands.

## Religion, Ritual, and Dance

Although we can account for various cultural influences in the folk dances, the strong African influence manifests itself very clearly through the transfer of elements from spiritual practices and social behaviors that were very much a part of the existence of the ex-slaves and free coloreds of Trinidad and Tobago. We recognize that the strongest bodily influence on the folk dances of Trinidad and Tobago is the slightly tilted forward torso, together with the bent knees, the parallel feet, and the placing and gestures of the hands that represent an African aesthetic.

It was the African religious beliefs and artistic expressions of drumming, dance, and song that served as a vehicle for diminishing the pain and suffering of the African slaves. Researchers believe that although the slaves were far removed from their homelands, the rituals they practiced allowed them to maintain a connectedness to their traditions. In his research findings on the island of Carriacou north of Grenada, Anthropologist Andrew Pearce talks about the significance of the Big Drum Dance, which was testimony to the preservation there of a sense of African nationhood. The ritual practices of wetting of the ring, passing the bouquet, and the towel dance are aspects of traditions that served as a symbolic honoring of deceased ancestors. Historical accounts of the migration of enslaved Africans have been our reference for identifying the connections between the islands of Grenada, Trinidad, and Tobago. What is evident is that a direct link exists between the Big Drum Dance of Carriacou and Saraka in Trinidad (where it is rare) and Tobago, where it is often called Salaka.

Dancing, as an integral part of life's expression in African society, is a fundamental element in the thanksgiving feast of Saraka/Salaka. At this feast the dancing normally starts after the more formal part of the ceremony. It is a celebration of the different African nations in song and dance. The drummers and singers first pay tribute to the Koromantees of the Ashanti of Ghana. The basic movement is a quick shuffle of alternating feet, moving forward and back to position. This develops into a lifting of one foot, placed behind the other while the support foot slides forward.

Three songs are sung for each nation, and individuals from the different nations are expected to participate in the dancing. Dance Congo, for the nation dance of the Congo of the Congo region, is done with a right and left side shuffle, with alternating hands punctuating the beats and describing inner circles and feet traveling diagonally to the sides, repeating right and left, on phrases of four counts. In dance Ibo for the Ibo of Nigeria, the hands are used simultaneously in a traveling movement, right and left. This basic direction describes a quick step shuffle while hands at waist level reach out and in. At a change in the rhythm, the knees are closed together while the dancers rise onto the balls of the feet, rocking with an upward thrust of the knees right and left.

For the Manding of the Mandingos of Senegal, the lead foot marks a strong stamping step forward on the first beat while the following foot echoes it. A sort of rocking motion that can develop into a slight jump is accomplished, with the attack on the first beat getting stronger as the dancer becomes more involved. The stately Temne for the Temne from Sierra Leone is danced with a flat shuffle, each foot marking one, two, right and left, describing outside circles, traveling in half turns, while the hands hold out the end of the skirt, or are poised in open position at waist level.

In recent times much has been researched and documented about the two main African religions brought to these islands, the Orisha religion, formerly known as Shango in Trinidad, from Yorubaland in Nigeria, and the related Rada rites from the kingdom of Dahomey, brought by one immigrant from Dahomey in the 1850s and maintained by one community in Belmont. Religious worship and rituals were able to survive amid much adversity as the slaves developed a form of masking after being forced to adopt the religious teachings of their masters. Giving praise and honoring the orishas or powers was done by creating a parallel diversionary association with the saints associated with Christianity. Arriving in a new environment hostile to their religious practices, enslaved people developed a new form. Herskovits reports on this in *Trinidad Village*: "the Negroes became

converts of the church and lived the faith, achieving this without inner conflict by identifying the Saints with their African Deities through a simple
syncretism" (1964, 304).

The religious rituals and traditions of sacrificing, praying, and manifestations were highlighted with drumming, dancing, and singing. The dancing
takes place after the private parts of the ritual, the calling of the ancestral
spirits, and the libation ritual (wetting the ground) are performed. The
dancing, referred to as manifestation, is full of energy, strength, sensuality,
and beauty as the person moves his/her body with the drum rhythms and
the style of the spiritual power he/she possesses.

Molly Ahye, in *Golden Heritage*, gives a vivid description of the style of
dancing of the major deities as the devotee is possessed by the power: Ogun
will assume the warrior personality of this deity and, with cutlass in hand,
dance as if doing battle. Shango executes his dance with powerful and swift
intricate footwork, erratic movements of the body, and hands in exacting
coordination. Yemonja is a water deity who in Trinidad dances with a symbolic oar of wood. She goes through movements simulating rowing and
other movements reminiscent of graceful sea creatures (1978, 78).

## Carnival and the Folk Dance

Festivals such as Carnival spawned a number of dance forms and styles
that are now important additions to the folk dance repertoire. The many
carnival character portrayals that emerged with the people were a source
of innovation that injected something incomparable into the festival from
its early days of promenading on the streets and visiting house to house by
the elite classes of society. One has only to witness the maneuvering of the
body and limbs as the dragon supported by his imps attempts to cross water.
Then there is the Jab Molassie or molasses devil, whose costume consists
of cut-off short pants and a bare back with black grease covering the body.
With pitchfork in hand, his antics are a pelvic circling and menacing body
action that is a frightening sight for most children. The tall stately presence
of the Moko Jumbie on stilts is said to be directly associated with African
masquerade (Alleyne-Dettmers 2002); this character would be seen striding
down the street, overpowering in his manner.

The early accounts of dance on the islands are from the writings of scholars who researched and documented Carnival celebrations of the early 1900s and the pre-emancipation era, 1783–1833. Moreau de Saint-Méry sums it up well: "The influence of the dance is well known in the colonies, particularly among countries where the Carnival is celebrated with balls" (1976, 33). In Trinidad and Tobago, one has to closely examine the structure and laws of the society that dictated the work habits, the social interaction, and the hierarchy in terms of class and color of people in discussing dance as a cultural habit. The Spanish Cedula of Population (1783) was responsible for the settling of the French white and colored planters and their slaves. The white and colored French planters established a fairly comfortable standard of living and sought to adopt the habits and style of the French court in their mode of dress, manner, and behavior.

The Carnival season, which lasted from Christmas to Ash Wednesday, was a time reserved for much partying and fun. The planters were known to amuse themselves with the staging of concerts, balls, dinners, hunting parties, and "fetes champetres." However, there were restrictions on the privileges afforded the free coloreds. They had to adhere to some of the stringent laws that were clearly enforced to maintain the divide of the society. The free coloreds were forbidden to wear masks. Although free to celebrate as they chose, they were not allowed to participate in the celebrations of the elite. If there was to be any dancing, they were obliged to obtain a fandango license.

The fandango license, a discriminatory regulation, made it necessary for "any free coloured proprietor wishing to give a dancing party in the night" to "first obtain permission to do so from the Commandant of the Quarter"; at the same time he was "forbidden under penalty of a fine of $25 to admit any slave to the party" (Ahye 1988, 11). The slaves were relegated to onlooker status or by special favor, which meant a slave could be asked to perform to entertain guests.

The British also established certain traditions on the islands that were enforced during the Christmas season. For the British, Christmas and New Year was a time for merriment and partying, and like the slaves of the older British West Indian colonies, those residing in Trinidad and Tobago were given the freedom at this time to engage in partying and parading in their restricted areas. Among the elite class of the period, Carnival was a time to host elaborate balls where masking and disguising were a common feature. The major part of the activities consisted of house-to-house visiting and street promenading, on foot or in carriages. It was also customary to play music and dance.

Certain elements of Carnival of yesteryear continue to be a major part of the celebrations today. What is important about Carnival celebrations, the feature that engages the focus of a dance researcher, is the dancing that was the highlight of the masked balls held at the large wooden houses of the masters and mistresses of the plantations. The significant feature of these displays was the introduction of manners, style, and formal behavior that became popular in the period of Louis XIV court dances. The curious slaves observed their masters and mistresses and later adapted their styles, fashions, and mannerisms.

At these balls the men and women got to display their ability as dancers, and the women got an opportunity to be regal in their fine clothing and jewelry. Here many of the court dances were introduced. The galliard, the pavane, the contredanse, and the most popular dance of the French court, the minuet, were danced. The technique of the minuet, a coupled line dance, showed off the grace and elegance of the women and the stately and sturdy manner of the gentlemen as they executed the mincing steps and grand bows and curtsies, weaving in and out of the intricate floor patterns with clarity and precision.

Other popular dances also performed by the British were the quadrille, the lancers, and the gigue or jig. The quadrille, of French origin and later adopted by the English, is a square dance done with four couples. The movements are a balancé, ronde, chaîné, step traversée, and presentée performed with continuous interchanging by the four couples, creating varying floor patterns in numbered figures. The lancers is said to have adopted some of the same characteristics and principles as the quadrille. Although I have not come across anything to suggest that the quadrille and lancers were danced in Trinidad, it is likely they would have been performed by the slaves who came to the island from Grenada. However, there is evidence that these dances, together with the jig, were danced in Tobago.

As the twentieth century approached, dance in the Carnival celebrations took on a different perspective as specific characters became a prominent feature of the celebration. The street parade was now filled with people of the low class of society, with the more affluent continuing to celebrate the Carnival in horse-drawn carriages and later on trucks. Characters such as Dame Lorraine, Jab Molassie, Moko Jumbie, Midnight Robber, Jab Jab, and

Dragon/Imps would display distinctive movements of the body and limbs in keeping with their costume and the mythological history of their origins.

The invention of the steel drum, along with sailor and military mas portrayals, brought a special style to the Carnival and a significant dance form to the folk dance repertoire. The sailors and ships' firemen were a prominent feature in the Carnival celebrations from as early as the 1940s, with a series of fancy footworks and antics that were a depiction of life on the ships.

### Sailors Ashore: The Visual Impact

The vivid memories I still cherish of the fancy sailors and firemen strutting their stuff in the streets of Port of Spain on Carnival Monday and Tuesday are from my first encounter with the dance of Trinidad and Tobago. My family resided in a small village, Tortuga, in the central part of Trinidad where I was born and spent what would be considered my impressionable years. Around the age of four, I remember making the trek to Port of Spain with my mother to witness the Carnival celebrations. We spent the time with a family on Quarry Street, Port of Spain, a community well known as the headquarters of some of the famous steel bands that played sailor mas. The area was the hub of activity on Carnival Monday and Tuesday as the bands of three or four thousand masqueraders descended on the capital city.

It was a delight to watch the sailors dressed in their lily white sailor costumes passing by chipping (a two-step shuffle movement) down the street to the slow and infectious music of the steel drums. At intervals the sailors from different bands would stop and display their unique talent for dancing in a manner that was fun, but a challenge for both bands. With a very stately and upright posture, they would execute some intricate movement patterns, each trying to be more creative than the other, the illusion being to mimic the rank and file of the military services and in particular the drunken sailors who hung around the bars and clubs in the western part of the island. Drunken sailors were a regular sight in the bars and brothels at Carenage, the village close to the United States naval base at Chaguaramas that was occupied during World War II.

Visually, it was very refreshing to witness the firemen masqueraders as they displayed their talents as dancers. The firemen, dressed in their black merino bell-bottom pants, armed with a replica of a fire poker (the instrument that stoked the fire on the steamships)in hand, and standing in a line that spanned the width of the road, would maneuver their bodies in a wiry fashion as they imitated the stoking actions. The gestures and antics associated with the stoking action were the highlight of the day as the firemen displayed their talents for dancing and choreography, all to the delight and amusement of the audience.

The changes in the Carnival celebrations represented a transformation, as the early times of segregation were now a thing of the past. The street parade that in early years did not allow for the slaves' participation was now filled with people dancing, singing, abandoning all restrictions, and adopting a mode of merriment previously frowned upon as rowdy and lewd. By the early twentieth century the Carnival celebrations had taken on a different look; masquerade on the streets was reflective of the traditions of the African people as well as those of Europeans, and inclusive of all other groups that one can say are recognizably Trinidadian, but the horse-drawn carriages prevalent in early times were still very much a part of the Carnival well into the 1950s.

## Changing Times

The transitional periods of governance affected the culture and, by extension, the folk dance, in a very significant way. Although the act of emancipation was enforced to give the slaves freedom of choice in many ways, dominance continued by the ruling fraction. This freedom for slaves did not have much effect on the class structure in the society. The colonial powers held control in all the islands of the Caribbean until independence was granted to some of them. Although the power to govern seemed to be out of colonial control, a hierarchical class structure continued that informed the cultural divisions in the society. A good example was the bond of state and church that seemed impossible to penetrate, as the control of government and education remained in the hands of the elite and the church, respectively. But the cultural forms, the music and dance that gave aesthetic value and meaning to the society, remained rooted in the lower classes.

This innate need of the slaves to engage in dancing, a fundamental element of African expression, was the foundation on which many of the folk dances were built. Slaves practiced their religious worship and rituals under a cloud of secrecy, fearing persecution until they were allowed the freedom to beat the drums and dance in honor of their ancestors. Creolization, the fusing of European and African cultures, allowed new dance forms to emerge, and their survival in this new environment confirmed the resourcefulness of the slaves. The following types of folk dance in Trinidad and Tobago can be identified by their dominant influences: African—nation dances, orisha dances, wake dances; French—bele, quadrille; Spanish—joropo, castillian, galleron, sebucan; British—lancers, jig, quadrille.

As the power of rule shifted, it led to the establishment of villages reflective of the dominant cultural traits of the people who settled there. Life habits of the villagers were now clearly defined. In areas on the coastline such as Carenage, Moruga, and Toco, work, food, and entertainment were centered around the water, while the villages inland were associated with growing and harvesting of staple crops and vegetables. Religion and spirituality continued to be a major source of hope for the communities. The more open practice of African religious rituals and practices that had been forbidden in the past remained a means of comfort and relief. Celebrating other aspects of life in a communal manner gave villagers a sense of purpose and belonging. It was not uncommon for drums to beat long into the night as elders who remembered the movement of the dances, the songs and chants of their ancestors, danced and sang while encouraging participation by the younger generation so that cultural forms would not be lost. Many rituals and traditions that survived were passed on from generation to generation. People in the communities carried on with their vibrant and enriching cultural forms; they danced and sang, performed their religious rituals, taught the young children dance games, and related stories about Anansi and other folk characters. Cultural change was inevitable, but village life established pivotal periods in the history and culture of the land.

## Beryl McBurnie's Legacy

Researchers from as far as North America visited villages in Trinidad and Tobago, spent time with the village folks, and learned about the vibrancy, aesthetic beauty, and power of folk dances in their natural environment to express joys and sorrows through movement, song, and drum rhythms. Visits to sacred shrines of the orishas in Laventille or Belmont, or to a wake in Moruga to witness the dancing of the bongo, or the observance of such things as the launching of a boat, a good season of food gathering, or success at sea for the fishermen would transfix observers as they witnessed the richness of movement and creativity ignited by the pulsating drums. One researcher who realized the wealth of culture waiting for all in the country to see was the late Beryl McBurnie. Because of Ms. McBurnie's determination, the cultural practices common in the villages were now staged for public viewing. This cultural awakening allowed for some momentous periods in our dance history that saw the folk dance emerge in new and exciting forms.

Beryl McBurnie and her Little Carib Dance Theatre were the first of many dance companies presenting the folk dances as theatrical items, removing them from their natural environment. Ms. McBurnie's pioneering work was of major significance in the presentation and performance of folk dances. Between the 1930s and 1950s, Beryl's work influenced many people in the Caribbean region and produced locally and internationally acclaimed dance leaders.

Beryl's passion for dance began in her parents' home in the middle-class Port of Spain suburb of Woodbrook, where she engaged local children in theatrical performances for their parents and friends. She became a teacher at Tranquility Girls School, where her love of the arts allowed her to express herself and to make a difference in many children's academic lives. At the school she quickly established herself as a leader and was actively involved in the preparation of school productions. Her interest in folk forms was fueled by the folklorist Andrew Carr, whom she accompanied on many field trips to the villages. It wasn't long before Ms. McBurnie took the raw materials and perfected the moves, adapted the appropriate drum rhythms and chants, gave them form and style, and presented them as dance productions to the general public.

Beryl's need for self-expression could only be realized by her leaving these shores, and in 1938 she left to study at Teacher's College, Columbia University. While studying in New York, she was influenced by some of the innovators and pioneers of modern dance, including Martha Graham and Charles Weidman. Developing her technical skills and learning about dance from a broader perspective only helped to enhance and give form and clarity to the folk dances. Miss McBurnie's eagerness to experiment and create new forms by using what she had learned abroad allowed her to present works influenced by modern dance and ballet. Her first public production on her return to Trinidad was *A Trip through the Tropics*. Patrons were treated to contemporary pieces presented alongside the folk dances. The program was a mix of "abstract fantasy," to classical composers Wagner, Beethoven, Bach, and Mendelssohn, and classic Caribbean adaptations of Shango, Cuban conga, and Haitian drama.

Establishing the Little Carib Dance Theatre as a home for dance was always a dream of Beryl's, and it became a reality when the first brick was laid on White Street, Woodbrook, in 1947. Although the first show presented there, a year later, was a precarnival show called *Belé*, the official opening of the Little Carib Theatre was highlighted with a production titled *Talking Drums*. The program presented dances that exhibited African retentions: the Awassa Dance of Suriname, the nation dances Koromantee and Pencow, and the wake dances limbo and bongo from Trinidad. Beryl's flirting with modern dance techniques produced the piece *Gasparee Cave Ballet*. Over the years her company shared its talents with international and national audiences and won rave reviews for its performances. Ms. McBurnie's unique choreographic style, showcased in pieces such as *Green Corner, Tobago Love,* and *Hosanna*, utilized folk dance movements to highlight social attitudes in theatrical presentations. Her choreography of folk dances such as La Reine, Shango, galleron, and joropo was innovative and aesthetically pleasing to the audiences who packed the concert halls. Beryl's generosity with sharing and passing on was not reserved exclusively for her dancers; she staged children's school rallies for visiting dignitaries, an effective method for instructing young people about the folk dances and their origins.

Ms. McBurnie left us a rich legacy of information and choreographic works, as well as making us proud of our folk dance heritage. Her achievements were recognized by an honorary doctorate from the University of the West Indies. She was fondly known as the "Grand Dame of Caribbean Dance." Her success as a creative teacher and choreographer was also realized as she saw many dancers who had excelled under her watchful eye become masters of the art both at home and abroad. Her booklet *Dance Trinidad Dance* is the first of its kind to give us some insight into the movement patterns of Trinidad folk dances. By the 1960s the popularity of the Little Carib Theatre dancers was waning as migration of some of the best dancers to Europe and North America was inevitable. We do acknowledge that our dance history is richer because of Beryl McBurnie's dedication, style, and creativity in the art form.

## Experiencing the Folk Dances

In the early 1950s my family moved to Port of Spain, and I experienced my first dance lesson. My brother, Desmond, played sailor mas with the then-famous Casablanca steel band, and I observed with very keen interest every sailor dance movement he was rehearsing for the big day. I would then dance all the moves I remembered in front of a mirror. This early exposure to the sailor dance, a major part of the steel bands' masquerade, engaged my curiosity for the dance, but this was quickly dissolved as any attempt to get involved was met with strong resistance from my parents.

Attending secondary school, however, I was once again exposed to dance. I was taught the bongo dance by the late Cyril St. Lewis for an islandwide competition among secondary school students who were members of a youth organization called the Land Rangers. The bongo is a funerary dance, which means the dance is done in honor of the dead, and is a significant element at wakes, gatherings at the home of the dead where family and friends engage in prayer, singing, and dancing. This dance is said to originate from West Africa, where death is not mourned, but celebrated. Molly Ahye explains in her book *Golden Heritage* the significance of funerary dances: "Because music and dance play an important part in all the rites of passage, it is believed that the deceased must be provided with the necessary conditions for a happy passage beyond" (1978, 93; see also Ahye 2002).

The ritual begins with the lighted flambeaux being placed at strategic points in the yard, illuminating the area with bright silhouetted shapes. The bongo is usually done as a circle dance. A circle is formed by the onlookers, the drummers, and the chorus as two male dancers enter the circle and display their agility, flexibility, stamina, and strength, executing their movements—sometimes jumps that explode in the air, or low Russian-type movements with some intricate footwork. A symbolic element of the bongo dance is the continuous crossing of the hands and feet. Dancing will continue for hours as dancers come forward to challenge each other in skill and ability. My introduction to folk dance by St. Lewis would later serve as the impetus for my participation, research, and documentation work as a member of his dance troupe.

Cyril St. Lewis's passion for folk dance forms originated in his early experiences growing up in Rio Claro, where he witnessed the bongo danced at wakes and the worship and rituals performed at the Shango yards in the

Figure 20.1. Hazel Franco in the joropo, performed with the Humming Bird Dance Theatre Company in 1965. Photo by Richardson Henry. Used by permission of Hazel Franco.

area. Mr. St. Lewis became a member of the Little Carib Dance Theatre very briefly before he ambitiously began his own company, the Humming Bird Dance Theatre Company. The period he spent as one of McBurnie's dancers had a profound impact on his style as a dance teacher and choreographer. He observed very closely Beryl's methods for transforming folk dances for the stage and her aptitude for creating new works portraying community life. Mr. St. Lewis grasped the opportunity to continue his work in dance by engaging young students in the Port of Spain schools whenever he was called upon to stage schoolchildren's presentations for visiting dignitaries.

As a member of Cyril St. Lewis's Humming Bird Dance Theatre Company, I was exposed to the basic steps, drum rhythms, chants, and music of the folk dances of Trinidad and some of the other Caribbean islands. I particularly enjoyed performing dances such as the bele, Shango, and joropo. I was fascinated by the Spanish influence on the peasant style and gaiety found in the joropo, a dance that originated in the plains of Venezuela. The movements of the joropo are punctuated by lots of stamping of feet and clapping of hands as male and female dancers interact with each other. The women, in their pretty floral skirts, with white blouses frilled at the neckline and ends of the sleeves, would hold the ends of their skirts in their hands to add more flair to the strong accentuated movements of the feet. The bele, with its elegant form and style, was always the most popular of all the dances.

The first performance of the Humming Bird Dance Theatre Company's *Iere Dances* (Iere is an Amerindian name for Trinidad) featured the dances of the Caribs and Arawaks and the settlers from Venezuela's joropo as part of a full-length program. Mr. St. Lewis's exceptional creative abilities in choreography and as a dance teacher were realized in the series of yearly productions staged from the inception of the company in 1962. Like Ms. McBurnie, he experimented with folk material as the basis for fusions with other dance forms. St. Lewis researched and studied the dances of other Caribbean islands, and, before long, they were incorporated into his yearly season. Dances such as the Cuban Naningo and Babaloo, and Haitian Damballa were now permanent works in his repertoire.

His studies, which took him to university in New York City, also added a new dimension to his choreographic works. The full-length dance drama *Bianchi* embraced folk forms while interjecting modern and jazz dance. The very simple story was about a young man who travels the world in search of his loved one, Bianchi. Finding her results in a grand wedding celebration. This full-length dance drama gave the audience a blend of dances of African, Spanish, French, and American influences, producing a choreographic spectacle. It was quite obvious that Ms. McBurnie and Mr. St. Lewis, with their worldly knowledge of dance and appreciation for professional standards, offered audiences some new and dynamic choreographic work that transformed the aesthetic quality of the folk dances with sporadic interjection of other dance styles.

## Independence and its Impact on the Folk Dance

There was a point in the country's history when the cultural forms particularly flourished. The steel band movement, with thousands of masqueraders parading in military and sailor costumes, was a dominant element on the streets during the 1930s to 1950s. Traditional carnival characters were taking center stage with their blend of drama, dance, and spectacle, while portrayals of historical facts were becoming a major aspect of Carnival celebrations. The dancing, singing, and making music that was a customary habit in the villages continued to be a major source for the portrayal of life in the communities; however, the country had to cope with the depletion of colonial power as the governing force. The world dynamics of rule were changing as the young intellectuals in society were demanding a voice. The emerging of a new political force in Dr. Eric Williams and his People's National Movement in Trinidad and Tobago brought changes that significantly affected the folk culture.

Dr. Williams and the People's National Movement formed the government in 1956, signaling a shift in dominance and control of the people's resources. On August 31, 1962, the twin island state of Trinidad and Tobago gained its independence from Great Britain. The move to independent status was a symbolic and historical period for the nation. The country was being led for the first time by a black premier who later became the first prime minister. His call to the nation was for unity, discipline, and tolerance to be exercised in achieving a better nation. The talk of nationalism and nationhood seemed a lot for the people to absorb and understand as they were encouraged to be creative and innovative in building a new society divorced from colonialism. This was a time for looking forward to development and growth as a nation, removing the shackles of colonialism, and forging a new identity. The prime minister recognized that the preservation of our traditional folk forms was crucial to the development of the culture if the intention was national pride.

In 1963, the Prime Minister's Best Village Trophy Competition was the vehicle chosen for the preservation of folk forms and cultural practices. Communities worked together in presenting the dances, songs, crafts, and local foods that were unique to their village life style. This competition was started so the villagers of Trinidad and Tobago would recognize their own potential and growth. The competition focused on arts and crafts in its inaugural year and added local food dishes and sweets and dances and music in subsequent years. It so grew from the arts and craft competition of 1963 that fifteen years later, in 1978, it had became a multifaceted competition with villagers displaying their talents in the additional areas of dramatic skits, culinary exhibitions, dressmaking, dress designing, village Olympics, and environmental sanitation. My recollection of the staging of the arts component in the competition is of a concert in which each village was judged on the performance of nine dances, eight songs including the national anthem, and three skits (on Carnival, folk characters, and a one-act play). Villagers were enthusiastic about the preparation and presentation of their folk traditions on stage, whether these creolized traditions stemmed originally from Africa, Europe, or India.

African religious rituals normally experienced in the yard and known to a few were now presented before an audience. A Shango dance would leave the audience spellbound. Dancers reenacted the ritual of preparation of the ground and calling the ancestral spirits through song before possession takes place. Audiences would get wrapped up in the rhythms of the drums as the dancer, with *cocoyea* (a type of straw) broom in hand, moved to the four corners, using sweeping motions. This would be followed by dancers performing the cleansing of the area with water. The drum rhythm would rise as the dancers went through a series of movements giving the illusion of possession. People now saw the need to immerse themselves in researching the folk forms and finding new and creative ways of presentation.

One of the most significant aspects of the Best Village competition was the overwhelming participation by villages that were predominantly East Indian. This participation fostered healthy competitive interrelations among villages, exposing the communities to the various folk forms that went with the cultural makeup of the village. Indian participation helped to dispel the gesturing by others who imitated Indian dance with perfunctory hand movements and neck glides from side to side. Everyone developed an increasing knowledge of the intricate patterns and different styles of Indian dances. Two folk dances that were very popular were the ghadka (stick dance) and jharoo (broom dance). Both were couple dances done in a circular formation in which the dancers created numerous floor patterns and designs with the hitting of the stick or broom.

In the development of folk dances to performance status, very little attention had been paid to Tobago's dance heritage. Apart from research by anthropologist Andrew Pearce and researcher J. D. Elder, little was written about the dances of Tobago. It was the Prime Minister's Best Village Trophy Competition and later the Tobago Heritage Festival, held in July, that brought the richness of Tobago's culture to the full view of the public. Videotaping of these festivals over the years has given us valuable archival information on the form and style of the dances and the songs and drum rhythms accompanying them. Although the quadrille, jig, and lancers reflect the influence of European culture, strong African retentions are very evident in the movement style and posture of the dances.

The Tobago jig is a combination of the form, movement style, dress, and mannerisms of both the European and the African. As first danced by the slaves, the jig's slight hop and rocking motion, alternating weight from left foot to right foot, can be attributed to a mimicking of the gestures and movement patterns of the masters and mistresses of the plantations, superimposed on the movement style and form of the African slaves. The formal wear, scissor-tailed coat and top hat by the men, and the finest of clothes with gloves by the women, is another element that showcased the interweaving of cultural influences in creating a new and exciting folk dance form. The accompaniment for this dance has maintained a European flavor, as the fiddle is the front instrument, played with the Tobago tambourine and a pair of steel triangles. The tambourine is made of goat skin and is considered a hand drum.

The Congo bele of Tobago bears no similarities in movement or form to the bele dance of Trinidad. It is the earthy and sensual quality of the Congo woman that is emulated and not the "mincing step, turn, point and bow" of the bele as described by Beryl McBurnie (n.d., 25), but the costume is the same douillette dress, fashioned after the French court style, worn by the bele dancers. The reel is also unique to Tobago and, like the jig, is a dance for two couples performed at various family occasions. The Tobago reel has specific spiritual functions based on ancestor cult worship, as indicated by Molly Ahye: "Before marriage it is customary that the Reel Dance be held in honour of the ancestors so that they can bless the young couple and offer spiritual guidance through divination. . . . At wakes also, the Reel Dance is performed to guide the soul of the deceased and to summon the ancestors to assist in this rite of passage" (1978, 99). Two couples would be chosen to dance and, with flat feet weaving intricate floor patterns, they would gesture with their bodies as though engaged in conversation with each other.

The Best Village competition went through a period of uncertainty, with a change in the political directorate and a shift in policy regarding culture. One saw a waning of support for the program, and the very low artistic standard left much to be desired. This was a harsh reality for the communities who cherished the opportunity to display their talents and preserve the folk forms by passing their cultural practices on to the younger generation, but they were not daunted by the cancellation of the competition for one year, 1987. On the contrary, the competition gained momentum once again as communities came out in support of continuity. The Folk Fair, Village Olympics, La Reine beauty pageant, and Beautification stayed the same, but a major change was instituted in the concerts. Villages were now judged in either of two categories: a theater production or the existing concert format. This was a welcome opportunity for those who felt compelled to write a play or to improve their skills in another area. Delving into the theater arena was not as simple as the concert; a lot more work lay ahead for staging a good production.

Certain dances were repeatedly performed in both the concert and theater productions, particularly the bele. The bele is a fusion of the rhythm, form, and style of the African with the flair and coquetry of the French, which makes a very good combination. Unlike pique, a flirtatious couples dance, bele in Trinidad is danced by women. Dressed in long, full, plaid dresses with frilled sleeves over a white frilled petticoat, and a brightly colored necktie or foulard, heads covered with the madras headtie, the dancers glide across the floor with intricate floor patterns and delicate heel and toe movements as they manipulate the overskirts, creating geometrical patterns in space. In the days before this dance was performed on stage, it was part of the Saraka feast. According to the late Jean Coggins-Simmons, the bele dance ritual is a thanksgiving and can be either a secular or religious event (personal interview, 1998).

One can distinguish five different styles of bele presented during a village performance with the ritual practices associated with the bele. The cabine (opening dance) is usually performed first by the Queen, who is escorted to the dancing area by the King. After performing her greeting dance, she retires and invites the rest of the gathering to dance. At some point during the dancing, a Queen will be chosen to be responsible for hosting the next bele feast. Some choreographers of the stage dance surprise the audience with an element of folklore, the entrance of La Diablesse. La Diablesse (the devil

Figure 20.2. Dancer Natakie Punter in the bele, performed by the Diego Martin Footprints Folk Performers in 2007. Photo by Nyoko Giles. Used by permission of Hazel Franco.

woman) is one of our famous folklore characters; her beauty attracts men who, if they are not aware, are led to their death. In today's competition, it is not uncommon to see changes in the costuming and in the sequence of the dance presentation, and the addition of chants, but, whatever the new form, it is a dance that shows the beauty and grace of the female dancer.

The Best Village competition is now the main vehicle for staged folk dances in Trinidad. Folk dance oriented companies no longer present a season in a theater, though there are modern dance companies, those that have not fallen by the wayside, that do.

## The 1970s Heralded Another Era of Innovation

The 1970s was a time of political and social growth for the nation. We were now an oil-rich country, but growth was also realized in the actions of the people. With a sense of the meaning of political power, people were now aware of their strength to make change from within the society. Needless to say, it was also a time of unrest in the country. The cry for black power sweeping the United States eventually reached us in the form of a call for African pride to take its rightful place. Black consciousness was the focus of the people of African descent as they marched and protested about the social issues plaguing society. Culturally, it was a time when creativity was at its highest, as was evident in the calypsos of the time. Brother Valentino echoed the words of Bob Marley, to emancipate ourselves from mental slavery. The Mighty Duke called on us to be proud because "Black is Beautiful." This political unrest provided a perfect backdrop for the emergence of the Astor Johnson Repertory Dance Company, which sought to uplift the people through dance.

The late Astor Johnson was simple and direct in his manner. His vision was to find a clearly defined direction for dance in Trinidad and Tobago that would encourage the practitioners of folk dances to strive for excellence and professionalism. His work addressed the role of women in the society, which led him to produce works identifying women as sensual, strong, and courageous. Astor's early association with dance was with the Julia Edwards Dance Group, a vibrant and exciting bunch of dancers known for their exhilarating performance of the limbo, Jab Molassie, and calypso dances. Astor's first thought of establishing a repertory dance company came out of a series of workshop classes he conducted while on holiday from his studies at Howard University in Washington, DC. In conversation with his very good friend Austin Forsyth, a dancer and one of the founding members of the company, he indicated that a repertory company would be the ideal tool for the advancement of dance as an art form. On his return to Trinidad after finishing his studies, with a few dancers who attended the workshop, including Forsyth, the Repertory Dance Company was born.

Their first production, a workshop/demonstration, was staged at the Town Hall in Port of Spain. Johnson's creative genius manifested itself in choreographic works that span a fourteen-year period until his untimely death in 1985. The use of modern dance movements and concepts and jazz dance styles together with the folk forms once again spoke to the need for a contemporary Caribbean dance form. His masterpiece, *Fusion*, engaged the audience with a series of duets, trios, and company work that displayed the strength, agility, and grace of the dancers as they sailed across the floor at exhilarating heights, combined with an earthy sensation as their feet stomped varying patterns in a dialogue with the floor. Before long, the Repertory Dance Company was attracting dancers from the Best Village groups and those returning from studies abroad.

In the fourteen years of its existence, under the artistic directorship of Astor Johnson (the company continued after his death), the Repertory Dance Company staged some memorable pieces of work that have their place in the history books of our dance heritage. *SHE* is danced in praise of the strength and beauty of the black woman. In the symbolic solo dance with the water goblet, with strands of connection to the water deity Oshun, *SHE* moves lightly across the floor with a series of hip thrusts that capture the sensuality of the black woman. Audiences were always in awe of the precision and clarity with which the dancers performed Astor's work. *Graveyard for the Living, Mantis, Colour Him Andre,* and *Blood Wedding* are pieces that once again display a unique blend of folk and other dance forms and the creative strengths of people who made a difference in the performance of the traditions.

## Conclusion

We cannot deny that some fought to broaden the scope of the traditional dance forms by engaging in innovative and creative work. From the depths of ancestral worship and the drudgery and pain of slavery, a dance form emerged with strands of European and American influences, but rooted in the customs of the people of Trinidad and Tobago. Like the slaves who superimposed the style and manner of European cultures on their existing African forms, Beryl McBurnie exposed the richness of talent of the village folk by infusing modern techniques and modifying the dances for the grand stage. She presented the traditional, the folk dances from other Caribbean islands, and contemporary choreographed pieces that dramatically delved into life experiences. Cyril St. Lewis followed in McBurnie's footsteps, but apart from performances of folk dances in new and exciting form, he introduced dance drama, while Astor Johnson sought to create a dance form that would determine a Caribbean dance aesthetic unique to the region.

The Prime Minister's Best Village Trophy Competition was a vehicle that one hoped would ensure preservation of the traditional forms. What has surfaced, however, is an emphasis on African retentions that has seen performances of some folk dances of previous years, such as Spanish-influenced ones, become rare or nonexistent. African consciousness, the height of cultural activism and the driving force of the 1970s, continued in many ways to be the main impetus. The emergence of Astor Johnson, whose choreographic works showcased the beauty of our Africanness, and the Best Village competition, which drew continued attention to the dances with a strong African base, are testimony to this trend in the dance. Clearly African cultural retentions were dominant in dances like the bele, bongo, kalenda, limbo, nation dances, and dances of the orishas, and they were now the popular dances presented to the public.

In examining the folk dances and their development, one recognizes a cyclical effect—these dances were the creation of African slaves whose cultural history embodied a spirituality punctuated by dance and music. The embracing of other cultures to create a new and exciting tradition started with the slaves observing and adopting some elements of European movement and gesture and evolved through innovation and creativity from the Beryl McBurnie era to Astor Johnson's. And African culture is once again at the core of a new form, a new tradition, as we continue the quest for that Trinidad dance aesthetic. Pivotal artists at pivotal periods served to set professional standards, allow for more creative and innovative work, and engage the interest of the wider society in knowing and appreciating their folk culture.

# 21

# A Narrative on the Framework of the Presence, Change, and Continuity of Indian Dance in Trinidad

RAVINDRA NATH "RAVIJI" MAHARAJ

I have always loved dancing, but cannot claim to be a trained dancer. Yet I have performed as a dancer, in Indian and African dance, on television, at formal occasions, at Best Village competitions, and at cooking nights in communities across Trinidad. I have always been a keen student of the art and the history of Indian dance. I also learned African dance from Daniel at Enterprise Community Centre and have performed in India. My wife, Sujata, who was trained in Benares, taught children folk dances. Nandaye and Mridulla, under her training, were the first dancers to win the Mastana Bahar Finals, a local competition, held once a week over several months and televised live. She has been a great source for my learning process.

## History

It is often acknowledged that nritya (mimed) dance has its origin in prehistoric communities, that dance's earliest impulse may have been to freely and spontaneously express play (*leela*) or a mood (*rasa*) as well as to propitiate the Divine and to engage in community making. Indian dance, however, affirms a divine origin to dance. Lord Shiva is well known as Nataraja—king of dance. Lord Shiva and Lord Vishnu are described as Adi Natya Guru and Adi Nritya Guru—first teachers of dance. Lord Krishna's Rasleela and dance on the serpent Kaliya's head form part of popular folk repertoires. Lord Ganesh and Mother Saraswati are propitiated by all dance students and teachers before beginning performances. In odissi dance, a *moorti* (statue of a deity) is ceremonially established at one of the corners of the front stage and an offering is made through dance before the performance begins. Mother Kali danced before and during the destruction of evil forces who threatened the earth.

The performance ground is consecrated before Ramdilla or Ramleela performances in which dance supports the peripatetic nature of the performance. In fact the "grong" (ground) is really a mythopoetic map of Lord Rama's journeys as well as a multilayering of the poles and lokas—worlds described with the aid of prescribed ceremonies on a large open-air performance space.

It is not surprising, then, to experience a close relationship between Hindu religious traditions and dance. This has been maintained in Trinidad and Tobago, so far from India, even today, more than 160 years after the first arrival of indentured laborers from India in Trinidad in 1845. These indentured laborers, the first source of Indian dance, came mostly from Bihar and Uttar Pradesh, which accounts for a religious, cultural, and language base that was Bhojpuri. Upon this base many layers were added through smaller numbers coming from various provinces in south India, hilly regions of east India, Punjab, and even Nepal.

But besides the enduring Hindu community folk forms like Ramdilla (the vernacular for Ramleela), other sources fed into the diversity of Indo-Trindadian dance. The entrance of Hindi film to post World War II Trinidad, some one hundred years after Indians first arrived, made a powerful impact on the folk traditions, religion, culture, language, music, dance, technology, and aesthetics. The Hindi film brought with it a silver screen version of cabaret, Arabian (Middle Eastern), and ballroom dancing of the West, and an urban attitude toward folk culture. The Hindi film capitalized on the longing for India, as it provided heroes, romance, styles (often copied from contemporary western film stars like Humphrey Bogart, or using music like country and western), fantasies, and scenes from the Indian landscape. All these invaded the susceptible imagination of self and thus the fabric of Indian culture in Trinidad and seeded it with artificial and alien energies that reshaped it. Because of the assimilative nature of Indian culture, Indian dance was in particularly heavy overdose.

At the same time, however, the Hindi film exposed the Indian population to film versions of folk dances and music. (It must be taken into consideration that India experienced a long history of invasion and foreign rule through which Middle Eastern and Islamic, and later Western and Christian, cultures and attitudes were nourished.) Hindi film also carried some impressions of classical dance that was, by then, all but a distant memory among descendants of the indentured workers, cut off as they were from cultural association with India and with little time for leisure. But Hindi films certainly left us with an impression of a dance that was templar, courtly, and complex. This thread would lead Indian dance in Trinidad and Tobago from folk drama and freestyle community dance at cooking nights, when the community would assemble to prepare the feast for weddings, to other types of performances, even to classical forms like kathak, bharata natyam, and odissi.

The folk-drama ensembles that thrived up to the early 1960s continued the traditions of *Harichandra, Sarwan Neer, Alla-Udal*—reenactments of Bhojpuri epics complete with texts, poetry, music, narrative styles, and dance traditions. The *bhatwan* (cooking nights for weddings), *yagna* (religious occasions spanning nine days and nights), and other special socioreligious occasions provided a natural space for their nurturance. It is important to note the nature of the space that provided their continuity; the ceremonial space was therefore largely responsible for sponsorship of Indian dance. On one hand, the purely religious space provided for the dance's discipline and purity, while on the other, the wedding allowed for some freedom of expression, and they both provided opportunity for creative expression in dance as well as remuneration in cash and kind and status for the performers.

Each folk drama had at its core very capable dancers, singers, and actors. Group dances such as Rasleela, Harvest Dance, and Jharoo dance were not only integrated into the folk dramas, they also found invitation at community events on their own merit as dance.

Dance played an important role in recruiting members for the folk dramas. While all the members would be costumed and face-painted, their roles all called for a level of dance competency, while singing and acting main roles were left to the seniors. Members were often recruited from participants in the freestyle community dancing sessions. In fact, to a large extent, free dance steps were mostly caught, netted from existing folk, appropriated from films, created, but hardly ever formally taught, but they were visually, unmistakably, aesthetically Indian.

## Teaching of Dance

Formal dance teaching may have been initiated by Anandi Seereeram, who, born in Benares (also called Varanasi, a home of Hindu learning, ceremonies, kathak dance, and North Indian music), came to Trinidad in 1947 as a young bride. Kolattam, Manipuri, and some folk dances were introduced by her in Trinidad. In later years her daughter continued her legacy.

With the coming of independence to Trinidad and Tobago in 1962, the question of identity and patriotism arose within the national community. With this, naturally, came the question of cultural identity. The Indian community, still attached emotionally to India as motherland, and to Indian culture, were taunted that they had a "going back mentality" and that their culture "was not national," because it was not indigenous. It was also refused a privileged position because it carried forward a different aesthetic and rhythm. The Indian community by and large refused to abandon Indian culture. Instead, a desire arose to have youths trained in "authentic Indian culture." Thus began the steep road to recover Indian dance.

The Indian Commission was established in Port of Spain in 1948 and upgraded to an Indian High Commission in 1961. In spite of its very cautious attitude, it became a constant reminder and a portal to India. Except for Hindi, in which Indo-Trinidadians seem to have lost interest in preference for competency in English, the Indian High Commission seemed to have a hands-off attitude about offering classes in Indian arts and culture. One of the early Hindi teachers brought by the Indian Council for Cultural Relations of the government of India was Harishankar Adesh. After his tenure ended, Adesh became a citizen of Trinidad and Tobago. He formed the Bharatiya Vidya Sansthaan (BVS) which continued to organize classes in Hindi and vocal (*kanth*) and instrumental (*vaadya*) music. He was the first person to establish the teaching of music in a systematic way, reinforced by a system of classes, camps, events, graduation exercises, and *guru-shishya parampara* (training under a guru); however, dance has been noticeably absent from the BVS syllabus. But the BVS raised the standard of music and music appreciation, which prepared the soil for classical dance.

Even before the advent of BVS, Indian music in Trinidad had received a push from an interesting quarter. Hindi films had become firmly established in Trinidad by the 1950s. Film songs introduced the harmonium and a move toward orchestra music. This dealt a powerful blow to the local folk traditions, but established an alternative film presence to Western films. It also established a link to playback singers of the Hindi films. At this time, the first steps on the island toward Indian musical orchestras or music bands slowly emerged; Naya Zamana, Nav Jawan, and Jit Seesahai began, backed with names that have become icons in Trinidad: Rahamat Ali, Jhagroo Kawal, Taran Persad, Narsaloo Ramaya, Ganga Persad, Ustad Nazir Mohammed, and the dance icon Champa Devi.

The harmonium linked a very important traditional genre to what was evolving as Indian orchestras. In the 1970s this genre came to be called "local classical," or tent singing, differentiating it from the folk and film songs. Some three decades later, when the Bhojpuri language was effectively lost and Indians sang Indian songs without understanding their meaning, they intensified their love of melody and to a lesser extent rhythm.

The period between the 1960s and early '70s is touted as the golden era of Hindi films. Several elements fell into place. Technology gifted the "mike," referring to the long and short horns that amplified the music from the records spawned by the film industry and "mike-man," an earlier version of the DJ. This trio of mike, mike-man, and film records both hurt Indian music and gave it a boost. The recorded music fascinated the local Indian community and raised the level of performance, but sidelined the traditional music makers; this accounted for much of the loss sustained by the folk and ceremonial music. But this period saw development of the orchestra, amplification of the music, and the iconic nature of the film songs. It also expanded the range of musical instruments beyond the *dholak* drum, *dhantaal* (a steel rod struck by horseshoe-shaped metal), *sarangee*, a bowed string instrument, and *jhaals* (finger cymbals).

The critical first step was introduction of the harmonium to Trinidad, which gathered around it the dholak drum, mandolin, violin, guitar, and singers of popular film songs. Leading Trinidadian singers and musicians were Taran Persad, Nazir Mohammed, Jit Seesahai, Chander Bally, Narsaloo Ramaya, Rhoda Asgarali, and Ganga Persad.

Among them Champa Devi emerged as the first queen of Indian dance in Trinidad. Champa Devi is a landmark for Indian dance and social change within the Indian community. She came at the time of the rise of Indian films and the wave of Indian orchestras. Public performance by an Indian woman was still frowned upon in the community, at a time when men used to don women's clothes to perform roles in dance or folk drama and women would dance only in private chambers. A female dancer was breaking ground and making an advance in woman's liberty long before the gender revolution formally began.

Champa Devi provided a transition from the idea of an Indian female dancer as a courtesan to a woman who was a performer of dance. One may suggest that with Champa, Indian dance became a performance for its own sake, advancing from dance either in the context of social and religious ritual or as a matter of what the British termed a "nautch" girl, a practice well known in North India. In later years, Nrityanjali, a local school of classical dance, officially celebrated Champa Devi's contribution to Indian dance at a public function.

By the 1950s, the impact of World War II on social transformation within the Indian community included lifting the *orhini* (veil) as well as many restrictions on women and an increasing drive for education for social mobility. The Indian community was changing rapidly; it was gaining in independence and confidence, and even raising a political profile. Importantly, women were being educated, first at the Christian schools and then at Hindu, Vedic, Islamic, and Kabir Panthi schools. This brought, incrementally, economic independence and social mobility. One of the most important transformations was the loosening of the tradition of reserve for women that had kept them away from the public spaces. Education, small business, Hindi films at the cinema, and entertainment provided important windows for women entering the public space apart from the traditional ceremonial community occasions. Dance was still, however, the preserve of men in disguise in women's roles. But Champa Devi had arrived and no one was immune.

Hindi films had by the '50s made singers Saigal, K. C. Dey, Manadey, Talat Mahamood, Pradeep, Rafi, Mukesh, Lata, Asha, Shamshad and Sooriya and Madhubala, Cuckoo, and Bharat Bhoosan household names. The opening up of Radio Trinidad and one Indian program on Fridays became a new community event. Hosted by Kamaluddin Mohammed, "Indian Talent on Parade" commanded large audiences when the few radios in the community were at high volume for the benefit of gatherings of clusters of new music lovers within earshot of the radio.

Music director and playback singer Hemant Kumar became popular with the film *Nagin* (Snake). The "been," a folk wind instrument identified with snake charmers in India, was used in a song and dance sequence that became a landmark. The film's snake dance was imitated across the community, so much so that its movement became an identifying feature of Indian dance. The snake dance, adapted by film and transported to Trinidad, has become so much a part of Indian dance movement that when Afro-Trinidadians imitate Indian dance they often turn to snake dance movements. This suggests that the snake dance has now received folk status in Trinidad. It serves as one example of the impact of Hindi film on Indian dance. And if the snake dance has become folk, so too has cabaret, Bollywood style.

Hindi film, as a source, was artificial, heavily imitative of the West and Middle Eastern countries, but it was the most popular ongoing link with India for the Indo-Trinidadian population. The Hindi films, which continue to mimic Western cultural forms, had a strong influence on the popular cultural imagination of the growing Indian population. In Hindi films, cabaret, Western ballroom, and what in Trinidad is called Arabian dancing forms were and continue to be more prominent than traditional Indian dance. These threads would also join the energies of the later chatnee (or chutney) culture arising within the music-dance-song culture of Indians in Trinidad.

Why India had to dip into Western and Arabian dance forms for Hindi film may well explain much about the nature of Indian dance in Trinidad. It is also interesting to note that Hindi film unwittingly provided a link back to classical dance.

Local interest in Indian culture was served another way. The Indian Council for Cultural Relations (ICCR) of the Ministry of External Affairs offered scholarships to foreigners in Hindi, dance, and vocal and instrumental music. Three persons initially received ICCR scholarships in the wake of Hemant Kumar's visit for performances and a competition in which he adjudicated. They were Rajkumar Krishna Persad in dance, Harry Mahabir in instrumental music, and Azeez Khan in classical Sangeet vocal music. Over the years more than twenty dance students have benefited from this scholarship scheme by ICCR.

Others like Sujata Maharaj, who went to India to pursue a first degree, went on to train in dance, also. Both Krishna Persad and Sujata opened dance schools in Central Trinidad, the former in bharata natyam and the latter in folk dance. Both returned in the early 1970s when I left for India for Hindu studies.

It is to Krishna we must turn to recognize our first local guru in Indian classical dance, in bharata natyam. He initiated the stone-breaking era of Indian classical dance. Rajkumar "Krishna" Persad of Penal in south Trinidad was one of many youths and elders performing in Rasmandali, an ensemble of respected Indian dancers based in Gopi Trace, Penal. The community, enthralled by the young dancer, bestowed on him the name Krishna, not only because he performed the role of Krishna in Rasmandali's rasleela depiction, but also because he was a handsome, graceful dancer. (I suppose his fair complexion had something to do with it, too.) He was the first person representing Indian dance in Trinidad abroad and was employed at the Ministry of Culture of Trinidad and Tobago.

Indian classical dance would really spring to life in Trinidad when Hans Hanoomansingh led a local organization, National Council of Indian Culture (NCIC), to intervene for classical Indian dance in the 1970s. NCIC employed the Pratap and Priya Pawar husband and wife team to teach kathak in Trinidad. Most of our classical dancers who are leading performers, teachers, and founders of schools of Indian dance were initiated in kathak at NCIC by Priya and Pratap. The NCIC was soon able to take Indian dance to another level when its students began performing at cultural programs, but the local audience needed another twenty years to provide a pool of patrons large enough to fill the halls for classical performance. This did come by the 1990s.

Indian dance may be divided into classical or shastra and folk dance or loka. The following eight types of dance from different parts of India have, over the years, been accepted as classical forms by Sangeet Natak Academy: bharata natyam, kathak, kathakali, kuchipudi, manipuri, mohiniattam, odissi, and sattriya. Bharata natyam, kuchipudi, and odissi are placed in the category of mandirs, very complex, religious dance forms that were once confined to the inner sanctorum of Hindu religious places.

A second category, darbari, refers to those classical forms that were performed at the royal courts. Kathak is placed in this category and was popular in the Moghul courts, though even kathak is filled with Hindu religious abhinaya danced mime. Kathak still seems to be the preferred dance form sent by Delhi to represent Indian dance at their cultural schools abroad, a preference also visible in Trinidad. In Trinidad, however, the classical forms visibly carried forward by trained teachers and classes are not only in kathak, but also in odissi, bharata natyam, and kuchipudi. Classical schools currently standing out with ongoing classes and annual concerts showcasing their students are the Nrityanjali Dance Theatre, founded by Satnarine (Sat) Balkaransingh (kathak) and Mondira Balkaransingh (odissi); the Sandra Sookdeo School of Performing Arts, founded by Sandra Sookdeo (odissi); Sangeet Mahavidyalaya, founded by Susan Mohip (kathak) and Rana Mohip (instrumental and vocal); and that of Rajesh Seenath, trained in kuchipudi. A plethora of dance schools today also teach dance to Bollywood music, but it is Michael Salikram's dance schools along with that of Indira Mahatoo that lead.

Loka nritya are folk dances rooted in the community that mark ceremonies of rites of passage, seasons, and the life of the people. Tribal or vanvasi dances are rooted among the tribal folks and may be considered separately, but the two forms seem to have some common threads.

## Folk Theater

Another source has cradled and transported Indian dance to Trinidad: Bhojpuri folk theater, popular in North India. This thread accounts for folk dramas of royalty and heroes such as Allah Udal, Harischandra, and Sarwan Neer, and for leelas, stories of the deities: Ramdilla (vernacular for Ramleela), and Krishna leela. Rajkumar Krishna Persad arose from the Krishna leela tradition to which the Rasmandali group belonged.

Krishna leela, a folk drama that allowed for a range of folk dances, was last performed at the Divali Nagar in Chaguanas, central Trinidad, in 2006. This performance was organized by Dr. Kusaal, whose family had hosted Krishna leela during the 1980s in their community, Mon Plaisir, five miles from Chaguanas. Krishna leela was popular in Penal in south Trinidad up to the 1980s.

On the other hand, Ramdilla is flourishing. Dow Village Ramdilla and Cedar Hill both claim to be the oldest venue, with origins in the mid-1880s. While the number of Ramdilla venues had dropped during the period 1970–1980, growth in Ramdilla venues picked up by the mid-1990s and peaked as we entered the new millennium, when there were approximately forty venues. Many strands of Indian culture registered an upswing in the mid-1990s for two reasons: the 150th anniversary of Indian arrival in 1995 and the advent of the first Indian as prime minister of Trinidad and Tobago.

Trinidad and Tobago boasts a form of Ramdilla that is perhaps extinct in India today. It is an open-air theater in which the epic Hindi poem is reenacted over a period of ten days. Tassa, a powerful drum ensemble that originated in North India, provides the main music for it. Dance plays a critical role in this form of faith-theater. Ramdilla formed the basis of Derek Walcott's construction of a metaphor for the Caribbean during his Nobel Prize address in 1992.

Ramdilla is open-air theater, set in a marked-off rectangular or spherical sanctified area, varying between 100 and 120 feet wide by 120 to 150 feet long. The performance area, called the Ramdilla grong, is really a mythopoetic map of the journeys of Rama, a divine king in ancient India considered the avatar of Lord Vishnu, one of the triad of Hindu male apex divinities. The reenactment traces Rama's journeys from north to south as an exile and back to north, returning to be crowned king of Ayodhya after having vanquished the demon king Ravan.

Dance plays a central role in moving the narrative of Rama's journeys and exploits. The peripatetic nature of the folk drama may well be the reason for the preservation of the two main dance steps. These dance steps seem to be preserved largely because of the necessity for covering distance to accommodate the journeys of Rama, the epic nature of which is symbolized by the large open field.

On the north of the field stands Ayodhya, the kingdom of King Dasharatha, father of Rama. On the south stands Lanka, home of the villain and tyrant king, Ravan. On the east the sacred text, *Ramcharitmanas* of Goswami Tulsidas, is established through prescribed ceremonies. The four poles are marked off by a bamboo fence ceremonially establishing the borders of the Ramdilla grong. The spectators stand outside the bamboo fence, and the costumed players perform inside barefooted. The narrator stands behind the text and chants it.

The tassa ensemble of bass, fuller, and cutter drums and a large pair of cymbals provides the rhythm for a processional dance from the assembly point to the Ramdilla grong. The performers bow to the Ramdilla grong before entering and perform *pradakshina*, a circumambulation of it. The players then assemble in lines facing the text for a ceremony called *arti*, with those who are ritually prepared waving lighted earthen lamps in brass plates filled with flowers. While the narrator proceeds to chant and interpret verses written in an Indian dialect, the performers mime the story and telegraph the emotion of the episode through rasa or mood by facial and eye expressions as well as body postures. Performers are rated by their ability to dance, mime, and portray the rasa or mood.

Dance plays an important role in Ramdilla. Since Rama conquers space through movement, the movement becomes divine. Two basic steps are universal to all traditional Ramdilla performances, performed on the earth and not on proscenium stages. The deva gati is used by the divinities for walking. Usually Mahadeo-Shiva and Parvati, his consort, circumambulate (right shoulder always facing the jharjhara pole or axis mundi of the Ramdilla grong, placed in the middle). Shri Ram and his brothers, Bharat, Lakshmana, Shatrughan, and Narad Muni, almost always maintain this highly stylized step for walking. It consists of the foot raised slowly with a high back-lift before moving forward and placing it on the ground. It interprets a movement of divinities or celestial beings whose footsteps are partly on earth, partly beyond the earth.

The other movement is the yatra gati, used when the characters need to portray long journeys. It is also used to provide the characters a chance to exhibit their dancing and athletic skills and heighten the emotion of the spectators, or to provide entertainment while transiting from episode to episode. It is basically a one-two-three step. Beginning with the left foot moving forward, the right foot moves only as far as the heel of the left foot. The left foot again moves forward before the right foot comes forward, this time ahead of the left foot. The left foot then comes as far as the heel and the right foot moves forward. This is repeated; it is used in reverse to move backward and adjusted to a swinging sideways orientation, as when engaging in battle or exhibiting dance skills. The body assumes different angles, levels, and postures to add style or telegraph certain moods, or just to display personal skills.

Choreographed dances, classical, filmi, and folk also find their way into the Ramdilla performance as celebratory interventions to mark the birth of Rama, the wedding of Sita and Rama, and the return of Rama and Sita, accompanied by Lakshmana and the monkey army, to Ayodhya after the defeat of Ravan. There is also reason for extended dance performances by professional dancers to celebrate the coronation of Rama as king of Ayodhya. Here the invitation to dancers outside the Ramdilla performers is viewed as a natural course of action, since the Ayodhya kingdom would, in the course of its celebrations, invite performers to Ayodhya. In any case, it is not seen as dance by outsiders, as the dancers are happy to make offerings of their art in the consecrated space offered to King and Lord Rama and Queen and Divine Mother Sita.

## Hosay

The pageantry of the Ramleela is matched by the annual Hosay, celebrated by one sect of the Islamic community. The festival has been reduced to two main venues: St. James, close to the capital city, Port of Spain, and Cedros at the opposite end of the country at the southwestern end of Trinidad.

Hosay is centered around a narrative of two brothers sacrificing their lives, one poisoned and the other in the battle of Karbala. The Hosay festival adheres to strict discipline and breathtaking artistry in the making of the *tadjas*, the elaborately decorated constructions commemorating the tomb of Hussein. The tassa ensemble plays as important a role in Hosay as it does in Ramdilla. It accompanies the procession of the flag night, when participants bear colorful flags as standards reminiscent of the Karbala war of the seventh century. Whenever the tassa rolls, people dance.

The tassa leads the procession through the streets of St. James and Cedros. Naturally there is dancing as people move along with the procession. The main dance really is the moon dance of the two crescent moons, one green, symbolizing the poison given to the elder brother, Hassan, and the other red, symbolizing the blood of Hussein, who died by sword. The moon dance is the outcome of the ritual of maneuvering the large crescent moons borne on the shoulders during the procession. Part of this maneuvering is a reenactment of the two brothers facing each other and embracing each other.

The firepass also provides for dance as part of Hosay. Firepass is the movement of two ends of a pole padded with cloth and lit. The dancer then moves to the rhythm of the tassa and demonstrates complex twirls of the fire pole around his head or body. The dancer also twirls the fire on the sides, with hands outstretched. Gatcar or Indian stick fights were also performed and symbolized the place of martial arts in the Hosay commemoration. Elders involved in Hosay would also emphasize that dance really has no place in Hosay because it is symbolic of a funeral procession. Although Hosay threatens from time to time to go the way of fete (party in Trinidad), with the pulsating rhythm of the tassa, alcohol, and dance, the somber funeral note at its core and strict religious discipline keep it from going that far, and not further. Dance therefore, though present, cannot prosper in the Hosay.

## Further Developments

The most dynamic form of Indian dance, song, and music today has inherited the convergence of the fertility dances of the wedding, which took place away from the gaze of the public at two different locations. In the *maati khod* (or *matikhor*), a prenuptial rite of harvesting earth as part of a fertility rite, a procession of women accompanied by tassa drums and chanters go to a selected spot near the water's edge, or in modern times, near a water tap. There, amid chanting of folk songs accompanied by the tassa or dholak drums playing rhythms called "ladies hand," the ceremony is performed by women. Earth is harvested and brought back to the wedding tent and interred in the altar. Ladies dance is part of the ritual. The ladies also have long sessions of festivity indoors on bhatwan or cooking night, which usually falls on a Saturday night.

By the late 1960s, with the loss of Bhojpuri language comprehension, music appreciation depended on melody and rhythm. The audience was increasingly pressuring for faster rhythms. At the same time, women were already integrated into the male audiences and socializing freely. At this time, the women's or "ladies hands" of Bhojpuri folk songs were welcomed in the men's space. Previously no male drummer of class would have been caught playing women's hands; it was considered beneath them. But times had changed; the cooking night music of the traditional pal saj variety was pressed by gender issues, and the traditional reserve was giving way. All this happened within the community and outside the formal commercialized or competitive staged music events. It spread fast and was soon reverberating in dance halls of Indo-Trinidadians in New York and Miami.

It was in the early 1980s that the name "chatnee" (or chutney) emerged from other contenders, meaning "hot one," "something hot," or "fas-han," as the name for this incipient music culture. The late cultural icon Moen Mohammed is credited with the official naming rights. Chatnee therefore is a convergence of several strands of Indian music, song, and dance, but with a distinct Bhojpuri flavor. It spread fast and overtook everything else.

In the mid-1990s, ethnic contentions rose between Africans and Indians

in Trinidad because of rising consciousness among Indians of the 150th anniversary of Indian arrival in 1995, coinciding with a general election toward
the end of that year. The loss of the largely Afro-based Peoples National
Movement and the political victory of the United National Congress, largely
based among Indians, saw high-decibel criticism of Basdeo Panday, the first
Indian prime minister, in the media.

At the same time, in the Indian-dominated Penal area, large concerts
were bringing in top Indian and African entertainers. Two chatnee songs
played important roles in these venues. Anand Yankaran, the son of a great
icon of local classical music, recorded "Nandalala," and his melodious voice
and infectious rhythm caused a breakthrough of Indian music into the Carnival space. Later, Sonny Mann, an elder in the Indian music arena, burst
through even more powerfully. His song "Lotay La," the melody of which
came from a Bhajan-religious song, took the Indian community by storm.
It even caught the ear of the African community. Sonny Mann then did a
remix of "Lotay La" and released it well before the next Carnival season.
"Lotay La" took over the Carnival circuit locally and abroad. For the first
time a singer was invited to perform an Indian song at a calypso tent, and a
Bhojpuri melody and lyrics joined the calypso rhythm. But it had to com-
promise its rhythm. "Lotay La" entered the road march race for Carnival.

At the same time, many Indian orchestras were introducing calypso
rhythms in their music. Virendra Persad, after winning the Mastana Bahar
finals, rose to the top as a young charismatic keyboard musician. He soon
took over the helm of Triveni Orchestra and led it from an Indian orchestra
to a Caribbean orchestra; the name was changed to Triveni Brass. Other Indian orchestras like Dil-E-Nadan, Log Boys, and others soon followed this
lead. A few years later, Karma appeared as a breakaway from the traditional
Indian orchestras. Today hardly any traditional orchestras can be found.

At this time, in some cultural spaces within the Indian community, there
is a blurring. The question is whether Indian culture is Indians playing any
music, singing any type of song, and dancing any type of dance, or is it when
they are practicing conventionally defined Indian culture?

All these transformation were reshaping the crucible for a new impulse
in dance among Indians in Trinidad. Many young Indians were increasingly influenced by Caribbean and American music. Further, Bollywood,
as a vehicle for Indian culture in Trinidad, became increasingly devoted

to Michael Jackson. As in previous decades, Indian movies set the tone for change in Indian culture, music, song, and dance.

Today, modern dance and Michael Jackson and others influence dance-makers for the main course of Indian dance. Another Michael, Michael Salickram of Trinidad and Tobago, steps in. Following the earlier trend of the 1970s of dancing to film music, best exemplified by the charismatic Baby Susan, Michael Salikram stepped into the vacuum created when Baby Susan left to study kathak in India. Salikram brought energy, crispness, drama, and disciplined group choreography to Indian filmi dance in the local variety. He rose in popularity even as many troupes sprang up across the country to fill the rising demand for Indian group dances. Salikram, imitating Bollywood, began using modern dance and integrating African movements into his dance. There was great approval. Salikram then suddenly ventured into learning classical dance from Sandra Sookdeo, a dance guru in central Trinidad and founder of Kala Mandir. His dance was now garnished with classical moods along with his penchant for speed and drama.

On the other hand, it is Baby Susan, now really Lady Susan, who transited from the self-taught filmi dance repertoire that made her the darling of all Trinidad. Her move to classical marked a maturing of her inner self. On returning home, she married Rana Mohip, one of the most accomplished Indian musicians in the Caribbean and a classical singer. The couple established Sangeet Mahavidyalaya, with classes at several venues. This music school therefore offers a wide range of expertise shaped by training in India. This is the only couple in Trinidad dedicated to playing and teaching such music for a living. Lately, for the first time, Susan, the classical dancer and teacher, has stepped forward to experiment with classical Indian dance on the nonclassical modern Caribbean pop stage. Susan choreographed the dance to accompany a performance by Rikki Jai, the top chutney singer, at one of the annual mega competitions.

Indian dance is now armed with trained personnel, wider appreciation, and an opportunity for Indian culture when culture is being viewed as capital. In the Caribbean, culture is also viewed as identity and a tool for self-affirmation. The Caribbean is also making moves to draw closer together in an increasingly globalized market-conscious world.

Will Indian dance take the Indian community further away from an Indian identity, or will it anchor the Indian community in a distinct selfhood?

Or will it offer a dual identity of Indian and Caribbean? Dance has the potential to lead the community down any or all three paths.

Here is where we must look in the direction of Susan, Sat, Salikram, and Sandra, all from different dance traditions, offering their energies through their art. Much will depend on the community's ability to give support, primarily through allowing their children to engage in culture as an important constituent of a healthy, confident person, negotiating the space we inhabit and call home and where dance and music embrace all its people.

# Bibliography

Abrahams, Roger D., and John F. Szwed. 1983. *After Africa: Extracts from British Travel Accounts and Journals of the Seventeenth, Eighteenth, and Nineteenth Centuries concerning the Slaves, their Manners, and Customs in the British West Indies*. New Haven: Yale University Press.

Achebe, Chinua. 1985 [1959]. *Things Fall Apart*. New York: Fawcett Books.

Aching, Gerard. 2002. *Masking and Power: Carnival and Popular Culture in the Caribbean*. Minneapolis: University of Minnesota Press.

AfricanRithyms.DancesGome. http://www.freewebs.com/tombotch/dancesandthier-meaning.htm>

Agorsah, E. Kofi. 1994. "Background to Maroon Heritage." In *Maroon Heritage: Archaeological, Ethnographic, and Historical Perspectives*, ed. E. Kofi Agorsah, 1–35. Barbados: Canoe Press/University of West Indies Press.

Ahye, Molly. 1978. *Golden Heritage: The Dances of Trinidad and Tobago*. Petit Valley, Trinidad: Heritage Cultures.

———. 1983. *Cradle of Caribbean Dance*. Petit Valley, Trinidad: Heritage Cultures.

———. 1988. *Trinidad Carnival. A republication of the Caribbean Quarterly, vol. 4, nos. 3 & 4*. Paria Publishing.

———. 2002. "In Search of the Limbo: An Investigation into Its Folklore as a Wake Dance." In *Caribbean Dance From Abakuá to Zouk: How Movement Shapes Identity*, ed. Susanna Sloat, 247–261. Gainesville: University Press of Florida.

Akrong, Isaac. 2003. "Kpanlogo Dance Today: a Documentation of the Evolution of a Ga Traditional Dance Form of Ghana, West Africa." Master's research project. York University, Toronto.

———. "Objectives." African Dance Ensemble. http://www.afridance.com.

Alarcón, Alexis. 1988. "Vodú en Cuba o vodú cubano?" Santiago de Cuba: *Del Caribe* 5(12): 89–90.

Aldrich, Elizabeth. 1991. *From the Ballroom to Hell: Grace and Folly in Nineteenth-Century Dance*. Evanston, Ill.: Northwestern University Press.

Alén Rodriguez, Olavo. 1986. "Les Afro-Français à Cuba." In *Les Musiques Guadeloupéennes dans le Champ Culturel Afro-Américain au Sein des Musiques du Monde*, ed. Marie-Céline Lafontaine, 165–173. Paris: Editions Caribéennes.

———. 1986. *La música de las sociedades de tumba francesa en Cuba*. Havana: Casa de las Americas.

———. 1991. "The Tumba Francesa." In *Essays on Cuban Music*, ed. Peter Manuel. Lanham, Md.: University Press of America.

Alleyne-Dettmers, Patricia T. 2002. "The Moko Jumbie: Elevating the Children." In *Caribbean Dance From Abakuá to Zouk: How Movement Shapes Identity*, ed. Susanna Sloat, 262–287. Gainesville: University Press of Florida.

Alonso Andreu, Guillermo. 1997. *The Arara in Cuba*. Trans. Carmen González. Havana: Editorial José Martí 1997. Originally published as *Los araráes en Cuba* (Editorial José Martí, 1992).

AM4 (Association Mi Mes Manmay Matnik). 1992a. *Notes Techniques sur les Instruments Tibwa et Tanbou Dejanbe*. Fort-de-France: A.M.4.

———. 1992b. *Pour le Renouveau du Kalennda-Bele: Danses Nationales Martiniquaises*. Fort-de-France: A.M.4.

———. 2003. *Souche: AM4 Vol. 6*. Fort-de-France: A.M.4.

American Rumba Committee. 1943. *The American Rumba*. New York: Rudor.

Anderson, Benedict. 1991. *Imagined Communities: Reflections on the Origin and Spread of Nationalism*. London: Verso.

Anon. 1994. "Dance." In *Grenada, Carriacou, Petit Martinique: Spice Island of the Caribbean*, 154–157. London: Hansib.

Anthony, A. B. Patrick. 1986. "Folk Research and Development: The Institutional Background to the Folk Research Center, St. Lucia." In *Research in Ethnography and Ethnohistory of St. Lucia*, ed. Manfred Kremser and Karl R. Wernhart. Vienna: Ferdinand Berger and Söhne. 37–56.

Armas Rigal, Nieves. 1991. *Los bailes de las sociedades de tumba francesa*. Havana: Editorial Pueblo y Educación.

Arroyo, Jossianna. 2002. "'Mirror, Mirror on the Wall': Performing Racial and Gender Identities in Javier Cardona's *You Don't Look Like*." In *The State of Latino Theater in the United States: Hybridity, Transculturation, and Identity*, ed. Luis A. Ramos García. New York and London: Routledge.

Asher, Kesi. 2005. "Africa Live in Kumina." *Jamaica Gleaner*. http://www.jamaica-gleaner.com/Sunday, October 9, 2005/ent/ent1.html

Atwood, Thomas. 1971 [1791]. *The History of the Island of Dominica*. London: Frank Cass & Co.

Averill, Gage. 1997. *A Day for the Hunter, A Day for the Prey: Popular Music and Power in Haiti*. Chicago: University of Chicago Press.

Avorgbedor, Daniel K. 2005. "Musical Traditions of Ewe and Related Peoples of Togo and Benin." In *The Ewe of Togo and Benin*, ed. Benjamin N. Lawrance, 197–214. Accra New Town, Ghana: Woeli Publishing Services.

Bhabha, Homi K., ed. 1990. *Nation and Narration*. London and New York: Routledge.

Banes, Sally. 1987 [1980]. *Terpsichore in Sneakers: Post-modern Dance*. Middletown, Conn.: Wesleyan University Press.

Barton, Halbert. 2002. "The Challenges of Puerto Rican Bomba." In *Caribbean Dance From Abakuá to Zouk: How Movement Shapes Identity*, ed. Susanna Sloat, 183—196. Gainesville: University Press of Florida.

Barz, Gregory, and Timothy Cooley, eds. 1997. *Shadows in the Field: New Perspectives for Fieldwork in Ethnomusicology*. New York: Oxford University Press.

Basso, Alessandra. 1995. "Las celebraciones ararás in Perico y Jovellanos." Unpublished master's thesis, CNSEA, Havana.

Bastide, Roger. 1971. *African Civilizations in the New World*. New York: Harper and Row.

Baxter, Ivy. 1970. *The Arts of an Island*. New Jersey: Scarecrow Press.

Beaudet, Jean-Michel. 1998. "French Guiana." In *The Garland Encyclopedia of World Music*. Vol. 2, *South America, Mexico, Central America, and the Caribbean*, ed. Dale A. Olsen and Daniel E. Sheehy, 434–440. New York: Garland.

Bellegarde-Smith, Patrick. 1990. *Haiti: The Breached Citadel*. Toronto: Canadian Scholars' Press.

Bergan, Laura Wilson. 1979. "Folk and Ethnological Dance in Barbados." Unpublished research paper prepared as part of the Colgate University program in Barbados.

Bertrand, Anca. 1966a. "Folklore à la Guadeloupe: Le Cercle de Culture Ansois." *Parallèles* 14: 19–21.

———. 1966b. "Love Games at Sainte Marie: Folk Orchestras in Martinique." *Parallèles* 15: 18–19.

Best, Curwen. 2001. *Roots to Popular Culture: Barbadian Aesthetics: Kamau Brathwaite to Hardcore Styles*. London and Oxford: Macmillan Education.

Bettelheim, Judith. 2001. "The Tumba Francesa and Tajona of Santiago de Cuba," "Carnival in Santiago de Cuba," and "Carnival in Santiago de Cuba at the End of the Millenium." In *Cuban Festivals: A Century of Afro-Cuban Culture*, ed. Judith Bettelheim, 94–153. Princeton, N.J.: Markus Wiener.

Bilby, Kenneth M. 1985. "The Caribbean as a Musical Region." In *Caribbean Contours*, ed. Sidney W. Mintz and Sally Price, 181–218. Baltimore: Johns Hopkins University Press.

———. 2003. "Performing African Nations in Jamaica," Séminaire d'ethnomusicologie caribéenne." http://pagesperso-orange.fr/lameca/dossiers/ethnomusicologie/bilby1_eng.html.

———. 2005. *True-Born Maroons*. Gainesville: University Press of Florida.

———. 2007. "Masking the Spirit in the South Atlantic World: Jankunu's Partially Hidden History." http://www.cis.yale.edu/glc/belisario/Bilby.pdf.

Bilby, Kenneth, and Morton Marks. 1999. *Dominica—Creole Crossroads*. Notes for compact disc. Caribbean Voyage Series. Rounder CD 11661–1724–2.

Blacking, John. 1973. *How Musical is Man*. Seattle: University of Washington Press.

Blérald-Ndagano, Monique. 1996. *Musiques et Danses Créoles au Tambour de la Guyane Française*. Cayenne: Ibis Rouge Editions/Presses Universitaires Créoles/ GEREC.

Borome, Joseph A. 1969. "How Crown Colony Government Came to Dominica by 1898." *Caribbean Studies* 9(3): 26–67.

Bourne, Luther, 1989. "The Early Days of BDTC." In *Twenty-one years of dance in*

*Barbados: The development of the Barbados Dance Theatre Company*, 9–11. Barbados: Lighthouse Communications Inc.

Brandel, Rose. 1973. *The Music of Central Africa: An Ethnomusicological Study*. The Hague: Martinus Nijhoff.

Brathwaite, Edward Kamau. 1979. "A Report on Cultural Formation in Barbados with Proposals for a Plan for National Cultural Development." Barbados: Ministry of Education and Culture.

———. 1995. *History of the Voice: The Development of Nation Language in Anglophone Caribbean Poetry*. London: New Beacon Books.

Browning, Barbara. 1998. *Infectious Rhythm: Metaphors of Contagion and the Spread of African Culture*. New York: Routledge.

Buckman, Peter. 1978. *Let's Dance: Social, Ballroom and Folk Dancing*. New York: Paddington Press.

Burrowes, Marcia. 2005. "The Cloaking of a Heritage: The Barbados Landship." In *Contesting Freedom: Control and Resistance in the Post-emancipation Caribbean*, ed. Gad Heuman and David Trotman, 215–234. Oxford: MacMillan Caribbean.

Butler, Judith. 1990. *Gender Trouble. Feminism and the Subversion of Identity*. New York and London: Routlege.

———. 1993. *Bodies That Matter. On the Discursive Limits of "Sex."* New York and London: Routlege.

Cable, George Washington. 1969 [1886]. "The Dance in Place Congo"; "Creole Slave Songs." In *The Social Implications of Early Negro Music in the United States*, ed. Bernard Katz, 32–68. New York: Arno Press. 32–68.

Cabrera, Lydia. *El Monte*. 1996. Havana: Editorial SI-MAR S.A.

Cally-Lézin, Sully. 1990. *Musiques et danses Afro-Caraïbes: Martinique*. Gros Morne, Martinique: Cally-Lézin.

*Canadian Ten Cent Ball-Room Companion and Guide to Dancing*. 1871. Toronto: Wm. Warwick, Publisher.

Caribbean Area. http://www.peakbagger.com/range.aspx?rid=19>

Carmichael, Mrs. 1969 [1833]. *Domestic Manners and Social Conditions of the White, Coloured, and Negro Populations of the West Indies*. New York: Negro Universities Press.

Carpentier, Alejo. 1979. *La Música en Cuba*. Havana: Letras Cubanas.

Carty, Hilary. S. 1988. *Folk Dances of Jamaica: An Insight*. London: Dance Books.

Caudeiron, Mabel "Cissie." 1988. "Music and Songs of Dominica." In Lennox Honychurch, *Our Island Culture*, 48–54. Barbados: Letchworth Press.

Cave, Rosita. 1979. "The History and Changing Focus of Dance in Barbados." Unpublished research paper, UWI, Cave Hill.

Chao Carbonero, Graciela. 1980. *Bailes Yorubas en Cuba*. Havana: Editorial Pueblo y Educación.

Chao Carbonero, Graciela, and Sara Lamerán. 1980. *Guía de estudio Folklore Cubano I-II-III-IV*. Havana: Editorial Pueblo y Educación.

Chatterjee, Partha. 1993. *The Nation and and Its Fragment: Colonial and Postcolonial Histories*. Princeton, N.J.: Princeton University Press.

Chernoff, John Miller. 1979. *African Rhythm and African Sensibility*. Chicago: University of Chicago Press.

Christa, Gabri. 2002. "Tambu: Afro-Curaçao's Music and Dance of Resistance." In *Caribbean Dance From Abakuá to Zouk: How Movement Shapes Identity*, ed. Susanna Sloat, 291–302. Gainesville: University Press of Florida.

Clark, VèVè A. 2002. "Katherine Dunham's Tropical Revue." In *Caribbean Dance From Abakuá to Zouk: How Movement Shapes Identity*, ed. Susanna Sloat, 305–319. Gainesville: University Press of Florida.

Clarke, Austin. 1994. "We is a wukking-up people!" *Sunday Sun*, August 7: 23A.

Collins, John. 1992. "Some Anti-Hegemonic Aspects of African Popular Music." In *Rockin' the Boat: Mass Music and Mass Movements*, ed. Reebee Garofalo, 185–194. Boston: South End Press.

———. 2004. *African Musical Symbolism in Contemporary Perspective: Roots, Rhythm and Relativity*. Berlin: Pro Business.

Collymore, F. A. 1970. *Barbadian Dialect*, 4th ed. Barbados: The Barbados National Trust.

Concepción, Alma. 2002a. "Dance in Puerto Rico: Embodied Meanings." In *Caribbean Dance from Abakuá to Zouk: How Movement Shapes Identity*, ed. Susanna Sloat, 165–175. Gainesville: University Press of Florida.

———. 2002b. "Gilda Navarra Before Taller de Histriones." In *Caribbean Dance from Abakuá to Zouk: How Movement Shapes Identity*, ed. Susanna Sloat, 176–182. Gainesville: University Press of Florida.

Cooper, Frederick. 2002. *Africa Since 1940: the Past of the Present*. New York: Cambridge University Press.

Corbea Calzado, Julio. 2004. "Historia de una familia haitano-cubana." Santiago de Cuba: *Del Caribe* 44: 62–70.

Courlander, Harold. 1954. *African and Afro-American Drums*. New York: Folkways FE 4502 C/D.

———. 1960. *The Drum and the Hoe: Life and Lore of the Haitian People*. Berkeley: University of California.

Cowley, John. No date. "Kalenda: A sample of the complex development of African-derived culture in the Americas." Manuscript.

———. 1996. *Carnival, Canboulay and Calypso: Traditions in the Making*. Cambridge: Cambridge University Press.

Crowell, Nathaniel Hamilton, Jr. 2002. "What Is Congolese in Caribbean Dance." In *Caribbean Dance From Abakuá to Zouk: How Movement Shapes Identity*, ed. Susanna Sloat, 11–20. Gainesville: University Press of Florida.

Crowley, Daniel J. 1957. "Song and Dance in St. Lucia," *Ethnomusicology* 1(9): 4–14.

Cruz, Eduardo Marrero. 2006. *Julián de Zulueta y Amondo: Promotor del Capitalismo en Cuba*. Havana: Ediciones UNIÓN.

Cruz Ríos, Laura. 2006. *Flujos inmigratorios franceses a Santiago de Cuba 1800–1868.* Santiago de Cuba: Editorial Oriente.

Curtin, Philip. 1969. *The Atlantic Slave Trade: A Census.* Madison: University of Wisconsin Press.

Cyrille, Dominique. 2002. "Sa Ki Ta Nou (This belongs to us): Creole Dances of the French Caribbean." In *Caribbean Dance From Abakuá to Zouk: How Movement Shapes Identity*, ed. Susanna Sloat, 221–244. Gainesville: University Press of Florida.

Cyrille, Dominique, and Julian Gerstin. 2001. "Kalenda: Resonances of Tradition." Paper presented to the Center for Black Music Studies, Port-of-Spain, Trinidad.

Dagan, Esther A., ed. 1997. *The Spirit's Dance in Africa: Evolution, Transformation and Continuity in Sub-Sahara.* Westmount, Quebec: Galerie Amrad African Arts Publications.

Daniel, Yvonne. 2002. "Cuban Dance: An Orchard of Caribbean Creativity." In *Caribbean Dance From Abakuá to Zouk: How Movement Shapes Identity*, ed. Susanna Sloat. Gainesville: University Press of Florida. 23–55.

———. 2005. *Dancing Wisdom: Embodied Knowledge in Haitian Vodou, Cuban Yoruba, and Bahian Candomblé.* Chicago and Urbana: University of Illinois Press.

David, Christine. 1994. "Carriacou Dance." In *Grenada, Carriacou, Petit Martinique: Spice Island of the Caribbean*, 162–169. London: Hansib.

———. 2006 [2004]. *Folk Traditions of Carriacou & Petite Martinique.* Carriacou: Christine David.

Davis, Martha Ellen. 1987. *La otra ciencia: el vodú dominicano como religión y medicina populares.* Santo Domingo: Universidad Autónoma de Santo Domingo.

———. 1998. "The Dominican Republic." In *The Garland Encyclopedia of World Music.* Vol. 2, *South America, Mexico, Central America, and the Caribbean*, ed. Dale A. Olsen and Daniel E. Sheehy, 845–863. New York: Garland Publishing.

———. 2002. "Dominican Folk Dance and the Shaping of National Identity." In *Caribbean Dance From Abakuá to Zouk: How Movement Shapes Identity*, ed. Susanna Sloat, 127–151. Gainesville: University Press of Florida.

———. 2007a. "La historia oral del son vivo de la capital dominicana." *Boletín del Archivo General de la Nación* 32 (117), 175–197.

———. 2007b. "*Vodú* of the Dominican Republic: Devotion to 'La Veintiuna División.'" *Afro-Hispanic Review* 26(1): 75–90.

Day, Charles William. 1852. *Five Years' Residence in the West Indies.* London: Colburn and Co.

De Leon, Rafael. 1986. *Calypso from France to Trinidad: 800 Years of History.* Trinidad: General Printers of San Juan.

Delgado, Celeste Fraser, and José Esteban Muñoz, eds. 1997. *Every-night Life: Culture and Dance in Latin/o America.* Durham, N.C.: Duke University Press.

Dixon Gottschild, Brenda. 1996. *Digging the Africanist Presence in American Performance: Dance and Other Contexts.* Westport, Conn.: Praeger Publishers.

———. 2002. "Crossroads, Continuities, and Contradictions: The Afro-Euro-Caribbean Triangle." In *Caribbean Dance from Abakua to Zouk: How Movement Shapes Identity*, ed. Susanna Sloat, 3–10. Gainesville: University Press of Florida.

Don, Esther. 2002. *USISTD American Rhythm Bronze Syllabus*. Houston: United States Imperial Society of Teachers of Dancing.

Dudley, Shannon. 2004. *Carnival Music in Trinidad: Experiencing Music, Expressing Culture*. New York and Oxford: Oxford University Press.

Duharte Jiménez, Rafael. 2001. *Santiago de Cuba y África: un diálogo en el tiempo*. Santiago de Cuba: Ediciones Santiago.

Dunham, Katherine. 1947. "The Dances of Haiti." *Acta Anthropologica* 2(4).

———. 2005. *Kaiso!: Writings by and about Katherine Dunham*, ed. VèVè A. Clark and Sara E. Johnson. Madison: University of Wisconsin Press.

Eldridge, Michael. 2002. "There Goes the Transnational Neighborhood: Calypso Buys a Bungalow." *Callaloo* 25(2): 620–638.

Eli Rodríguez, Victoria, Olavo Alén, et. al. 1997. *Instrumentos de la Música Folclórico-Popular de Cuba*. Havana: Centro de Investigación y Desarrollo de la Música Cubana: Editorial de Ciencias Sociales.

Eltis, David. 2000. *The Rise of African Slavery in the Americas*. Cambridge: Cambridge University Press.

Eltis, David, Stephen D. Behrendt, David Richardson, and Herbert S. Klein. 1999. *The Trans-Atlantic Slave Trade: A Database on CD-ROM*. Cambridge: Cambridge University Press.

Emery, Lynne. 1988. *Black Dance in the U.S. From 1619–1970*. Princeton, NJ: Princeton Book Company/Dance Horizons.

"Encyclopedia of Cajun Culture." http://www.cajunculture.com/Other/creolization.htm>

Engel, Lyle Kenyon, ed. 1962. *The Fred Astaire Dance Book*. New York: Pocket Books.

Epstein, Dena. 1977. *Sinful Tunes and Spirituals: Black Folk Music to the Civil War*. Urbana: University of Illinois Press.

Eskamp, Kees, and Frank de Geus. 1993. "The Pelvis as Shock Absorber: Modern and African Dance." *Journal of Popular Culture* 27(1): 55–65.

Fage, J. D., with William Tardoff. 1999. *A History of Africa*, 4th ed. London: Routledge.

Fernández Martinez, Mirta. 2005. *Oralidad y Africania en Cuba*. Havana: Editorial de Ciencias Sociales.

Fiehrer, Thomas. 1991. "From Quadrille to Stomp: The Creole Origins of Jazz." *Popular Music* 10(1): 21–38.

Flanders Crosby, Jill. 2007. "A Felt Authentic Grounding: Intersecting Theories of Performance, Authenticity and Tradition." Paper presented at the annual meeting of Congress on Research in Dance, New York, NY, Nov. 8–11.

———. 2008. *West African Dance and Music in the United States and Cuba: Looking at Social and Concert Jazz Dance and at Cuban Religious and Social Dances*. London: Dancing at the Crossroads Publications.

Floyd, Samuel A., Jr. 1999. "Black Music in the Circum-Caribbean." *American Music* 17(1): 1–37.

Forman, Murray. 2002. *The 'Hood Comes First: Race, Space, and Place in Rap and Hip-Hop*. Middletown, Conn.: Wesleyan University Press.

Franco, Hazel. 1999. "Cross-Cultural Influences in the Bele Dance of Trinidad." Master's research project. York , Toronto.

Frank, Henry. 2002. "Haitian Vodou Ritual Dance and Its Secularization." In *Caribbean Dance From Abakuá to Zouk: How Movement Shapes Identity*, ed. Susanna Sloat, 109–113. Gainesville: University Press of Florida.

Frow, John. 1995. *Cultural Studies and Cultural Value*. Oxford: Clarendon Press.

Fryer, Peter. 2000. *Rhythms of Resistance: African Musical Heritage in Brazil*. Hanover, N.H.: Wesleyan University Press/University Press of New England.

Ga. http://www.hoasogli.com/african/ga.htm

Gabali, Jocelyn. 1980. *Diadyéé*. Paris: Imprimerie Edit.

Gavua, Kodzo, ed. 2000. *A Handbook of Eweland*. Vol. 2, *The Northern Ewes in Ghana*. Accra: Woeli Publishing Service.

Gerstin, Julian. 2000. "Musical Revivals and Social Movements in Contemporary Martinique: Ideology, Identity, Ambivalence." In *The African Diaspora: A Musical Perspective*, ed. Ingrid Monson, 295–328. New York: Garland.

———. 2004. "Tangled Roots: Kalenda and Other Neo-African dances in the Circum-Caribbean." *New West Indian Guide* 78(1&2): 5–41.

———. 2007. "The Allure of Origins: Neo-African Dances in the French Caribbean and the Southern United States." In *Just Below South: Intercultural Performance in the Caribbean and the U.S. South*, ed. Jessica Adams, Michael P. Bibler, and Cécile Accilien, 123–145. Charlottesville: University of Virginia Press.

Gerstin, Julian, and Dominique Cyrille. 2001. *Martinique: Canefields and City Streets*. In the CD series, *Caribbean Voyage: The 1962 Field Recordings of Alan Lomax*. Rounder 11661-1730-2.

Ghana History. *Ghana Web*. http://www.ghanaweb.com/GhanaHomePage/history/.

Gilkes, Al. 1994. "No ring bang no wuk up." *Sunday Sun*, July 31, 48.

Gilroy, Paul. 1993. *The Black Atlantic: Modernity and Double Consciousness*. Cambridge, Mass.: Harvard University Press.

———. 2007. *Black Britain: A Photographic History*. London: Saqi Books.

Glissant, Edouard. 1989. "Theater, Consciousness of the People." In *Caribbean Discourse: Selected Essays*. Charlottesville: University Press of Virginia.

———. 1989. "Introductions." In *Caribbean Discourse: Selected Essays*. Charlottesville: University Press of Virginia.

Gómez Nava, Raimundo. 2005. "Lo Haitiano en lo Cubano." In *De Dónde son los Cubanos*, ed. Graciela Chailloux Laffita, 5–51. Havana: Editorial de Ciencias Sociales.

Griffith, Glyne, ed. 2001. *Caribbean Cultural Identities*. Lewisburg, Pa.: Bucknell University Press.

Guanche, Jesus. 1983. *Procesos Etnoculturales de Cuba*. Havana: Editorial Letras Cubanas.

Guanche, Jesus, and Dennis Moreno. 1988. *Caidije*. Santiago de Cuba: Editorial Oriente.

Guerra, Ramiro. 1989. *Una metodología para la danza moderna*. Havana: Coleccion Estudios Teóricos. Instituto Superior de Arte.

———. 1989. *Teatralización del folklore y otros ensayos*. Havana: Editorial Letras Cubana.

———. 1999. *Caliban danzante*. Caracas: Monte Avila Editores Latinoamericana.

———. 1999. *Coordenadas danzarias*. Havana: Ediciones UNION.

———. 2000. *Eros baila. Danza y sexualidad*.(Premio Alejo Carpentier). Havana: Editorial Letras Cubanas.

———. 2003. *El síndrome del placer*. Santa Clara, Cuba: Editorial Capiro.

———. 2003. *De la narratividad al abstraccionismo*. Havana: Centro de Investigación y Desarrollo de la Cultura Cubana Juan Marinello.

———. 2003. *Apreciación de la danza*. Havana: Editorial Letras Cubanas.

Guilbault, Jocelyne. 1985. "A St. Lucian 'Kwadril' Evening." *Latin American Music Review* 6(1): 31–57.

———. 1993. *Musical Traditions of St. Lucia, West Indies*. Smithsonian Folkways C-SF 40416.

———. 1998a. "Dominica." In *The Garland Encyclopedia of World Music*. Vol. 2, *South America, Mexico, Central America, and the Caribbean*, ed. Dale A. Olsen and Daniel E. Sheehy, 840–844. New York: Garland.

———. 1998b. "Guadeloupe." In *The Garland Encyclopedia of World Music*. Vol. 2, *South America, Mexico, Central America, and the Caribbean*, ed. Dale A. Olsen and Daniel E. Sheehy, 873–880. New York: Garland.

———. 1998c. "St. Lucia." In *The Garland Encyclopedia of World Music*. Vol. 2, *South America, Mexico, Central America, and the Caribbean*, ed. Dale A. Olsen and Daniel E. Sheehy, 942–951. New York: Garland.

———. 2002. "The Politics of Calypso in a World of Music Industries." In *Popular Music Studies*, ed. David Hesmondhalgh and Keith Negus, 191–204. London: Arnold.

Hagedorn, Katherine J. 2001. *Divine Utterances: The Performance of Afro-Cuban Santería*. Washington, D.C.: Smithsonian Institution Press.

Hall, Stuart. 2001. "Negotiating Caribbean Identities." In *New Caribbean Thought: A Reader*, ed. Brian Meeks and Folke Lindahl. Jamaica: University of West Indies Press.

Hall-Alleyne, Beverly. 1982. "Asante Kotoko: The Maroons of Jamaica." *ACIJ Newsletter* 7, 3–40.

Hamilton, Beverley. 1988. "Marcus Garvey and Cultural Development in Jamaica: A Preliminary Survey." In *Garvey: His Work and Impact*, ed. R. Lewis and P. Bryan, 87–111. Kingston: University of the West Indies, Institute of Social and Economic Research and Department of Extra Mural Studies.

Hamm, Charles. 1979. *Yesterdays: Popular Song in America*. New York: W. W. Norton.

Handler, Jerome S., and Charlotte J. Frisbie. 1972. "Aspects of Slave Life in Barbados: Music and Its Cultural Context." *Caribbean Studies* 11(4): 5–46.

Harewood, Susan. 2006. "Transnational Soca Performances and Gendered Re-narrations of Caribbean Nationalisms." *Social and Economic Studies* 55(1 & 2).

———. 2008. "Policy and Performance in the Caribbean." *Popular Music* 27: 209–223.

Harris, Col. C.L.G. 1994. "The True Traditions of my Ancestors." In *Maroon Heritage: Archaeological, Ethnographic, and Historical Perspectives*, ed. E. Kofi Agorsah, 36–63. Barbados: Canoe Press/University of West Indies Press.

Harris, Wilson. 1998. "Creoleness: The Crossroads of a Civilization?" In *Caribbean Creolization: Reflections on the Cultural Dynamics of Language, Literature,and Identity*, ed. Kathleen M. Balutansky and Marie-Agnès Sourieau. Gainesville: University Press of Florida.

Hartman, Saidya. 1997. *Scenes of Subjection: Terror, Slavery and Self-making in Nineteenth Century America*. New York and London: Oxford University Press.

Hearn, Lafcadio. 1923 [1890]. *Two Years in the French West Indies*. New York: Harper & Bros.

———. 1977 [1924]. *Esquisses Martiniquaises*. French translation by Marc Loge. Paris: Annuaire International des Français d'Outre-Mer.

Helg, Aline. 1995. *Our Rightful Share: The Afro-Cuban Struggle for Equality, 1886–1912*. Chapel Hill: University of North Carolina Press.

Herskovits, Melville J., and Frances S. Herskovits. 1964 [1947]. *Trinidad Village*. New York: Knopf.

Higman, B. W. 1984. *Slave Populations of the British Caribbean, 1807–1834*. Baltimore: Johns Hopkins University Press.

Hill, Donald R. 1974. "Music for the Old Parents: The Folk Religion of Carriacou As Expressed in the Big Drum Dance." Unpublished paper delivered at the annual meeting of the American Folklore Society.

———. 1977. "The Impact of Migration on the Metropolitan and Folk Society of Carriacou, Grenada." *Anthropological Papers of the American Museum of Natural History* 54(2).

———. 1980. Liner notes. *The Big Drum and Other Ritual and Social Music of Carriacou*. New York: Folkways FE 34002.

———. 1993. *Calypso Calaloo: Early Carnival Music in Trinidad*. Gainesville: University Press of Florida.

———. 1998. "West African and Haitian Influences on the Ritual and Popular Music of Carriacou, Trinidad, and Cuba." *Black Music Research Journal* 18(1/2): 183–202.

Hill, Errol. 1972. *The Trinidad Carnival: Mandate for a National Theatre*. Austin: University of Texas Press.

Hintzen, Percy C. 2000. "Afro-Creole Nationalism as Elite Domination: The English-Speaking West Indies." In *Foreign Policy and the Black (Inter)National Interest*, ed. Charles P. Henry, 185–215 . Albany: State University of New York Press.

Honychurch, Lennox. 1984. *The Dominica Story: A History of the Island*, 2nd ed. Roseau, Dominica: The Dominican Institute.

———, ed. 1988. *Our Island Culture*. Barbados: Letchworth Press.

———. 1991. *Dominica: Isle of Adventure*. London: The Macmillan Press.

———. "Africa and Dominica" in "Dominica: Art, Articles, Culture, History and Resources." http://www.lennoxhonychurch.com/africa-Dominica.cfm

———. "Edward le Blanc, Mabel 'Cissie' Caudeiron, and the Creation of Creole Nationalism in Dominica" in "Dominica: Art, Articles, Culture, History and Resources." http://www.lennoxhonychurch.com/article.cfm?Id=384.

Honorat, Michel Lamartinière. 1955. *Les Danses folkloriques haitiennes*. Port-au-Prince: Imprimerie de l'État.

Hulme, Peter, and Neil L. Whitehead, eds. 1992. *Wild Majesty: Encounters with Caribs from Columbus to the Present Day, An Anthology*. New York: Oxford University Press.

Hurbon, Laënnec. 1995. "American Fantasy and Haitian Vodou." In *Sacred Arts of Haitian Vodou*, ed. Donald Cosentino. Los Angeles: UCLA Fowler Museum of Cultural History.

Jahn, Janheinz. 1961. *Muntu: An Outline of the New African Culture*. New York: Grove Press.

Jallier, Maurice, and Yollen Lossen. 1985. *Musique aux Antilles: Mizik bô kay*. Paris: Editions Caribéennes.

Jamaica, Ethnic Origins. Wikipedia. http://en.wikipedia.org/wikGomi/Jamaica#Ethnic_origins>.

James, Joel, José Millet, and Alexis Alarcón. 1992. *El Vodú en Cuba*. Santiago de Cuba: Casa del Caribe.

Jegede, Dele. 2000. "Art." In *Africa*. Vol. 2, *African Cultures and Societies Before 1885*, ed. Toyin Falola. Durham, N.C.: Carolina Academic Press.

Jesse, Rev. C. 1963. "The Spanish Cedula of December 23, 1511 on the Subject of the Caribs." *Caribbean Quarterly* 9(3).

John, Suki. 2002. "The Técnica Cubana." In *Caribbean Dance From Abakuá to Zouk: How Movement Shapes Identity*, ed. Susanna Sloat, 73–78. Gainesville: University Press of Florida.

Johnson, Sara E. 2005. "*Cinquillo* Consciousness: The Formation of a Pan-Caribbean Musical Aesthetic." In *Music, Writing, and Cultural Unity in the Caribbean*, ed. Timothy J. Reiss, 35–38. Trenton: Africa World Press.

Jones, Leroi [Amiri Baraka]. 1963. *Blues People: Negro Music in White America*. New York: William Morrow.

Joseph, May. 1998. "Transatlantic Inscriptions: Desire, Diaspora, and Cultural Citizenship." In *Talking Visions: Multicultural Feminism in a Transnational Age*, ed. Ella Shohat. Cambridge, Mass.: MIT Press.

Kasinitz, Philip. 1992. "Carnival: Community Dramatized." In *Caribbean New York: Black Immigrants and the Politics of Race*. Ithaca: Cornell University Press.

Katz, Bernard, ed. 1969. *The Social Implications of Early Negro Music in the United States*. New York: Arno Press.

Kubik, Gerhard. 1990. "Drum Patterns in the *Batuque* of Benedito Caxias." *Latin American Music Review* 11(2): 115–181.

———. 1994. *Theory of African Music*. Wilhelmshaven: Florian Noetzel Verlag.

———. 1998. "Central Africa: An Introduction." In *The Garland Encyclopedia of World Music*. Vol. 1, *Africa*, ed. Ruth M. Stone, 650–680. New York: Garland Publishing, Inc.

Labat, Jean Baptiste. 1972 [1724]. *Nouveaux voyages aux isles de l'Amérique*. Fort-de-France: Editions des Horizons Caraïbes.

Lafontaine, Marie-Céline. 1986. "Unité et Diversité des Musiques Traditionelles Guadeloupéennes." In *Les Musiques Guadeloupéennes dans le Champ Culturel Afro-Américain au Sein des Musiques du Monde*, ed. Marie-Céline Lafontaine, 71–92. Paris: Editions Caribéennes.

Lamb, William. [1898?]. *Everybody's Guide to Ball-Room Dancing*. London: W. R. Russell.

Latrobe, Benjamin Henry. 1905. *The Journal of Latrobe: Being the Notes and Sketches of an Architect, Naturalist and Traveler in the United States from 1796 to 1820*. New York: D. Appleton.

Lavelle, Doris. 1965. *Latin and American Dances*. London: Sir Isaac Pitman & Sons.

Lawrence, Benjamín N. 2005. *The Ewe of Togo and Benin*. Accra New Town, Ghana: Woeli Publishing Services.

Leaf, Earl. 1948. *Isles of Rhythm*. New York: A. S. Barnes.

Lent, John A., ed. 1990. *Caribbean Popular Culture*. Bowling Green, Ohio: Bowling Green State University Popular Press.

Lewin, Olive. 1998. "Jamaica." In *The Garland Encyclopedia of World Music*. Vol. 2, *South America, Mexico, Central America, and the Caribbean*, ed. Dale A. Olsen and Daniel E. Sheehy, 896–913. New York: Garland.

———. 2000. *"Rock It Come Over:" The Folk Music of Jamaica*. Kingston: University of the West Indies Press.

Leymarie, Isabelle. 2001. "De la rumba brava à la rumba de salon." In *Danses latines: Le désir des continents*, ed. Élisabeth Dorier-Apprill, 94–103. Paris: Éditions Autrement.

Lieth-Philipp, Margot. 1988. "Music and Folklore in the U.S. Virgin Islands." Liner notes to Mary Jane Soule, *Zoop Zoop Zoop: Traditional Music and Folklore of St. Croix, St. Thomas, and St. John*. New World Records 80427–2.

Liverpool, Hollis "Chalkdust." 2001. *Rituals of Power & Rebellion: The Carnival Tradition in Trinidad and Tobago 1763–1962*. Chicago; Trinidad and Tobago: Research Associates School Times Publications; Frontline Distribution.

Lokaisingh-Meighoo, Sean. 1997. "Dialectics of Diaspora and Home: Indentureship, Migration and Indo-Caribbean Identity." MA thesis, York University, Toronto. Ann Arbor: UMI Dissertation Services.

———. 2001. "The Diasporic Mo(ve)ment: Indentureship and Indo-Caribbean Identity." In *Nation Dance: Religion, Identity, and Cultural Difference in the Caribbean*, ed. Patrick Taylor, 171–192. Bloomington/Indianapolis: Indiana University Press.

Lomax, Alan. 1970. "The Homogeneity of African-Afro-American Musical Style." In *Afro-American Anthropology: Contemporary Perspectives*, ed. Norman Whitten and John Szwed. New York: Free Press.

Macdonald, Annette. 1978. "The Big Drum Dance of Carriacou." *Revista/Review Interamericana* 8(4): 570–576.

Malm, Krister. 1983. *An Island Carnival: Music of the West Indies*. Los Angeles: Nonesuch Explorer.

Malnig, Julie, ed. 2008. *Ballroom, Boogie, Shimmy Sham, Shake: A Social and Popular Dance Reader*. Urbana: University of Illinois Press.

Manning, Frank E. 1990. "Overseas Caribbean Carnivals: The Art and Politics of a Transnational Celebration." In *Caribbean Popular Culture*, ed. John A. Lent. Bowling Green, Ohio: Bowling Green State University Popular Press.

Marshall, T. 1990. "A ship on land?" *Insight Guide Barbados*. APA Publications.

Martínez Furé, Rogelio. 1963. "De paleros y firmas se trata." *Revista Unión*.

———. 1979. *Diálogos Imaginarios*. Havana: Editorial Letras Cubanas.

Martínez Gordo, Isabel. 1989. *Algunas consideraciones sobre Patois cubain de F. Boytel Jambú*. Havana: Editorial Academia.

Masters, Ryan. 2008. "African Dance Ensemble Set to Shake Lula." *The Ethnic Umbrella*, February 9.

McAlister, Elizabeth. 2002. *Rara!: Vodou, Power, and Performance in Haiti and Its Diaspora*. Berkeley: University of California Press.

McBurnie, Beryl. n.d. *Dance Trinidad Dance: Outlines of the Dances of Trinidad*. Port of Spain: Guardian Commercial Printery.

McDaniel, Lorna. 1992. "The Concept of Nation in the Big Drum Dance of Carriacou, Grenada." In *Musical Repercussions of 1492: Encounters in Text and Performance*, ed. Carol E. Robertson, 395–411. Washington, D.C.: Smithsonian Institution.

———. 1998a. *The Big Drum Ritual of Carriacou: Praisesongs in Rememory of Flight*. Gainesville: University Press of Florida.

———. 1998b. "Grenada (and Carriacou)." In *The Garland Encyclopedia of World Music*. Vol. 2, *South America, Mexico, Central America, and the Caribbean*, ed. Dale A. Olsen and Daniel E. Sheehy, 864–872. New York: Garland.

———. 1998c. "Trinidad and Tobago." In *The Garland Encyclopedia of World Music*. Vol. 2, *South America, Mexico, Central America, and the Caribbean*, ed. Dale A. Olsen and Daniel E. Sheehy, 952–967. New York: Garland.

McLeod, Marc Christian. 2000. "Undesirable Aliens: Haitian and British West Indian Workers in Cuba, 1898 to 1940." Doctoral diss., University of Texas at Austin. Available online from ProQuest.

Meeks, Brian, and Folke Lindahl, eds. 2001. *New Caribbean Thought: A Reader*. Jamaica: University of West Indies Press.

Michalon, Josy. 1987. *La Ladjia: Origine et practiques*. Paris: Editions Caribéennes.

Miller, R. S. 2005. "Performing Ambivalence: The Case of Quadrille Music and Dance in Carriacou, Grenada." *Ethnomusicology* 49(3): 403–440.

Millet, José, and Rafael Brea. 1989. *Grupos folklóricos de Santiago de Cuba*. Santiago de Cuba: Editorial Oriente.

———. 1995. "Carnivals of Santiago de Cuba," *Journal of Caribbean Studies*, 10(1&2), 30–49.

Mintz, Sidney W., and Richard Price. 1992 [1976]. *The Birth of African-American Culture: An Anthropological Perspective*. Boston: Beacon Press.

Mitchell, Dayo Nicole. 2005. "The Ambiguous Distinctions of Descent: Free People of Color and the Construction of Citizenship in Trinidad and Dominica, 1800–1838." PhD diss., University of Virginia.

Mohanty, Chandra Talpade. 1998. "Crafting Feminist Genealogies: On the Geography and Politics of Home, Nation, and Community." In *Talking Visions: Multicultural Feminism in a Transnational Age*, ed. Ella Shohat. Cambridge, Mass.: MIT Press.

Moore, Joseph Graessle. 1954. *Religion of Jamaican Negroes: A Study of Afro-Jamaican Acculturation*. PhD diss., Northwestern University. Ann Arbor, Mich.: University Microfilms.

Moore, Robin D. 1995. "The Commercial Rumba in Afrocuban Arts as International Popular Culture." *Latin American Music Review* 16(2): 165–198.

———. 1997. *Nationalizing Blackness: Afrocubanismo and Artistic Revolution in Havana, 1920–1940*. Pittsburgh: University of Pittsburgh Press.

Moreau de Saint Méry, Médéric Louis Elie. 1976 [1796]. *Dance: an article drawn from the work by M.L.E. Moreau de St.-Méry*. Trans. Lily and Baird Hastings. Brooklyn: Dance Horizons.

Mottley, Elombe. 2003. *Identities Volume 1: A collection of Newspaper Columns*. Barbados and Jamaica: Fatpork Ten-Ten Productions.

Mousouris, Melinda. 2002. "The Dance World of Ramiro Guerra: Solemnity, Voluptuousness, Humor, and Chance." In *Caribbean Dance From Abakuá to Zouk: How Movement Shapes Identity*, ed. Susanna Sloat, 56–72. Gainesville: University Press of Florida.

Mukuna, Kazadi wa. 1978. *Contribução bantu na música popular brasileira*. São Paolo: Editora Parma Ltd.

Murray, Arthur. 1938. *How to Become a Good Dancer*. New York: Simon & Schuster.

———. 1942. *How to Become a Good Dancer*. New York: Simon & Schuster.

———. 1954. *How to Become a Good Dancer*. New York: Simon & Schuster.

Nettleford, Rex. 1985. *Dance Jamaica: Cultural Definitions and Artistic Discovery: The National Dance Theatre Company of Jamaica, 1962–1983*. New York: Grove Press.

———. 1988. "Implications for Caribbean Development." In *Caribbean Festival Arts: Each and Every Bit a Difference*, ed. John W. Nunley and Judith Bettelheim, 183–197. Seattle: University of Washington Press.

———. 1993. "Fancy Dress and the Roots of Culture: From Jonkonnu to Dancehall," *Sunday Gleaner*, July 18: 1D, 6D.

———. 2002. "Jamaican Dance Theatre: Celebrating the Caribbean Heritage." In *Caribbean Dance From Abakuá to Zouk: How Movement Shapes Identity*, ed. Susanna Sloat, 81–94. Gainesville: University Press of Florida.

Nketia, J. H. Kwabena. 2005. *Ethnomusicology and African Music (Collected Papers): Modes of Inquiry and Interpretation*. Vol. 1. Accra: Afram Publications.

Nwauwa, Apollos O. 2000. "The Europeans in Africa: Prelude to Colonialism." In *Africa*. Vol. 2, *African Cultures and Societies Before 1885*, ed. Toyin Falola. Durham, N.C.: Carolina Academic Press.

Olivacce-Marie, Ophelia. 1977. "Dominican Folk Songs." Thesis, Commonwealth Youth Programme.

Oliver, Cynthia. 2002. "'Winin' Yo' Wais'": The Changing Tastes of Dance on the U.S. Virgin Island of St. Croix." In *Caribbean Dance From Abakuá to Zouk: How Movement Shapes Identity*, ed. Susanna Sloat, 199–218. Gainesville: University Press of Florida.

Orovio, Helio. 1981. *Diccionario de la música cubana: biográfico y técnico*. Havana: Editorial Letras Cubanas.

Ortiz, Fernando. 1947. *Cuban Counterpoint: Tobacco and Sugar*. New York: A. A. Knopf.

———. 1950. *La africanía de la música folklórica de Cuba*. Cárdenas y Cia

———. 1951. "Del folklore antillano afro-francés." *Bohemia* 43(34) August 26: 36–38, 116–117.

———. 1952–55. *Los Instrumentos de la Musica Afrocubana*. 5 volumes. Havana: Direccion de Cultura del Ministerio de Educacion.

———. 1975. *Los Negros Esclavos*. Havana: Editorial de Ciencias Sociales.

———. 1981 [1951]. *El baile y el teatro de los negros en el Folklore de Cuba*. Havana: Editorial Letras Cubana.

Osabu-Kle, Daniel T. 2000. "The African Reparation Cry: Rationale, Estimate, Prospects and Strategies." *Journal of Black Studies*, 30(3): 331–350.

Pearse, Andrew. 1955. "Aspects of Change in Caribbean Folk Music." *UNESCO International Folk Music Journal* 7: 29–36.

———. 1956. Liner notes. "The Big Drum Dance of Carriacou." Ethnic Folkways FE4011.

Pedro, Alberto. 1967. "La semana santa haitiano-cubana." *Etnologia y Folklore*, Academia de Ciencias de Cuba, July–December: 49–78.

Pérez Fernández, Rolando Antonio. 1986. *La binarización de los ritmos ternarios africanos en América Latina*. Havana: Ediciones Casa de las Américas.

Philip, M. Nourbese. 1997. "African Roots and Continuities: Race, Space, and the Poetics of Moving." In *A Genealogy of Resistance: and Other Essays*. Toronto: Mercury Press.

Phillip, Daryl. n.d. *Bele in Dominica*. Roseau: Committee for Progress in Democracy.

Phillip, Daryl, and Gary Smith. 1998. *The Heritage Dances of Dominica*. Dominica: Dominica Division of Culture.

Pichardo, Esteban. 1985 [1836]. *Diccionario provincial casi razonado de vozes y frases cubanas*. Havana: Editorial de Ciencias Sociales.

Pierre. 1948. *Latin and American Dances for Students and Teachers*. London.

Pinnock, Thomas Osha. 2002. "Rasta & Reggae." In *Caribbean Dance From Abakuá to Zouk: How Movement Shapes Identity*, ed. Susanna Sloat, 95–106. Gainesville: University Press of Florida.

Price, Sally, and Richard Price. 1980. *Afro-American Arts of the Suriname Rain Forest*. Los Angeles: Museum of Cultural History/Berkeley: University of California Press.

Price-Mars, Jean. 1928. *Ainsi parla l'oncle . . . : essais d'ethnographie*. Port-au-Prince: Imprimerie de Compiègne.

Pugliese, Patri J. 2005 [1998]. "Country Dance." In *The International Encyclopedia of Dance*, ed. Selma Jean Cohen et. al. Oxford University Press. (e-reference edition. http://www.oxford-dance.com/entry?entry=t171.e0422 ).

Ramos Venereo, Zobeyda. 1997. "Tambores de tahona." In *Instrumentos de la Música Folclórico-Popular de Cuba*, ed. Victoria Eli Rodríguez et. al., Vol. 1, 262–268. Havana: Centro de Investigación y Desarrollo de la Música Cubana, Editorial de Ciencias Sociales.

Ramsey, Kate. 1997. "Vodou, Nationalism, and Performance: The Staging of Folklore in Mid-Twentieth-Century Haiti." In *Meaning and Motion: New Cultural Studies in Dance*, ed. Jane C. Desmond. Durham, N.C.: Duke University Press.

Rawley, James A. 1981. *The Transatlantic Slave Trade: A History*. New York: W. W. Norton.

Reader, John. 1997. *Afrca: A Biography of the Continent*. New York: Vintage.

Reckord, Verena. 1997. "Reggae, Rastafarianism and Cultural Identity." In *Reggae, Rasta, Revolution: Jamaican Music From Ska to Dub*, ed. Chris Potash. New York and London: Schirmer Books & Prentice Hall International.

Reyes, Carla. 1993. "Investigation into Dancehall," research paper in Dance and Theatre Production, Jamaica School of Dance, Edna Manley College for the Visual and Performing Arts, Jamaica.

Reyes, Clara. "Clara Reyes gives insight into the Ponum Dance," in "Ponum." NAGICO newletter online, html version, page 4. www.nagico.cm/pdf/newsletter>

Rice, Timothy. 1997. "Toward a Mediation of Field Methods and Field Experience in Ethnomusicology." In *Shadows in the Field: New Perspectives for Fieldwork in Ethnomusicology*, ed. Gregory F. Barz and Timothy J. Cooley. New York: Oxford University Press.

Richards, Mike. 1989. "The BDTC and Barbados' Cultural Development." *Twenty-one Years of Dance in Barbados: The Development of the Barbados Dance Theatre Company*, 19–23. Barbados: Lighthouse Communications.

Richardson, P. J. S. 1960. *The Social Dances of the 19th Century*. London: Herbert Jenkins.

Rivera-Servera, Ramón H. 2002. "A Dominican York in Andhra." In *Caribbean Dance*

*From Abakuá to Zouk: How Movement Shapes Identity*, ed. Susanna Sloat, 152–161. Gainesville: University Press of Florida.

Roach, Joseph. 1996. *Cities of the Dead: Circum-Atlantic Performance*. New York: Columbia University Press.

Roberts, John Storm. 1972. *Black Music of Two Worlds*. New York: William Morrow.

Rohlehr, Gordon. 1990. *Calypso and Society in Pre-Independence Trinidad*. Port of Spain, Trinidad: G. Rohlehr.

———. 1998. "We Getting the Kaiso We Deserve: Calypso and the World Music Market." *The Drama Review: TDR* 42(3)(T159).

———. 2001. "Calypso and Caribbean Identity." In *Caribbean Cultural Identities*, ed. Glyne Griffith. Lewisburg, Pa.: Bucknell University Press.

Rose, Tricia. 1994. *Black Noise: Rap Music and Black Culture in Contemporary America*. Middletown, Conn.: Wesleyan University Press.

Rosemain, Jacqueline. 1986. *La Musique dans la société Antillaise, 1635–1902*. Paris: L'Harmattan.

———. 1990. *La Danse aux Antilles: Des rythmes sacrés au zouk*. Paris: L'Harmattan.

———. 1993. *Jazz et biguine: Les musiques noires du Nouveau Monde*. Paris: L'Harmattan.

Ryman, Cheryl. 1980. "The Jamaican Heritage in Dance." *Jamaica Journal* 44: 2–13. Kingston: Institute of Jamaica Publications.

———. 1984. "Kumina—Stability and Change." *ACIJ Research Review* 81(128). Kingston: African-Caribbean Institute of Jamaica.

———. 2003. "Jamaican Body Moves: Source and Continuity of Jamaican Movement." In *Tapestry of Jamaica: The Best of Skywritings, Air Jamaica's Inflight Magazine*, ed. Linda Gambrill, 170–171. Kingston and Oxford: Macmillan Caribbean.

———. 2004. "Bouyaka Boo-ya'h-kah: A Salute to Dancehall." *Discourses in Dance* 2(2): 5–7. London: Laban.

Sánchez-Carretero, Cristina. 2005. "Santos and Misterios as Channels of Communication in the Diaspora: Afro-Dominican Religious Practices Abroad." *Journal of American Folklore* 118(469): 308–326.

Sanderson, Tessa. "Strictly African Dancing—Biographies." BBC. http://www.bbc.co.uk/pressoffice/pressreleases/stories/2005/06_june/20/dancing_biographies.shtml.

Santos, Caridad. 2002. *Danzas Populares Tradicionales Cubanas*. Centro Juan Marinello.

Shay, Anthony. 2002. *Choreographic Politics: State Folk Dance Companies, Representation and Power*. Middletown, Conn.: Wesleyan University Press.

Sheehy, Daniel. 1998. "The Virgin Islands." In *The Garland Encyclopedia of World Music*. Vol. 2, *South America, Mexico, Central America, and the Caribbean*, ed. Dale A. Olsen and Daniel E. Sheehy, 968–974. New York: Garland.

Simón, Pedro, ed. 1986. *Alicia Alonso, diálogos con la danza*. Havana: Editorial Letras Cubanas.

Simpson, George. E. 1956. "Jamaican Revivalist Cults." *Social & Economic Studies* 5(4): 321–442.

Sloat, Susanna, ed. 2002. *Caribbean Dance From Abakuá to Zouk: How Movement Shapes Identity*. Gainesville: University Press of Florida.

———. 2002a. "Islands Refracted: Recent Dance on Caribbean Themes in New York." In *Caribbean Dance From Abakuá to Zouk: How Movement Shapes Identity*, ed. Susanna Sloat, 320–335. Gainesville: University Press of Florida.

Smith, Ronald R. 1985. "They Sing with the Voice of the Drum: Afro-Panamanian Musical Traditions." In *More than Drumming: Essays on African and Afro-Latin American Music and Musicians*, ed. Irene V. Jackson. Westport: Greenwood Press.

Southern, Eileen, and Josephine Wright. 2000. *Images: Iconography of Music in African-American Culture, 1770s-1920s*. New York: Garland.

Spencer, Flora (1974). *Crop Over: An Old Barbadian Plantation Festival*. Barbados: Commonwealth Caribbean Centre.

Spitzer, Nick. 1976. *Zodico: Louisiana Creole Music*. Somerville, Mass.: Rounder Records.

Stanley Niaah, Sonjah. 2004. "Making Space: Dancehall Performance and its Philosophy of Boundarylessness." *African Identities* 2(2): 117–132.

———. 2004a. "Kingston's Dancehall: A Story of Space and Celebration." *Space and Culture* 7(1): 102–118.

Stanley Niaah, Sonjah, and Donna Hope. 2007. "Canvasses of Representation: Stuart Hall, the Body and Dancehall Performance." In *Caribbean Reasonings: Culture, Race, Politics and Diaspora*, ed. Brian Meeks. Kingston: Ian Randle Publishers.

Stein, Robert Louis. 1979. *The French Slave Trade in the Eighteenth Century: An Old Regime Business*. Madison: University of Wisconsin Press.

Stephenson, Richard M., and Joseph Iaccarino. 1980. *The Complete Book of Ballroom Dancing*. New York: Doubleday.

Strobel, Desmond F. 2005 [1998]. "Quadrille." In *The International Encyclopedia of Dance*, ed. Selma Jean Cohen et. al. Oxford University Press. (e-reference edition. http://www.oxford-dance.com/entry?entry=t171.e0422).

Stubbs, Norris. 1973. *A Survey of the Folk Music of Dominica*, ed. Daniel Caudeiron. Roseau: Dominica Arts Council.

Sublette, Ned. 2004. *Cuba and its Music*. Chicago: Chicago Review Press.

Szwed, John F., and Morton Marks. 1988. "The Afro-American Transformation of European Set Dances and Dance Suites." *Dance Research Journal* 20(1): 29–36.

Tabanka Crew. http://www.tabankacrew.no/caribdance/kumina/index.html>.

"The Uncrowned King of the Dancehall: Montana Interviews Bogle." 2002. http://www.chicagoreggae.com/bogle.htm.

Thomas, Hugh. 1997. *The Slave Trade: The Story of the Atlantic Slave Trade 1440–1870*. New York: Simon and Schuster.

———. 1998 [1971]. *Cuba, or, The Pursuit of Freedom*. New York: DaCapo Press.

Thompson, Robert Farris. 1966. "An Aesthetic of the Cool: West African Dance." *African Forum* 2(2): 85–102.

———. 1974. *African Art in Motion: Icon and Art.* Los Angeles: University of California Press.

———. 1993. *Face of the Gods: Art and Altars of Africa and the African Americas.* New York: The Museum for African Art.

———. 2002. "Teaching the People to Triumph Over Time: Notes from the World of Mambo." In *Caribbean Dance From Abakuá to Zouk: How Movement Shapes Identity*, ed. Susanna Sloat, 336–344. Gainesville: University Press of Florida.

Tishken, E. Joel. 2000. "Indigenous Religions." In *Africa*. Vol. 2, *African Cultures and Societies Before 1885*, ed. Toyin Falola. Durham, N.C.: Carolina Academic Press.

Trouillot, Michel-Rolph. 1994. "Culture, Color, and Politics in Haiti." In *Race*, ed. Steven Gregory and Roger Sanjek. New Brunswick: Rutgers University Press.

Turner, Rasbert. 2006. "Dance of Death?—Beacon Hill Residents Blame 'Dutty Wine' for Teen's Death." *Daily Gleaner*, October 30.

Uri, Alex, and Françoise Uri. 1991. *Musiques et musiciens de la Guadeloupe: Le chant de Karukera.* Paris: Con Brio.

Vázquez, Viveca. *Riversa*, CD-ROM. Designed by María de Mater O'Neill and DMZ-Digital Media Zone. (San Juan, Puerto Rico: El cuarto del quenepón and DMZ, 1997).

Vázquez Millares, Angel. 1963. *Música y Folklore Bantú.* Ediciones del CNC.

Vega Drouet, Héctor. 1998. "Puerto Rico." In *The Garland Encyclopedia of World Music.* Vol. 2, *South America, Mexico, Central America, and the Caribbean*, ed. Dale A. Olsen and Daniel E. Sheehy. New York: Garland.

Vélez, María Teresa. 2000. *Drumming for the Gods: The Life and Times of Felipe García Villamil, Santero, Palero, and Abakuá.* Philadelphia: Temple University Press.

Veloz [Frank] and Yolanda [Veloz], with Willard Hall. 1938. *Tango and Rumba: The Dances of Today and Tomorrow.* New York: Harper & Brothers.

Vergés Martinez, Orlando. 2002. "La haitianidad en el contexto de la cultura popular tradicional cubana." Santiago de Cuba: *Del Caribe* 52: 3–5.

Vinueza, María Elena. 1988. *Presencia Arara en la Musica Folclórica de Matanzas.* Havana: Casa de las Americas.

Walcott, Derek. 1992. Nobel Lecture. http://nobelprize.org/nobel_prizes/literature/laureates/1992/walcott-lecture.html>

Washburne, Christopher. 1997. "The Clave of Jazz: A Caribbean Contribution to the Rhythmic Foundation of an African-American Music." *Black Music Research Journal* 17(1): 59–80.

Wason, Janet. 1987. "Recherches et Études sur les Danses Folkloriques de la Dominique." Report 221/8601–12. Paris: Agence de Cooperation Culturelle et Technique.

Webster, J. B., and A. A. Boahen. 1980 [1967]. *The Revolutionary Years: West Africa since 1800 (The Growth of African Civilisation).* London: Longman.

Welsh Asante, Kariamu. 1985. "Commonalities in African Dance: An Aesthetic Foundation." In *African Culture: The Rhythms of Unity*, ed. Molefi Kete Asante and Kariamu Welsh Asante. 71–82. Westport, Conn.: Greenwood Press.

White, Garth. 1984. "The Development of Jamaican Popular Music, Part 2. Urbaniza-

tion of the Folk, the Merger of Traditional and the Popular in Jamaican Music."
*ACIJ Research Review* 1.

Whylie, Marjorie, and Maureen Warner-Lewis. 1994. "Characteristics of Maroon Music from Jamaica and Suriname." In *Maroon Heritage: Archaeological, Ethnographic, and Historical Perspectives*, ed. E. Kofi Agorsah, 139–148. Barbados: Canoe Press/ University of West Indies Press.

Wilcken, Lois. 2002. "Spirit Unbound: New Approaches to the Performance of Haitian Folklore." In *Caribbean Dance From Abakuá to Zouk: How Movement Shapes Identity*, ed. Susanna Sloat. Gainesville: University Press of Florida.

Williams, Eric. 1993 [1962]. *History of the People of Trinidad and Tobago*. Brooklyn: A & B Books.

Wirtz, Kristina. 2004. "Santeria in Cuban National Consciousness." *The Journal of Latin American Anthropology* 9(Fall): 409–438.

## Discography

Beenie Man. 1994. "World Dance." *Strictly the Best*, Vol. 13 [CD]. NY: VP Records.

Captain Barkey. 1996. "Go Go Wine." *Strictly the Best*, Vol. 17. VP Records.

Elephant Man. 2003 "Pon di River, Pon di Bank." *Good 2 Go*. Atlantic Records.

———. 2003. "Fan dem off." *Good 2 Go*. Atlantic Records.

———. 2003. "Blasé." *Good 2 Go*. Atlantic Records.

———. 2003. "Signal di Plane." *Good 2 Go*. Atlantic Records.

———. 2002. "Wining Queen." Studio 2000 [single].

Grace Jones. 1985. "Slave to the Rhythm." *Slave to the Rhythm* [CD] NY: Polygram.

Johnny P. 2000 [1991]. "Bike Back." *Punanny* [CD]. NY and UK: Greensleeves Records.

Shabba Ranks. 1993. "Girls Wine." *Rough and Ready*, Vol. 2.

# About the Contributors

Ga-La–born Isaac Nii Akrong is a teacher of many aspects of West African performance, including Ghanaian and Mande dances and music and their historical context. Akrong holds a diploma in theatre arts from the University of Ghana and an M.A. in dance ethnology from York University in Toronto, where he is now a Ph.D. candidate in ethnomusicology. He is working on Hip life music and dance from Ghana, has published text and audio on Kpanlogo dance from Ghana, has launched the Humanity in Harmony festival at York, and directs the African Dance Ensemble (ADE), based in Toronto. For further information please visit http://www.afridance.com.

Celia Weiss Bambara is a dancer and choreographer who has performed with Haitian and contemporary companies JAKA and Shirley Martin Dancers, among others, collaborated with Haitian and African artists, and performed her work in Los Angeles, Chicago, Iowa, Haiti, Jamaica, and Cuba. She has a Ph.D. in dance history and theory from the University of California– Riverside and was a postdoctoral fellow at the University of Illinois, Chicago, where she is now a visiting lecturer in the African American Studies Department. Her research addresses African diasporic cultural production, processes of transformation in the expressive arts, and the impact of travel and collaboration on performance. Celia teaches Haitian and African-based contemporary dance in Chicago and is investigating new ways of making dance with her company, the CCBdance Project. She has an essay published in *Australasian Drama Studies* and an article forthcoming in the *Journal of Haitian Studies*.

Graciela Chao Carbonero has been teaching and researching dance for forty years and is an adjunct regular professor of the Higher Institute of Arts in Havana. She studied ballet and music, trained as a teacher of traditional dances, danced with the Conjunto Folklórico Nacional, and has published teaching texts on traditional dances. Her book *De la Contradanza Cubana al Casino* was recently published, and her next work, *El baile de y para los orishas en el tambor de santo*, will be soon. Melba Nuñez Isalbe graduated as a translator and interpreter from the School of Foreign Languages at the University of Havana in 1997.

Martha Ellen Davis, anthropologist and ethnomusicologist, is advisor and researcher in oral history at the National Archives of the Dominican Republic and faculty affiliate in anthropology and music at the University of Florida. She is the author of three books, two documentaries, and numerous articles on the traditional musical and religious musical culture of the Dominican Republic, and has also conducted field research in Spain and the Canary Islands, Puerto Rico, and Brazil. Her book on Dominican Vodú, *La otra ciencia* (1987) received the National Nonfiction Award of the Dominican Republic.

Nicolás Dumit Estévez is an interdisciplinary artist who has exhibited and performed extensively in the United States as well as internationally. He often locates his projects outside the gallery context to interact directly with an audience in spaces of public access, inviting them to take an active role in his work and thereby affect the development of the piece. In doing so, latex gloves, plastic knives, whips, bananas, or disposable smocks are used on the subjects being examined: social rituals, prejudices, cultural clichés, and professional roles. While ephemeral by nature, his projects gain permanence through audio, photographs, props, drawings, costumes, videos, and texts. Estévez lives and works in the South Bronx. http://pleasedtomeetyou.org/

Jill Flanders Crosby is a professor in the Department of Theatre and Dance at the University of Alaska–Anchorage. She has been conducting fieldwork in Ghana since 1991 and in Cuba since 1997 and received a Fulbright Senior Research Grant in 1998 for her work in Ghana. Her other research, choreographic, and performance interests include music-based jazz dance. She has taught at the University of Ghana and offered classes in jazz dance for DanzAbierta of Havana, Cuba.

Hazel Franco, an M.A. graduate of York University, Toronto, in dance ethnology, has established herself at the forefront of dance in Trinidad and Tobago as a dancer, choreographer, educator, and researcher. Hazel is artistic director of the Festival Dance Ensemble, which has participated in international festivals in Brazil, South Africa, and French Guiana. As a dance ethnologist, she has presented papers on various aspects of Trinidad and Tobago's folk dances at conferences all over the world. Hazel is coordinator of the Dance and Dance Education Certificate Programme of the Department for Creative and Festival Arts, University of the West Indies, St. Augustine, Trinidad, a board member of World Dance Alliance America, and a member of the International Dance Council.

Julian Gerstin, Ph.D., is a percussionist specializing in the music of Martinique, Cuba, and Ghana. He lived in Martinique in 1993–95, studying bele drumming and dance and the revival of this tradition. Currently he teaches at Keene State College and the Vermont Jazz Center, and he performs with the Caribbean/Middle Eastern/jazz ensemble As Yet Quintet and the Afrocuban dance ensemble Grupo Palo Santo.

Ramiro Guerra introduced contemporary dance in Cuba and created a style synthesizing Graham technique with Cuban folklore that became a national dance style. He received an honorary doctorate in the arts in 1989 and the national prize for education in 2007, both from the National Institute of Arts, and the national prize for dance in 1999 from the Ministry of Culture. He has published eight books on dance, one of which, *Eros baila, Sexualidad y danza*, received the most prestigious award for literature in Cuba. He continues as a researcher, conference participant, and promoter of dance and was president of the jury of the first Caribbean Biennial of Dance in 2008. Melinda Mousouris is based in New York and writes about dance and Cuban culture.

Susan Harewood's research focuses on communication, popular music, performance, and gender. Her work has appeared in a number of academic journals and edited collections. She is an assistant professor at the University of Washington, Bothell.

John Hunte is a Ph.D. cultural studies candidate at the University of the West Indies–Cave Hill, Barbados, conducting research on dance in Barbados and focusing this study through the lens and perception of men who dance onstage. He locates himself in his research as an accomplished dancer and arts activist, having studied in Jamaica and the United States and worked in various places around the world. Hunte performs, choreographs, teaches, and consults for various local, regional, and international institutions.

Susan Homar is a full professor at the University of Puerto Rico's Comparative Literature Department, where she teaches contemporary literature as well as dance history and theory. She is working on a book on the development of theatrical dance in Puerto Rico and how it came out of and reflects the political and cultural history of the island in the 1950s. To make dance accessible to a wider audience, both popular and scholarly, she is also developing a digital archive and Web site on the history of dance on the island.

Tania Isaac is a choreographer and writer based in Philadelphia. A former member of Urban Bush Women and Rennie Harris Puremovement and now a member of David Dorfman Dance, she has toured her own company, TaniaIsaacDance, internationally and has received numerous grants and awards, among them a Choreographic Fellowship at the Maggie Allessee National Center for Choreography. She is the 2008 recipient of a Pennsylvania Council on the Arts Individual Fellowship Award. http://www.taniaisaacdance.org.

Annette C. Macdonald is professor emerita of dance at San Jose State University and a documentary filmmaker. With Allegra Fuller Snyder she produced, codirected, and edited the award-winning film *When the Fire Dances Between The Two Poles: Mary Wigman 1886–1973*. She was consultant and researcher for the PBS Dance in America documentary *Free to Dance* and is producing a documentary film of the life and work of the great choreographer/dancer Jack Cole.

Ravindra Nath Maharaj, known as Raviji, is from Caparo, a village in central Trinidad and Tobago, and grew up in a family steeped in Hindu traditions and Indian culture. He taught at primary school before pursuing Hindu studies in Varanasi, India. He has been active in community life for three decades and has been actively experimenting with many Hindu/Indian festivals with an eye on ethnic and cultural diversity and social consciousness. He is the president of The Kendra, Association of Traditional Religions—

Astrel, director of Bal Ramdilla, board member of the University of Trinidad and Tobago, and a columnist at the *Trinidad Guardian*.

Juliet McMains, Ph.D., is the author of the book *Glamour Addiction: Inside the American Ballroom Dance Industry*, which won the 2008 Congress on Research in Dance Outstanding Publication Award. As a DanceSport competitor, she has twice been a U.S. National Rising Star finalist and has won professional competitions in the United States and Canada. She is assistant professor in the Dance Program at the University of Washington.

Cynthia Oliver is an award-winning choreographer/performing artist. She has danced with numerous international touring companies, including David Gordon Pick Up Co., Ronald K. Brown/Evidence, and Bebe Miller Co., and has performed in the theater works of Laurie Carlos and Ntozake Shange, among others. She holds a Ph.D. in performance studies from New York University and is associate professor of dance at the University of Illinois, Urbana-Champaign.

Xiomarita Pérez is a teacher of dance and a widely published writer in the Dominican Republic on traditional Dominican culture. She was a member for twenty-seven years of Ballet Folklórico UASD and was the first director of Dirección Nacional de Folklore, DINAFOLK. She is the founding director of the Escuela Dominicana de Ritmos Folklóricos y Populares in Santo Domingo and the author of *Consultorio Folklórico*. Maria Lara Soto is a Dominican healer in New York and a descendent of Dominican healers.

Cheryl Ryman was a principal dancer with the National Dance Theatre Company of Jamaica and studied and researched dance and music in Ghana. As a research fellow with the African Caribbean Institute of Jamaica for ten years and in work beyond that, she has produced a significant body of dance research that dates back to the 1970s. This includes a dance map of Jamaica, ethnographies of Kumina and Jonkonnu, and work on the dance aesthetics of traditional and popular forms. A Ph.D. candidate in cultural studies at the University of the West Indies– Mona, Ryman is also involved in film and television and in developing the Outameni Experience, a tourist attraction that celebrates the history and culture of Jamaica.

Susanna Sloat is a writer and an editor and arts consultant in New York City who has written about many kinds of dance. She is the editor of *Caribbean Dance from Abakuá to Zouk: How Movement Shapes Identity*, for which she won the de la Torre Bueno Prize for 2003.

Sonjah Stanley Niaah is the inaugural Rhodes Trust Rex Nettleford Fellow in Cultural Studies (Caribbean) 2005, and is Lecturer in Cultural Studies at the University of the West Indies at Mona. Her book *DanceHall: Performance Geographies from Slave Ship to Ghetto* encompasses her research interests in Black Atlantic performance geographies, including Jamaican dancehall, blues, and South African kwaito space and culture; the city and the performing body; alternative productions of celebrity; and rituals in everyday life. Stanley Niaah has presented and published papers in numerous academic conferences and journals. She is an associate editor of *Wadabagei: A Journal of the Caribbean and its Diasporas* and serves on the editorial board of *Cultural Studies*.

Grete Viddal is a Ph.D. candidate in Harvard University's Department of African and African American Studies. She has traveled to Cuba and Haiti to study folkloric dance and ritual belief systems. Her doctoral research is based in the eastern provinces of Cuba, host to waves of migration from Haiti, and explores how folkloric performance groups, religious practitioners, government programs, academic institutes, tourism, and transnational contacts shape local culture and interface with Haitiano Cubano identity.

Janet Wason holds an M.F.A. in dance history from York University, Toronto, Ontario. She has researched, performed, and taught in the areas of sixteenth-century European court dance and nineteenth-century ballroom dance. Janet works as coordinator of library services for persons with disabilities at the University of Waterloo, Ontario.

# Index